MODERNIST AND FUNDAMENTALIST DEBATES IN ISLAM

A READER

Edited by

MANSOOR MOADDEL

and

KAMRAN TALATTOF

First published in 2002 by PALGRAVE MACMILLAN™
175 Fifth Avenue, New York, N.Y. 10010 and
Houndmills, Basingstoke, Hampshire, England RG21 6XS.
Companies and representatives throughout the world.

PALGRAVE MACMILLAN is the global academic imprint of the Palgrave
Macmillan division of St. Martin's Press, LLC and of Palgrave Macmillan Ltd.
Macmillan® is a registered trademark in the United States, United Kingdom and
other countries. Palgrave is a registered trademark in the European Union and other
countries.

ISBN 0–312–21580–0 hardback
ISBN 1–4039–6092–5 paperback

Library of Congress Cataloging-in-Publication Data
Contemporary debates in Islam : an anthology of modernist and
    fundamentalist thought / edited by Mansoor Moaddel and Kamran
    Talattof.
      p. cm.
    Includes bibliographical references and index.
    ISBN 0-312-21580-0 (cloth)
    1. Islam—20th century. 2. Islam—Essence, genius, nature.
3. Islamic fundamentalism. I. Moaddel, Mansoor. II. Talattof,
Kamran.
  BP163.C64   1999
  297.2'7—dc21   99–18673
                                                            CIP

Design by Letra Libre, Inc.

First Palgrave Macmillian edition: October 2002
10 9 8 7 6 5 4 3 2 1

TO MARJAN, CHRISTINE,
ARJANG, PAYVAND, AND ARMIN

CONTENTS

PART ONE: ISLAMIC MODERNISM

I. JURISPRUDENCE, RATIONAL SCIENCES, AND DIFFERENTIATION OF KNOWLEDGE

II. ISLAM AND POLITICS

PART TWO: ISLAMIC FUNDAMENTALISM

I. JURISPRUDENCE, BASES OF LAW, AND RATIONAL SCIENCES

II. ISLAM AND POLITICS

III.   ISLAM AND WESTERN CIVILIZATION

IV.   WOMEN AND THE HIJAB

PREFACE

IN THIS VOLUME WE INTRODUCE READERS TO TWO DIVERSE discourses in contemporary Islamic sociopolitical thought. We try to illustrate that Islam is not a monolithic religion, and, like any system of ideas, it is subject to change according to changes in social conditions. We also show that "Islam versus the West" is not simply a debate between Islamic fundamentalism and the Western world. It is rather an ideological/theological debate within Islam itself. Our broader objective, however, is to contribute to the existing debates on the determinants of ideological production. To this end, we have organized the views of Muslim scholars in terms of a series of historically significant issues that have appeared in the Islamic world since the second part of the nineteenth century. We believe that modernist and fundamentalist discourses were formulated around these issues. How wars of positions over these issues would lead to different, if not opposing, ideological resolutions within the same system of thought is a problem that needs to be analyzed in terms of the parameters of the socioeconomic, political, and cultural contexts within which Muslim ideological producers offer their ideas. Before doing so, however, we felt it is necessary to offer the community of scholars in the areas of Islamic/Middle Eastern studies as well as cultural sociology an explanation of the manner in which we reached our conception of Islamic modernism and fundamentalism, and for that matter, of the dependent variable—ideological production.

This work reflects the editors' common interest in the question of ideology. It is a part of Mansoor Moaddel's larger work on the determinants of ideological production in the Islamic world, which has been supported by two grants from the National Science Foundation (SBR 96–01439, SBR 92–13209), one grant from the United States Institute of Peace (USIP–080–965), fellowships from the National Endowment for the Humanities, the United States Information Agency, and Eastern Michigan University. It also reflects Kamran Talattof's thematic concerns in his project on the role of ideology in the formation of literary history and cultural change supported by grants from the University of Michigan and Princeton University. The opinions expressed in this book do not necessarily reflect the views of the NSF and other institutions that support this study.

CREDITS AND ACKNOWLEDGMENTS

WE WOULD LIKE TO THANK NEDA SAAB FOR HER contribution in improving the translations of the Arabic articles and Kazim Saeed for his help in the translations of Sir Sayyid Ahmad Khan's articles from Urdu. We are thankful to Christine Dykgraaf and Nathan Willis for their assistance in the preparation of this volume. We are also grateful to the Graduate School of Eastern Michigan University and Princeton University for providing financial support toward the publication of this book. In translating the articles by Sayyid Ahmad Khan, we have tremendously benefited from an earlier translation by John Wilder. Selected Essays By Sir Sayyid Ahmad Khan From the Journal Tahzib al-Akhlaq, unpublished M.A. Thesis, Hartford, Connecticut: Hartford Seminary Foundation, 1972. Finally, we are thankful to all the publishers that granted us permission to reprint material:

NOTE ON TRANSLATIONS, TRANSLITERATION, AND EDITING

IN TRANSLITERATING THE NAMES OF AUTHORS and individuals and the titles of books and other writings, we have adopted the Library of Congress system of transliteration without the diacritical marks. The only exceptions may include names and titles that are directly quoted from other sources or in the articles included. Except for some modifications, the translations done for this book are kept within the bounds of literal translation trying to remain as faithful as possible to the original. In some instances, translated articles that are quoted from other sources have been shortened and modified in terms of their grammar and fluency.

CONTEMPORARY DEBATES IN ISLAM: MODERNISM VERSUS FUNDAMENTALISM

AN ANTHOLOGY OF ISLAMIC THOUGHT

THIS BOOK PRESENTS A SERIES OF ARTICLES, TREATISES, and exposés on historically significant issues written by prominent theologians, scholars, and academics in the Islamic world from the last quarter of the nineteenth century to the late twentieth. These works constitute only a small sample of the vast array of intellectual products of Muslim scholars in this period. They display those diversities in theme and orientation that demonstrate the dynamic nature of the religion of Islam, far from its image that has been portrayed in certain media as a monolithic and stagnated system of ideas. This dynamism is naturally a function of the changing social conditions in time and space.

From the wide spectrum of ideas extant in the contemporary Islamic intellectual repertoire, these articles are carefully selected to represent two distinct and contrasting episodes in Islam's historical development. The first, covering a period between the late nineteenth and early twentieth century, consisted of a set of interrelated discourses that sought to bridge Islam with modernity. They were advanced by a group of prominent Muslim theologians, notably in India and Egypt. These scholars critically examined the classical conceptions and methods of jurisprudence and devised a new approach to Islamic theology and Quranic exegesis. This new theological movement, which was nothing short of an outright rebellion against the Islamic orthodoxy, displayed an astonishing compatibility with the nineteenth-century Enlightenment. The central theological problem that engaged its thinkers revolved around the question of the validity of the knowledge derived from sources external to Islam and the methodological adequacy of the four traditional sources of jurisprudence: the Quran, the dicta attributed to the Prophet (*hadith*), the consensus of the theologians (*ijma*), and juristic reasoning by analogy (*qiyas*). They resolved to reinterpret the first two sources and transform the last two in order to formulate a reformist project in light of the prevailing standards of scientific rationality and modern social theory. Such prominent intellectuals and theologians as Sayyid Jamal al-Din al-Afghani, Sayyid Ahmad Khan, Chiragh Ali,

Muhammad Abduh, Amir Ali, and Shibli Nu'mani, and their associates and disciples presented Islamic theology in a manner consistent with modern rationalist ideas and deist religion. These theologians were impressed by the achievements of the West, ranging from scientific and technological progress, the Newtonian conception of the universe, Spencer's sociology, and Darwinian evolutionism, to Western style of living. They all argued that Islam as a world religion was thoroughly capable of adapting itself to the changing conditions of every age, the hallmarks of the perfect Muslim community being law and reason.

In Egypt, the Islamic modernists tackled such perplexing issues as the rise of the rational sciences and their implications for the Islamic belief system, the historical roots of Muslim decadence, the apparent contradiction between the Islamic law and the principles of social organization underpinning the progress of European civilization, and such other controversial issues as the maltreatment of women in Islamic societies, and the Islamic theory of sovereignty and political leadership. The philosophic and political writings of al-Afghani, the modernist Quranic exegesis of Muhammad Abduh, the apologetics of Farid Wajdi, the Islamic feminism of Qasim Amin, and the controversial thesis of Abd al-Raziq were all produced to answer the burning questions facing Islam in a distinctly new historical context. Likewise, the modernist interpretation of Islam became popular among a group of Indian Muslims following the devastating consequences of the Sepoy rebellion of 1857–58. It was epitomized in Sir Sayyid Ahmad Khan's natural theology, the different modernist trends of such associates of his as Chiragh Ali's radical modernity, Shibli Nu'mani's and Amir Ali's hagiographies and rationalist approach toward historical Islam, and Mumtaz Ali's feminism. Islamic modernism in Iran was not as strong. The major modernist attempt transpired in the face of the devastating traditionalist critiques of the Constitutional Revolution (1905–11) when Ayatollah Na'ini defended the legitimacy of constitution-making from the Shi'i standpoint.

The second episode came in pari passu with the decline of liberal-nationalism between 1930s and 1950s (depending on the country) and its end almost always through right- or left-wing military coups. In marked contrast with the previous ideologies, this new discourse categorically rejected the Western model and outlook. Such precursors of fundamentalism as Ayatollah Khomeini and Ayatollah Motahhari from Iran, Hasan al-Bana and Sayyid Qutb from Egypt, Abul Ala Maududi from Pakistan, Mustafa as-Siba'i from Syria, Abbasi Madani, Shaikh Nahnah, and Ali Belhaj from Algeria insisted on unconditional fealty to Islam and questioned the validity of any sources of learning that were outside the Islamic cosmological doctrine. Ayatollah Khomeini advanced a theory of Islamic State based on the governance of the jurisprudent. While Islamic modernism aimed at rationalizing religious dogma to show its consonance with modernity, fundamentalism aimed at Islamizing all social institutions. And, while Islamic modernism had a predominantly social orientation, a distinctive feature of the fundamentalist movement was a high level of political activism aiming to seize state power. In fundamentalism, the political reorganization of society is the necessary step in its overall Islamization project.

The use of the concept of fundamentalism to capture a diversity of Islamic movements is considered problematic by a notable group of academic scholars and

Islamic activists. It has been argued that the concept is only applicable to a particular religious movement in Christianity in the twentieth century, which has no affinity with the existing Islamic movement, and that the concept carries a negative connotation. We realize the inadequacy of the concept. Unfortunately, the alternatives suggested in the literature, such as Islamic radicalism, revivalism, self-reassertion, and Islamism, are no less disputable. The word "Islamist," currently in vogue, could be applied to the pro-West Islamic thinkers as well as to the anti-West Muslim militants. Even if one considers Islamists to be those who, in recent decades, use Islam as a political ideology, the categories of Islamic modernism and Islamism are not exclusive enough to capture the remarkable differences between the two discourses. However defined and conceptualized, the movements noted as modernism and fundamentalism point to the existence of two distinct discourses in contemporary Islam. They may be somewhat clearly distinguished by the thinkers' position on a number of historically significant issues. Five of these issues have become particularly important in the intellectual landscape of the Islamic countries: (i) Islamic jurisprudence, its relationship with the rational sciences, and the notion of differentiation of knowledge; (ii) the relationship between Islam and politics and the proper form of government; (iii) the idea of civilization, the nature of Western society, and the relevance of the dar ul-Islam versus dar ul-harb binary; (iv) the status of women and gender relation in Islam; and (v) forms of representative behavior and lifestyle (style of dress, social mannerisms, customary behaviors in various settings).

The emergence of these issues was a result of the ideological contentions in the Islamic world that involved, in different periods, ideological groups such as the followers of the Enlightenment, secularists, Westernizers, Christian evangelicals, the ideologues connected to the bureaucratic-authoritarian states, liberal-nationalists, socialists, and the orthodox ulama. These ideological contentions were of course related to broader social processes that involved the decline of the old social institution, the development of capitalism, state and class formation. The modernist or fundamentalist exposé is an Islamic resolution of these issues. In their efforts to formulate a distinctly Islamic response to the problems facing their communities, these thinkers could not and would not violate such core principles of Islam as God's unity, the Quran being His word that descended to the people through Prophet Muhammad, and other fundamental religious dogma explicitly stated in the Quran. Beside the fact that they were devout Muslims, violating such principles meant that they would lose the right to speak as Muslims. Other principles, concepts, propositions, and methodological presuppositions that were added to the Islamic intellectual repertoire in the course of history were subject to re-examination.

Generally, the Islamic modernists: accepted an evolutionary view of history with the West being at the pinnacle of the world civilization; praised the Western model; in varying degrees subscribed to the Newtonian conception of the universe; reformulated Islamic methodology in a manner congruent with the standards of nineteenth-century social theory; and affirmed the validity of the scientific knowledge, even though it was not based on Islam; favored democracy and constitutionalism, and the *de facto* separation of religion from politics; and formulated a modernist discourse on women by rejecting polygamy and male domination. The Islamic fundamentalists, in contrast, rejected the notion of social evolution and portrayed the West as having an aggressive political system, exploitative and materialistic economic institutions, and decadent culture. Rather than attempting to reform and modernize Islam, they aimed at Islamizing virtually all social institutions. They rejected the separation of religion from politics, defended Islamic political hierarchy in society, and male domination and polygamy in the family.

Neither fundamentalism nor modernism should be considered as rigid categories. Given favorable sociopolitical and cultural conditions, a formerly strong fundamentalist movement could transform in a modernist direction. The Jordanian branch of the Muslim Brothers, having been favorably received by the ruling elite since its establishment in the country in the 1940s, and being involved in somewhat pluralistic debates since the launching of democratization by the late King Hussein in 1989, displayed many features of modernism. Likewise in Iran, after almost two decades of radical politics, a fairly strong modernist trend is emerging among the country's Shi'i thinkers that proposes, among other things, a notion along with the Tocquevillian view of the compatibility of religion and democracy. On the other hand, the political complications during and after the Constitutional Revolution (1905–11), ethnic strife, and the rise of secular despotism under Reza Shah were not favorable to the strengthening of Shi'i modernism. In all likelihood, the events surrounding the life and work of Ayatollah Na'ini were quite relevant in his attempt first to establish the compatibility of Shi'i political theory with a constitutional government and then in abandoning his political modernism to become a traditional source of emulation.

CULTURAL STUDIES AND SOCIOLOGY OF ISLAM

This book intends to advance knowledge of Islam and the relationship between Islamic thought and historically significant issues. The articles are the outcome of Muslim attempts to address these issues as the relationship is the point of intersection between broader social processes and religious change. The source and historical dynamics that led to the rise and crystallization of these issues were often outside the realm of Islamic political thought and were the cause of their historical discontinuity. Therefore, our historical presentation of the discourses of Islamic modernism and of fundamentalism is also a proposition—namely, ideological change, including changes in Islamic thought, is a discontinuous process that proceeds in an episodic fashion. These two diverse discourses are related to the broader sociocultural and political changes that have engulfed the Islamic countries since the nineteenth century. The breakdown of the traditional order preconditioned the rise of Islamic modernism and resulted in the decline of the ulama institutional basis and thus the weakening of a serious barrier to ideological innovation. It also accelerated the process of social transformation involving the rise of merchants and landowners as well as the emergence of the modern bureaucratic and military apparatus of the state. Although class formation was historically associated with the rise of Islamic modernism, it appears that the breakdown of the old regime and the formation of the modern states were more important factors that mediated social change and the production of the new discourse.

The traditional order in India, Egypt, and Iran was undermined by the gradual intensification of economic, political, and cultural crises in the course of the seventeenth century and thereafter, leading to a fundamental social transformation. It involved the integration into the world economy, the development of capitalism, and the emergence of the modern social institutions. On the nature of the crises that brought down the formidable bureaucratic and military organizations of the "Islamic" empires and on the patterns of social transformation, historians debate each case, let alone having consensus on the causes of change that were common to all. Nevertheless, after the tumult of economic dislocation was replaced by some degree of serenity and the chaos of conflicts gave way to a more clear configuration of political and social hierarchies, the picture that emerged in nineteenth-century India, Egypt, and Iran showed similar types of actors whose varying levels of resources and political alliance broadly accounted for the variations in culture production among these countries. These actors were the ulama, merchants/landowners, the state, and the colonial power.

The decline of the Mughal Empire and its eventual disintegration following the devastation of the mutiny of 1857–58 marked a definite end to the Muslim supremacy in India and ushered in a new episode in India's history. At the same time, commercialization and the development of capitalism in the subcontinent made available new forms of resources for culture production. These were as much the intended consequence of British rule in India as it was the unintended results. The British reformist policies also undermined the traditional bases of power of the ulama and set the stage for the rise of the Islamic modernist movement.

A new episode in Egypt began following the French invasion of the country in 1798–1801. The rise of Muhammad Ali to power marked the development of a strong regime capable of exercising central authority. He centralized state power, bringing under the firm control of the government some of the major institutions of the traditional society. He eliminated tax farming and effectively dispossessed the old mamluk ruling class and the ulama. Between 1810 and 1815, his government initiated a comprehensive system of state trading monopolies, creating modern industry. Muhammad Ali also expanded a European-style educational system in the country. The decline of Muhammad Ali's power in 1840 and the subsequent breakdown of the state monopoly system provided favorable conditions for the growth of modern social classes, including merchants and landowners. All these had positive effects on the development of new culture production.

The situation in Iran was quite different. The newly consolidated Qajar dynasty was a weak form of traditional absolutism with no serious interest in modernization. In contrast with their Indian and Egyptian counterparts, the power of the Iranian ulama grew considerably in the nineteenth century principally due to the strengthening of their ties to the merchants and the guilds. In the nineteenth century, foreign economic competition and the state's failure to protect domestic commercial interests adversely affected these classes. As a result, these classes engaged in protest activities that gained increasing momentum in the last quarter of the nineteenth century and culminated in the Constitutional Revolution of

1905–11. Hence a strong basis was formed for the ulama to play an influential role in politics and, occasionally, lead protest movements in the late nineteenth century and thereafter. Ironically, though, the ulama sociopolitical bases of power-ties to the state and different social classes-also became a source of disunity and political division. This disunity was best reflected in the emergence of opposing factions in the Tobacco Movement (1890–92) and the Constitutional Revolution, when a group of the ulama supported the Revolution, while others remained royalists. The latter resisted constitutional change so fiercely that the leaders of the Revolution ended up executing one of the most prominent outspoken critics of modernism, Shaikh Fazlullah Nuri. It was after the revolution, notably under the Reza Shah rule, that Islamic conceptual scaffolding was to lose its relevance in the making of the state and social institutions.

An important part of the social transformation of the nineteenth century was the flooding of the cultural landscape of the Islamic world by diverse ideological currents. The transfer of meaning from Europe diversified the structure of ideological contention that intensified debates about theological, philosophical, and social issues, bringing about a pluralistic cultural environment in a number of Islamic countries. This pluralism did not simply mean the presence of different ideological groups in society. And, for highbrow culture producers, scholarly debates were not simply the clashes of ideas. The debates were also over the codes and conceptual framework in terms of which ideas were expressed. Such binaries of the Islamic orthodoxy as *wahy* versus *aql*, *shari'ah* versus *jahiliyya*, *dar ul-Islam* versus *dar ul-harb*, and *khilaphat* versus *sultana* run into direct collisions with alternative sets of codes in the discourse of the followers of the Enlightenment, British Westernizers, Christian evangelicals such as *human reason* versus *superstition*, *scientific rationality* versus *traditionalism*, *civilization* versus *savagery*, *gender equality* versus *male domination*, *freedom* versus *despotism*, *Christendom* versus *Heathendom*. Cultural pluralism signified conceptual pluralism as well. These diverse discourses shaped Islamic modernism in India, Egypt, and Iran. Al-Afghani's modernist exposé on the role and function of religion; Sayyid Ahmad Khan's natural theology and rationalist interpretations of religious dogma; Abduh's modernist exegesis of the Quran; Shibli's, Chiragh Ali's, and Amir Ali's analysis of historical Islam; Mumtaz Ali's and Qasim Amin's formulation of Islamic feminism; and Chiragh Ali's and Abd al-Raziq's re-examination of Islamic political theory were all, as it were, formulated within the context of criticisms leveled against Islam and Islamic history by such diverse ideological contenders as the followers of the Enlightenment, Westernizers, the think-tanks connected to European colonialism, the Christian missionaries, and, of course, the orthodox ulama.

The sociocultural and political context within which the Islamic fundamentalist discourse was produced was quite different from that of Islamic modernism. It emerged in such countries as Egypt, Iran, Pakistan, and Syria following the military coups that effectively ended the period of somewhat liberal nationalism. In these countries as well as in post-revolutionary Algeria, this context was characterized by the rise of the bureaucratic-authoritarian state that extensively intervened not only in the economic but in the cultural spheres as well. The state's intervention in cultural affairs politicized culture production. The domination of society by the all-encompassing ideology of the state provided a clear target for the opposition groups in their mobilization efforts against the ruling elite. Secular education, cultural modernization, patrimonial policies, and "feminism from above" all became points of contention around which the pioneers of Islamic fundamentalism formulated the idea of Islamic community and the West, the Islamic state, the notion of Islamic economy, gender relations, and Islamic sciences.

The solidification and strength of the post-1950s fundamentalism appear to be a function of the nature of the state. Fundamentalism in pre-revolutionary Iran, Syria, and Algeria was most militant and mastered the support of a significant section of the population because of these states' extensive intervention in economic and cultural sectors. The state having a well-defined ideology provided a monolithic target against which the Islamic opposition developed their ideas of a virtuous Islamic state. In an important respect, the Islamic fundamentalists' view of politics mirrors the very structure of hierarchy against which they were fighting for decades. The ideology of the Egyptian state, in contrast, was subject to a discontinuous change from a semi-constitutional monarchy until 1952, a socialist oriented secular state under Nasser, to that of promoter of capitalism with a positive tendency toward both the West and Islam under Sadat. For the Muslim Brothers, therefore, the state ideology was a moving target. As a result, the historical trajectory of the Islamic fundamentalist movement in Egypt became more complex than that of Iran and Syria. The Society of the Muslim Brothers was not initially a revolutionary organization. Nor did it have a clear idea about its role in society. The program of the Society was articulated in the course of the first ten years of its activities. Even then, it only offered a general sketch of its programs. It was after the government blocked their participation in the political process that the Brothers begin to engage in radical political activities. In contrast to all, the Jordanian ruling elite patronized, and maintained a working relationship with, the Brothers, a factor that explains the predominately moderate and peaceful nature of the Jordanian Islamic movement.

PART I: AN OVERVIEW OF ISLAMIC MODERNISM: THE CONTRIBUTORS IN CONTEXT

INDIA AND THE ALIGARH MOVEMENT

Sayyid Ahmad Khan (1817–98): A pioneer of Islamic modernism in India, Sayyid Ahmad Khan was influenced by the problems of the Muslim community as well as the significant events of his time, the most important of which were the startling effects of the tumultuous days of the Mutiny. His ideas, however, were developed in relation to the existing intellectual problems and the issues raised by the missionaries, British civil servants and Westernizers, and scientific discoveries that challenged Islamic knowledge. For him, the ulama were ill-equipped to deal with the intellectual problems that had besieged Islam. To reconcile Islamic tenets with the principles of natural law, he refused to accept the orthodox methods of reasoning. The Quran, he said, was the sole authority in all matters of judgment. He enunciated the principle that he would accept only the explanation of the Quran by reference to the Quran itself, not to any tradition or the opinion of any scholar (Dar 1957, p. 140). To bring Quranic exegesis into the framework of natural theology, Sayyid Ahmad Khan established the premises that God as the creator of the universe sent prophets to guide mankind; the Quran is the word of God revealed to Muhammad through revelation (*wahy*); there is nothing in the Quran that is incorrect or anti-historical; and God has also created the laws of nature. His natural theology sought a correspondence between the Quran, as the word of God, and nature, as the work of God. These having one Creator cannot contradict each other. Revelation and natural law were thus identical (Ahmad 1967, pp. 42–3; Malik 1980, p. 29). In another article, he went as far as claiming, "Islam is nature and nature is Islam" (Dar 1957, pp. 149–50; Hali 1979, p. 172).

Sayyid Ahmad Khan spoke favorably for intellectual pluralism. "When people are forced to hear arguments on both sides of a matter," said he (1972, p. 85), "there is always hope of justice, but when they hear only one side, falsehoods become obdurate and turn into prejudice." In his commentary on the Bible, he did not accept that the Bible was altered and tampered with. In his view, belligerent disputations among the Muslims and Christians over the issue of abrogation were nothing more than argument about words, and much of the evidence the Christians had taken from the Bible to attack the tenets of Islam was based on misunderstanding (Hali 1979, p. 75). He also criticized the Indian Muslims who "have always considered and believed the Scriptures to be a worthless, fabulous and useless collection of books; and that this mischievous belief of theirs has sometimes been supported and strengthened by the imprudent and immature arguments proceeding from some missionaries" (cited in Arnold 1866, p. 481).

Moulavi Chiragh Ali (1844–95): As Sayyid Ahmad Khan's associate, Chiragh Ali followed a similar approach in rationalizing religious dogma. He examined the traditional sources of the Islamic law and methods to overcome the rigidity of the traditional theologians (Ahmad 1967, pp. 54–8). Rejecting all classical sources of jurisprudence except the Quran, Chiragh Ali constructed a new basis for the law. "There are," said Chiragh Ali, "certain points in which the Muhammadan Common Law is irreconcilable with the modern needs of Islam . . . and requires modifications. The several chapters of the Common Law, as those on political Institutes, Slavery, Concubinage, Marriage, Divorce, and the Disabilities of non-Moslem fellow-subjects are to be remodelled and re-written in accordance with the strict interpretations of the Quran" (Chiragh Ali 1883, p. xxvii).

Chiragh Ali's modernist exposé was developed in response to critics of Islam. One such critic was Reverend MacColl (1881), who had argued that reforms in Islam were not possible because Islamic states were branches of cosmopolitan theocracy bounded together by a common code of essentially and eternally unchangeable civil and religious rules. Chiragh Ali (1883, pp. 3–8) rejected MacColl's argument by making a distinction between the Muhammadan Revealed Law of the Quran and the Muhammadan Common Law that was developed in the course of Muslim history. Islamic jurisprudence, he argued, was compiled at a very late period, and as such it cannot be considered essentially and eternally unchangeable.

This distinction between the revealed law and the common law of Islam not only enabled Chiragh Ali to refute MacCall's claim on the rigidity of Islam, but also set the theological basis for his reinterpretation of the Quran in terms of the standards of modernity. For Chiragh Ali, "the fact that Muhammad did not compile a law, civil or canonical, for the conduct of the believers, nor did he enjoin them to do so, shows that he left to the believers in general to frame any code, civil or canon law, and to found systems which would harmonize with the times, and suit the political and social changes going on around them" (p. 11). For him, this new basis of Muslim law was rational, dynamic, progressive, and in tune with the standards of the modern civilized world. In terms of such standards Chiragh Ali addressed the Orientalists' and the missionaries' criticisms of Islam on the issues of polygamy, *jihad*, religious intolerance, slavery, and concubinage.

Popular *jihad* was a sore point in Muslim-Christian history and a source of often strident Western criticism of Islam. It was claimed that in his zeal to spread Islam, Muhammad, holding the Quran in one hand and the scimitar in the other, pursued wars of conquest against the Quriesh, other Arab tribes, the Jews, and Christians. They further claimed that Islam was an intolerant religion, and Muhammad himself plotted the assassinations of his enemies and was cruel to his prisoners. Chiragh Ali's strategy to reject these claims proceeded by first analyzing the historical context within which Muhammad's alleged actions had taken place. Then by recourse to international law, religious liberty, and the legitimacy of defending one's freedom—that is, the dominant mores of modern diplomacy—he claimed that Muhammad's conduct was justified. He argued that "neither of the wars of Muhammad were offensive, nor did he in any way use force or compulsion in the matter of belief" (Chiragh Ali 1977, p. i). Muhammad and his followers were severely oppressed at intervals and were under a general persecution in Mecca by the Qureish. Under the natural and international law, Muhammad and his followers had every reason to wage war against their persecutors to obtain their civil rights and religious freedom in their native city (p. ii).

'Allama Shibli Nu'mani (1851-1914): Among the outstanding members of Aligarh movement, Shibli was the most conservative. The greater bulk of his work was historical and hagiographical, dealing with the biographies of significant personalities in Islam. He was annoyed by anti-Islamic work of the Orientalists, and much of his historical writings were directed at refuting their claims regarding the nature of the early Islamic movement and responding to various charges made against Islam on the treatment of Christians and Jews living under its domain and on slavery. In his view, "the moral portrait of the Prophet which the historians of Europe have been presenting (may God protect us!) is a picture of evils of all kinds" (Shibli 1970, p. 5).

His approach toward Islamic history was influenced by the investigative methods of Western scholarship, and often in terms of some of the normative criteria in vogue in Europe. He criticized both the early writers of the life of the Prophet for being preoccupied with only reporting the facts and the European historians for exerting themselves to find out the cause of every event by far-fetched guesses and conjectures. The former did not at all care how these facts would affect their religion and history. The latter, on the other hand, were influenced by self-interest and particular viewpoint (Shibli 1970, pp. 59–60). Shibli is set to rectify both these problems at once by elaborating a proper method of writing on the life of Prophet Muhammad. He had read the work of virtually all European authors on Islam that were accessible to him in India (pp. 94–5). While Shibli believed that religious and political prejudices of European authors were the main cause of their distortions of Islamic history, he also considered their reliance on less authentic sources and their invalid principles of scrutinizing evidence additional reasons for their incorrect portrayal of the Prophet (pp. 95–98). Despite his methodological affinity with Western historiography, Shibli did not consider his principle of rationalist analysis of historical Islam and normative framework to be modern originated from Western civilization, but something that had always been implicit in Islam. In a nutshell, the influence of modernism may be discerned from his works, even though he seemed unwilling to admit this fact.

The Aligarh Movement, Modernization, and Policy Frame: Two major periodicals, *Aligarh Institute Gazette* and *Tahzib al-Akhlaq*, were founded by Sayyid Ahmad Khan and constituted the mouthpiece of the modernist discourse underpinning the Aligarh movement. The modernist discourse provided the basic parameters and conceptual framework for the framing of the religious, social, political, and economic program of the Aligarh movement. A most complete exposition of this policy frame and collective identity was presented in a long article, "The Present Economical Condition of the Musalmans of Bengal," which appeared in several issues of *The Aligarh Institute Gazette* (anonymous 1887, pp. 1022–1109). The article began by pointing to the poverty of Indian Muslims and their weak economic situation vis-à-vis the Hindus who controlled the banking system, wholesale trade, and landed property. The author's solutions to the problems of Muslims were sought in terms of nineteenth-century conception of laissez-faire capitalism, dissolution of the connection of religion with customary, social, and political laws, the promotion of pure religion, and the formulation of modern social laws.

Amir Ali (1849–1928): The Islamic modernist movement was not confined to the Aligarh School. In Calcutta, another Muslim tradition of modernism, Westernization, and loyalism to the British emerged. A distinctive feature of the Calcutta Islamic modernism was that its chief precursors, like Karmat Ali and his disciple Amir Ali, were orthodox Shi'i (Ahmad 1967, p. 86). Amir Ali was an effective writer. His *Spirit of Islam* ran to nine editions between 1922 and 1961, and *A Short History of the Saracens* to 13 between 1889 and 1961 in Great Britain.

In his discussions of such issues as slavery, polygamy, and life after death, Amir Ali made reference to other religions, thus giving a comparative perspective to his theological exposition. A spirit of religious tolerance and moderation permeated his presentation of Islam and Islamic history. One of Amir Ali's pioneering contributions to Islamic political theory was his attempt at theological resolution of the problem of succession to Muhammad that constituted one of the most ignitable points of contention between the Sunni and Shi'i. A committed Shi'i, Amir Ali made a distinction between the Shi'i notion of apostolical Imamat and the pontifical caliphate of Abu Bakr, Omar, and Osman who preceded Ali. The Imamat, for the Shi'i, descended by Divine appointment in the apostolic line. Ali was thus the first rightful Caliph, the Imam of the Faithful. For Amir Ali, however, the two forms of leadership, apostolic and pontifical, can coexist and even fulfill positive functions for Muslims as evidenced by Ali being the principal advisers to Abu Bakr and Omar (Amir Ali 1972, pp. 122–8).

Amir Ali's approach in presenting his views on such issues as women, slavery, and others raised by the evangelical polemics is informed by an evolutionary conception of human society. This evolutionary history is naturally experienced by adherents of all religions. This approach allowed him to go on the offensive against his ideological adversaries. The historical Judaism, Christianity, and other religions had displayed many instances of immorality, oppression, and cruelty against humans. Female infanticide, for example, which was common among the pagan Arabs, must have also been common in the seventh century of the Christian era. Whether it was under Zoroastrians or Christendom the conditions of women during the centuries preceding the advent of Islam was deplorable (Amir Ali 1922, pp. xxxiii, lii). Further, "concubinage, the union of people standing to each other in matrimony, existed among the Arabs, the Jews, the Christians, and all the neighboring nations. The Prophet did not in the beginning denounce the custom, but toward the end of his career he expressly forbade it" (p. 247).

ISLAMIC MODERNISM IN EGYPT

Rafi' al-Tahtawi [Rifa'a Badawi] (1801–73) was Egypt's first modern thinker. Among the seventeen books he wrote altogether, two books—*Takhlis al-ibriz il atalkhis Bariz* (The Extraction of Pure Gold from the Report of Paris), and *Manahij al-albab al-misriyya fi mabahij al-adab al-'asriyya* (The Paths of Egyptian Hearts in the Joys of the Contemporary Arabs)—represent the core of his thoughts and at the same time reflect the influence of eighteen-century French Enlightenment. Some of the views of the Enlightenment thinkers were not too far fetched for Tahtawi, who was brought up in the tradition of Islamic political thoughts. The views that an individual realizes his/her potential within the context of social life, that a good society is based on justice, that the purpose of government is the welfare of the ruled, or that a good legislator, as in Rousseau's conception, is one with the intellectual ability to frame good laws in religious symbols that the general public can understand and recognize as valid were all consistent with the views of Muslim philosophers on the role of the Prophet. Other views that influenced Tahatawi, such as the notion that the people should participate in governmental affairs, that they should be educated for this purpose, that laws must change according to circumstances, and that laws that are good in one time and place may not be so at others, were quite new for the ulama of Egypt. Tahtawi's views about nation, country, and nationalism were derived from Montesquieu. In Paris he met Orientalists, such as Silvestre de Sacy, and through them he became aware of the discoveries of the Egyptologists. His awareness of ancient Egypt and its glories filled his mind and became an important element in his thought.[1]

Tahtawi was not an uncritical French admirer. He disapproved of their avarice and believed that their men were slaves to their women. Nevertheless, he commended their cleanliness, the education of their children, their work ethic, and their intellectual curiosity. In spite of what he had seen in Paris, his view of the State was not that of a nineteenth-century liberal. His was a conventional Islamic view. The ruler possesses absolute executive power, but his use of it should be tempered by respect for the law and those who preserve it. In presenting his views on different subjects, his methodically styled expressions were often accompanied by a verse from the Quran or a dicta from the Prophet. This was to ensure that his modern views would not appear contrary to Islam. To encourage his fellow Muslims to travel abroad for the acquisition of knowledge, he presented a hadith from the Prophet that instructed the Muslims to seek knowledge even if that meant traveling to China (Hourani 1983, pp. 70–73).

As a first step towards a systematic introduction of rational sciences to the learned Egyptians, he clarified a distinction, one unfamiliar in Muslim academia, between the scientists who knew *rational* knowledge (i.e., science) and the ulama, who are scholars of *religious* knowledge (i.e., theology). The differentiation of knowledge, which had been an important characteristic of modernity, was, of course, contrary to the traditional Islamic conception of knowledge, which sought its roots in divine revelation, and to the practice of the orthodox ulama, who had often embodied both rational and religious scholarships. Tahtawi informed his readers that one should not assume that French scientists were also priests. Priests were only knowledgeable on religious matters, even though some might also be scientists. In France, there were not very many scientists who were also familiar with Christian theology. He believed that this fact explained why the Christians had surpassed the Muslims in sciences: The Europeans had emphasized the rational sciences (*Ulum-i Ma'aqul*), while Al-Azhar in Cairo and other Muslim universities in Syria and Tunisia were all pre-occupied with traditional sciences (*Ulum-i Manqul*).

In his view, the ulama were not simply the guardians of a fixed and established tradition. Well-versed in the religious law, a Shafi'i by legal rite, he believed that it was a necessary and legitimate practice to adapt the Shari'a to new circumstances. He thus came very close to natural theology when he suggested that there was not much difference between the principles of Islamic law and those principles of "natural law" on which the codes of modern Europe were based. This suggestion implied that Islamic law could be reinterpreted in the direction of conformity with modern needs, and he suggested a principle that could be used to justify this: It is legitimate for a believer, in certain circumstances, to accept an interpretation of the law drawn from a legal code other than his own. One important implication of this assertion was that the gate of independent reasoning (*ijtihad*) that had been considered closed for centuries by many traditionalists was no longer an acceptable methodological premise. It was, however, for the later generation of Islamic scholars to push it open (p. 75).

On issues related to women, Tahtawi believed that girls must be educated as well as boys and on the same footing. For him, polygamy was not forbidden, but

Islam only allows it if the husband is capable of doing justice between his wives. This point was taken up and turned into a virtual prohibition by later writers (p. 78).

There thus appeared for the first time in the writings of Tahtawi many themes that were later to become familiar in Arabic and Islamic thought: that, within the universal umma, there were national communities demanding the loyalty of their subjects; that the object of government was human welfare in this world as well as in the next; that human welfare consisted in the creation of civilization, which was the final worldly end of government; that modern Europe, and specifically France, provided the norms of civilization; that the secret of European strength and greatness lied in the cultivation of the rational sciences; that the Muslims, who had themselves studied the rational sciences in the past, had neglected them and fallen behind because of the domination of Turks and Mamlukes; and that they could and should enter the mainstream of modern civilization by adopting the European sciences and their fruits (p. 82).

Sayyid Jamal al-Din al-Afghani (1839–97): Islamic modernism in the Middle East is associated with the life and work of Afghani. In contrast with many of his contemporaries, Afghani's name is not attached to the Islamic history of only one country in the region. He was frequently on the move from this country to the next. His stay in Egypt for eight years is seen as the most fruitful period in his career. Although politically he displayed a strong anti-West stance, intellectually some of the crucial elements in his views on religion and society were developed in relation to and influenced by the modernist discourse of nineteenth-century Europe. One such element was Guizot's (1890) idea of civilization. Afghani subscribed to evolutionary thinking and the belief in human intellect as the prime mover of social progress and human civilization. Thus when he spoke of the decline of Islam, he did not mean Islam as a religion, but as a civilization (Hourani 1983, pp. 114–5). This notion is echoed in *al-Urwa al-wuthqa* (The Indissoluble Bond, 1884), an Arabic periodical published in Paris through the joint efforts of Afghani and Abduh.

Where Afghani's commitment to modernity and human reason is revealed in no uncertain term is in his exchange with Renan (1883), who had criticized Islam and early Arabs for being hostile to scientific and philosophical inquiry (Keddie 1968, p. 85). Afghani criticized Renan for advancing a racist argument, that the Arabs by nature were hostile to science. He contended that all peoples in their early stage of development were incapable of accepting reason to distinguish good from evil. Hence, the presence of prophets or teachers become necessary to guide these peoples.

Muhammad Abduh (1849–1905): Although he was Afghani's disciple and associate, Abduh later on abandoned the oppositional politics of his mentor altogether and began to emphasize social issues and educational reforms. Instead of anti-British political agitation, Abduh believed that priority must be given to education so that individuals could perform the duties of a representative government with intelligence and firmness. Both the government and the people must become accustomed gradually to the giving and receiving of advice, and if the country were ready for participation in the government, there would be no point in seeking such participation by force of arms. It is to be feared, he concluded, that this uprising will bring about the occupation of the country by foreigners (Adams 1933, pp. 55, 64; Cromer 1908, pp. 179–81; al-Manar 1906, pp. 413, 462; Hourani 1983, pp. 158–9; Enayat 1977, pp. 120–3).

Abduh was influenced by the Enlightenment discourse. He was an admirer of Herbert Spencer whom he visited in Great Britain, and translated his *Education* into Arabic. He had read Rousseau's *Emile*, the novels of Tolstoy as well as his didactic writings, Strauss's *Life of Jesus*, and the work of Renan. He had some contact with European thinkers, wrote to Tolstoy on the occasion of his excommunication from the Russian church, and traveled to Europe, whenever he could, to renew his soul, as he said, and because it revived his hopes about the future of the Muslim world (Adams 1933, p. 67; al-Manar 1906, p. 66; Hourani 1983, p. 135). Generally, the ideas of the French Enlightenment were in vogue among the new generation of intellectuals; the knowledge of the French was widespread—Montesquieu and Voltaire had been translated. "The ideas of positivism, in their original or a distorted form, were widespread. Some Egyptians indeed had drunk at the fountainhead: there is extant a copy of Comte's *Discours sur l'ensemble du positivisme*" (Hourani 1983, p. 138). As a result, in Abduh's view, a duality had emerged in Egypt's cultural landscape. One was a younger generation who had embraced all ideas of Europe, and the other, the conservatives who had resisted all change. Bridging the gap between these two intellectual orders was one of Abduh's central projects. His intellectual solution to this distinctly Muslim problem, however, was formulated in terms of the French Enlightenment. He doubted the possibility of transplanting European laws and institutions to Egypt. Abduh viewed Egypt's cultural predicament from Comtean perspective—the construction of a universally acceptable system of ideas that were to transcend both the rationalist zeal of the French Revolution and those who wanted to return to the old order. Abduh was preoccupied to show that Islam contained the universalistic creed that could link the two cultures and form a moral basis for modern Egypt (Hourani 1983, pp. 139–40; Adams 1933, pp. 97–9; Cromer 1908, pp. 180–1).

Muhammad Farid Wajdi (1875–1954): The civilized order in Europe, having its own laws to be discovered by sociology in contradistinction with the revealed laws of Islam, was an empirical fact that Afghani, Abduh, and other modernist thinkers had to reckon with. For if a non-Islamic order had surpassed Muslims in science and technology, understanding its sociological laws would not only uncover the secrets of its progress but also reveal the existence of a new mode of social organization that has yielded a better society than that of the Muslims. How could one reconcile the tension between the new mode of social organization that had produced civilization and the Islamic teachings that, in the Muslim view, were far superior to those of Europe? Wajdi (1899) attempted to overcome the tensions between the two by a simple apologetic assumption that Islam was a perfect model of civilization. Its central premise was that everything the modern world had discovered and approved was foresighted in the Quran and hidden in its verses: "There is no principle that has been discovered by experience and no theory that has been established by the testimony of the sense, which have had an influence in the progress of man and in uplifting civilization, but are an echo of a verse from the Kur'an or of a tradition of the Prophet; so that the observer imagines that all effort and energy on the part of the scholars of the world toward the uplift of mankind have no other purpose than to bring practical proof of the truth of the principles of Islam" (cited in Adams 1933, p. 244; Hourani 1983). While for Abduh a true society was based on the teaching of Islam, in Wajdi there was a subtle change in the relationship between the two, and a true Islam became in conformity with civilization. By implication, *dar ul-harb* vs. *dar ul-Islam* duality became irrelevant.

Qasim Amin (1865–1908) *and Islamic feminism:* Although Egyptian modernists were in favor of improving the conditions of women, Amin's *Tahrir al-mar'a* (The Liberation of Women, 1992 [1899]) represented one of the most systematic efforts to defend the compatibility of Islam with gender equality. Like other thinkers, Amin developed his ideas within the context of the existing debates about Egypt and Islam. His assessment of the situation of women in his country echoed much of the critiques of the missionaries, the British colonial administrators, and the followers of the Enlightenment. The intellectual context of Amin's exposé on women was also characterized by the rise of gender awareness among educated women. Egypt in the 1890s witnessed the rise of such women's publications as *al-Fatah* (The Young Woman, 1892), *al-Firdaus* (Paradise, 1896), and *Mir'at al-Hasana* (Mirror of the Beautiful, 1896) (Baron 1994, pp. 14–16). A more proximate factor that stimulated Amin's interests in women and his writing of *Tahrir al-mar'a* was the critiques leveled against Egypt's backwardness, the low status of women and the use of the veil by Duc d'Harcourt, a French writer. In his reply to d'Harcourt, Amin defended the use of the veil and criticized the promiscuity and laxity of European social life. From that time he began to study European views on woman and, as a result, became convinced that the advancement of Egypt lay in the uplift of its women (Adams 1933, p. 22).

Ali Abd al-Raziq (1888–1966) *and Re-examination of the Islamic Political Theory:* Abd al-Raziq's secular interpretation of Islamic political theory in his *Al-Islam wa usul al-hukm* (Islam and the Fundamentals of Authority, 1925) was a bold attempt to disengage the theological support that underpinned the Islamic notion of politics. The debate over the caliphate and the nature of the authority in Islam was as old as the Islamic movement itself. When the issue resurfaced in the early twentieth century, its discursive context was characterized by secularism, treating religion and politics as distinct spheres of human intellectual endeavors and practices. Al-Raziq's contribution to this debate went far beyond the assessment of the necessity of the caliphates—he questioned whether there had ever been an Islamic system of government. For al-Raziq, the concept of caliphate itself was un-Islamic—hence problematizing what had been taken for granted by virtually all Islamic political theorists. In his view, the caliphate had no basis either in the Quran, the Tradition, or Consensus among the Muslims. Theoretically, the caliphate was a vice-gerency on behalf of the Prophet and embodies both religious and secular authorities, and held by those who had succeeded him. They were given absolute authority in both spheres, except that they were required to rule in accordance with the *shari'ah*. Nevertheless, the examination of the evidence presented in support of this institution provided an insufficient basis to sustain the claim of this form of government. "If we were to collect all his direct teachings on the question of government, we would get little more than a fraction of the principle of law and organizations needed for maintaining a state" (cited in Ahmed 1960, p. 118). Raziq thus argued that the chief purpose of Muhammad was purely spiritual not political. It was not Muhammad's intention to establish an empire. Nor did his mission require him to exercise power over his followers or opponents. The political changes Muhammad brought about in the life of the Arabs were the incidental consequences of his moral revolution. He then attacked the historical experience of the caliphate by declaring that the institution had hindered the progress of the Muslims. It had been the sources of all corruption in Muslim history and an instrument of obstruction against intelligent thinking. Religion had therefore nothing to do with one form of government rather than another, and there was nothing in Islam that hindered Muslims to destroy the old and establish a new political system on the basis of newest concepts and experiences (Adams 1933, pp. 259–68; Ahmed 1960, pp. 117–19; Hourani 1983, pp. 185–8, Enayat 1982, pp. 62–8).

PART II: AN OVERVIEW OF ISLAMIC FUNDAMENTALISM: THE CONTRIBUTORS IN CONTEXT

Ishaq Ahmad Farhan (1934-) was born in Ein Karen, West Bank Palestine, and received his elementary education in Palestine. He was granted a scholarship to pursue his studies at the American University of Beirut. He obtained his MS in Chemistry in 1958. Continuing his education in the United States, he obtained a Master's degree in Literature in 1962 from Columbia College and a Doctorate in Education in 1964.

Dr. Farhan was appointed Minster of Education in 1970. In 1972 he was appointed Minister of Religious Affairs, but resigned from his post in 1973 in protest to Jordan's participation in the 1973 Vienna Conference. He was also Director of the Royal Scientific Society, 1975–78, and president of the University of Jordan, 1976–78. He was an appointed member of the Consultative National Council and a member of Upper House.

Dr. Farhan joined the Muslim Brothers in 1948. His membership was suspended in 1970 due to his participation in the government of Wasfi Al-Tal, but he was reinstated in 1980. He announced his withdrawal from the MB's Executive Office shortly after he declared the formation of the Islamic Action Front Party.

The Society of the Muslim Brothers was founded by Hasan al-Banna in Egypt in 1928. By the late 1930s, it had grown to become one of the most important politico-religious organizations in the country. A branch of the Muslim Brothers was also established in Syria. It was organized into the Islamic Socialist Front in

November 1949. Mustafa as-Siba'i, the leader of the Front, declared that he would work for the realization of Islamic socialism that had been advocated by the Prophet. The Brothers in both countries, however, have had belligerent relationships with their regimes. Another branch of the Muslim Brothers was established in Jordan in 1945. The Brothers' history in Jordan, in a marked contrast with that of their Egyptian and Syrian counterparts, has been one of moderation and unprecedented peaceful cohabitation with the state.

The Islamic Salvation Front (FIS) was created in 1989 in Algeria. The FIS was led by Abbassi Madani and Ali Belhaj. The governing principle of the Islamic state, for the FIS, was the shura. Ali Belhaj rejected democracy because he believed it was based on people's sovereignty and not that of God. He favored the execution of Islamic criminal sentencing, and limited role for women in society. The views of Abbasi Madani—a veteran of the Algerian independence movement and a Ph.D. from London—were more moderate. The FIS was successful at the polls in the first round of elections for the National Assembly in 1991. To prevent the FIS victory in the second round in 1992, the army displaced the Benjedid's regime. The army intervention, however, unleashed a cycle of violence between the military and the Islamic groups such as the GIA and the MIA, which has so far claimed tens of thousands lives.

Sayyid Qutb (1906–66), a novelist, poet, educator, and journalist, was a leader of the Muslim Brothers in Egypt. Qutb believed that Islam alone could deliver mankind from its "rubbish heap" of godless ideologies. In some of his works, Qutb tried to prove that the methodology of Islam could explain the harmony between "nature" and its functioning on the planet earth. In *Milestones*, Qutb outlined the stages in the establishment of a true Islamic life. For him, "the first part of the first pillar of Islam is a dedication of perfect servitude to God alone, and witness to this meaning and requirement is given by the recital of 'There is no god except God.' The second part of this pillar is that for knowing the details of this servitude and its true and correct way one has to refer to the Messenger of God (S.A.W). Witnessing 'Muhammad (S.A.W.) is the Messenger of God' refers to this. The practical shape of absolute servitude to God is that Allah alone should be deemed the Lord (the worshipped) in faith, practice and law" (Qutb 1988. p. 193). In his *Ma'alim fi al-Tariq*, he countered the perception that Islam pales next to what the West had to offer: "There is nothing in Islam for us to be ashamed of or defensive about. . . . During my years in America, some of my fellow Muslims would have recourse to apologetics as though they were defendants on trial. Contrariwise, I took an offensive position, excoriating the Western jahiliyya, be it in its much-acclaimed religious beliefs or in its depraved and dissolute socioeconomic and moral conditions: this Christian idolatry of the Trinity and its notions of sin and redemption which make no sense at all; this Capitalism, . . . that animal freedom which is called permissiveness, that slave market dubbed 'women's liberation'" (Qutb, 1964. pp.214–5 in Sivan 1990). One of the most controversial theses advanced by Qutb was that the existing order in all Muslim countries was in a state of ignorance *(jahiliyya)* similar to that of pre-Islamic ear, and called upon Muslims for its overthrow.

Sayyid Abul A'la Maududi (1903–79) was a prominent Islamic thinker from the Indian subcontinent. He began his journalistic career in 1929, editing first the *al-jama'a*, the organ of the orthodox *Jam'iyyat al-ulama-I Hind*, and then in 1932 starting the *Tarjuman al Quran*, an exegetical journal propagating his revivalist fundamentalism in religion and politics, a movement which he and his party described as the "Islamic Renaissance" (Ahmad 1967, p. 208). He founded the organization of Jama'at-i Islami in 1941 to further the idea that only authentic Islam—not Indian nationalism—could answer Muslims' social problems. He came to advocate an Islamic state in Pakistan, to which members of the organization fled after the Indian partition of 1947 (Ahmad and Grunebaum, 1970. p. 20). In his book *A short History of the Revivalist Movement in Islam* (1986), he claimed that Imam al-Ghazali confronted Greek philosophy and removed its effects from Muslim thought. In his view, al-Ghazali revealed the rational effects of the principles of belief, reopened the spirit of *ijtihad*, arranged the programs of education, introduced the moral principles of Islam, and invited the government and officials to follow Islam (Esposito 1983; Adams 1966). However, he criticizes al-Ghazali for his lack of knowledge of the hadith and his inclination toward Sufism. He divided religious reformers into three groups: first, scholars who had revealed the true knowledge transmitted by the Ahl-i Sunna *mujtahids;* second, heretic Muslim reformers who believed and respect the Quran and *hadith;* third, the religious reformers who were disbeliever. Criticizing Western influence on the new generation, Maududi stated "Western thought and Western civilization influenced them so deeply that they started looking at everything from the western angle, and pondered on every issue with a western mind. It became impossible for them to think and to observe independently keeping their approach free of western domination" (Maududi 1992, pp. 112–3).

Imam Ruhullah Khomeini (1902–89) believed that faith in the oneness of God, the mission of the Prophet of Islam, and the Holy Quran, as well as the acceptance of tenets of Islam are the solid pillars under which all Muslims need unite to face their enemies. Before the Iranian Revolution, he depicted the Shah's government, the United States, the West in general, and the Soviet Union as enemies. He announced, "If the religious leaders have influence, they will not permit this nation to be the slave of Britain one day, and America the next" (Khomeini 1981, p. 181). He believed the divine Islamic laws to be utterly progressive and comprehensive in any age. With such beliefs, Khomeini campaigned against the Western influence in Iran and in particular opposed its West-allied Pahlavi regime. In 1962 he denounced a bill for the establishment of provincial and city councils and universal suffrage, and accused the Shah of pursuing martial law and committing atrocities. Khomeini, then in exile, gained popular support and successfully led the revolutionary movement of 1977–79 that toppled the late Shah of Pahlavi. Ayatollah Khomeini wrote widely on religion, jurisprudence, philosophy, Gnosticism, and ethics (Abrahamian 1993; Ruhani 1993; Moin 1991).

Abd al-Latif Sultani (d.1984), an imam and schoolteacher, was a founder of the modern Algerian Islamic movement along with Muhammad Shannon. In his life, he was engaged in a constant campaign against "corruptive" Western, as well as socialist, elements in cultural and political dealings. He did not adopt the principles of Islamic socialism, as did many of his colleagues after coming to peaceful terms with the FLN regime (Ruedy 1994, p. 80). In 1974, he wrote a treatise against Houari Boumediene and all he stood for entitled *Mazdakism is the Source of Socialism*. In it he wrote, "The same harmful effects which were produced by the Mazdak sect in Persian society (licentiousness, usurpation, injustice, etc....) are reproduced [in the modern age] by socialism and Communism in the countries which are afflicted by them. Injustice and debauchery in all forms are common there. Liberties which call on the good and fight against evil are smothered there, while those who want to do evil or aid it are given complete freedom" (cited in Burgat and Dowell 1997, p. 251). He equated Algeria's liberal, innovation-prone leaders with the followers of Mazdak, a fifth century Persian heretic (p. 250). Shortly before his death, he published another book on the principles of Islamic beliefs (Sultani 1982).

Murtaza Mutahhari (1920–79), a close associate of Ayatollah Khomeini, taught Islamic theology at Tehran University and was involved in oppositional activities against the Shah's government. Mutahhari was assigned by Khomeini to organize a Revolutionary Council at the time of the Iranian Revolution. Although Mutahhari was engaged in political activities, his prominence arose from his philosophical writings most notably his criticism of materialism. He published numerous books and articles on Islamic topics. His work *Materialism and Fundamentals of Islamic Thought* presents his philosophical and methodological principles as well as his cultural views (Mutahhari 1985; Davari 1988). After the Revolution, when Islamic veiling was enforced, Ayatollah Mutahhari's book *The Problem of Veiling* (1969) became the standard Islamic fundamentalist exposé on women's social role. Mutahhari wrote, "If a woman leaves her house covered, not only does it not detract from her human dignity, but it adds to it. Take a woman who leaves her home with only her face and two hands showing and from her behavior and the clothes she wears there is nothing which would cause others to be stimulated or attracted toward her. That is, she does not invite men to herself" (Mutahhari 1987. pp. 47–64).

Ali Shariati (1933–77), a college professor and Islamic scholar, studied in Iran and then went to graduate school at the Sorbonne in Paris to study sociology. While studying in Europe, he became acquainted with the ideas of Jean-Paul Sartre and Franz Fanon. Upon returning to Iran, he promoted revolutionary action for social justice and freedom. His lectures at Housseini-e Ershad Religious Institute were popular. In his writings, he presented a new picture of Islam to encourage intellectuals and the younger generation to use this faith in their struggle toward social change. His main concern was with explaining the problems of Muslim societies by arguing that a new Islamic approach was necessary to solve those problems. He rejected the traditional view that Islam was only a set of formulas about ablution and menstruation. In his promotion of political activity, he represented Imam Husayn as a model of sacrifice for social freedom. He believed in a less determinative role for God in people's lives; an idea that was not welcomed by the mainstream clergy. He tirelessly rejected Western and Marxist views about religion and social life. He wrote, "*Economism* is the fundamental principle of the philosophy of life in Western industrial capitalist society, where, as Francis Bacon put it, 'Science abandons its search for truth and turns to the search for power.' The material 'needs' that are generated every day and progressively find increase (so that the scope of consumption may be enlarged in quantity, quality, and variety alike, to feed the vast engines of production as they race on in delirium), transform people into worshippers of consumption" (Shariati 1980, p. 32). In brief, "for Shariati religion is the most effective weapon to fight imperialism and Western cultural domination" (Moaddel 1993, p. 152).

Jalal Al-i Ahmad (1923–69) was an erstwhile journalist and the youngest writer to establish himself as a fiction writer and essayist between 1941 and 1953 in Iran. Before the 1953 coup d'état and during a relatively democratic period, he advocated nationalistic views and criticized tradition and backwardness. Then, when new sociopolitical conditions prompted intellectuals to develop a strong anti-Western sentiment, Jalal Al-i Ahmad became an advocate of committed literature. His loyalties began with the Tudeh Party, and then shifted to the Third Force (a small political group that separated from the Tudeh Party and supported Mossadeq's national government). Later, he devoted himself exclusively to writing. He acted as a spokesperson for his contemporaries in the 1950s and 1960s. Islam played an important role in his ideological commitment during this period. He was one of the few prominent authors who openly supported Islam as a potential force for fortifying the movement against foreign domination and as a means of defining Iranian cultural identity (Talattof 1999). He believed that Iranians should return both to Persian culture and Shiism to find an identity (Al-i Ahmad 1979 and 1982). In *Plagued by the West*, he claimed that consumerism and women's emancipation were the result of the subversive Western influence on pure, indigenous Iranian-Islamic culture (Al-i Ahmad, 1982). In *Mudir-i Madrisih* (The School Principle), Al-i Ahmad patronizes an anti-American sentiment in defense of Islamic society. The narrator tells a teacher who has been run over by an American car "don't you know you shouldn't be on the streets? Don't you know that the streets, the traffic lights, the civilization, the asphalt all belong to those who, driving in their cars, have spread all over the world" (Al-i Ahmad 1976)? With this sort of writing, he disseminated the idea that intellectuals should recognize Islam as a major unifying element in their culture, differentiating them from the West.

NOTES

1. Hourani, *Arabic Thought*, p. 70; Enayat, *Sayri*, p. 28; Ahmed, p. 13. According to Ahmed, "Ria'ah and his pupils translated 2,000 books and pamphlets on a variety of subjects. Many of them were published by the official printing press established by Muhammad Ali" (p. 10).

I. JURISPRUDENCE, RATIONAL SCIENCES, AND DIFFERENTIATION OF KNOWLEDGE

CHAPTER 1

RELIGION VERSUS SCIENCE

Sayyid Jamal al-Din al-Afghani

Excerpt from Nikki R. Keddie, ed. *An Islamic Response to Imperialism: Political and Religious Writings of Sayyid Jamal al-Din al-Afghani.* Berkeley and Los Angeles: University of California Press, 1968, pp. 181–87.

M. RENAN WANTED TO CLARIFY A POINT OF THE HISTORY of the Arabs that had remained unclear until now and to throw a living light on their past, a light that may be somewhat troubling for those who venerate these people, though one cannot say that he has usurped the place and rank that they formerly occupied in the world. M. Renan has not at all tried, we believe, to destroy the glory of the Arabs, which is indestructible; he has applied himself to discovering historical truth and making it known to those who do not know it, as well as to those who study the influence of religions on the history of nations, and in particular on that of civilization. I hasten to recognize that M. Renan has acquitted himself marvelously of this very difficult task, in citing certain facts that have passed unnoticed until this time. I find in his talk remarkable observations, new perceptions, and an indescribable charm. However, I have under my eyes only a more or less faithful translation of this talk. If I had had the opportunity to read it in the French text, I could have penetrated better the ideas of this great thinker.

He receives my humble salutation as an homage that is due him and as the sincere expression of my admiration. I would say to him, finally, in these circumstances, what al-Mutanabbi, a poet who loved philosophy, wrote several centuries ago to a high personage whose actions he celebrated: "Receive," he said to him, "the praises that I can give you; do not force me to bestow on you the praises that you merit."

M. Renan's talk covered two principal points. The eminent philosopher applied himself to proving that the Muslim religion was, by its very essence, opposed to the development of science, and that the Arab people, by their nature, do not like either metaphysical sciences or philosophy. This precious plant, M. Renan seems to say, dried up in their hands as if burnt up by the breath of the desert wind. But after reading this talk one cannot refrain from asking oneself if these obstacles come uniquely from the Muslim religion itself or from the manner in which it was propagated in the world; from the character, manners, and aptitudes of the peoples who adopted this religion, or of those on whose nations it was imposed by force. It is no doubt the lack of time that kept M. Renan from elucidating these points; but the harm is no less for that, and if it is difficult to determine its causes in a precise manner and by irrefutable proofs, it is even more difficult to indicate the remedy.

As to the first point, I will say that no nation at its origin is capable of letting itself be guided by pure reason. Haunted by terrors that it cannot escape, it is incapable of distinguishing good from evil, of distinguishing that which could make it happy from that which might be the unfailing source of its unhappiness and misfortune. It does not know, in a word, either how to trace back causes or to discern effects.

This lacuna means that it cannot be led either by force or persuasion to practice the actions that would perhaps be the most profitable for it, or to avoid what is harmful. It was therefore necessary that humanity look outside itself for a place of refuge, a peaceful corner where its tormented conscience could find repose. It was then that there arose some educator or other who, not having, as I said above, the necessary power to force humanity to follow the inspirations of reason, hurled it into the unknown and opened to it vast horizons where the imagination was pleased and where it found, if not the complete satisfaction of its desires, at least an unlimited field for its hopes. And, since humanity, at its origin, did not know the causes of the events that passed under its eyes and the secrets of things, it was perforce led to follow the advice of its teachers and the orders they gave. This obedience was imposed in the name of the supreme Being to whom the educators attributed all events, without permitting men to discuss its utility or its disadvantages. This is no doubt for man one of the heaviest and most humiliating yokes, as I recognize; but one cannot deny that it is by this religious education, whether it be Muslim, Christian, or pagan, that all nations have emerged from barbarism and marched toward a more advanced civilization.

If it is true that the Muslim religion is an obstacle to the development of sciences, can one affirm that this obstacle will not disappear someday? How does the Muslim religion differ on this point from other religions? All religions are intolerant, each one in its way. The Christian religion, I mean the society that follows its inspirations and its teachings and is formed in its image, has emerged from the first period to which I have just alluded; thenceforth free and independent, it seems to advance rapidly on the road of progress and science, whereas Muslim society has not yet freed itself from the tutelage of religion. Realizing, however, that the Christian religion preceded the Muslim religion in the world by many centuries, I cannot keep from hoping that Muhammadan society will succeed someday in breaking its bonds and marching resolutely in the path of civilization after the manner of Western society, for which the Christian faith, despite its rigors and intolerance, was not at all an invincible obstacle. No, I cannot admit that this hope be denied to Islam. I plead here with M. Renan not the cause of the Muslim religion, but that of several hundreds of millions of men, who would thus be condemned to live in barbarism and ignorance.

In truth, the Muslim religion has tried to stifle science and stop its progress. It has thus succeeded in halting the philosophical or intellectual movement and in turning minds from the search for scientific truth. A similar attempt, if I am not mistaken, was made by the Christian religion, and the venerated leaders of the Catholic church have not yet disarmed so far as I know. They continue to fight energetically against what they call the spirit of vertigo and error. I know all the difficulties that the Muslims will have to surmount to achieve the same degree of civilization, access to the truth with the help of philosophic and scientific methods being forbidden them. A true believer must, in fact, turn from the path of studies that have for their object scientific truth, studies on which all truth must depend, according to an opinion accepted at least by some people in Europe. Yoked, like an ox to the plow, to the dogma whose slave he is, he must walk eternally in the furrow that has been traced for him in advance by the interpreters of the law. Convinced, besides, that his religion contains in itself all morality and all sciences, he attaches himself resolutely to it and makes no effort to go beyond. Why should he exhaust himself in vain attempts? What would be the benefit of seeking truth when he believes he possesses it all? Will he be happier on the day when he has lost his faith, the day when he has stopped believing that all perfections are in the religion he practices and not in another? Wherefore he despises science. I know all this, but I know equally that this Muslim and Arab child whose portrait M. Renan traces in such vigorous terms and who, at a later age, becomes "a fanatic, full of foolish pride in possessing what he believes to be absolute truth," belongs to a race that has marked its passage in the world, not only by fire and blood, but by brilliant and fruitful achievements that prove its taste for science, for all the sciences, including philosophy (with which, I must recognize, it was unable to live happily for long).

I am led here to speak of the second point that M. Renan treated in his lecture with an incontestable authority. No one denies that the Arab people, while they were still in the state of barbarism, rushed into the road of intellectual and scientific progress with a rapidity only equaled by the speed of their conquests, since in the space of a century, they acquired and assimilated almost all the Greek and Persian sciences that had developed slowly during several centuries on their native soil, just as they extended their domination from the Arabian peninsula up to the mountains of the Himalaya and the summit of the Pyrenees.

One might say that in all this period the sciences made astonishing progress among the Arabs and in all the countries under their domination. Rome and

Byzantium were then the seats of theological and philosophical sciences as well as the shining center and burning hearth of all human knowledge. Having followed for several centuries the path of civilization, the Greeks and Romans walked with assurance over the vast field of science and philosophy. There came, however, a time when their researches were abandoned and their studies interrupted.

The monuments they had built to science collapsed and their most precious books were relegated to oblivion. The Arabs, ignorant and barbaric as they were in origin, took up what had been abandoned by the civilized nations, rekindled the extinguished sciences, developed them, and gave them a brilliance they had never had. Is not this the index and proof of their natural love for sciences? It is true that the Arabs took from the Greeks their philosophy as they stripped the Persians of what made their fame in antiquity; but these sciences, which they usurped by right of conquest, they developed, extended, clarified, perfected, completed, and coordinated with a perfect taste and a rare precision and exactitude. Besides, the French, the Germans, and the English were not as far from Rome and Byzantium as were the Arabs, whose capital was Baghdad. It was therefore easier for the former to exploit the scientific treasures that were buried in these two great cities. They made no effort in this direction until Arab civilization lit up with its reflections the summits of the Pyrenees and poured its light and riches on the Occident. The Europeans welcomed Aristotle, who had emigrated and become Arab; but they did not think of him at all when he was Greek and their neighbor. Is there not in this another proof, no less evident, of the intellectual superiority of the Arabs and of their natural attachment to philosophy? It is true that after the fall of the Arab kingdom in the Orient as in the Occident, the countries that had become the great centers of science, like Iraq and Andalusia, fell again into ignorance and became the center of religious fanaticism; but one cannot conclude from this sad spectacle that the scientific and philosophic progress of the Middle Ages was not due to the Arab people who ruled at that time.

M. Renan does do them this justice. He recognizes that the Arabs conserved and maintained for centuries the hearth of science. What nobler mission for a people! But while recognizing that from about A.D. 775 to near the middle of the thirteenth century, that is to say during about five hundred years, there were in Muslim countries very distinguished scholars and thinkers, and that during this period the Muslim world was superior in intellectual culture to the Christian world, M. Renan has said that the philosophers of the first centuries of Islam as well as the statesmen who became famous in this period were mostly from Harran, from Andalusia, and from Iran. There were also among them Transoxianan and Syrian priests. I do not wish to deny the great qualities of the Persian scholars nor the role that they played in the Arab world; but permit me to say that the Harranians were Arabs and that the Arabs in occupying Spain and Andalusia did not lose their nationality; they remained Arabs. Several centuries before Islam the Arabic language was that of the Harranians. The fact that they preserved their former religion, Sabaeanism, does not mean they should be considered foreign to the Arab nationality. The Syrian priests were also for the most part Ghassanian Arabs converted to Christianity.

As for Ibn-Bajja, Ibn-Rushd (Averroes), and Ibn-Tufail, one cannot say that they are not just as Arab as al-Kindi because they were not born in Arabia, especially if one is willing to consider that human races are only distinguished by their languages and that if this distinction should disappear, nations would not take long to forget their diverse origins. The Arabs who put their arms in the service of the Muslim religion, and who were simultaneously warriors and apostles, did not impose their language on the defeated, and wherever they established themselves, they preserved it for them with a jealous care. No doubt Islam, in penetrating the conquered countries with the violence that is known, transplanted there its language, its manners, and its doctrine, and these countries could not thenceforth avoid its influence. Iran is an example; but it is possible that in going back to the centuries preceding the appearance of Islam, one would find that the Arabic language was not then entirely unknown to Persian scholars. The expansion of Islam gave it, it is true, a new scope, and the Persian scholars converted to the Muhammadan faith thought it an honor to write their books in the language of the Quran. The Arabs cannot, no doubt, claim for themselves the glory that renders these writers illustrious, but we believe that they do not need this claim; they have among themselves enough celebrated scholars and writers. What would happen if, going back to the first period of Arab domination, we followed step by step the first group from which was formed this conquering people who spread their power over the world, and if, eliminating everything that is outside this group and its descendants, we did not take into account either the influence it exercised on minds or the impulse it gave to the sciences? Would we not be led, thus, no longer to recognize in conquering peoples other virtues or merits than those that flow from the material fact of conquest? All conquered peoples would then regain their moral autonomy and would attribute to themselves all glory, no part of which could be legitimately claimed by the power that fructified and developed these germs. Thus, Italy would come to say to France that neither Mazarin nor Bonaparte belonged to her; Germany or England would in turn claim the scholars who, having come to France, made its professorships illustrious and enhanced the brilliance of its scientific renown. The French, on their side, would claim for themselves the glory of the offspring of those illustrious families who, after [the revocation of] the edict of Nantes, emigrated to all Europe. And if all Europeans belong to the same stock, one can with justice claim that the Harranians and the Syrians, who are Semites, belong equally to the great Arab family.

It is permissible, however, to ask oneself why Arab civilization, after having thrown such a live light on the world, suddenly became extinguished; why this torch has not been relit since; and why the Arab world still remains buried in profound darkness.

Here the responsibility of the Muslim religion appears complete. It is clear that wherever it became established, this religion tried to stifle the sciences and it was marvelously served in its designs by despotism.

Al-Siuti tells that the Caliph al-Hadi put 5,000 philosophers to death in Baghdad in order to destroy sciences in the Muslim countries down to their roots. Admitting that this historian exaggerated the number of victims, it remains nonetheless established that this persecution took place, and it is a bloody stain for the history of a religion as it is for the history of a people. I could find in the past of the Christian religion analogous facts. Religions, by whatever names they are called, all resemble each other. No agreement and no reconciliation are possible between these religions and philosophy. Religion imposes on man its faith and its belief, whereas philosophy frees him of it totally or in part. How could one therefore hope that they would agree with each other? When the Christian religion, under the most modest and seductive forms, entered Athens and Alexandria, which were, as everyone knows, the two principal centers of science and philosophy, after becoming solidly established in these two cities its first concern was to put aside real science and philosophy, trying to stifle both under the bushes of theological discussions, to explain the inexplicable mysteries of the Trinity, the Incarnation, and Transubstantiation. It will always be thus. Whenever religion will have the upper hand, it will eliminate philosophy; and the contrary happens when it is philosophy that reigns as sovereign mistress. So long as humanity exists, the struggle will not cease between dogma and free investigation, between religion and philosophy; a desperate struggle in which, I fear, the triumph will not be for free thought, because the masses dislike reason, and its teachings are only understood by some intelligences of the elite, and because, also, science, however beautiful it is, does not completely satisfy humanity, which thirsts for the ideal and which likes to exist in dark and distant regions that the philosophers and scholars can neither perceive nor explore.

CHAPTER 2

ISLAMIC REVEALED LAW VERSUS ISLAMIC COMMON LAW

Moulavi Chiragh Ali [Maulavi Cheragh Ali]

Excerpt from Maulavi Cheragh Ali. "The Possibility of Reforms, Political and Social, in Islam." In *Proposed Political Legal, and Social Reforms in the Ottoman Empire and Other Muhammadan [Mohammadan] States*. Bombay: Education Society's Press, 1883. pp. 1–13.

1. THE REV. MALCOLM MACCOLL SAYS THAT WHAT WE call Mussulman states are only branches of a cosmopolitan theocracy, and are all bound by one common code of civil and religious rules and dogmas that are essentially and eternally unchangeable; that what seemed to the infallible Pontiff of Islam good to decree twelve centuries ago for the guidance of rude and ignorant Arabs must rule for ever the conduct of the Mussulman world; and that, the inviolable sanctity of his decrees is guarded by a most powerful and wealthy corporation, whose duty and interest it is to prevent the introduction of any of those reforms which European cabinets periodically recommend to the favorable consideration of the Sultan.[1]

2. The Muhammadan states are not usually considered theocratic in their system of government. The first four or five khalifates were of a republican nature, and after them, the system of government was changed with the Ommiade dynasty into monarchy and despotism. The early khalifas were appointed by election. Moávia, the sixth khalifa, made the succession hereditary amongst his own descendants. All the khalifas, sultans, and malicks after the republican period are accepted as monarchs and despots. The first four or five khalifas are called *Khulafai-Rashedeen*. Those following them are termed *Moolkan Azoozan*, the tyrannous kings or despots, and *Khulafai-jour*, the oppressive khalifas.

Two Muhammadan kings may be professors of the same religion, but that does not prevent them from having political differences and even hostilities with each other. Indian history furnishes abundant examples of instances of this nature.

3. There was no common code or law book for the guidance of the government during the republican period, nor during the Ommiade dynasty. There was even a total absence of any canon or ecclesiastical law books in those periods, except the Muhammadan Revealed Law of the Quran.

After the overthrow of the Omiade dynasty in 136 A.H., the Abbasides became khalifas, and the great want of a common code of law was felt. It was required partly for the guidance of government, and the security of person and property, as well as partly to coincide with the wishes of the despots, and to sanction their arbitrary and capricious acts by means of an appeal to the examples of the earlier generations of Islam, whose men were thought most pious by the people in general. Every exertion was made to deduce all the accidents of common life from the Quran by fortuitous interpretation, illustration, construction, and corollary, however repugnant such deductions might be to reason and modesty. False traditions were foisted upon people to corroborate the acts of their rulers. Circumstances, which had never existed, were invented to support the policy of conquest or arbitrary aggressions of the reigning monarchs of the Abbaside dynasty.

4. Still there was no common code of civil and canon law. Some private persons supplied the want to a certain extent of collecting the various traditions, which were in existence; and thus they were enabled to form judgments on matters of jurisprudence for their own private use. Ingenuity and labor were lavishly used in drawing elaborate distinctions, and demonstrating points of casuistry or unimportant trivialities from some single words or half sentences of the Quran, irrespective of their classical or literal meanings and contexts. These self-constituted lawgivers rarely attended the courts of the Abbaside khalifs, and they never gave them their notes and collections for circulation, so that they might be adapted to the use of the common folk. They hesitated, nay, they feared very much to lead or force people against their conscience, and to fabricate occurrences and examples that had never happened.

5. Aboo Haneefa, the famous legist, the head and founder of the *Ahlar-rái* branch of Jurisprudence, was offered the office of a kázee by Hobaira, the governor of Koofa, but he persisted in refusing to accept it, and was scourged. Khalifa Mansoor, the second of the Abbaside dynasty, tried to induce him to accept the same office, but as he still refused, he was thrown into prison, where he was confined till his death in 150 A.H. Imám Aboo Yoosoof, a disciple of Aboo Haneefa, was exalted by Hároon Arrasheed, the fifth khalifa of the Abbaside dynasty to the post of *Kázee-al-Kozát*, literally "judge of judges," or the chief justice. He was the first individual who ever filled that important post. He instituted courts of judicature for the sole purpose of hearing and determining causes. Before him there was no judicial system of law and courts in practice; all disputes being decided among the Arabs in a summary way by appeal to the chief of the tribe, and to the Imám of the city or district, who, in the absence of a common code of jurisprudence, gave his decision in accordance with the customs and usages of the country. Aboo Yoosoof, though he differed in a variety of decisions from his master, Aboo Haneefa, professed to be guided by his opinion, and appointed kázees to the districts on the understanding that they should decide the cases in conformity with the opinions of Aboo Haneefa. Thus he introduced and enforced the private opinions

of Aboo Haneefa in the matter of jurisprudence, which he, Aboo Haneefa, was so reluctant to do. Imám Muhammad, another disciple of Aboo Haneefa, was deputed by the same Khalifa Hároon Arrasheed to superintend the administration of justice in the province of Khorásán. Though he differed in many points from the opinion of his master, Aboo Haneefa, and his fellow pupil, Aboo Yoosoof, the system of Jurisprudence practiced by these two Judges has gone under the name of Hanafia (called by English writers Haneefa) school, notwithstanding their dissent from Aboo Haneefa, and from each other. The opinions of Aboo Haneefa thus became paramount in the matter of Jurisprudence in Asia, or in only those provinces that were under the jurisdiction of Aboo Yoosoof. In Africa and Spain, the opinions of Aboo Haneefa were not adhered to, and in Asiatic provinces also they were not yielded a ready compliance by the Moslems, in the private exercise of civil and common law, and in matters of practical divinity. In the law-courts only were the decrees passed according to the opinions of Aboo Haneefa and Aboo Yoosoof.

6. Yet there was no book of written law or codes, nor was any mention made of the private opinions of several Imáms who had voluntarily prosecuted the cause of jurisprudence as binding on the people or the government in general. This was the case up to the end of the second century. The third and the fourth centuries of the Muhammadan era passed on, and still no standard or common code of Jurisprudence was in force.[2]

7. Now, it will appear from the above remarks that the Rev. Mr. MacColl is altogether under a false impression when he speaks of a common code of civil and religious rules and dogmas as *essentially and eternally unchangeable*. The common code of Islam, or the Muhammadan system of jurisprudence, is the unwritten law of the Muhammadan community, compiled at a very late period, so that it cannot be considered as *essentially and eternally unchangeable*; nor can it be binding on any other nation than the Arabs, whose customs, usages, and traditions it contains, and upon which it is based. The Muhammadan Common Law is not to be confounded with the Muhammadan Revealed Law. The Muhammadan Common Law is the unwritten law that has been compiled from a very few verses of the Quran, as well as from the customs and usages of the country, supported by traditions contradictory in themselves, and based on the *Ijmaa*, or the unanimous consent of the Moslems. It is impossible to trace the origin of these early rulings, for they are based chiefly on the analogy of some admitted or acknowledged casuistry, and thus it is but a simple truth to say that such decisions or rulings can in no wise [sic] be *essentially and eternally unchangeable*.

8. Those writers are greatly mistaken who either confound the Quran, the Muhammadan Revealed Law, with *Fiquah* or *Cheriat (Cheri)*, the Muhammadan Common or Civil Law; or think that the Quran contains the entire code of Islam; or that the Muhammadan Law, by which is invariably meant the Muhammadan Common Law, is infallible and unalterable. The Muhammadan law books, the fundamental codes of Islam, take very little or nothing from the Quran, and all the Muhammadan jurists, casuists, *mooftis*, and *moojtahids*, have by a tacit consent removed the law points from the text of the sacred book to the jurisdiction of the canon or civil law. Muhammadans rely principally on the later lego-religious

books instead of the Quran. Sir George Campbell, M.P., the late Lieutenant-Governor of Bengal, who had a very long practice in dealing with the Muhammadan community in India, and who lately traveled in European Turkey, has fully ascertained the real state of things on this subject. His remarks are as follows:

> The Quran is by no means a clear and simple book like our Testament—far from it; it is difficult to make much of it, and Mahammedans rely principally on the later lego-religious books. It is somewhat as if we had no Bible, and were obliged to get our Christianity from the works of the Fathers only—a state of things which leaves room for much dispute, and renders it possible to find texts for almost anything.[3]

The Rev. Mr. Edward Sell has taken the same view. He says: "So far from the Quran alone being the *sole* rule of faith and practice to Muslims, there is not one single sect amongst them whose faith and practice are based on it alone."[4]

The Honourable Dr. Hunter is also near the truth when he says: " . . . The Quran was long ago found inadequate to the necessities of Civil Polity, and a system of Canon and Public Law has been developed from it to suit the exigencies of Musalman nations."[5]

But of all authors I have hitherto the honor of quoting, I will now cite the opinions of one [Cyrus Hamlin] on this subject, whose long stay and deep acquaintance of the Muhammadan world entitles his words to a greater veracity and respect. He speaks of the Quran:

> All the world, excepting those who have resided in Turkey and have there examined the subject, knows beyond all possibility of doubt that the Quran is the law of Mussulmans, and that it is administered by priests ! The most respectable Reviews assert it almost every month. Mr. Bosworth Smith, an ardent friend of the Mussulmans, and Mr. Freeman, an ardent enemy, both receive it as true. Both are guilty of the same degree of ignorance. The Mussulman code of law, as reduced by Ibrahim Haleby, by direction of Solyman the Magnificent, is accepted as law by all Mussulmans. With its accepted commentaries, it forms many volumes, each one larger than the Quran, and treating upon scores of subjects not referred to in the Quran. The Quran has but little in it that is capable of being law. Where it states a principle capable of being so viewed, it stands as the highest authority, and the codified law will be in accord with it. But how can it be authority in those things to which it makes no reference? Even the whole ritual of prayer is governed by this code and not by the Quran ; and so of very many of the religious observances most strictly held.[6]

Further on the author writes:

> Tradition, rather than the Quran, has formed both law and religion for the Moslems. One is astounded at the temerity, or shall we say ignorance, of J. Bosworth Smith, in taking the Quran as containing the whole of Islam. He might well take the four Gospels as containing the Whole Roman Catholic system, Jesuits and all.[7]

9. Islam is capable of progress, and possesses sufficient elasticity to enable it to adapt itself to the social and political changes going on around it. The Islam, by which I mean the pure Islam as taught by Muhammad in the Quran, and not that Islam as taught by the Muhammadan Common Law was itself a progress and a change for the better. It has the vital principles of rapid development, of progress, of rationalism, and of adaptability to new circumstances. What the Rev. Mr. Mac-Coll calls "the inviolable and absolutely unchangeable law of Islam," and which, he argues, impels the *Ulema* to resist the introduction of European reforms, is only the Muhammadan Common Law, which can in no way be considered infallible. The Common Law of Islam is the *Leges non-Scripta*, and consists of general or particular customs, and certain peculiar or ecclesiastical laws. The only infallible law is *Leges Scripta*, or the Quran.

10. The Rev. Mr. MacColl writes: "The institutions of every Mussulman state are necessarily built upon the Quran, and the Quran, being, for every Moslem the last expression of the Divine Will, reform is not only superfluous, but presumptuous in addition."[8]

The institutions of the Muhammadan Common Law, called the *Cheriat* or *Cheri*, are not necessarily built upon the Quran. Very few points of the civil and canon law of the Muhammadan Common Law are founded upon the Quran; all other points of civil and ecclesiastical law being based on general and particular Arab customs. Some of them are reformed and improved while others are simply put down as they were proved, found at the time, to be generally practiced, and to be a necessary and inseparable part of the Arab institutions. Had the Prophet thought it incumbent on him to frame a civil and canon law, other than the Revealed one, he would have done so, but in fact he did not accomplish any such thing. "Spiritual power in Islam," says Ubicini truly, "begins and ends with Mohamed," and I agree with the Rev. Mr. MacColl when he says that "there is no hint of spiritual succession in the Quran, and Mahammad himself excluded any such idea when he was asked to appoint a successor."[9] This, together with the fact that Muhammad did not compile a law, civil or canonical, for the conduct of the believers, nor did he enjoin them to do so, shows that he left to the believers in general to frame any code, civil or canon law, and to found systems which would harmonize with the times, and suit the political and social changes going on around them.

11. The *Lex non-Scripta*, or the Common Law of Islam, is an unwritten law, that is, not written by Muhammad the Prophet, nor dictated by him, nor compiled in his time, nor compiled even in the first century of the Hejira, comprising those principles, usages, and rules of conduct applicable to the government and security of person and property, which do not depend for their authority, and are not based upon any existing, express and positive, declaration of the Quran or the Revealed Law. It comprises, and mainly consists of old-established Arab civil institutions, customs, and the traditionary [*sic*] sayings of the Prophet—most of them not genuine—and of his companions; and, of considerations to humanity, reason, common sense, and also the principles of moral fitness, and public convenience included in the words *Ijmaa*, and *Kias*. It also consists in great part of the opinions of famous lawyers and text-writers of the Abbaside age, and was committed to

writing after the Commonwealth of Islam ceased to be a republican government, i.e., the undivided Khalifat; and after the overthrow of the Omayya dynasty of the Khalifs from Asia and Africa, but has never been fully acted upon in the times of the Abbaside Khalifs. The Muhammadan Common Law, in its features and principles, resembles very much the Jewish oral law or *Mishna*, and the Roman Civil or Common Law.

12. The Rev. Mr. MacColl in the *Review* referred to above says:

> To talk, therefore, of any reforms under the Sultan's direct rule which shall alter in any material degree the condition and *status* of the Christian population is in truth to talk nonsense. No reforms of the kind are possible. For the dominions of the Sultan are merely a part of one vast theocratic power which claims divine sanction to reduce all mankind to the alternative of embracing Islam or submitting to servitude or death: servitude in the case of Jews or Christians; death in the case of all other non-Mussulman people, and of Christians who take up arms in defense of their liberty.[10]

That the Muhammadan states are not theocratic in their system of government has already been explained and proved. There is no precept in the Muhammadan Revealed Law, the Quran, which places before all mankind the alternative of embracing Islam or submitting to servitude. Had there been any such decree in it, that would have been tantamount to intoleration, but, on the contrary, the Quran in a good many passages in the Meccan and Medanite suras enjoins universal toleration. None of the genuine traditions, as they are technically called, instructs the reduction of all mankind to the alternative of embracing Islam, or submitting to servitude or death.

NOTES

1. *The Contemporary Review* for August 1881, page 267.
2. Compare Shah Valiullah's *Hojjatil Báligha*, chapter IV of the Supplement, page 158.
3. *A Handy-book on the Eastern Question*; by Sir G. Campbell, M. P. London: 1876, page 26.
4. *The Faith of Islam*; by the Rev. Edward Sell, London: 1880, page I.
5. *Our Indian Musalmans*; by W. W. Hunter, LL.D., London: 1871, page 139.
6. *Among the Turks*; by Cyrus Hamlin; London: 1878, pages 82–83. 2m.
7. Ibid., p. 335.
8. *The Contemporary Review* for August 1881, page 268.
9. Ibid.
10. Ibid., page 270.

CHAPTER 3

THE RATIONALISTIC AND PHILOSOPHICAL SPIRIT OF ISLAM

Amir Ali

Excerpt from Sayyid Amir Ali. "The Rationalistic and Philosophical Spirit of Islam." In *The Spirit of Islam: A History of the Evolution and Ideals of Islam.* London: Christophers, 1922, pp. 403–410.

God changes not as to what concerns any people until they change in respect to what depends upon themselves

LIKE ALL OTHER NATIONS OF ANTIQUITY, THE PRE-ISLAMIC Arabs were stern fatalists. The remains of their ancient poetry, sole record of old Arab thought and manners, show that before the promulgation of Islam the people of the Peninsula had absolutely abandoned themselves to the idea of an irresistible and blind fatality. Man was but a sport in the hands of Fate. This idea bred a reckless contempt of death, and an utter disregard for human life. The teachings of Islam created a revolution in the Arab mind; with the recognition of a supreme Intelligence governing the universe, they received the conception of self-dependence and of moral responsibility founded on the liberty of human volition. One of the remarkable characteristics of the Quran is the curious, and, at first sight, inconsistent, manner in which it combines the existence of a Divine Will, which not only orders all things, but which acts directly upon men and addresses itself to the springs of thought in them, with the assertion of a free agency in man and of the liberty of the intellect. Not that this feature is peculiar to the Moslem scripture; the same characteristic is to be found in the Biblical records. But in the Quran the conception of human responsibility is so strongly developed that the question naturally occurs to the mind, How can these two ideas be reconciled with each other? It seems inconsistent at first sight that man should be judged by his works, a doctrine which forms the foundation of Islamic morality, if all his actions are ruled by an all-powerful Will. The earnest faith of Mohammed in an active ever-living Principle, joined to his trust in the progress of man, supplies a key to this mystery. I propose to illustrate my meaning by a reference to a few of the passages which give expression to the absolutism of the Divine Will and those which assert the liberty of human volition: "And God's ordering is in accordance with a determined decree; ... and the sun preceding to its place of rest—that is an ordinance (taqdir) of the Almighty, the All-wise;[1] ... and among His signs is the creation of the heavens and the earth and of the animals which He hath distributed therein, which He has sovereign power to gather when He will;[2] ... and do they not see that God who created the heavens and earth, and faltered not in creating these, has power to vivify the dead—nay, He has sovereign control over all things;[3] and other things which are not at your command, but which are truly within His grasp, inasmuch as God is sovereign disposer of all things ('ala kul-i shi'y qadiran);[4] nor is there anything not provided beforehand by Us, or which We send down otherwise than according to a fore-known decree;[5] ... the secrets of the heavens and the earth are Gods; ... God has all things at command;[6] ... and profound to them a similitude of this present life, which is like water sent down by Us from heaven, so that the plants of the earth are fattened by it, and on the morrow become stubble, scattered by the winds,—God disposes of all things;[7] ... and it pertains to God's sovereignty to defend them;[8] ... God creates what He will;[9] ... and who created all things, and determined respecting the same with absolute determination;[10] ... and thy Lord is a supreme sovereign;[11] ... behold thou the imprints of the mercy of God: how He vivifies the earth, after it has died—in very deed, a restorer of life to the dead is there, and all things are at His bidding;[12] ... to God belongs whatsoever is in the heavens and whatsoever is on the earth; and whether ye disclose that which is within you or conceal it, God will reckon with you for it; and He pardons whom He will, and punishes whom He will—inasmuch as God is Supreme Sovereign;[13] ... say thou: O God, Sovereign Disposer of dominion, Thou givest rule to whom Thou wilt, and takest away power from whom Thou wilt, Thou exaltest whom Thou wilt, and humblest whom Thou wilt: all good is at Thy disposal—verily, Thou art a Supreme Sovereign;[14] ... God punishes whom he will, and pardons whom He will;[15] ... to God belongs dominion of the heavens and the earth, and whatsoever they contain is His, and He is Sovereign over all things.[16] ... Verily, God accomplishes what He ordains—He hath established for everything a fixed decree;[17] ... but God has the measuring out (yuqaddar) of the night and the day;[18] ... extol the name of Thy Lord, the Most High, who made the world, and fashioned it to completeness, who fore-ordained, and guides accordingly;[19] ... as for the unbelievers it matters nothing to them whether thou warnest them or dost not warn them; they will not believe; God hath sealed up their hearts and their ears;[20] ... and the darkness of night is over their eyes;[21] ... and God guides into the right path whomsoever He will;[22] ... God is pleased to make your burdens light inasmuch as man is by nature infirm.... God changes not as to what concerns people until they change in respect to what depends upon themselves;[23] . . . say thou: Verily, God leads astray whomsoever He will, and directs to Himself those who are penitent."[24]

It will be noticed that, in many of these passages, by "the decree of God" is clearly meant the law of nature. The stars and planets have each their appointed course; so has every other object in creation. The movements of the heavenly bodies, the phenomena of nature, life and death, are all governed by law. Other passages unquestionably indicate the idea of Divine agency upon human will; but they are again explained by others, in which that agency is "conditioned" upon human will. It is to the seeker for Divine help that God renders His help; it is on the searcher of his own heart, who purifies his soul from impure longings, that God bestows grace. To the Arabian Teacher, as to his predecessors, the existence of an Almighty Power, the Fashioner of the Universe, the Ruler of His creatures, was an intense and vivid reality. The feeling of "an assured trust" in an all-pervading, ever-conscious Personality has been the motive power in the work of every age. To the weary mariner, "sailing on life's solemn main," there is nothing more assuring, nothing that more satisfies the intense longing for a better and purer world, than the consciousness of a Power above humanity to redress wrongs, to fulfill hopes, to help the forlorn. Our belief in God springs from the very essence of Divine ordinances. They are as much laws, in the strictest sense of the word, as the laws which regulate the movements of the celestial bodies. But the will of God is not an arbitrary will: it is an educating will, to be obeyed by the scholar in his walks of learning as by the devotee in his cell.

The passages, however, in which human responsibility and freedom of human will are laid down in emphatic terms define and limit the conception of absolutism. "And whosoever gets to himself a sin, get it solely on his own responsibility;[25] . . . and let alone those who make a sport and a mockery of their religion, and whom this present world has deluded, and thereby bring to remembrance that any soul perishes for what it has got to itself;[26] and when they commit a deed of shame they say: We have found that our fathers did so, and God obliges us to do it; say thou: Surely, God requireth not shameful doing:[27] . . . they did injustice to themselves;[28] yonder will every soul experience that which it hath bargained for;[29] . . . so then, whosoever goes astray, he himself bears the whole responsibility of wandering."[30]

Man, within the limited sphere of his existence, is absolute master of his conduct. He is responsible for his actions, and for the use or misuse of the powers with which he has been endowed. He may fall or rise, according to his own "inclination." There was supreme assistance for him who sought Divine help and guidance. Is not the soul purer and better in calling to its Lord for that help which He has promised? Are not the weak strengthened, the stricken comforted—by their own appeal to the Heavenly Father for solace and strength? Such were the ideas of the Teacher of Islam with regard to Divine sovereignty and the liberty of human volition. His recorded sayings handed down from sources which may be regarded as unquestionably authentic, help in explaining the conception he entertained about freewill and predestination (qadaa wa qadr or jabr wa ikhtiyaar). Not only his own words, but those of his son-in-law, "the legitimate heir to his inspiration," and his immediate descendants, who derived their ideas from him, may well furnish us with a key to the true *Islamic* notion on the question of the free agency of man—a subject that has for ages, both in Islam and in Christianity, been the battle-ground of sectarian disputes. In discussing this subject, we must not, however, lose sight of the fact that most of the traditions that have supplied to Patristicism its armory of weapons against the sovereignty of reason, bear evident traces of being 'made to order.' They tell their own story of how, and the circumstances under which, they came into existence. Some of the traditions that purport to be handed down by men who came casually in contact with the Teacher, show palpable signs of changes and transformations in the minds and in the memories of the mediaries. The authentic sayings, however, are many, and I shall refer only to a few to explain what I have already indicated, that in Mohammed's mind an earnest belief in the liberty of human will was joined to a vivid trust in personality of the Heavenly Father. Hereditary depravity and natural sinfulness were emphatically denied. Every child of man was born pure and true; every departure in after-life from the path of truth and rectitude is due to education. "Every man is born religiously constituted; it is his parents who make him afterwards a Jew, Christian, or a Sabæan, like as ye take up the beast at its birth—do ye find upon it any mutilation, until ye yourselves mutilate it?"[31] Infants have no positive moral character: for about those who die in early life, "God best knows what would have been their conduct" [had they lived to maturity]. "Every human being has two inclinations,—one prompting him to good and impelling him thereto, and the other prompting him to evil and thereto impelling him;[32] but the godly assistance is nigh, and he who asks the help of God in contending with the evil promptings of his own heart obtains it." "It is your own conduct which will lead you to paradise or hell, as if you had been destined therefor." No man's conduct is the outcome of fatality, nor is he borne along by an irresistible decree to heaven or hell; on the contrary, the ultimate result is the creation of his own actions, for each individual is primarily answerable for his future destiny. "Every moral agent is furthered to his own conduct," or, as it is put in another tradition: "Every one is divinely furthered in accordance with his character."[33] Human conduct is by no means fortuitous; one act is the result of another; and life, destiny and character mean the connected series of incidents and actions which are related to each other, as cause and effect, by an ordained law, "the assignment" of God. In the sermons of the Disciple we find the doctrine more fully developed. "Weigh your own soul before the time for the weighing of your actions arrives; take count with yourself before you are called upon to account for your conduct in this existence; apply yourself to good and pure actions, adhere to the path of truth and rectitude before the soul is pressed to leave its earthly abode; verily, if you will not guide and warn yourself, none other can direct you."[34] "I adjure you to worship the Lord in purity and holiness. He has pointed out to you the path of salvation and the temptations of this world. Abstain from foulness, though it may be fair-seeming to your sight; avoid evil, however pleasant. . . . For ye knoweth how far it takes you away from Him. . . . Listen, and take warning by the words of the Merciful Guardian."[35] . . . And again, O ye servants of my Lord, fulfil the duties that are imposed on you, for in their neglect is abasement: your good works alone will render easy the road to death. Remember, each sin increases the debt, and makes the chain [which binds you] heavier. The message of mercy has come; the path of truth is clear; obey the command that has been laid on you; live in purity, and work in piety, and ask God to help you in your endeavors, and to forgive your past transgressions."[36] "Cultivate humility and forbearance: comport yourself with piety and truth. Take count of your actions with your own conscience (nafs), for he who takes such count reaps a great reward, and he who neglects incurs great loss. He who acts with piety gives rest to his soul; he who takes warning understands the truth; he who understands it attains the perfect knowledge." These utterances convey no impression of predestinarianism; on the contrary, they portray a soul animated with a living faith in God, and yet full of trust in human development founded upon individual exertion springing from human volition. Mohammed's definition of reason and knowledge, of the cognition of the finite and infinite, reminds us of Aristotelian phraseology and thought, and Ali's address to his son may be read with advantage by the admirer of Aristotelian ethics.

The *Ihtijaj ut-Tabrasi* [37] supplies further materials to form a correct opinion on the question of predestinarianism in Islam. The Caliph Ali was one day asked the meaning of Kaza and Kadar; he replied, "The first means obedience to the commandments of God and avoidance of sin; the latter, the ability to live a holy life, and to do that which brings one nearer to God and to shun that which throws him away from His perfection. . . . Say not that man is *compelled*, for that is attribution of tyranny to God; nor say that man has absolute discretion,[38]—rather that we are furthered by His help and grace in our endeavors to act righteously, and we transgress because of our neglect (of His commands)." One of his interlocutors, 'Utba ibn Rabi'a Asadi, asked him once as to the meaning of the words "there is no power nor help but from God," (la hawla wa la qawat illa bil-Allah). "It means," said the Caliph, "that I am not afraid of God's anger, but I am afraid of his purity; nor have I the power to observe His commandment, but my strength is in His assistance."[39] . . . God has placed us on earth to try each according to his endowments. Referring to the following and other passages of the Quran, the Caliph went on to say, "God says, 'We will try you to see who are the *strivers* (mujaahidin) [after truth and purity], and who are the forbearing and patient, and We will test your actions' . . . and 'We will help you by degrees to attain what ye know not." . . . These verses prove the liberty of human volition."[40] Explaining the verse of the Quran, "God directs him whom He chooses, and leads astray him whom He chooses," the Caliph said that this does not mean that He compels men to evil or good, that He either gives direction or refuses it according to His caprice, for this would do away with all responsibility for human action; it means, on the contrary, that God points out the road to truth, and lets men choose as they will.

NOTES

*The following are references to the Avran. The first number refers to the Surasaid, the second number refers to the Ayahs.

1. XXXVI. 38.
2. XLII. 28.
3. XLVI. 29.
4. XLVIII. 21.

5. XV. 21.
6. XVI. 77.
7. XVIII. 45.
8. XXII. 40
9. XXIV. 45.
10. XXV. 2.
11. XXV. 54.
12. XXX. 50.
13. II. 284.
14. III. 25.
15. V. 18.
16. V. 120.
17. LXV. 3.
18. LXXIII. 20.
19. LXXXVII. 1–3.
20. II. 5–6.
21. II. 7.
22. XIII. 31.
23. XIII. 11.
24. XIII. 27.
25. IV. 111.
26. VI. 70.
27. VII. 29.
28. IX. 70.
29. X. 30.
30. X. 108.
31. A Hadith.
32. Bukhari's *Collections*, chapter on the Hadîs, "He is secured whom God helps"; reported by Abu Sa'îd al-Khuzri.
33. A Hadith.
34. *Nahj ul-Balaghat*, p. 43 (a collection of the sermons of the Caliph Ali by one of his descendants, named Sharif Riza, mentioned by Ibn-Khallikân), printed at Tabriz in 1299 A.H.
35. Ibid. p. 136.
36. *Nahj ul-Balâghat*, p. 170.
37. *Evidences of Tabrasi*, a collection of traditions by the Shaikh ut-Tabrasi.
38. That is, to decide what is right and what is wrong.
39. *Ihtijâj ut-Tabrasi*, p. 236.
40. Ibid., p. 237.
41. Ibid.

CHAPTER 4

THE SOCIOLOGICAL LAWS OF THE QURAN

Muhammad Abduh

Excerpt from Muhammad Abduh. "Quranic Exegesis" (Tafsir al-Quran al-Hakim). *al-Manar,* vol. 8, no. 24, pp. 921–30, February 10, 1906. Translated by Kamran Talattof.

THE EXCERPTS FROM PREVIOUS TEACHINGS OF Imam Abduh at al-Azhar on the sociological laws and rules are derived from his exegesis of the Quranic parable ("Talout") and can be categorized as follows.

First, when a nation's independence is threatened by external aggression, and its rights are forsaken, an anti-aggression sentiment is likely to arise. This sentiment is directed toward trying to find a leader who can represent the unity of the nation. Nations then learn that the way to freedom is through finding this leader, like the situation of the ancient Israelites when the philistines persecuted them.

Second, the nation's realization of its rights and independence is best represented by the efforts of its notables. When the number of notables increases within a nation, they will seek a ruler who will lead them, as was the case, for example, with the early Israelites.

Third, this desire for independence grows first among the notables, and then spreads among the common people. When this feeling and realization evolve into overt action, the imposters will be exposed. Only truthfulness will reap rewards.

Fourth, it is normal that people differ in choosing their leader. This disagreement could be a cause of discord. Thus, any nation should have a referee accepted by most of the people. The Israelites resorted to their prophet to choose their leaders. Islam devised the "bay'a," which is an act of allegiance to the leader selected by the notables.

Fifth, people do not follow things that are contrary to their interests. Every individual has an opinion about politics and the social organization of the nation.

Although social science is more complex than sciences in which people readily recognize their incompetence, they do not hesitate to express opinions about social or political issues. Thus, many Muslims now believe that the call to caliphate, which is in accordance with religious laws, is against their interests, considering such an advocate not only their enemy but an enemy to Islam as well.

Sixth, at the stage of darkness, nations believed that the most legitimate rulers were the wealthiest people and those with a noble lineage. This is wrong because wealth and lineage are false honors. The real honor is the possession of knowledge and morality. While Islam did not give power to a specific family, it did not completely rule out lineage, either. The right of Imamate belongs to the Quraish, the Prophet's tribe.

Seventh, conditions to be respected when choosing a ruler are indicated in the following verse: "Allah selected him [Talout] among you and gave him more knowledge and more physical power."

Eighth, "Allah gives his power to whom He wants." Allah's will is executed when his general commands are followed. The situation of a nation changes when people themselves change and when people take away power from the unjust and grant it to those who are worthy. Such interpretation applies to the Muslim's conditions. Other nations dominated the Muslims according to God's general justice and His wise laws, which are described in the Quran. They themselves have forsaken God's commands. If they repent and return to good deeds, God will forgive them.

Ninth, it is a common rule that any soldier must obey his superior. Yes, this rule is correct only on the condition that this superior accepts the advice of those who possess knowledge.

Tenth, sometimes a few people who obey their leader and are persevering and united may gain victory over a bigger crowd who also obey their leader but lack perseverance and unity.

Eleventh, faith in God is one among the sources of patience and endurance in war.

Twelfth, prayer during the fight is helpful in gaining a victory.

Thirteenth, conflicts among nations are a reflection of the general laws. This is what contemporary scientists (or philosophers) call "survival of the fittest." They consider war as natural in humankind because it is a secondary principle of the "survival of the fittest" law. The Quranic verse "Were it not for the restraint of one by means of the other, imposed on men by God, verily the earth would be ruled by the fittest," does not refer only to what is done during war, but it is a general statement concerning any kind of conflict between people that requires resistance and fighting. Some imposters to social science mistakenly think that the general law of the survival of the fittest was, in effect, brought about by contemporary materialists and that it is contrary to the guidance of religion. If they truly knew the meaning of humankind, they would not have claimed that.

Fourteenth, the Quranic verse confirms the principle that social scientists call natural selection or the survival of the fittest. God says that humankind's desire for good purposes and truth protects the earth from corruption and helps goodness prevail. God allowing Muslims to fight, in Surat al-Hajj, verses 39–41, further supports this: "Permission is granted those (to take up arms) who fight because they were oppressed. God is certainly able to give help to those who were driven away from their homes for no other reason than they said: 'Our Lord is God.'" And if God had not restrained some men through some others, monasteries, churches, synagogues, and mosques, where the name of God is honored most, would have been razed. God will surely help those who help him—verily God is all-powerful and all-mighty—those who would be firm in devotion, give zakat, enjoin what is good, and forbid what is wrong. We gave them authority in the land. The rest is with God. This reveals how the struggle for survival and the defense of the good lead to the survival of the fittest and the preservation of the best.

Further evidence of this principle in the Quran is verse 17 in Surat al-Ra'd: "He sends down water from the skies, which flows in channels according to their capacity, with the scum borne on the surface of the torrent, as rises the scum when metals are heated on the fire for making ornaments and household utensils. This is how God determines truth and falsehood. The scum disappears like the foam on the bank, and that which is useful to man remains on the earth. That is how God sets forth precepts of wisdom." This indicates that the flow of incidents and the fire of strife push away evil's "foam," which is harmful to society. The soil[1] in which civilization flourishes remains fertile and the good continue seeking righteousness, which is an adornment of mankind. There are other verses that prove that good triumphs over evil and they will be explained and clarified in their proper place later, if time allows and if God is our aid in that.

NOTE

1. Ibliz is the mud brought by the Nile when it floods. This is also called al-Tami where the name of something specific is used to denote a more general thing.

CHAPTER 5

THE NECESSITY OF
RELIGIOUS REFORM

Muhammad Abduh

Excerpt from Muhammad Abduh. "The True Reform and its Necessity for Al-Azhar" (al-Islah al- Hakiqiqi wa al-Wajib lil al-Azhar). *al-Manar,* vol. 10, no. 28, (February 1906), pp. 758–65. Translated by Kamran Talattof.

LIKE ALL OTHER EASTERN NATIONS, EGYPT CONSTITUTED a religious community bounded together by the Shari'ah. It had built its ethics and its civilization on religion. Religion is the organizing principle of all its affairs—it dictates man's private and public conduct, the king's orientation toward his subjects and the subjects' toward their king. Ask an Egyptian, Why do you speak the truth? Why do you try to be fair in your judgment? Why are you honest whenever you are trusted? Why are you not vulgar? Why do you avoid misdeeds and do not lie to, treat unfairly, or mistrust others? He will answer you that God recommends those good qualities and interdicts the misdeeds. Whether he is a scholar or a student, he will be able to recite to you Quranic verses and sayings of the Prophet that support his statement, such as "God recommends fairness and charity and visitation of relatives, and interdicts vulgarity, unfairness, and oppression." Likewise, and for the same purpose, he may recall the following hadith: "There are three signs distinguishing the hypocrite: He lies when he talks, he does not fulfill his promises, and he betrays when trusted."

If the spirit of religion is not strengthened among the Egyptians, and if religion is weakened, these moral qualities will also collapse. Religion is the basis on which moral conduct has been built. Moral conduct will disappear when religion collapses. The same thing will happen if religion is deformed by introducing into its core any innovations or superstitions. The nation will be weakened. For this reason, it has been a mandatory duty of Egyptian rulers to care about religion in order to avoid any weakness of faith within the nation and to hinder innovations in religion that could distort its beauty. Should any change or innovation be allowed to happen, religion would not fulfill its function as a means of power and safety.

Since al-Azhar and other religious establishments are the locales of religion in Egypt and the place where the clergymen are educated, they must be the focus of interest and must be reformed. This is the reason for the precursor reformists: Sheikh Jamal al-Din al-Afghani and the master Imam [Muhammad Abduh] and others who looked toward al-Azhar. They wished to reform the nation through the reformation of al-Azhar and to bring progress to the nation through the progress of al-Azhar. But al-Azhar resisted the reformists and rejected reformation. The cause of this refusal is that al-Azhar Ulama had no knowledge except that of their own sciences through their own textbooks, which are taught at al-Azhar. The press had yet to diffuse both long-withheld books and the intellectual products of other nations. They did not acknowledge the existence of any other science but their own knowledge, or any education but their own education. They thus believed that whoever touched them intended to inflict misdeeds and deformation.

That was the dominant belief. There was no recognized institute but al-Azhar and no science except for what was thought there. There was no Ulama but those at al-Azhar. Because of such understandings, al-Azhar rejected what the reformists were willing to do for its reformation. Therefore, the reformists had no choice but to find new schools that claimed the same objectives as al-Azhar.

They did so even though they knew there was little benefit to be expected from their projects, because al-Azhar, by virtue of its religious and historical position, would remain the primary authority in religious matters. The nation took its religious beliefs from al-Azhar and adopted convictions about life and society from it as well. Those schools founded in contest to al-Azhar did not have a comparable enough position to even influence society. The reformists, therefore, simply created the new schools to apply some pressure, hoping that al-Azhar would come back under their control and be totally reformed.

That was the situation of al-Azhar in the remote past. Later, however, it accepted reformation because its horizon broadened under the influence of publication of books of the Salaf [early generations of Islam] and the sciences of other peoples. a-Azhar came to learn that there was other science besides its own, and that there were books other than its own. It also saw its "sons" retiring because they had not been armed with the necessary, new weapons. But the reforms in Dar al-Ulum and the school of religious law [Madrasat al-Qada' al-Shari'] were so limited in their effectiveness that they failed to change their outer appearances and to reach the core of these institutes.

Up to the present day, the reformation of Dar al-Ulum, the school of religious law, and other religious institutes has been limited to the introduction of some new sciences and the rewriting of some textbooks. Despite this, the sciences themselves remain the same. Perhaps this type of reform was convenient at that time because it avoided rough change and because it accorded to the needs of that epoch. But now, since the nation has developed, times have changed, and new ways of life need a new type of education. It is a duty, in the interest of Egypt and the Islamic world, to reform the subject and themes of sciences. The reformation should include the content of the books and even the names of the sciences themselves. It could even change the content of specific sciences. The only thing that remains, then, is a title to be applied to this totally different content.

The reformation must be done on a long-term basis and go far beyond the superficial reforms proposed so far. However, an old law established the authority of his majesty the king and the president of the council of ministers upon the religious institutes. This president is accountable to the assembly of deputies, and the assembly has expressed more than once its willingness to reform al-Azhar and the religious institutes. The commission of "Awqaf" and institutes also expressed the same wish when presenting al-Azhar's budget report. It had requested that the government set a commission, including some deputies to write the proposal of reformation, which would be presented to the next session of the Parliament.

Since I have been studying al-Azhar and the religious institutes over the past quarter of a century, I have thoroughly searched for the cause of its illnesses and discovered its sickness and its remedies. I have been watching for an appropriate time for the rulers to start a serious reform of al-Azhar and the religious institute, and I think a good opportunity now exists. The rulers have shown their wish to make these reforms by designating a commission to work on the project. I wish to present to the rulers a summary of my version of the reforms, which is the result of my efforts and hard work. I wish to present the general principles of this reformation. If it benefits the nation, and if the reform of al-Azhar helps the progress of the nation, I will present a detailed version of such reform.

I will restrict myself to the reformation of the sciences. I leave the administrative reformation to whoever is more competent. This is a general presentation of what I believe to be beneficial reforms. The reformation that I propose to the rulers considers the development of science and distinguishes its different states: when science was in its height and when it declined, when it was controlled by powerful peoples and when it was in the hands of those less powerful. This reformation is professional, brave, and wise.

It is professional because it follows religion through its different periods, and observes it during the first epoch, when religion was new and beautiful and was the source of power, glory, and happiness to its followers. It also observes religion as it was mixed with innovations and many of its traditions transformed, and as people adopted traditions introduced into religion as valid parts thereof. It also observes the history of the different doctrines and different Islamic groups and distinguishes between that which is true and useful and that which is false and harmful.

It is courageous because it intends to extract from the foundations all those innovations and superstitions attributed to religion that really have nothing to do with it. The reformation will replace them with original holy principles. It will bring religion back to the epoch of the precursors, transforming it to its initial image, which was light, happiness, and compassion for humankind. It will take from the different Islamic groups whatever is true and useful, and reject whatever is false and harmful.

The reformation is a wise idea because it does not intend to make changes by surprise, constraint, and oppression, but will induce changes progressively. It will not introduce anything until it is proved true and necessary and is accepted by the majority. Reformation by means of kindness and patience is better and more fruit-ful than reformation by means of violence. In this way, it is also more likely to bring peace and quietness.

By the means of these reformations, Egypt will become the teacher of Islamic culture and an example to be followed in the Orient.

The reform will be founded on two principles. The first principle is that science has not yet reached its perfect state. Sciences, however, are developing toward, not away from, progress and perfection. The second principle is that ethics, laws, religions, beliefs, science and all that is in the universe exist for the benefit of humankind and for its happiness.

The proposed reform is not only a reform of the religious institutes, but is an important social revolution that has benefits and importance in social life, particularly in Egypt, and in Islamic life in general. It observes all of the Oriental and Western nations and finds that the former are subject nations while the latter are independent nations. It finds the Oriental nations as having no ambition, little hope of life, and as willing to accept inferiority, while the Western nations have the highest and noblest objectives. It finds that the Oriental nations are lazy, accustomed to quietness and rest, and that their souls are imbibed with despair and boredom. These nations are actually sleeping and are not willing to wake up. The Western nations are full of will and endurance, accustomed to effort and hardships, with hope and ambition, and smiling at life while life smiles at them.

In studying the cause of social illnesses in the Orient, it can be found that among the causes are the beliefs and opinions introduced into Islam by different groups like the Sufis and others. These beliefs and opinions took root in the souls of Oriental people and have wrought harmful results. The reformation will extract these beliefs from the nation. It will replace them with authentic Islamic beliefs: those that call for resolution, work, perseverance, and determination in this life. This reform will prepare al-Azhar's Ulama to be helpful in the achievement of this objective. They are the focus of hope for this reformation. I will give an example of one of these opinions to help people realize what benefits the nation will gain, and what harm will be avoided in the event this reform is implemented.

Sufis have introduced one of these opinions: faith in God [tawakul ala Allah] is in contradiction with saving and making money, seeking work, and utilizing modern medical care. The believer in God, they would have us accept, would not be a true believer until he "cut off all means of livelihood." Faith in God is also in contradiction with precaution, prevention, and carefulness. In their opinion, faith in God implies a disregard for the consequences of one's worldly actions and a rejection of carefulness. To support this opinion, they present what Abu Daoud Darani has been reported as saying: "If we have real faith in God, we will neither build walls nor put locks on the doors because of fear of thieves." They also report that Abu Yakub al-Zayyat had been asked about faith. He gave away a dirham [drachma] before answering the question. By doing so, he showed he had good faith [he is a mutawakil, a trusting person]. He then commented that he had been ashamed of himself to talk about tawakul [trusting] while owning something. They report that Di al-Noun al-Misri said he traveled a lot but experienced tawakul only one time: "I was traveling by sea and the boat broke. I clung onto a piece of wood. I then thought, if God decided you will sink, this piece of wood will not be helpful anymore. I therefore left the piece of wood and I was thrown by the ocean onto the shore."

This doctrine is in contradiction with religion and reason, and it is a cause of the humiliation of nations. It is in contradiction with religion because religion says "Get ready by whatever means of power you can," "When prayer is done disperse through land and seek the gift of God," "Be careful," and "Consult about the matters."

It is in contradiction with reason because wise men recommend to practice saving, making money, and following a means of livelihood. They also say, "No wisdom is better than precaution." They ask that one analyze matters with deep reflection and put this reflection in practice with willingness after safe recognition of areas of hope and fear.

This approach leads to the weakness of the nation: it promotes laziness, which makes the nation weak and thus likely to be dominated by those who have been ready, those who know the means of success and employ them. This doctrine has been transmitted from generation to generation, and been spread within the nation to the point that it is even expressed in poetry and idioms. The reform will clean up the nation from this and other similar doctrines. This is neither the first nor the last. There are other doctrines that cause similar harm but our purpose here was to give an example not to analyze.

Thus, the objectives of this reform are:

First, to educate judges who have the status of Mujtahid [a clergy entitled to decree an independent judgement on a matter of theology or law], or at least followers who are able to analyze the arguments of the Mujtahid they follow. They will, therefore, conduct trials based on Ijtihad or consensus, and not based on imitation, the way it is now. The early Muslims agreed to prohibit the judges from action based solely on imitation. They said that imitation was the province of the people, not of the judges or Muftis. They stated that there was no difference between an animal and a human being that imitates.

Second, to educate competent teachers of the Arabic language and religion, and try to make the teacher of religion practice its morality himself, to act as an example for other people. The teacher of Arabic must be a capable writer and speaker of good Arabic, for his students will learn this skill by means of exchange with him. Teaching language will be, in this case, both theoretical and practical at the same time. Sometimes, spoken language will progress to the level of written language, making it easy for people to benefit from written language.

Third, to make preachers and counselors [social workers] aware of the city and household policies and of what consitutes a happy city and a happy household. They will have to know people's temper and the means of persuasion needed to guide the citizens to whatever brings them happiness. They will captivate the citizens by preaching and guidance in order to help them achieve happiness and peace. They will have to avoid imitation the way it is practiced now, during the epoch of decadence and backwardness; speeches are now being given that have no purpose but to reject life.

Fourth, to make clergymen in Egypt responsible for morality. In the same way that the health service is responsible for the bodily health of the people of Egypt, the clergymen would be responsible for their moral health. Clergymen will be prepared to spread strong will, healthy character, and love of homeland, altruism, cooperation, and solidarity within the nation. They will also explain to the Egyptians that they constitute one physical entity, every organ works for the benefit of all and the suffering of one organ is the suffering of all. They will fight immoral behavior, like envy, hate, weak will, and egoism, which are destructive to society. Finally, the clergymen will be responsible for the poor worker who spends his earnings on cocaine, opium, hashish, wine, and other dangerous drugs. The program of reform will inculcate the Azhari love of humankind and society. Those associated with it will sacrifice themselves for the happiness of the society and for the spreading of good morality. They will have a strong desire to save those who are wounded by these dangerous sicknesses and murderous vices like wine, gambling, and drugs. They will give those wounded efficient medicines when they are asked to do so. Otherwise, they will go to these unfortunate people, they will knock on their doors and places of entertainment, and present them with guidance. By doing so, the clergymen will produce in the nation what no other group would be able to do. They will serve society, a service could be provided by no other means. They could be compared to the physicians who strengthen bodies, because they build morality[1] in the nation and educate its souls. A nation's worth is its morality. By defying morality one nation can dominate another nation and exploit it in the same way people exploit animals. This is the production, which could not be upgraded by any other production. Whenever a nation develops and progresses, it will appreciate the value of morality and therefore appreciate the value of its clergymen.

Fifth, to arm the clergymen with genuine science and to give them the ability to resurrect their nation from inherited beliefs. These beliefs have remained from the old generation, are in contradiction with religion, are fatal to the nation, and weaken the nation's morality. It is likely that they were the main factors leading to the weakness of the Orient and its descent into the abyss in which it is now struggling.

Sixth, to free minds from the constraints of imitation and to lead them to the universe of freedom of thought and deduction. The object is to teach the art of intellectual production and initiation of scientific movement in the fields of ethics, sociology, religion, language, and philosophical sciences, such as those that came to being during the flourishing epochs of al-Ma'mun and others.

This reform is the result of 25 years of careful study, verification, precision of observation, independence of opinion, and freedom of thought. This science is not known except by the one who has been mastering it and has had the chance to follow its precepts. If the rulers want a reform like this one, they need to devote themselves to it for a long time and exert a great effort and power.

We owe a heavy duty toward our nation and that duty consists of regenerating it by regenerating the causes of life and glory in it. Destiny allowed us to carry out this duty because of what we knew about the causes of its weakness and the solutions to these problems. We support with great effort this endeavor and we ask the rulers to help us fulfill our duty.

NOTE

1. *al-Manar:* This is also true for physical health. Anyone who follows the guidelines of religion concerning prohibition of alcoholic beverages, drugs, and libertine behavior, and concerning cleanliness of the body, clothes, location, and all such things is less likely to be exposed to illness and therefore to need physicians. Following religion is the best way to prevent illness before it happens.

CHAPTER 6

METHODOLOGY OF HISTORICAL WRITING

'Allama Shibli Nu'mani

Excerpt from 'Allama Shibli Nu'mani *Sirat un-Nabi*, vol. I. Translated by M. Tayyib Bakhsh Budayuni. Delhi: Idarah-i Adabiyat-i Delli, reprint 1983, pp. 36–63.

AUTHENTICITY OF THE SOURCES

THE EVENTS OF THE LIFE OF THE HOLY PROPHET were first put into writing almost 100 years after his death. Hence the writers had no written sources to fall back upon except memorized traditions.

In a similar situation, when facts have to be recorded long after their occurrence, people generally pick up all sorts of street gossip, without ever caring to know even the names of the reporters. At the most, out of a worthless heap of hearsay, a selection is made in the light of circumstances or on grounds of probability. Shortly after, this worthless collection passes for a piece of interesting historical literature. European history is a collection of this type of material.

THE ISLAMIC METHOD OF JUDGING THE NARRATORS

Muslims alone, among the nations of the world, may claim the credit of having established a far superior standard of writing history. The first principle the Muslim historians laid down was that the incidents to be incorporated should be such as have been reported by a person who has personally witnessed the affair. If this is not the case, the name of all the intermediaries have to be serially mentioned up to the man who had been an actual participator or eye-witness. The important thing was to see the type of persons the reporters were, what calling they followed, what character they bore, how they stood in the matter of memory and judgment, and whether they were reliable or untrustworthy, had a keen intellect or a shallow mind, and were well-informed or ignorant. It was almost impossible to know all these details. Still, hundreds of workers in the field devoted their lives to this arduous task. They went from door to door, traveled from place to place, met persons who had anything to narrate, and gathered all possible information regarding their life and character. If the person had been dead, inquiries were made from those who had known him when living.

ASMA AL-RIJAL

These inquiries gave birth to a new branch of knowledge known as "Asma' al-Rijal" (Biographies of the narrators of the Prophet's sayings). To this colossal store-house we are indebted for exhaustive information with respect to at least 100,000 narrators; and if the opinion of Sprenger is to be accepted, to not less than five times that number.[1]

These traditionists, without being influenced by the position or status of a man, gathered all relevant information, detected the innermost moral weaknesses and laid bare every shortcoming, sparing neither kings nor religious heads. Thus, hundreds of books were written, of which we give a brief description here:

The first book on the subject, i.e., on the critical study of the lives of the narrators, was written by Yahya ibn Sa'id al-Qattan (d. 198 A.H.). He was a scholar of such a high caliber that a man like the Imam Ibn Hanbal said of him: "Never have I seen the like of him." After Yahya this branch of knowledge gained wide popularity and many books were produced. A few of the most prominent among them are:

Rijal 'Uqaili (called *Kitab al-du'afa*)
It dealt with the narrators whose reliability were questionable. The author died in 322 A.H.–934 C.E.
Rijal Ahmad (d. 216 A.H.–874 C.E.)
The full name of the book was "*al-Jarh wal-ta'dil.*" (Scrutiny and Criticism).
Rijal al-Imam 'abd al-Rahman ibn Hatim al-Razi (d. 327 A.H.–939 C.E.)
It is a voluminous book (Printed in Hyderabad 1354 A.H.).
Al-Kamil of Ibn 'Adi
It was the most famous book on the subject. Later traditionists have all drawn from it as their main source (for a copy see Top Kapu, iii. 2943).
Rijal of al-Daraqutni
Al-Imam al-Daraqutni (d. 385 A.H.–995 C.E.) was a well-known traditionist. The book deals particularly with the weak narrators (ed. Wajahat Hussain, 1934).

Most of these books are now no longer available. Later writings based on them are, however, available.

The most comprehensive and authentic work in this category is *Tahdhib al-kamal* by al-Mizzi Yusuf ibn al-Zaki (d. 742 A.H./1341 C.E.). Ala al-Din Mughlata'i (d. 762 A.H./1361 C.E.) completed it in thirteen volumes. Al-Dhahabi (d. 748 A.H./1347 C.E.) brought out an abridged version of this book. Many other traditionists also produced its abridged versions or companion-books. Based on this material, Ibn Hajar at last compiled a voluminous work, *Tahdhib al-tahdhib*, running into 12 volumes. It has recently been published from Hyderabad Deccan (India). The author remarks that it took him eight years to compile it. Another popular work in this line is the *Mizan al-i'tidal* by Al-Dhahabi, to which Ibn Hajar has made further additions in his book *Lisan al-Mizan*.

BOOKS ON RIJAL CONSULTED BY US

Of these sources we have made use of the following books:

Tahdhib al-kamal
tahdib al-tahdhib
Lisan al-Mizan
Taqrib
Ta'rikh Kabir
Ta'rikh Saghir (both by al-Imam al-Bukhari)
Thiqat by Ibn Hibban
Tadhkirat al-Huffaz by al-Dhahabi
Mushtabih al-Nisba by al-Dhahabi
Ansab by al-Sam'ani
Tahdhib al-Asma.

THE FIRST PRINCIPLE

The principle of investigation has been laid down by the Quran itself. The Quran says, "O you who believe, if an evil-doer comes onto you with a report, then inquire strictly" (49: 6). A saying of the Prophet, too, confirms this: "If one relates whatever one hears from others, it is enough for him to be regarded as a liar."

THE SECOND PRINCIPLE

The best principle of investigation in order to ascertain the truth of a report is to see whether the statement stands to reason.

This principle, too, has been, enunciated by the Quran. When the hypocrites started a calumny against 'A'isha (wife of the Prophet), they advertised and propagated this in a way that some of the Companions of the Prophet were misled. The

Sahih of al-Bukhari and the *Sahih* of Muslim both state that even Hassan, the poet, was led to believe it; and consequently was ordered to be punished for libel. The Quran says: 'Verily those who brought forward the calumny were a small band among you" (24:11). The author of *Tafsir al-Jalalain*, a famous commentary of the Quran, while explaining the word *"minkum"* (from among you), says that by this is meant a group of Muslims. One of the verses of the Quran that exonerates 'A'isha and declares her chastity runs thus: "And wherefore, when ye heard it, did ye not say, it is not for us to speak thereof, hallowed be Thou, that is a slander mighty" (24: 16). In accordance with the general principle, the procedure for an inquiry would have been to ascertain the name of the reporters and then to see if they were trustworthy. This done, their statements were to be taken. God, however, says that it ought to have been discarded as a baseless calumny. This establishes the principle that an incident that sounds so highly incredible ought to be rejected outright as false.

Thus the method of inquiry called *"Diraya"* (judging the truth of a report in the light of one's previous knowledge and experience) had made a beginning even in the days of the Companions of the Prophet.

Some *fuqaha'* (jurists) are of the opinion that ablution, or *wudu*, has to be performed again if one takes anything cooked on fire. When Abu Huraira attributed this saying to the Prophet in the presence of 'abd Allah ibn 'Abbas, the latter said that if it were so, ablution would no longer stand even if one drank water heated on a fire.[2] Not that 'abd Allah ibn 'Abbas considered Abu Huraira a weak narrator, yet he was not prepared to accept this report as it was against Diraya (common knowledge and experience). In his opinion, Abu Huraira might have erred in grasping the actual meaning.

Side by side with the compilation of books on traditions, the traditionists were engaged in framing the principles of Diraya. A few of these principles are given here:

Ibn al-Jauzi says that if you find any Hadith to be contrary to reason and against the accepted principles, then know for certain that it is fabricated. You need not bother about narrators' reliability or unreliability. Similarly, reports that are contrary to our experience and observation and do not admit of any interpretation need not be accepted. Similar is the case with the sayings that threaten people with severe chastisement for trivial errors, or which promise enormous rewards for insignificant acts of virtue (such sayings are mostly currently among the preachers from the pulpit and the unlettered), or the traditions that border on absurdity, e.g., the saying that one should not eat a gourd without slaughtering it. Consequently, some of the traditionists hold that the absurdity of the statement is in itself an argument for the falsehood of the reporter. The presumptions given above relate to the reports, but they may as well relate to the reporters, for example, the story of Ghiyath and Caliph Mehdi. The same presumption should hold good relating to the reporter if he narrates a tradition that has not been narrated by any one else and the person has not even seen the person he narrates from, or when he is the single reporter while the nature of the report warrants the knowledge of the fact to others as well (as Khatib al-Baghdadi has elucidated the point in the early chapters of his book *al-Kifaya*), or the reported incident, if true, ought to have been narrated by hundreds of persons, for example, if someone says that an enemy prevented the pilgrims from making the holy pilgrimage."[3]

The sum and substance of the foregoing discourse is that the following categories of reports are to be discredited without an inquiry into the characters of their narrators:

1. The traditions that are contrary to reason.
2. The traditions that go against the accepted principles.
3. The traditions that belie common observation and physical experience.
4. The traditions that contradict the Quran or a Mutawatir Hadith (repeatedly corroborated tradition), or go against a decided consensus of opinion (*Ijma' Qati'*) and do not conform to any interpretation.
5. The tradition that threatens severe punishment for a minor fault.
6. The tradition that sounds absurd and nonsense, e.g., "Eat not a gourd without slaughtering it."
7. The tradition that promises big rewards for trivial acts of piety.
8. A tradition narrated by a single person who has never personally contacted the man from whom he narrates.
9. A tradition concerning an incident so noteworthy that, if it had actually taken place, it ought to have been related by many, and yet there is but a single narrator to report it.

Mulla 'Ali al-Qari, in his book *al-Moudu'at*, has elaborated certain criteria for judging the authenticity of a Hadith, and has cited examples, which we summarize hereunder:

1. Any Hadith full of nonsense that the Prophet could never have uttered; for instance, the saying "If one recited '*La Ilaha Ill-Lallah—Muhammad Rasul Allah*' (There is no god but Allah and Mohammed is His Messenger), god creates out of his words a birth with 70 tongues, each tongue having 70,000 words of the Kalima."
2. Any Hadith that runs contrary to observation and experience, e.g., "Brinjal is the cure for all diseases and ailments."
3. Any Hadith that cancels another Hadith of established authenticity.
4. Any Hadith that states something against actual experience, e.g., "One should not take one's bath in water heated in the sun, as it causes leprosy."
5. Any Hadith that does not sound like a prophet's utterance, e.g., "Three things improve eyesight, namely, green meadows, flowing water, and a beautiful face."
6. Any Hadith that predicts the future, specifically the exact date and time, e.g., such an incident is to occur on such and such a day, in such and such a year.
7. Any Hadith that looks like the words of a physician, e.g., "Harisa [a kind of sweet preparation consisting of wheat, meat, butter, cinnamon and aromatic herbs] gives vigor to a man" or that "a Muslim is sweet and loves sweets."

8. Any Hadith that is obviously wrong, e.g., "'Iwaj ibn 'Unaq was 3,000 yards [2,742.8 meters] in height."
9. Any Hadith that contradicts the Holy Quran, e.g., the saying that the life of the world is to be 7,000 years. Were it true, anybody could tell when the Day of Judgment would come, although it is established from the Quran that no mortal knows when the Last Day will come.
10. Any Hadith concerning Khidr.
11. Any Hadith whose language is vulgar.
12. Any Hadith that describes that efficacy and merits of the various chapters of the Holy Quran, though many such traditions are found in the commentaries of al-Baidawi and the *Kashshaf*.[4]

It was on the basis of these principles that the traditionists rejected many sayings, for instance, the Hadith that the Prophet had exempted the Jews of Khaibar from the payment of Jizya (capitation tax), and had given them a written document to this effect. Mulla 'Ali al-Qari, while rejecting this saying, has given the following reasons:

1. Sa'd ibn Mu'adh is said to have been one of the witnesses to the document; whereas Sa'd ibn Mu'adh had breathed his last in the battle of the Trenches (much earlier than the battle of Khaibar).
2. The scribe of the document is said to have been Mu'awiyah. But Mu'awiyah embraced Islam after the conquest of Mecca (long after the battle of Khaibar).
3. Jizya had not been enforced or sanctioned till that time. It was enforced after the battle of Tabuk.
4. The document is reported to stipulate that no forced labor would be exacted from the Jews of Khaibar. As a matter of fact, forced labor was not in vogue then.
5. The people of Khaibar had offered a stiff opposition to Islam and so they could not have been exempted from the payment of Jizya.
6. The tribesmen living in distant parts of Arabia who had not shown much hostility to Islam were not exempted; how, then, could the Jews of Khaibar be exempt from its payment?
7. Exemption from the payment of Jizya would mean that the Jews of Khaibar had been friendly to Islam and, as such, deserving of concession. But the fact was that, shortly after, they had to be banished from their land.

REVIEW

In the preceding pages we have given a brief and plain history of the *Sira* literature. We now wish to discuss its various aspects.

There are hundreds of books on *Sira* now available, but the ultimate sources to which they are all indebted are: Ibn Ishaq, Ibn Sa'd, al-Waqidi, and al-Tabari.

Books other than these are later products and draw from them the facts they record—here we are not taking into account the Hadith literature. Thus it is necessary to review these four books critically and exhaustively.

Of these al-Waqidi deserves no notice. Traditionists are all agreed that al-Waqidi coined and fabricated traditions—a fact borne out by his book itself. His descriptions of very minor incidents are so replete with varied and interesting detail, the likes of which no pen, however masterly, can so vividly describe even the events to which the writer had been an eye-witness.

The other three writers are quite reliable. Ibn Ishaq, though criticized by the Imam Malik[5] and some other traditionists, holds a high place; and a traditionist like the Imam al-Bukhari, in his "*al-Juz' al-Qira'a*" (chapter on reading), has quoted many a saying from him.

As to Ibn Sa'd and al-Tabari no one has anything to say against them. Unfortunately, however, their personal integrity and position of authority do not guarantee the authenticity of their works on *Sira*. They were not eye-witnesses to any incident and have consequently quoted others, many of who are untrustworthy. Moreover, the original book of Ibn Ishaq is not traceable here. What we have is its version as edited and altered by Ibn Hisham. But Ibn Hisham has reproduced Ibn Ishaq's book as re-written by Ziyad al-Bakka'i, for he had no direct access to it. Ziyad al-Bakka'i himself is a respectable author; but he falls short of the high criteria of the traditionists. Ibn Madini (the teacher of al-Bukhari) says that al-Bakka'i was a weak narrator and so he had to give him up. So does Abu Hatim discard him as a source worth quoting. Al-Nasa'i, too, regards him as unreliable.

More than half of the reports related by Ibn Sa'd have been borrowed from al-Waqidi: hence they deserve no better respect than the reports of al-Waqidi himself. As regards the other sources utilized by him, some are reliable, others not. Similarly, most of the chief narrators that feed al-Tabari are untrustworthy, such as Salama Abrash, Ibn Salama, and others. Thus the books on *Sira* do not stand on a par with the traditions in authenticity. Only those statements that may stand scrutiny are worth recording.

SIRA COMPARED WITH TRADITIONS

The reason for the inferior authenticity of books of *Sira* is that research and scrutiny were exclusively confined to the saying of the Prophet on Law (Fiqh). It was supposed that the traditions bearing upon the dos and don'ts were to be critically examined, while the rest, dealing with the life land virtues of the Prophet, did not demand a very severe and cautious scrutiny. Zain al-Din al-'Iraqi, a prominent traditionist, in the preface to his book *al-Sira al-Mauzuma*, says: "A lover of this branch of learning (*Sira*) should remember that books on *Sira* incorporate all sorts of reports, *Sahih* as well as *Munkar.*"

It was for this reason that many inauthentic sayings dealing with the status and excellence of the Prophet, or with the meritoriousness of his pious acts, got currency. Even learned scholars had no objection to incorporating them in their books. The great scholar Ibn Taimiyya, in his book *at-Tawassul* says: "This Hadith has been quoted by authors who have written on supererogatory services and prayers; for instance, the work of Ibn al-Sini and Abu Nu'aim, with all other books of that type, contain a large number of fabricated traditions that are quite unreliable; and this is the agreed opinion of all the scholars."[6]

Al-Hakim, in his *Mustadrak*, has quoted a tradition to the effect that when Adam committed the Original Sin, he prayed to God in these words: "O God, forgive me for the sake of Muhammad." At this God asked Adam how he came to know of Muhammad? Adam replied that on the pedestal of the 'Arsh (heavenly seat of God) he has seen inscribed the Kalima (There is no god but Allah and Muhammad is His Messenger); and added that this had led Him to believe that he whose name God associated with his own name must certainly be dearest to him. God replied that Adam was right and that if Muhammad had not been there, He would not have created Adam. This tradition has been quoted by al-Hakim with the comment that it is an authentic report. Ibn Taimiyya, having quoted the comment of al-Hakim says: "Al-Hakim has faith in sayings of this type. Leading traditionists declare it to be baseless. They are of the opinion that many of the sayings approved by al-Hakim are coined and forged. Similarly, there are many traditions in *Mustadrak* which are held to be true by al-Hakim, while recognized traditionists declare them to be forged." On another occasion he refers to the book of Abu Sheikh al-Isphahani and says: "And in it there are many sayings that are true and authentic as also many that are fabricated, weak and absurd. The same may be said of the reports quoted by Khaithamah ibn Sulaiman, exalting and eulogizing the faithful Companions of the Prophet. The same is true of the reports that have been recorded in a separate book by Abu Nu'aim al-Isphahani dealing with the virtues of the Companions. And so are the traditions quoted by Abu Bakr al-Khatib, Abu al-Fadl, Abu Musa Madyani, Ibn 'Asakir, al-Hafiz, 'abd al-Ghani and other eminent writers."[7]

It is to be noted that Abu Nu'aim, Ibn 'Asakir, Khatib al-Baghdadi, al-Hafiz, 'abd al-Ghani, and others were leading traditionists; still they freely quoted weak traditions while dealing with the accomplishments of the Caliphs and the Companions of the Prophet. The only explanation is to be found in the belief that strict care and caution had to be observed only when quoting the traditions telling what is lawful and what is forbidden. In matters other than these, they thought it enough to quote the names of those from whom they narrated and did not care for a critical study and scrutiny.

Mulla 'Ali al-Qari, in his *Maudu'at*, says that in the city of Baghdad a preacher narrated a Hadith that on the Day of Judgment God will seat Muhammad by His side on the 'Arsh. Al-Imam Ibn Jarir was indignant when he heard it, and at his door he hung a placard bearing the words: "None can sit by the side of God." At this the people of Baghdad were so infuriated that they pelted the house of Ibn Jarir with stones till the walls were covered.

One thing is worth mentioning here. Al-Bukhari and Muslim are by general consent the greatest masters of this branch of knowledge. They had a sincere love and a profound sense of reverence for the Prophet, which is another reason for their superiority over the rest of the traditionists. With all that, they have no space for the exaggerated sayings in exaltation of the Prophet that have been reported by al-Baihaqi, Abu Nu'aim, al-Bazzar, al-Tabarani, and others. Even some of the sayings that one finds in the works of al-Nasa'i, Ibn Majah, al-Tirmidhi, and others are missing there. This proves that the number of overstatements declines with the progress of critical scrutiny. For instance, al-Baihaqi, Abu Nu'aim, Ibn 'Asakir and Ibn Jarir relate that on the day of the Prophet's birth 14 minarets of the imperial palace of Persia fell to the ground, the holy fire in the Zoroastrian synagogue died out, and the sea of Tabriyah (Lake Sawa) dried up. But al-Bukhari or Muslim, or any other of the Six Authentic Books of Hadith has nothing to say of this story.

Books on *Sira* so far written are generally based on al-Tabarani and others of the same class. Consequently, they contain quite a large number of fabricated reports. This led the traditionists to declare that *Sira* books contain all sorts of reports.

The principles set forth by the traditionists were mostly overlooked by the biographers. The first Principle was that there should be no break in the chain of the narrators right up to the original source. But all the incidents relating to the birth of the Prophet have a link or two missing in the chain. None of the Companions of the Prophet was old enough to report at the time of the Prophet's birth. The oldest among the Companions was Abu Bakr; but he too was two years younger than Him. This resulted in giving currency to baseless stories concerning the birth of the Prophet, most of which have disconnected chains. For instance there is the story quoted by Abu Nu'aim, said to be reported by the mother of the Prophet, that at the time of the birth of the Prophet, a large number of small birds flocked into the house; and their beaks were made of emeralds and their tongues of rubies; then a patch of white cloud was seen in the sky floating very low and that this patch descended down and took away the holy babe; then a voice was heard announcing that the holy babe should be shown to all the seas, that all should know him. Most of the Maghazi literature is based on al-Imam al-Zuhri. But al-Zuhri's reports mentioned in the *Sira* of Ibn Hisham and the *Tabaqat* of Ibn Sa'd are mostly disconnected, with gaps in the chain of narrators.

DISREGARD OF TRADITIONS
BY THE "SIRA" WRITERS

It is surprising that eminent writers, like al-Tabari and others, while writing on *Sira* did not seek help from the standard books on traditions. There are many important events about which one may get valuable information from the books on traditions and thus solve many problems. But books on *Sira* and history show that their authors have taken no notice of these facts. For example, there is a controversy as to which party was the first to start hostilities after the migration of the Prophet to Medina. From the way the historians and writers on *Sira* have presented facts, one is led to conclude that it was the Prophet who struck first. But the *Sunan* of Abu Dawud records an authentic report definitely saying that before the battle of Badr, 'abd Allah ibn Ubayy, the famous hypocrite of Medina, had received a letter from the Quraish of Mecca asking him to turn Muhammad (peace and blessing of Allah be upon him) out of Medina, else they (the Quraish) would come and exterminate them (the Medinites) all as well as the Prophet.[8] The historical and biographical literature has not a word to say of this threat.

Some of the writers realized this fault; and on a close examination of the traditions, they had to admit that a large number of reports, clearly contradicted by the authentic traditions, had been wrongly incorporated in books on *Sira* and needed correction. But correction was not possible for them because the books had already gone into circulation. Ibn Hajar quotes a passage from al-Dimyati and then writes: "The above passage points to the fact that al-Dimyati had to revise his opinion regarding many incidents that he had endorsed in pursuance of *Sira*-Writers against the testimony of authentic traditions. This he did before attaining maturity in this art. But the book had gone into circulation, and he could not make any corrections.[9]

FALSE PLAY OF SIRA-WRITERS

The later writers on *Sira* have all drawn from the ancients. As the names of the early writers were supposed to guarantee truth, readers were led to take all the contents of the later *Sira* literature as true facts. Unfortunately, the original sources were not within reach; so the readers could not trace out the narrators. Consequently, these statements found their way into all *Sira* literature. For instance, sayings reported by al-Waqidi were regarded by all as untrue; but the same traditions, when they were mentioned in the name of Ibn Sa'd, were believed to be authentic. When the original book by Ibn Sa'd was available, only then was it found that almost all the material contained in it had been borrowed from al-Waqidi.

PRINCIPLES OF NARRATION
SOMETIMES NOT FOLLOWED

The principles set forth for judging the veracity of the narrators were, in some cases, ignored in respect of the Companions. For example, there are many grades of narrators. Some have a retentive memory, keen intelligence, and discerning mind, some possess these qualities to a lesser degree, while others possess them still less. These differences are noticed in all kinds of narrators; and the Companions of the Prophet were no exception. It was on this basis that 'A'isha criticized the reports narrated by Ibn 'Umar, while 'Abu Huraira was criticized both by 'A'isha and 'abd Allah ibn 'Abbas. This we have already spoken of.

This gradation among the narrators forms the basis of many of the questions of great consequence. When two reports disagree and the integrity of the narrators on either side is not to be questioned, the caliber and the status of the narrators is the deciding factor; and the report made by the superior set is declared to be more authentic. But this criterion is dropped in the case of the Companions. Suppose there is a report made by 'Umar and a contradictory one is made by a Bedouin who had chanced to see the Prophet only once. As Companions, both are supposed to stand on the same footing. Al-Mazari, the famous traditionist, who is often quoted by al-Nawawi in his commentary on the *Sahih* of Muslim, has criticized this indiscriminate application of the principle of equality. Ibn Hajar, in the preface to his *Isaba*, has quoted al-Mazari saying, "The dictum that the Companions of the Prophet are all equally judicious does not apply, in our opinion, to a man who may have seen the Prophet by chance or visited him with a purpose and then turned back immediately. By Companions we mean persons who were regularly in attendance on him, who helped him and who followed the Light that he had brought unto them; and verily such men are successful."[10]

Traditionists in general have disagreed with this view of al-Mazari. In fact al-Mazari made a mistake in denying judiciousness to any other than the close Companions of the Prophet. This opposition by the traditionists was, therefore, justified. But we could doubt that the reports of Abu Bakr, 'Umar, 'Uthman, and 'Ali do not stand on a par with the reports made by a Bedouin? This fact is to be kept in mind particularly when problems of Fiqh (Islamic Jurisprudence) are involved, or where the issues are subtle and deep.

CAUSAL RELATIONS IGNORED

Generally the writers on *Sira* do not concern themselves with causes and effects, which they seldom seek to interrelate. The Europeans, on the other hand, have carried things too far. The European mind seeks a cause for each effect; and weaves into a connected chain of events a whole guesswork of far-fetched possibilities and probabilities. His personal bias and objectives mold his writings, as he sets before himself a particular aim and makes the whole revolve round it; the facts he describes are all directed to serve the end in view. On the contrary, the Muslim historian tries to find out facts, impartially and with utmost integrity, little caring for their bearing on history or his religious convictions. His main object is the discovery of truth; and at the altar of truth he will sacrifice even his beliefs and national interests.

But there the pendulum swings to the other extreme. In his extravagant love for factual description, untinged by subjective color, he ignores the concomitant facts that could evidently explain their effects. He passes on leaving the incidents half-said, dull, and dry. For instance, while giving the description of a battle, he will start saying that the Prophet sent an army at such and such time against such and such tribe, without giving the reasons that made the expedition necessary. Average readers are led to suppose that non-Muslims could be attacked and destroyed without rhyme or reason, and that the mere fact that they happened to be infidels was sufficient grounds for an attack. Consequently, critics ascribe the spread of Islam to the sword. But a close study reveals that in all cases wars were made upon those hostile tribes that had been found making preparations for an attack on the Muslims.

NATURE OF THE REPORT AND
THE STATUS OF THE NARRATOR

It is to be noted that the position and status of the narrator must vary according to the nature and importance of the incident. Suppose a man, generally regarded as trustworthy, narrates an ordinary incident that commonly occurs and may occur at any time; his version may then be accepted without any hesitation. But if the same narrator narrates an extraordinary incident that runs counter to general experience and cannot be reconciled to the attendant circumstances, it should then require a stronger evidence and the reporter has to be uncommonly judicious, discerning, and scrupulous, far above average. He should possess a deeper insight than an ordinary witness.

For instance, a commonly debated question is this: Is it necessary to impose an age limit for narrators? Most traditionists hold that a five-year-old child may narrate a tradition or may later on report an incident he had experienced at the age of five; and his narration ought to be accepted.[11] For example, there is the case of Mahmud ibn Rabi' who at the time of the Prophet's death was five years old. Once the Holy Prophet, by way of sporting with him, spat on him the washing of his gargle. This incident was narrated by him when he was a young man; and people made no objection. This proves that a report relating to incidents witnessed at this stage of life might be admissible. But some traditionists differ. The author of the *Fath al-Mughith* says: "Some people hold that such a narration should not be accepted; they are not inclined to accept a narration referring to the experience of a minor. The followers of Imam al-Shafi'i hold this view. 'abd Allah ibn Mubarak too hesitated in accepting the narration of a child."[12]

But the pros and cons are both open to discussion. For example, if a child reports that such and such person, whom he had seen, had a hairy head, or that he was old, or that the man used to carry him in his arms, then there is no reason to disbelieve him. But if this child narrated how a certain gentleman had explained a delicate problem of religious law it would be highly doubtful if he had properly grasped the thing explained. The scholars of Fiqh had this point in mind. The author of the *Fath al-Mughith* who had quoted from *Sharh al-Muhadhdhab*, says: "It is permissible to accept the version of a grown-up child concerning observable facts only; but reporting a Hadith or a legal verdict, the narration of children should in no way be depended on."[13]

Unfortunately, this principle was not universally accepted. The author of the *Fath al-Mughith* says: "Dabt (comprehension) is of two kinds—external or literal Dabt and essential or appreciative. External or literal Dabt relates to the dictionary meanings of words, whereas the essential or appreciative Dabt extends to their implications in relation to Fiqh. The comprehension of Dabt considered necessary for a narrator, is the external or literal one. This school holds that it was valid if a narrator narrated the sense of a report when he did not remember the actual words. This was the main reason why the narrators could be suspected of having altered the sense owing to want of knowledge or lack of memory; and hence the Companions of the Prophet did not narrate many traditions, for it is difficult to retain the sense of words intact in reproduction. But traditionists do not follow such a rigid course in the case of a child (of course a sensible child). They hold that a child when he is able to listen and talk, and bear company to his elders, can easily narrate what he has heard or seen and his report may be relied on."[14]

There is another problem: Should a report made by a Companion of the Prophet not well-versed in Fiqh fail to conform to the rules of inductive inference, as set forth by religious law or Shari'ah, would it then be incumbent to act upon it? Bahr al-'Ulum, commenting on the view of al-Imam Fakhr al-Islam in the matter, says: "The reasons why al-Imam Fakhr al-Islam holds this view is that people have generally reproduced the sense not the actual words, verbal reproduction is rare; and one incident has been narrated in different words, not even synonymous. Not only that we meet metaphorical expressions. Hence the narrator, if not a scholar of Fiqh, may err in understanding the legal significance of the report. But this does not imply imputation of a false statement to a Companion."[15]

The traditionists were not ignorant of the principle that the character of evidence must vary in accordance with the character of the report. Al-Imam al-Baihaqi, in his *Madkhal*, quotes Ibn Mahdi as saying: "When we quote from the Prophet injunctions forbidding or allowing, we make a thorough examination of the sources and the status of the narrators; but when we come to the traditions expounding the merits and excellence of persons and things or announcing rewards or punishments in the Hereafter, we relax our criteria for the sources and sometimes overlook the status of narrators.[16]

Al-Imam Ibn Hanbal says: "Ibn Ishaq is a narrator on whose reports we can depend so far as Maghazi are concerned. But where there is a question of legal and religious injunctions, then we require men like this," and saying this, he closed his fist tight.[17]

This means that in view of the importance of a report, the traditionists took into account the status of the narrators. It was on this account that al-Imam Ibn Hanbal declared Ibn Ishaq to have been dependable with respect to military history, but was not to be relied upon in matters of Fiqh.[18] This is simply a restatement of the principle that the character of the sources must correspond to the nature of the incident; and that the evidence required must vary with the importance of the event. But legal injunctions are not the only important things.

The Hanafi school did realize that the nature of the event was very important. Hence they said we must ascertain, when faced with an improbable report, whether the narrator is learned in Fiqh and capable of giving a ruling. In the book *al-Manar* it is stated thus: "If the narrator happens to be a man of established fame for his knowledge of Fiqh and his proficiency in passing judgment, like the first Four Caliphs or like the 'Ibad Allah ('abd Allah ibn 'Umar, 'abd Allah ibn 'abbas, 'abd Allah ibn Zubair and 'abd Allah ibn 'Amr ibn al-'As), his narration need not be disputed and circumstantial consideration should not be allowed to disqualify it. This is a view contrary to that held by al-Imam Malik. But when the narrator happens to be a man who, though otherwise dependable and judicious, knows nothing of Fiqh, just as Anas and Abu Huraira were, then it will be binding to follow the saying only when it is warranted by circumstantial evidence available; if not, circumstantial consideration should not be unnecessarily set aside."[19]

The question whether Abu Huraira was a man of Fiqh or not is debatable. Some scholars hold him to be an authority. But this is a side issue; for it is the principle and not the personality that is under discussion.

SUBJECTIVE ELEMENT IN A REPORT

A very important and highly debatable question arises when we try to differentiate the objective truth for the subjective additions by a narrator. Scrutiny sometimes reveals that much of what the narrator is describing as a fact is mostly his won imagination. There are many such examples; we cite only a few of them.

When the Prophet, displeased with his wives, began to live in seclusion, it was rumored that he had divorced them all. 'Umar heard of it and came to the Prophet's mosque. He saw people assembled there talking of divorce.[20] 'Umar himself went to the Prophet and asked him if it was a fact. The Prophet said he had not divorced them. This Hadith has been mentioned in the *Sahih* of al-Bukhari in several places, with slight differences in words. The version in the chapter on "Nikah" (Marriage Contract) is commented upon by Ibn Hajar thus: "The rumor that gains currency, though repeated by many, need not be necessarily true unless ultimately based on observation by the ear or the eye. Thus it is probable that the particular Ansari and the rest of the Companions whom 'Umar had seen talking it over the pulpit, may have believed the rumor, because some person seeing the Prophet living in separation from his wives, which was not his custom, had supposed that the Prophet had divorced his wives so he gave publicity to his conjecture. People then started repeating it to one another. This man who first of all set it afloat must have, in all probability, been a hypocrite."[21]

Just think of the Companions assembled in the mosque of the Prophet, and all relating the Prophet's divorce of his wives. The Companions of the Prophet are all trustworthy and reliable men; and a large number of them are narrating this incident. But inquiry later on proves the story to have been a mere conjecture. Ibn Hajar has very courageously declared the originator of the rumor to have been a hypocrite.

There are similar incidents concerning 'A'isha, of which one is known as the incident of "*Ifk*" (false accusation). Ibn Hajar's remarks are equally applicable to these reports. They must have been the malicious imputations of some hypocrite that got currency among the Muslims in general.

EXTERNAL INFLUENCE ON HISTORICAL NARRATIONS

It is a recognized fact that history telling has always been susceptible to external influences, the most powerful of them being the influence of the government. Muslim historians, however, will always claim credit that their pen had never bowed down to the sword.

Traditions were first formed in book form in the days of the Umayyads, who, for about 90 years, throughout their vast dominions stretching from the Indus in India to Asia Minor and Spain, insulted the descendants of Fatima and got 'Ali openly censored in Friday sermons at the mosques. They had hundreds of sayings coined to eulogize Amir Mu'awiyah. Under the 'abbasids, predictions relating to each Caliph by name made their way into Hadith literature. But what was the result? In the very days of these Caliphs, traditionists boldly declared that such sayings were coined and absolutely baseless. Today we find none of this rubbish in the Hadith literature. The 'abbasids and the Umayyads, who in their own days were regarded as the 'Shadow of God' and the 'Vicegerents of the Prophet,' are now seen in their true perspective. Once a poet read out a panegyric in praise of the famous Caliph Mamun al-Rashid, saying that had the caliph been there at the time of the Prophet's death, the question of succession would never have cropped up; and both parties would have chosen him as their first Caliph. Just then in the open court there stood up a man who said, "He is telling a falsehood for the great grandfather of the Caliph was there when the Prophet died; but who cared to take notice of him." He meant 'abbas, the ancestor of the 'abbasid caliphs. Mamun had to appreciate this irrefutable, though disrespectful, reply.

Nevertheless, this extensively operative factor could not remain totally ineffective; and in the books on Maghazi one may easily discern the traces of its influence. The old method of writing history was to describe battles and military exploits in lengthy detail, while administrative measures and social conditions were either entirely neglected or dealt with in a manner so discursive and unappealing that they easily escaped notice. When, later on, Muslim authors took to writing, they had no better models before them. The first influence of the Maghazi models is to be seen in Sira receiving the name of Maghazi, just as the biographies of kings and emperors were given the names of *Shah-Nameh* or *Jang-Nameh*. Accordingly, early books on like *Sira Sira* of Musa ibn 'Uqba and *Sira* of Ibn Ishaq are known as books of Maghazi. Like in history books, incidents have been described in chronological order, year by year, with warfare occupying a prominent place, and chapters begin with the name of some battle as the heading.

This method, though not quite proper even for a political history, was decidedly unsuited to the biography of a Prophet. A Prophet may have to indulge in warfare, when he appears to us as a conqueror or a general: but this is not the true picture of a Prophet. Piety, sanctity, forbearance, generosity, love of humanity, and altruism are the weft and warp that make up the texture of his personality. Even when one is misled to take him for an Alexander, a penetrating eye may easily see that it is not Alexander, but an angel from heaven.

That is why the style of Maghazi differs from that of books on *Sira*. Biographers say when the Prophet laid siege to the fortress of Banu Nadir, he ordered their groves to be cut down. (The Holy Quran, too, makes a brief reference to it). They also speak of the Jews having protested against this order as unfair and inhumanitarian. But they do not explain the reasons and pass on.

CIRCUMSTANTIAL EVIDENCE AND ITS VALUE

Another great problem is whether a report that contradicts reason or an established fact, or surpasses all likelihood in view of circumstances definitely known, is to be accepted simply on the ground that the narrator's integrity is recognized and the chain of reporters unbroken. Ibn al-Jauzi has declared that reports that go against reason should be rejected without inquiring into the character of their narrators. But the controversy does not end here. Reason is an elusive term. Advocates of the school that relied on reports argue that the word "reason," when allowed an extensive application, is sure to give anybody a free license to reject any report on the grounds that, in his opinion, it did not stand to reason.

The fact is that it is hard to decide the controversy one way or the other. Generally it is recognized that a report of which the narrators are all persons of sound integrity and the chain is unbroken is not to be rejected, although it does not stand to reason. The following instances will be useful:

1. The report to the effect that the Prophet, when offering his prayers, was made by Satan to utter words "*Tilka al-Gharanig al-Ula*" in praise of idols, was discredited by all the traditionists as weak and baseless. The traditionists argued that had it been the case that many Muslims must have been led astray; but nothing like this happened. Ibn Hajar, in his *Fath al-Bari*, comments on this argument and says: "Such arguments cannot hold on principle, for a report received through various and several sources is an argument in itself, meaning that there is something of truth in it."[22]

2. In the *Sahih* of al-Bukhari there is a report that the Prophet Abraham told a lie on three occasions. Al-Imam al-Razi rejected this report saying that it forced one to grant that a Prophet could lie; he thinks it safer to suppose that any of the narrators was a liar. Al-Qastallani, quoting the view of al-Imam al-Razi, says: "The view of al-Imam al-Razi is unacceptable, because the report, part of which is fully corroborated, is not the only report that ascribes a false utterance to the Khalil (Abraham). How can we condemn the reporter, when there are these clear words of Abraham, viz., 'This is the work of the greatest of them,' 'I am in a wretched condition,' and 'Sarah is my sister.' In all these three sentences, certainly Abraham did not mean what the words outwardly indicate."[23]

Let us be content with these two instances, though many more could be added.

NOTES

1. A famous German orientalist, who served at the Asiatic Society, Calcutta, for a long time. A. G. Sprenger brought out the edition of the book Isaba. In its preface, he says that he had found no other nation having developed so splendid a branch of knowledge as the Asma' al-Rijal. He has further remarked that it was owing to this development that we get exhaustive knowledge of about 500,000 narrators.
2. *Sahih of Tirmidhi*, chapter on "Wudu."
3. The original book, *Fath al-Mughith*, Lucknow edition, is full of mistakes. Unfortunately, I had to follow its text. In fact, these principles have been framed by the traditionists and not by Ibn al-Jauzi.
4. *Maudu'at*, Mujtaba'i Press, Delhi, p. 92.
5. Here I beg to differ. The fact that the Imam Malik differed with some of the views and opinions held by Ibn Ishaq. But soon after this difference, the Imam Malik realized his own mistake; and had the greatness of withdrawing his earlier remarks about him. The Imam Malik is also reported to have written about this to Ibn Ishaq and along with his letter he also sent to him some gifts, which Ibn Ishaq accepted. This shows that al-Imam Malik held Ibn Ishaq very high in his opinion—Translator.
6. *Al-Tawassul*, Minar Press, p. 99.
7. No note attended this quote in the original text.
8. We shall discuss this in detail when dealing with the battle of Badr.
9. *Al-Zurqani*, vol. III. p. 11.

10. *Isaba*, Preface, pp. 10,11.
11. There seems to be some ambiguity or expression here. With all that, the issue involved relates to an experience at the age of five reported in after years, not to a child of five appearing as a reporter (translator).
12. For details see *Fath al-Mughith* (Lucknow edition), pp. 166–8.
13. Ibid., p. 122.
14. Ibid.
15. *Sharh Muslim*, p. 432.
16. *Fath al-Mughith*, p. 120.
17. Ibid.
18. Al-Imam Malik and not al-Imam Ibn Hanbal. See my previous note.
19. *Nur al-anwar*, pp. 176, 177.
20. *Sahih of al-Bukhari*, chapter on "Ila."
21. *Fath al-Bari*, Cairo edition, vol. IX, p. 257.
22. Ibid., vol. VIII, p. 333.
23. *Al-Qastallani*, vol. V, p. 280.

II. ISLAM AND POLITICS

CHAPTER 7

WAR AND PEACE: POPULAR JIHAD

Moulavi Chiragh Ali

Excerpt from Moulavi Chiragh Ali. "The Popular Jihad or Crusade; According to the Muhammadan Common Law." In *A Critical Exposition of the Popular "Jihad."* Karachi, Pakistan: Karimsons, 1977. pp. 114–61.

89. THE QURAN ENJOINED ONLY DEFENSIVE WARS

ALMOST ALL THE COMMON MUHAMMADAN AND EUROPEAN writers think that a religious war of aggression is one of the tenets of Islam, and prescribed by the Quran for the purpose of proselytizing or exacting tribute. But I do not find any such doctrine enjoined in the Quran, or taught, or preached by Muhammad. His mission was not to wage wars, or to make converts at the point of the sword, or to exact tribute or exterminate those who did not believe his religion. His sole mission was to enlighten the Arabs to the true worship of the one God, to recommend virtue and denounce vice, which he truly fulfilled. That he and his followers were persecuted, that they were expelled from their houses and were invaded upon and warred against; that to repel incursions and to gain the liberty of conscience and the security of his followers' lives and the freedom of their religion, he and they waged defensive wars, encountered superior numbers, made defensive treaties, securing the main object of the war, i.e., the freedom of their living unmolested at Mecca and Medina, and of having a free intercourse to the Sacred Mosque, and a free exercise of their religion: all these are questions quite separate and irrelevant, and have nothing to do with the subject in hand, i.e., the popular *Jihad*, or the crusade for the purpose of proselytizing, exacting tribute, and exterminating the idolaters, said to be one of the tenets of Islam. All the defensive wars, and the verses of the Quran relating to the same, were strictly temporary and transitory in their nature. They cannot be made an example of, or be construed into a tenet or injunction for aggressive wars, nor were they intended so to be. Even they cannot be an example or instruction for a defensive war to be waged by the Muhammadan community or commonwealth, because all the circumstances under which Muhammad waged his defensive wars were local and temporary. But almost all European writers do not understand that the Quran does not teach a war of aggression, but had only, under the adverse circumstances, to enjoin a war of defense, clearly setting forth the grounds in its justification and strictly prohibiting offensive measures.

90. COMMON LAW AND JIHAD

All the fighting injunctions in the Quran are, in the first place, only in self-defense, and none of them has any reference to make warfare offensively. In the second place, it is to be particularly noted that they were transitory in their nature, and are not to be considered positive injunctions for future observance or religious precepts for coming generations.[1] They were only temporary measures to meet the emergency of the aggressive circumstances. The Muhammadan Common Law is wrong on this point, where it allows unbelievers to be attacked without provocation. But this it places under the category of a non-positive injunction. A positive injunction is that which is incumbent on every believer. But attacking unbelievers without any provocation, or offensively, is not incumbent on every believer. The *Hedaya* has: "The sacred injunction concerning war is sufficiently observed when it is carried on by any one *party* or *tribe* of *Mussulmans*; and it is then no longer of any force with respect to the rest."[2]

91. JIHAD WHEN POSITIVE

The Muhammadan Common Law makes the fighting only a positive injunction "where there is a *general summons* (that is, where the infidels invade a *Mussulman* territory, and the *Imam* for the time being issues a general proclamation, requiring all persons to stand forth to fight) for in this case war becomes a positive injunction with respect to the whole of the inhabitants,"[3]—this is sanctioned by the Law of Nations and the Law of Nature.

92. THE HEDAYA QUOTED AND REFUTED

The *Hedaya*, or a Commentary of the Muhammadan Common Law by Nuraddin Ali of Murghinan (died in 593 A.H.) has: "The destruction of the sword[4] is incurred by the infidels, although they be not the first aggressors, as appears from the various passages in the sacred writings which are generally received to this effect."[5]

This assertion is not borne out by the sacred injunction of the Quran, and, on the contrary, is in direct contradiction to the same. There are several passages in the Quran, already quoted on pages 16–25, which expressly forbid the taking of offensive measures, and enjoin only defensive wars. There are some other passages which are not so expressive as the several others referred to above, or in other words, are not conditional. But the law of interpretation, the general scope and tenor of the Quran, and the context of the verses and parallel passages, all show that those few verses which are not conditional should be construed as conditional in conformity with other passages more clear, expressive, and conditional, and with the general laws of scriptural interpretation. Now, the author of the Hedaya and other writers on the Common Law quote only those few passages from the Quran which are absolute or unconditional, and shut their eyes against those many conditional verses and general scope and tenor of the Quran.

Limited, or *Conditional*	General, or *Absolute*
Sura XXII, 39–42.	Sura II, 245, (read together with 247.)
Sura II, 186–189, 212, 214.	Sura IX, 124.
Sura IV, 76, 77, 78, 86, 91, 92, 93.	
Sura VIII, 39–41, 58–66, 73, 74.	The context, parallel passages and their
Sura, IX, 1–15, 29, 36.	history, show them to be limited and
Quoted in pages 16–25, 35.	conditional, in conformity with the
	general scope of the Quran.

93. RULE OF INTERPRETATION

Now, there are only two verses in the Quran (Sura II, v. 245, and Sura IX, v. 124) containing an absolute or non-conditional injunction for making war against the unbelievers. Perhaps you may be able to detach some more sentences, or dislocate some half verses from amongst those given under the head of conditional. But these absolute, as well as those detached and dislocated parts of some other verses will not, by any rule of interpretation, show absolute injunction to wage war against the unbelievers without any provocation or limitation. There is a rule in the exegesis of the Quran, as well as in other Scriptural interpretations, that when two commandments, one conditional, and the other general or absolute, are found on the same subject, the conditional is to be preferred, and the absolute should be construed as conditional, because the latter is more expressive of the views of the author than the general, which is considered as vague in its expression.

The rule is: Where a passage which is ambiguous, or which contains any unusual expression, or in which a doctrine is slightly treated, or is in general terms, must be interpreted agreeably to what is revealed more clearly in other parts, or where a subject is more clearly discussed. A single or general passage is not to be explained in contradiction to many others restricted, conditional, and limited consistently with them, and with proper reservations.

94. THE COMMON LAW AND ITS COMMENTATORS

It is not to be wondered that the Muhammadan legists or the compilers of the Common Law are wrong in this point. Because, as a rule, or as a matter of fact, they have compiled the Common Law from different sources irrespective of the Quran, and the commentators of the Common Law take the trouble of vindicating its views, principles, and casuistries, and justifying the Moslem conquests under the Khalifs by the authority of the Quran. Then only they commit the unpardonable blunder of citing isolated parts of solitary verses of the Quran, which are neither expressive enough nor are in general terms. In doing so, they avoid the many other conditional and more explicit verses on the same subject.

95. *KIFAYA* QUOTED

The author of *Kifaya*, a commentary on the *Hedaya*, who flourished in the seventh century of the Hegira, remarks on the words of the text, " The destruction of the sword is incurred by the infidels, although they be not the first aggressors," already quoted in the 92nd paragraph, and says: "Fighting against the infidels who do not become converts to Islam, and do not pay the capitation-tax, is incumbent, though they do not attack first." The author of the *Hedaya* has mentioned this aggressive measure specially, because apparently the words of God, " if they attack you then slay them,"[6] indicate that the fighting against the unbelievers is only incumbent when they fight first, but, however, such is not the case. It is incumbent to fight with them, though they be not the aggressors.[7]

96. FURTHER QUOTATION

The same author writes in continuation of the above quotation, and attempts to reconcile his theory with the numerous precepts of the Quran, which do not permit the war of aggression: "Know, that in the beginning the Prophet was enjoined to forgive, and withdraw from those who joined other gods with God. God said, 'wherefore dost thou forgive with kindly forgiveness, and withdraw from those who join other gods with Me.'"

"Then He enjoined him to summon the people to the faith by kind warning and kind disputation, saying 'Summon thou to the way of thy Lord with wisdom and kindly warning: dispute with them in the kindest manner.' "

"Then He allowed fighting, when they, the unbelievers, were the aggressors, and said: 'A sanction is given to those who have fought because they have suffered outrages;' i.e., they are allowed to fight in self-defense. And God said, If they attack you, then kill them ' (II, 187); and also said, 'If they lean to peace, lean thou also to it.' (VIII, 63)."

"Then he enjoined to fight aggressively during a certain period. God said, 'And when the sacred months are passed, kill them who join other gods with God, wherever ye find them, and seize them' (IX, 5)."

"After this He enjoined for fighting absolutely, at every time and in every place. God said, 'And do battle against them until there be no more (fitnah) persecution' (II, 189; VII, 40)."

97. THE *KIFAYA* REFUTED

Here the author of *Kifaya* has contrived to make out by way of subterfuge and sophistry five successive periods of the policy of the Quran regarding warfare against the unbelievers:

First Period	Forgiveness and withdrawal.	Sura XV, 85. VI, 106.
Second Period	Summoning	Sura XVI, 126.
Third Period	Fighting in self-defense	Sura XXII, 40. II, 187. VIII, 63.
Fourth Period	Fighting aggressively during certain times	Sura, IX, 5.
Fifth Period	Aggressive fighting absolutely	Sura II, 189. VIII, 40.

He is wrong in history, chronology, as well as in understanding the general scope of the Quran and the tenor of the Suras. He does not regard even the context of the verses quoted.

The verses containing injunctions for turning aside, shunning, forgiving, passing over, and withdrawing are found even in the later period of the Medinite Suras—(*Vide* Sura II, 103; V, 16, 46 ; Sura IV, 66, 83; and VII, 198). They have nothing to do either with war or peace.

The summoning of people to the faith of God was the chief duty of the Prophetical office, and was not confined to any special period, and was alike during times of war and peace. Even during the actual warfare it was incumbent on the Prophet to give quarters to the enemy, if he desired, to listen to his preachings—(*Vide* Sura IX, 6).

98. S. IX, V. 5, DISCUSSED

The fifth verse of the ninth Sura is by no means an injunction to attack first or wage an aggressive war. This verse is one of the several published at Medina after the Meccans had violated the treaty of Hodeibia and attacked the Bani Khozaa, who were in alliance with Muhammad. The Meccans were given four months' time to submit, in default of which they were to be attacked for their violation of the treaty and for their attacking the Bani Khozaa. They submitted beforehand, and Mecca was conquered by compromise. The verses referred to above (Sura IX, 1–15, etc.) were not acted upon. So there was no injunction to wage an aggressive war. This subject has been discussed on pages 51–5 of this work, and the reader is referred to them for fuller information.

99. SURA II, V. 189, DISCUSSED

The 189th verse of the second Sura is not at all a war of aggression. The verses in 186, 187, 188 and 189, if read together, will show that the injunction for fighting, is only in defense. The verses are:

186. And fight for the cause of God against those who fight against you: but commit not the injustice *of attacking them first;* verily God loveth not the unjust.
187. And kill them wherever ye shall find them; and eject them from whatever place they have ejected you; for *(fitnah)* persecution is worse than slaughter; yet attack them not at the sacred Mosque, until they attack you therein, but if they attack you, then slay them: such is the recompense of the infidels!
188. But if they desist, then verily God is Gracious, Merciful—
189. And do battle against them until there be no more *(fitnah)* persecution and the only worship be that of God: but if they desist, then let there be no hostility, save against wrong-doers.

100. SURAS II, 189; VIII, 40, ARE DEFENSIVE

Besides, this verse as well as the fortieth verse of Sura VIII have indications in themselves of their relating to a defensive war. As the torture, aggression, in short, the persecutions suffered by the Moslems from the Koreish, are very clearly indicated by the word *fitnah* in these two verses, the object of fighting or counter-fighting by the Moslems is plainly set forth, which is to suppress the persecutions.

They have clear reference to the persecution, to stop or remove which they enjoined fighting, and this was fighting in self-defense obviously.

They also show that the Meccans had not desisted from persecuting and attacking the Moslems, and therefore a provision was made that if they discontinue their incursions, there will be no more hostility. This is quite sufficient to show that these verses relate to the defensive wars of Muhammad.

101. ALL INJUNCTIONS LOCAL AND FOR THE TIME BEING

Lastly, supposing the Quran permitted waging aggressive wars against the Meccans, who were the first aggressors, this does not corroborate the theory or principle of the Common Law of making lawful aggressive wars in the future on the authority of these verses, as all of them in the Quran on the subject of war relate only to Pagan Arabs, who had long persevered in their hostility to the early Moslems or to the Jews, who, being in league with the Moslems, went over to their enemies, and aided them against the Moslems. These verses are not binding on other persons, who are not under the same circumstance as the Moslems were under at Medina. [See paragraph 90.]

102. AINEE QUOTED AND REFUTED

Another commentator of the *Hedaya*, Ainee[8] (who died in 855) follows *Kifaya* already quoted, and mentions some other verses of the Quran on the war of aggression, which the author of *Kifaya* has left uncited in his work. They are as follow:

> " ... Then do battle with the ringleaders of infidelity,—for no oaths are binding on them—that they may desist."—(Sura IX, 12).
> "War is prescribed to you, but from this ye are averse."—(Sura II, 212).
> "March ye forth, the light and heavy, and contend with your substance and your persons on the Way of God."—(Sura IX, 41).

The first verse when it is complete runs thus: "But if, after alliance made, they break their oaths and revile your religion, then do battle with the ringleaders of infidelity,—for no oaths are binding on them—that they may desist"; and fully shows by its wording that it relates to the war of defense, as the breaking of alliances, and reviling of the Moslem religion were the grounds of making war with the object in view that the aggressors may desist. This verse is one of those in the beginning of the ninth Sura, which have already been discussed.—(*Vide* pages 51–55).

The second verse (II, 212) does not allow a war of aggression, as the next verse (II, 214) expressly mentions the attacks made by the aggressors on the Moslems. It has been quoted at full length on page 18.

The third verse (IX, 41) was published on the occasion of the expedition of Tabuk, which was certainly a defensive measure, and has been discussed on pages 51 to 55.

103. SARAKHSEE QUOTED AND REFUTED

Sarakhsee generally entitled *Shums-ul-a-imma* (the Sun of the Leaders), who died in 671 A. H., as quoted by Ibn Abdeen in his *Radd-ul-Muhtar*,[9] makes several stages in publishing the injunctions for fighting. He writes: "Know thou, that the command for fighting has descended by degrees. First the Prophet was enjoined to proclaim and withdraw, 'Profess publicly then what thou hast been bidden and withdraw from those who join gods with God' (XV, 94). Then he was ordered to dispute kindly; 'Summon thou to the way of thy Lord with wisdom and with kindly warning: dispute with them in the kindest warning' (XVI, 126). Then they were allowed to fight, 'A sanction is given to those who are fought ... '(XXII, 40). Then they were allowed to fight if they (the unbelievers) attacked them, 'If they attack you, then kill them, (II, 187). After this they were enjoined to fight on the condition of passing over the sacred months, 'And when the sacred months are passed, then kill the polytheists' (IX, 5). After this they were enjoined to fight absolutely, 'And fight for the cause of God ... ' (II, 186, 245). And thus the matter was settled."

There was no injunction for fighting absolutely or aggressively in the Quran. I have already explained the 5th verse of the ninth Sura as not allowing an offensive war. And the same is the case with the 186th verse of the second Sura, which has in itself the condition of fighting against those only who fought against the Moslems. The other verse, 245th, of the same Sura is restricted by the 186th verse, (and is explained by the 245th verse), which refers to the defense measures. This verse is quoted on page 19 of this work.

104. IBN HAJAR QUOTED AND REFUTED

Shahabudeen Ahmed-bin-Hajr Makki writes: "Fighting was prohibited before the Hegira, as the Prophet was enjoined only to preach and warn and to be patient in the persecutions of the unbelievers in order to conciliate them. After this, God gave sanction to the Moslems for fighting, (after that had been prohibited in seventy and odd verses), when the unbelievers were the aggressors, and said, 'And fight for the cause of God against those who fight against you' (II, 187). And it is a genuine tradition from Zohri that the first revealed verse sanctioning it was, 'A sanction is given to those who are fought, because they have suffered outrages' (XXII, 40): that is a sanction was given for fighting on the ground of the word 'fought'. Then the war of aggression was made lawful in other than the sacred months, 'When the sacred months are over ... ' (IX, 5). After this, in the eighth year of the Hegira, after the victory of Mecca, the fighting was enjoined absolutely by the words of God; 'March ye forth, the light and the heavy' (IX, 41); and 'attack those who join gods with God in all' (IX, 36). And this is the very verse of the sword, and some say the preceding verse is the verse of the sword, while others think that both bear on the same subject, i.e., of the sword."[10]

105. IBN HAJAR REFUTED

I have already explained the several verses quoted by the author in the preceding paragraphs, but have only to pass remarks on the only verse, i.e., (IX, 36), which the authors cited have not dared to mention, because it goes contrary to their assertion. Perhaps it is a slip in the rapidity of Ibn Hajar's remarks, for which he may be excused. But I will not hesitate in saying that generally the Muhammadan legists, while quoting the Quran in support of their theories, quote some dislocated portion from a verse without any heed to its context, and thus caused a great irreparable mischief by misleading others, especially the European writers, as it is apparent from the testimony of Mr. Lane quoted in paragraph 113 of this work.

The verse referred to by the author mentioned in the last paragraph, Ibn Hajar Makki, is as follows: "Attack you those who join gods with God in all, as they attack you in all."—(IX, 36). This speaks evidently of the defensive war, and has not the slightest or faintest idea of a war of aggression on the part of Tabuk.

106. HALABI QUOTED

Nooruddeen Ali Halabi (died 1044 A.H.), the author of *Insan-ul-Oyoon*, a biography of the Prophet, writes: "It is not hidden that the Prophet for ten and odd years was warning and summoning people without fighting, and bearing patiently the severe persecutions of the Meccan Arabs and the Medinite Jews on himself and on his followers, because God had enjoined him to warn and to have patience to bear the injuries by withholding from them, in accordance with His words, 'Withdraw from them' (V, 46); and 'endure them with patience' (XVI, 128; XVIII, 27; XXXI, 16; LII, 48; and LXXIII, 10). He also used to promise them victory. His companions at Mecca used to come to him beaten and injured, and he used to tell them, 'Endure with patience, I am not commanded to fight,' because they were but a small party at Mecca. After this, when he was settled at Medina after the Hegira and his followers became numerous who preferred him to their fathers, children and wives, and the unbelievers persisted in their idolatry, charging him with falsehoods, then God permitted his followers to fight, but against those *only* who used to fight against them (the Moslems), and were aggressors, as he said, 'If they fight you then kill them' (II, 187). This was in the year of Safar A.H. 2.... Then the whole Arab host marched against the Moslems to fight against them from every direction. The Moslems passed in the same state, and longed to pass peaceful nights without fear from anybody except from God. Then it was revealed, 'God hath promised to those of you who believe and do the things that are right, that he will cause them to succeed others in the land, as he gave succession to those who were before them, and that He will establish for them that religion which they delight in, and after their fears He will give them security in exchange' (XXIV, 54). After this to attack first was allowed against those who had not fought, but in other than the sacred months, viz., *Rajab, Zulkada, Zulhijja,* and *Mohurram,* according to the precept, 'And when the sacred months are passed, kill those who join gods with God ... '(IX, 5). Then the order became incumbent after the victory of Mecca, in the next year, to fight absolutely without any restriction, without any regard to any condition and time, by the words of God, 'Attack those who join gods with God in all [times], at any time (IX, 36). So it is known that the fighting was forbidden before the Hegira up to the month of Safar in its second year, as the Prophet was in this period ordered to preach and warn without any fighting, which was forbidden in seventy and odd verses. Then it was permitted to fight against *only* those who fought against them. Then it was allowed to fight against those who fought aggressively in other than the sacred months. After this it was enjoined absolutely to wage war against them whether they did or did not fight, at all times, whether during the sacred months, or others of the year."[11]

107. HALABI REFUTED

Neither the fifth verse or the ninth Sura, nor the thirty-sixth of the same, allowed war of aggression. Both of them were published on the occasions of defensive wars, and the party against whom they were directed were the aggressors. All the verses quoted by Halabi, bearing on the subject, have been discussed and explained in the forgoing pages, from 92 to 106.

108. AINEE AGAIN QUOTED AND REFUTED

Ainee, the author of the commentary on the *Hedaya*, called *Binayah*, in justifying the war of aggression against the unbelievers, quotes two verses from the Quran,[12] and two traditions from the Prophet,[13] and says, "If it be objected that these absolute injunctions are restricted by the word of God, 'If they attack you, then kill them' (II, 187), which shows that the fighting is only incumbent when the unbelievers are the aggressors in fighting, as it was held by Souri, the reply is that the verse was abrogated by another, 'So fight against them until there be no more persecution' (II, 189), and 'fight against those who do not believe in God' (IX, 29)."[14] But he is wrong in asserting that the verse II, 187 was abrogated by II, 189, and IX, 29. There is no authority for such a gratuitous assumption. And besides, both these verses (II, 189, and IX, 29) relate to defensive wars as it has been already explained in paragraphs 96–99.

109. CONTINUATION OF THE ABOVE

The verse 189 shows by its very wording the existence of *fitnah* or persecution, torture, and fighting on the part of the aggressors. By suppressing the Meccans' persecution, the Moslems had to regain their civil and religious liberty, from which they were so unjustly deprived. And this war of the Moslems to repel the force of their aggressors was the war of defense and protection enjoined in the verse. The 29th verse of the ninth Sura appertains to the expeditions of Tabuk, if not to that of Khyber. These expeditions were of a defensive character.[15]

110. TRADITIONS QUOTED AND REFUTED

The jurists further quote a tradition from the compilation of Abu Daood that the Prophet had said, "The Jihad will last up to the day of the Resurrection." But in the first place, Jihad does not literally and classically mean warfare or fighting in a war. It means, as used by the classical poets as well as by the Quran, to do one's utmost; to labor; to toil; to exert oneself or his power, efforts, endeavors, or ability; to employ oneself vigorously, diligently, studiously, sedulously, earnestly, or with energy; to be diligent or studious, to take pains or extraordinary pains.[16]

In the second place, Yezid bin Abi Shaiba, a link in the chain of the tradition, is a *Mujhool*,[17] i.e., his biography is not known, therefore his tradition can have no authority.

There is also another tradition in Bokharee to the effect that the Prophet had said, "I have been joined to fight the people until they confess that there is no god but the God." This tradition goes quite contrary to the verses of the Quran which enjoin to fight in defense, that is, until the persecution of civil discord was removed.[18] Thus it appears that either the whole tradition is a spurious one, or some of the narrators were wrong in interpreting the words of the Prophet.

111. EARLY MOSLEM LEGISTS
QUOTED AGAINST JIHAD

That the Quran did not allow war of aggression either when it was revealed, or in the future the early jurisconsults did infer from it, will be further shown from the opinions of the early Moslems; legists of the first and second century of the Hegira, like Ibn (son of) Omar the second Khalif, Sofian Souri, Ibn Shobormah, Ata, and Amar-bin-Dinar. All these early legists held that the fighting was not religiously incumbent *(wajib)*, and that it was only a voluntary act, and that only those were to be fought against who attacked the Moslems.[19]

112. BIOGRAPHICAL SKETCHES
OF THE LEGISTS

I will give here short biographical sketches of the legists named above.

(1) "Abu Abd-ur-Rahman Abdullah ibn Omar ibn-al-Khattab was one of the most eminent among the *companions* of Muhammad by his piety, his generosity, his contempt of the world, his learning and his virtues. Though entitled by birth to aspire to the highest places in the empire, he never hearkened to the dictates of ambition; possessing a vast influence over the Moslims by his rank, his instruction, and his holy life, he neither employed nor abused it in favor of any party, and during the civil wars which raged among the followers of Islamism, he remained neutral, solely occupied with the duties of religion. For a period of thirty years persons came from all parts to consult him and learn from him the Traditions. . . . He died in Mekka 73 A.H.(692–3 C.E.) aged 84 years. . . ."[20]

(2) Ata Ibn abi Rabah—"He held a high rank at Mekka as a juris-consult, a *Tabi*, and a devout ascetic; and he derived *(his knowledge of the law and the Traditions)* from the lips of Jabir Ibn Abd Allah al-Ansari, and Abd Allah Ibn Abbas, Abd Allah Ibn Zubair, and many others of Muhammad's companions. His own authority as a traditionist was cited by Amr ibn Durar, Al-Aamash, Al-Auzai, and a great number of others who had heard him teach. The office of *Mufti* at Mekka devolved on him and on Mujahid, and was filled by them whilst they lived. . . . He died in 115 A.H.(733–4 C.E.); some say 114 at the age of eighty-eight years."[21]

(3) Amr Ibn Dinar—"He is counted among the most eminent of the Tabis, and considered as a traditionist of very highest authority. He was only one of the Mujatahid Imams. Died 126 A.H.(743–4 C.E.), aged eighty years."[22]

(4.) "Abd Allah Ibn Shuburma ibn Tufail ad-Dubbi, a celebrated Imam and Tabi, was an eminent jurisconsult of Kufa. He learned the Traditions from Ans, As-Shabi, and Ibn Sirni, and his own authority was cited for Traditions by Soffian Ath-Thauri, Sofyan ibn Oyaina, and others. His veracity and his eminence as a doctor of the law was universally acknowledged. He was abstemious, intelligent, devout, generous, of a handsome countenance, and possessed a talent for poetry. He acted under the Khalif Al-Mamun, as kadi of the cultivated country (Sawad) around Kufa. Born 92 A.H., (710–1 C.E.); died 144 A.H.(761–2 C.E.)."[23]

(5.) "Sofyan Ath-Thauri (As-Sauri) was native of Kufa and a master of the highest authority in the Traditions and other sciences; his piety, devotion, veracity, and contempt for worldly goods were universally acknowledged, and as an Imam, he is counted among the *Mujtahids*. . . . Sofyan ibn Oyaina declared that he did not know a man better informed than Sofyan Ath-Thauri respecting what was permitted and what was forbidden by the law. . . . Sofyan was born 95 A.H. (713–4 C.E.). Other accounts place his birth in 96 or 97. He died 161 A.H. (713–4 C.E.) at Basra. . . . It has been stated by some that Sofyan died 162 A.H., but the first is the true date."[24]

113. EUROPEAN WRITERS' MISTAKE

That it is a mistake on the part of the European writers to assert that the Quran allows wars of aggression or, in other words, to wage war against the unbelievers without any provocation, is shown by the testimony of Mr. Urquhart and Mr. Edward William Lane. The latter writes: "Misled by the decision of those doctors, and an opinion prevalent in Europe, I represented the laws of 'holy war' as more severe than I found them to be according to the letter and spirit of the Kuran, when carefully examined, and according to the Hanafee code. I am indebted to Mr. Urquhart for suggesting to me the necessity of revising my former statement on the subject; and must express my conviction that no precept is to be found in the Kuran, which, taken with the context, can justify unprovoked war."[25]

114. SIR WILLIAM MUIR QUOTED

I will quote several remarks of European writers, including clergymen and Indian missionaries, to show how astray they go in attributing to the Quran and Muhammad the wars of aggressions and compulsory proselytizing. Sir William Muir represents the principles of Islam as requiring constant prosecutions of war, and writes: "It was essential to the permanence of Islam that its aggressive course should be continuously pursued, and that its claim to an universal acceptance, or at the least to an universal supremacy, should be enforced at the point of the sword. Within the limits of Arabia the work appeared now to be accomplished. It remained to gain over the Christian and idolatrous tribes of the Syrian desert, and then in the name of the Lord to throw down the gauntlet of war before the empires of Rome and Persia, which, having treated with contempt the summons of the Prophet addressed to them in solemn warning four years ago, were now rife for chastisement."[26]

The occasion to which Sir W. Muir refers here was to wipe out the memory of the reverse at Muta. The expedition to Muta was occasioned by the murder of a messenger or envoy dispatched by Muhammad to the Ghassanide prince at Bostra. A party was sent to punish the offending chief, Sharahbil. This could, by no means, be maintained as a warlike spirit or an aggressive course for the prosecution of war, or for enforcing the claim of universal supremacy at the point of the sword.

115. ISLAM NOT AGGRESSIVE

That Islam as preached by Muhammad was never aggressive has been fully shown in several places of the Quran. During the whole time of his ministry, Muhammad was persecuted, rejected, despised and at last made an outlaw by the Koreish at Mecca, and a fugitive seeking protection in a distant city; exiled, attacked upon, besieged, defeated, and prevented from returning to Mecca or visiting the Holy Kaaba by the same enemies at Mecca and other surrounding tribes who had joined them, and even from within Medina plotted against by the Jews who were not less aggressive toward him than their confederates of Mecca, the Koreish, whom they had instigated to make war on him and had brought an overwhelming army, had proved traitors, and even more injurious than the Koreish themselves. Consequently, he was constantly in dangers and troubles, and under such circumstances it was impossible for him to be aggressive, to get time or opportunity to pursue any aggressive course, or enforce, at the point of the sword, any attempt of his for universal acceptance, or universal supremacy even if he had designed so. But it was far from his principles to have cherished the object of universal conquest. "That Islam ever stepped beyond the limits of Arabia and its border lands," admits Sir. W. Muir in his Rede Lecture for 1881, just twenty years after be had written the passage I am dealing with, "was due to circumstances rather than design. The faith was meant originally for the Arabs. From first to last, the call was addressed primarily to them." He writes in a footnote of the same lecture (page 5): "It is true that three or four years before, Mahmet had addressed dispatches to the Kaiser, and the Chosroes, and other neighboring potentates, summoning them to embrace the true faith. But the step had never been followed up in any way."[27]

116. MR. FREEMAN QUOTED

Mr. Freeman writes regarding Muhammad: "Mahomet had before him the example of Mosaic Law, which preached a far more rigorous mandate of extermination against the guilty nations of Canaan. He had before him the practice of all surrounding powers, Christian, Jewish, and Heathen; though, from the disaffection of Syria and Egypt to the orthodox throne of Constantinople, he might have learned how easily persecution defeats its own end. . . . Under his circumstances, it is really no very great ground to condemnation that he did appeal to the sword. He did no more than follow the precedents of his own and every surrounding nation. Yet one might say that a man of such mighty genius as Mahomet must have been, might have been, fairly expected to rise Superior to the trammels of prejudice and precedent."[28]

Muhammad never professed to have followed the footsteps of Moses and Joshua in waging wars of extermination and proselytism. He only appealed to the sword in his and his followers' defense. Never did he seem to have been anxious to copy the practice of the surrounding nations, Christians, Jews, and Egyptians. His wars of defense, as they certainly all were, were very mild, specially with regard to the treatment of children, women, and old men who were never to be attacked; and above all, in the mildness shown toward the captives of war who were either to be set free or ransomed—but were never to be enslaved—contrary to the practice of all the surrounding nations. This virtual abolition of slavery[29] has been a great boon to mankind in general as a beneficial result of Muhammad's wars of defense.

117. THE REVD. STEPHENS QUOTED

The Reverend Mr. Stephens writes: "In the Quran, the Mussulman is absolutely and positively commanded to make war upon all those who decline to acknowledge the Prophet until they submit, or, in the case of Jews and Christians, purchase exemption from the conformity by the payment of tribute. The mission of the Mussulmen, as declared in the Quran, is distinctly aggressive. We might say that Mahomet bequeathed to his disciples a roving commission to propagate his faith by the employment of force where persuasion failed. '0 Prophet, fight for the religion of God'—'Stir up the faithful to war,' such are commands which Mahomet believed to be given him by God. 'Fight against them who believe not a God, nor the last day'—'Attack the idolatrous in all the months,' such are his own exhortations to his disciples."[30]

The Reverend gentleman is very much mistaken in his assertions against the Quran. There is no absolute or positive command in the Quran for a war of aggression or compulsory proselytism. The sentences quoted by Mr. Stephens are but mutilated verses forcibly dislocated from their context. A disjointed portion of a verse, or a single sentence of it cannot be brought forth to prove any doctrine or theory. Due regard must be made for the context, the general scope, and parallel passages. The verses referred to by Mr. Stephens are Sura IV, 86, and Sura IX, 29, 36. All these have been quoted in full and discussed elsewhere.[31] They relate only to defensive wars.

118. MR. BOSWORTH SMITH QUOTED

Mr. Bosworth Smith says: "The free toleration of the purer among the creeds around him, which the Prophet had at first enjoined, gradually changes into intolerance. Persecuted no longer, Mohammed becomes a persecutor himself; with the Quran in one hand, the scimitar in the other, he goes forth to offer to the nations the threefold alternative of conversion, tribute, death."[32]

Muhammad never changed his practice of toleration nor his own teachings into intolerance; he was always persecuted at Mecca and Medina, but, for all we know, he himself never turned a persecutor. The three-fold alternative so much talked of, and so little proved, is nowhere to be found in the Quran. This subject has been fully discussed in paragraphs 34–39.

119. MR. G. SALE QUOTED

Mr. George Sale, in his celebrated preliminary discourse to the translation of the Quran, writes, referring to the thirteenth year of Muhammad's mission: "Hitherto Mohammed had propagated his religion by fair means, so that the whole success of his enterprise, before his flight to Medina, must be attributed to persuasion only, and not to compulsion. For before this second oath of fealty or inauguration at al-Akaba, he had no permission to use any force at all; and in several places of the Quran, which he pretended were revealed during his stay at Mecca, he declares his business was only to preach and admonish; that he had no authority to compel any person to embrace his religion; and that whether people believed or not, was none of his concern, but belonged solely to God. And he was so far from allowing his followers to use force, that he exhorted them to bear patiently those injuries which were offered them on account of their faith; and when persecuted himself chose rather to quit the place of his birth and retire to Medina, than to make any resistance. But this great passiveness and moderation seems entirely owing to his want of power and the great superiority of his oppressors for the first twelve years of his mission; for no sooner was he enabled by the assistance of those of Medina to make head against his enemies, than he gave out, that God had allowed him and his followers to defend themselves against the infidels; and at length, as his forces increased, he pretended to have the divine leave even to attack them, and to destroy idolatry, and set up the true faith by the sword; finding by experience that his designs would otherwise proceed very slowly, if they were not utterly overthrown, and knowing on the other hand that innovators, when they depend solely on their own strength, and can compel, seldom run any risk; from whence, the politician observes, it follows, that all the armed prophets have succeeded, and the unarmed ones have failed. Moses, Cyrus, Theseus and Romulus would not have been able to establish the observance of their institutions for any length of time had they not been armed. The first passage of the Quran, which gave Mohammed the permission of defending himself by arms, is said to have been that in the twenty-second chapter: after which a great number to the same purpose were revealed.

> That Mohammed had a right to take up arms for his own defense against his unjust persecutors, may perhaps be allowed; but whether he ought afterwards to have made use of that means for the establishing of his religion, is a question which I will not here determine. How far the secular power may or ought to interpose in affairs of this nature, mankind are not agreed. The method of converting by the sword gives no very favorable idea of the faith which is so propagated, and is disallowed by every body in those of another religion, though the same persons are willing to admit of it for the advancement of their own; supposing that though a false religion ought not to be established by authority, yet a true one may; and accordingly force is as constantly employed in these cases by those who

have the power in their hands as it is constantly complained of by those who suffer the violence.[33]

I do not agree with these words of Mr. George Sale regarding Muhammad, "and at length, as his forces increased, he pretended to have the divine leave even to attack them, and to destroy idolatry, and set up the true faith by the sword"; he never attacked the Koreish or others except in his own defense. The destruction of idolatry was the chief mission of Muhammad, and that even was not resorted to by force of arms. There were neither compulsory conversions nor does his history point to any extirpation of the idolater's at the point of sword from their native countries, as the chief objects of his mission. The persecutions and civil discord were to be removed or put a stop to, and force was used to repel force but nothing more. Conversion by the sword was not enforced on any proselyte by Muhammad.

120. MAJOR OSBORN QUOTED

Major Osborn has drawn a very dark picture of what he calls " The Doctrine of Jehad," in his *Islam under the Arabs.*[34] The defensive wars of Muhammad are explained by him as "means of livelihood congenial to the Arab mind, and carrying with it no stain of disgrace or immorality. This was robbery. Why should not the faithful eke out their scanty means by adopting this lucrative and honorable profession, which was open to everyone who had a sword and knew how to use it? . . . Surely, to despoil these infidels and employ their property to feed the hungry and clothe the naked among the people of God, would be a work well pleasing in His sight. . . . And thus was the first advance made in the conversion of the religion of Islam with the religion of the sword" (pages 46–47). After this the Major writes again: "The ninth Sura is that which contains the Prophet's proclamation of war against the votaries of all creeds other than that of Islam " (page 52). Then he quotes several verses, some of them, half sentences, violently distorted, from the eighth and ninth Suras, in a consecutive form without giving the numbers. These are Sura IX, 20, 34, 35, 82, 121; Sura VIII, 67; Sura IX, 36, 5, 29, 19; Sura XLVII, 4; Sura IX, 5; and Sura VIII, 42. Lastly, the learned Major concludes by saying: "Such was the character of the Sacred War enjoined upon the Faithful. It is Muhammad's greatest achievement and his worst. When subjected himself to the pains of persecution he had learned to perceive how powerless were torments applied to the body to work a change of conviction in the mind. 'Let there be no violence in religion' had then been one of the maxims he had laid down. 'Unto every one of you,' he had said in former days, speaking of Jews and Christians, 'have we given a law, and an open path; and if God had pleased He had surely made you one people; but He hath thought fit to give you different laws, that He might try you in that which He hath given you respectively. Therefore, strive to excel each other in good works; unto God shall ye all return, and then will He declare unto you that concerning which ye have disagreed.' But the intoxication of success had long ago stilled the voice of his better self. The aged Prophet standing on the brink of the grave, and leaving as his last legacy a mandate of universal war, irresistibly recalls, by force of contrast, the parting words to his disciples of another religious teacher that they should go forth and preach a gospel of peace to all nations. Nor less striking in their contrast is the response to either mandate; the Arab, with the Quran in one hand and the sword in the other, spreading his creed amid the glare of burning cities, and the shrieks of violated homes, and the Apostles of Christ working in the moral darkness of the Roman world with the gentle but irresistible power of light, laying anew the foundations of society, and cleansing at their source the polluted springs of domestic and national life."

121. MAJOR OSBORN REFUTED

The learned author quoted above has either misunderstood the character of the wars of the Prophet of Islam, or has grossly misrepresented it. He errs in two points: First, he makes the wars as wars of conquest, compulsion, and aggression, whereas they were all undertaken in the defense of the civil and religious rights of the early Moslems, who were, as I have said before, persecuted, harassed, and tormented at Mecca for their religion, and after a long period of persecution with occasional fresh and vigorous measures, were condemned to severer and harder sufferings, were expelled from their homes, leaving their dear relations, and religious brethren to endure the calamities of the persecution, and while taking refuge at Medina were attacked upon [*sic*] by superior numbers, several of the surrounding tribes of Arabs and Jews joining the aggressive Koreish, making ruinous inroads and threatening the Moslems with still greater and heavier miseries. From this statement it will appear that these wars were neither of conquest nor of compulsory conversion. The second great mistake under which Major Osborn seems to labor is that he takes the injunctions of war against the Meccans or other aggressors as a general obligation to wage war against all unbelievers in the Moslem faith. In fact, these injunctions were only against those aggressors who had actually committed great encroachments on the rights and liberties of the early Moslems, and had inflicted very disastrous injuries on them. These injunctions had and have nothing to do with the future guidance of the Moslem world.

122. THE IXTH SURA OF THE QURAN

It is a great misrepresentation on the part of Major Osborn to assert that "the ninth Sura is that which contains the Prophet's proclamation of war against the votaries of all creeds other than that of Islam." No statement could be farther from the truth than this of his. The ninth Sura, or, more correctly, the beginning or opening verses of it, contain the Prophet's proclamation of war against those of the Meccan idolaters, who, in violation of the treaty of Hodeibia, had attacked the Moslems.[35] They were allowed four months' time (IX, 2, 5) to make terms. They submitted, and Mecca was taken by compromise, in consequence of which the threatened war was never waged. Those who had not broken their treaties were especially mentioned, with whom the proclamation or the period allowed for peace had no connection.[36] Thus it is quite clear that the proclamation of war was only against the violators and aggressors, and not against the votaries of all creeds other than that of Islam. I have further discussed the ninth Sura in paragraph 40 of this work. The other verses of this Sura refer to the expedition of Tabuk, which was purely defensive in its nature as has been described in paragraph 33 of this book (see also paragraph 42).

123. THE REVEREND WHERRY QUOTED

The Reverend E. M. Wherry, M.A., in his note on Sale's Preliminary Discourse, says: "Though Muhammad undoubtedly took Moses as his pattern, and supposed himself following in his footsteps when he gave the command to fight against the infidels, yet there is no comparison between them whatever so far as warring against infidels is concerned. The Israelites were commanded to slay the Canaanites as divinely ordained instruments of *destruction*; but Muhammad inaugurated war as a means of proselytism. The Israelite was not permitted to proselytize from among the Canaanites, (Exod. XXIII, 27–33), but Muslims are required to proselytize by sword-power."[37]

Muhammad never had said that he did follow the footsteps of Moses in giving the command of fighting in self-defense, and in repelling force by force. There could be no comparison whatsoever between the wars of Moses, which were merely wars of conquest, and those of Muhammad, waged only in self-defense. Muhammad did not inaugurate his career by prosecuting war as a means of proselytism, and never did he proselytize any one by the sheer strength of the sword. Mr. T. H. Horne, M.A., writes regarding the expiration of the Canaanites: "After the time of God's forbearance was expired, they had still the alternative, either to flee elsewhere, as in fact, many of them did, or to surrender themselves, renounce their idolatries, and serve the God of Israel. Compare Deut. XX, 1–17."[38] This was certainly compulsory conversion and proselytizing at the point of the sword.

124. EXAMPLE CITED FROM THE JEWISH HISTORY

There is only one instance in the Quran in which an example is cited for the war of defense by Muhammad, from the Jewish History. It is the asking of the children of Israel their prophet Samuel to raise up a king for them to fight in their defense against the Philistines, who had very much oppressed the Israelites. Saul killed Goliath, called *Jalut* in the Quran, which was in defense of the Israelites. I have quoted the verses relating to the above subject from the Quran (Sura II, 247 and 252) on page 19 of this work.

"Hast thou not considered the assembly of the children of Israel after *the death* of Moses, when they said to a prophet of theirs, 'Raise up for us a king; we will do battle for the cause of God?' He said, 'May it not be that when fighting is ordained you, ye would not fight?" They said, 'And why should we not fight in the cause of God, since we are driven forth from our dwellings and our children ?'. . . .

This shows that what the Quran or Muhammad took as an example from the history of the Jews was only their defensive war.

125. MOSAIC INJUNCTIONS

It is very unfair of the Christians to make too much of the wars of Muhammad, which were purely of a defensive nature, and offer apologies for the most cruel wars of conquest and extermination by Moses, Joshua and other Jewish worthies under the express commands of God.—(*Vide* Numbers XXXI; Dent. XXI, etc.) But see what Mr. Wherry says. He writes in his comments on the 191st verse of the second Sura of the Quran: "(191). *kill them*, etc. Much is made of expressions like this, by some Christian apologists, to show the cruel character of the Arabian prophet, and the inference is thence drawn that be was an impostor and his Quran a fraud. Without denying that Muhammad was cruel, we think this mode of assault to be very unsatisfactory to say the least, as it is capable of being turned against the Old Testament Scriptures. If the claim of Muhammad to have received a divine command to exterminate idolatry by the slaughter of all impenitent idolaters be admitted, I can see no objection to his practice. The question at issue is this. Did God command such slaughter of idolaters, as he commanded the destruction of the Canaanites or of the Amalekites? Taking the stand of the Muslim, that God did so command Muhammad and his followers, his morality in this respect may be defended on precisely the same ground that the morality of Moses and Joshua is defended by the Christian."[39]

126. THE REVD. T. F. HUGHES QUOTED

The Revd. T. P. Hughes in his *Notes on Muhammadanism* writes: "Jihad (lit. 'an effort') is a religious war against the infidels, as enjoined by Muhammad in the Quran." (Surat-un-Nisa (VI). "Fight therefore for the religion of God."

> "God hath indeed promised Paradise to every one. But God hath preferred those who *fight for the faith.*" (IV, 97), Surat-ul-Muhammad (XLVII).

> "Those who *fight in the defense of God's true religion*, God will not suffer their works to perish" (XLVII, 5).[40]

The first verse quoted by Mr. Hughes appertains to the war of defense. The verse in itself has express indications of its relating to the war of defense, but Mr. Hughes was not inclined, perhaps, to copy it in full. He merely quotes half a sentence, and shuts his eyes from other words and phrases of the same verse. The verse has been quoted on page 20. It is as follows: "Fight then on the path of God: lay not burdens on any but thyself; and stir up the faithful. The powers of the infidels, God will happily restrain; for God is stronger in prowess, and stronger to punish."—(Sura IV, 86).

The severe persecution, the intense torture and mighty aggression of the Meccans and their allies is referred to in the original word *Bass*, rendered *prowess* into English and referred to in the previous verse 77, which shows that the war herein enjoined was to restrain the aggressions of the enemy and to repel force by force.

It is very unfair on the part of the Revd. T. P. Hughes to twist or dislocate half a sentence from a verse and put it forth to demonstrate and prove a certain object of his.

127. MEANING OF JIHAD

The second verse quoted by the same author is a mere mistranslation. There is no such word in the original which admits of being rendered as "fighting." The true translation of the sentence quoted above from Sura IV, verse 97, is as follows: " Good promises hath he made to all. But God hath assigned to the *strenuous* a rich recompense above those who sit still at home."

The word rendered "*strenuous*" is originally "mojahid" (plural " Mojahidin," from Jihad), which in classical Arabic and throughout the Quran means to do one's utmost, to make effort, to strive, to exert, to employ one's-self diligently, studiously, sedulously, earnestly, zealously, or with energy, and does not mean fighting or warfare. It was subsequently applied to religious war, but was never used in the Quran in such a sense.[41]

128. SURA XLVII, V. 5

The third instance quoted by Mr. Hughes is also a mistranslation of a sentence in verse 5, Sura XLVII. The original word is "*kotelu*," which means "those who are *killed*" and not "those who *fight*," as explained and translated by the author. The correct rendering of the sentence is this: "And those who are killed, their work God will not suffer to miscarry."

Some read the word "*katalu*," which means "those who fought," but the general and authorized reading is "*kotelu*," i.e., "Those who are killed." Even if it be taken for granted that the former is the correct reading, it will be explained by several other verses which mean fighting in defense and not fighting aggressively, which not only has been never taught in the Quran but is always prohibited (II, 186). The verse to that effect runs thus: "And fight for the cause of God against those who fight against you; but commit not the injustice of attacking them first. Verily God loveth not the unjust." (II, 186).

This verse permitted only defensive war and prohibited every aggressive measure. All other verses mentioned in connection with fighting on the part of the Moslems must be interpreted in conformity with this.

129. THE REV. MR. MALCOLM MACCOLL QUOTED

The Rev. Malcolm MacColl writes: " The Quran divides the earth into parts: Dar-ul-Islam, or the House of Islam ; and Dar-ul-Harb, or the House of the enemy. All who are not of Islam are thus against it, and it is accordingly the duty of the True Believers to fight against the infidels till they accept Islam, or are destroyed. This is called the Djihad or Holy War, which can only end with the conversion or death of the last infidel on earth. It is thus the sacred duty of the Commander of the Faithful to make war on the non-Mussulman world as occasion may offer. But Dar-ul-Harb, or the non-Mussulman world, is subdivided into Idolaters and Ketabi, or "People of the Book," i.e., people who possess divinely inspired scriptures, namely, Jews, Samaritans, and Christians. All the inhabitants of Dar-ul-Harb are infidels, and consequently outside the pale of Salvation. But the Ketabi are entitled to certain privileges in this world, if they submit to the conditions which Islam imposes. Other infidels must make their choice between one of two alternatives—Islam or the sword. The Ketabi are allowed a third alternative, namely, submission and the payment of tribute. But if they refuse to submit, and presume to fight against the True Believers, they lapse at once into the condition of the rest of Dar-ul-Harb, and may be summarily put to death or sold as slaves."[42]

I am very sorry the Rev. gentleman is altogether wrong in his assertions against the Quran. There is neither such a division of the world in the Quran, nor are such words as "Dar-ul-Islam" and "Dar-ul-Harb" to be found anywhere in it. There is no injunction in the Quran to the True Believers to fight against the infidels till they accept Islam, failing which they are to be put to death. The words "Dar-ul-Islam" and "Dar-ul-Harb" are only to be found in the Muhammadan Common Law, and are only used in the question of jurisdiction. No Moslem magistrate will pass a sentence in a criminal case against a criminal who had committed an offense in a foreign country. The same is the case in civil courts.[43] All the inhabitants of Dar-ul-Harb are not necessarily infidels. Muhammadans, either permanently or temporarily by obtaining permission from the sovereign of the foreign land, can be the inhabitants of a Dar-ul-Harb, a country out of the Moslem jurisdiction, or at war with it.

130. THE UNTENABLE THEORIES OF
THE COMMON LAW AND CONCLUSION

It is only a theory of our Common Law, in its military and political chapters, which allow waging unprovoked war with non-Moslems, exacting tribute from "the people of the Book," and other idolaters, except those of Arabia, for which the Hanafi Code of the Common Law has nothing short of conversion to Islam or destruction by the sword. As a rule, our canonical legists support their theories by quotations from the Muhammadan Revealed Law, i.e., the Quran, as well as from the Sunnah, or the traditions from the Prophet, however absurd and untenable may be their process of reasoning and argumentative deductions. In this theory of waging war with, and exacting tribute or the capitation-tax from, the non-Moslem world, they quote the ninth and other Suras. These verses have been copied and explained elsewhere in this book. The casuistic sophistry of the canonical legists in deducing these war theories from the Quran is altogether futile. These verses relate only to the wars waged by the Prophet and his followers purely in their self-defense. Neither of these verses had anything to do with waging unprovoked war and exacting tributes during Muhammad's time, nor could they be made a law for future military conquest. These were only temporary in their operations and purely defensive in their nature. The Muhammadan Common Law is by no means divine or superhuman. It mostly consists of uncertain traditions, Arabian usages and customs, some frivolous and fortuitous analogical deductions from the Quran, and a multitudinous array of casuistical sophistry of the canonical legists. It has not been held sacred or unchangeable by enlightened Muhammadans of any Moslem country and in any age since its compilation in the fourth century of the Hejira. All the *Mujtahids*, *Ahl Hadis*, and other non-Mokallids had had no regard for the four schools of Muhammadan religious jurisprudence, or the Common Law.

SURA XLVIII, 16 AND SURA XLVII, 4 AND 5

Sura XLVIII, 16, is not generally quoted by the canonical legists in support of their theory of Jehad, but by some few. It is not in the shape of a command or injunction; it is in a prophetical tone: "Say to those Arabs of the desert who stayed behind, Ye shall be called forth against a people of mighty valor; Ye shall do battle with them, or they shall submit (*Yoslemoon*). . . ."[44]

The verses 4 and 5 of Sura XLVII, like all other verses on the subject, appertain to the wars of defense, and no one has ever quoted them for wars of aggression. These verses have already been quoted on page 85. The abolition of future slavery as enjoined in the fifth verse has been treated separately in Appendix B. The Arabs, like other barbarous nations round them, used either to kill the prisoners of war or to enslave them; but this injunction of the Quran abolished both of these barbarous practices. The prisoners henceforward were neither to be killed nor enslaved, but were to be set at liberty with or without ransom.

NOTES

1. Ata, a learned legist of Mecca, who flourished at the end of the first century of the Hegira, and held rank there as juris-consult, (*vide* para. 112) held that Jihad was only incumbent on the Companions of the Prophet, and was not binding on any one else after them. See para. 112, and *Tafsir Majma ul-Bayan* by Tabarsi under Sura II, 212.
2. The *Hedaya* or Guide; or [A Commentary on the Mussulman Laws], translated by Charles Hamilton; Vol. II, Book IX, ch. I, p. 140, London, MDCCXCI.
3. Ibid., p. 141.
4. "Arab Kattal; meaning war in its operation, such as fighting, slaying," etc.
5. The *Hedaya*, Vol. II, p. 141.

6. Sura II, 187.
7. The *Hedaya*, with its commentary called *Kifaya*, Vol. II, p. 708. Calcutta Medical Press, 1834. As a general rule the Muhammadan authors do not refer to the verses of the Quran by their number. They generally quote the first sentence, or even a portion of it. The numbers of verses are mine. I have followed Fluegel and Rodwell's numbers of verses in their editions and translations of the Quran.
8. *Binayah*, a commentary of the *Hedaya*, by Ainee. Vol. II, Part II, p. 789.
9. Part III, p. 219.
10. *Tuhfatul Muktaj fi Sharah-al-Minha*j, Part IV, p. 137.
11. *Insan-ul-Oyoon*, Part II, chapter on "Campaign," pp. 289, 291.
12. Sura IX, 5 and 12. These verses have been discussed on pages 51–55.
13. "The Jihad will last till the day of the Resurrection." "I have been enjoined to fight the people until they confess there is no god but the God." For these traditions see the next paragraph.
14. *Vide* Ainee's Commentary of the Hedaya, Vol. II, Part II, p. 790.
15. *Vide*, speaks of this on pages 37 and 41.
16. *Vide*, Appendix A.
17. *Vide* Ainee's Commentary on the *Hedaya*, Vol. II, Part II, p. 798.
18. *Vide* Sura II, 189; VIII, 40.
19. *Vide* Kazee Budrudeen Mahmood bin Ahmed Ainee's (who died in 855 A.H.) Commentary on the *Hedaya*, called *Binayah*, and generally know by the name of Ainee, Vol. II,. "Book of Institute," pp. 789–90
20. *Tabakat al-Fokaha*, vol. 5.
21. *Ibn Khallikan's biographical Dictionary*, translated from the Arabic by Baron MacGuckin De Slane; Vol. II, pp. 203–4, London, MDCCCXLIII.
22. *Tabakat al-Fokaha.*
23. *Tabal-Fak. Al-Yadfi.*
24. *Ibn Khallikan's Biographical Dictionary*, translated from the Arabic by Baron MacGuckin De Slane, Vol. 1, pp. 576–8, London, MDCCCXLIll.
25. *The Modern Egyptians* by Edward William Lane, Vol. I, fifth edition, London, 1871, p. 117.
26. *Muir's Life of Mahomet*, Vol. IV, pp. 251–2.
27. "The Early Caliphate and Rise of Islam," being the Rede Lecture for 1881, delivered before the University of Cambridge by Sir William Muir, K.C.S.I., LL.D., London, 1881, p. 5.
28. *The History and Conquests of the Saracens* by Edward A. Freeman, D.C.L., LL.D., London, 1877, pp. 41–42.
29. *Vide* Sura XLVIII, 5, and Appendix B.
30. *Christianity and Islam: The Bible and the Quran* by the Rev. W. R. W. Stephens, London, 1877, pp. 98–9.
31. *Vide* paragraphs 17, 29, 126.
32. *Mohammed and Mohammedanism*, lectures delivered at the Royal Institution of Great Britain in February and March 1874 by R. Bosworth Smith, M.A. Second edition, London, 1876 p. 137.
33. *The Quran* by George Sale. The "Chandos Classics." The Preliminary Discourse, Section II, pp. 37–8.
34. *Islam Under the Arabs* by Major Osborn, London: Longmans, Green & Co., 1876, pp. 46–54.
35. Sura IX, 4, 8, 10, 12, & 13, *vide* pp. 23–5.
36. *Vide* Sura IX, 4, 7, quoted above, pp. 23–4.

37. *A Comprehensive Commentary on the Quran: Comprising Sale's Translation and Prelimi-nary Discourse with Additional Notes and Emendations,* by the Reverend E. M. Wherry, M.A., London: Trubner & Co., 1882, p. 220.

38. *An Introduction to the Critical Study and Knowledge of the Holy Scripture* by Thomas Hartwell Horne, Esq. M.A., Vol. II, London, 1828, p. 524.

39. *Commentary on the Quran* by the Reverend Wherry, p. 358.

40. *Notes on Muhammadanism: Being Outlines of the Religious System of Islam* by the Rev-erend T. P. Hughes, M.R.A.S., C.M.S., Missionary to the Afghans, second edition, 1877, p. 206.

41. *Vide* Appendix A.

42. *The Ninteenth Century,* London, December 1877, p. 832.

43. This subject has been fully treated in my "The Proposed Political, Legal, and Social Reforms in Moslem States," Bombay Education Society Press, 1883, pp. 22–5.

44. Sir W. Muir, with other European translators of the Quran, translates the word "they shall profess Islam" (*The Life of Mahomet,* Vol. IV, p. 39, footnote). It ought to be translated "they shall submit." There is a difference of opinion among the com-mentators and canonical legists on this word. Some translate the word Yoslemoon as "shall profess Islam," and others "shall submit." This difference in the interpretation of the same word is merely of a sectarian nature, each party wishing to serve their own purpose. Those legists who held that the polytheists and idolaters may either be fought against or be submitted to the authority of Islam by being tributaries, took the word in its proper sense of submission. Those who held that "the people of the Book" ought only to be made tributaries, while all other idolaters and polytheists should be compelled either to perish or to embrace Islam, interpret the word techni-cally to mean the religion of Islam. But as the verse is not a legal command, we con-demn at once the casuistic sophistry of the legists.

CHAPTER 8

THE PROBLEM
OF CALIPHATE

Ali Abd al-Raziq

Excerpt from Ali Abd al-Raziq. "The Unity of Religion and Arabs." *al-Islam wax-Usul al-Hukm* (Islam and the Fundamentals of Authority). Cairo: Matba'at Misr, 1925, pp. 81–89. Translated by Kamran Talattof.

1. ISLAM IS NOT A RELIGION
SOLELY FOR THE ARABS

ISLAM AS WE KNOW IS A SUBLIME CALLING SENT by God for the benefit of the entire world, East and West, Arabs and non-Arabs, men and women, rich and poor, knowledgeable and illiterate. It is a unified religion, with which God wanted to bind people together not forsaking any part of the world. Islam has never been a call exclusively for the Arabs, an exclusive Arab unity, or an exclusive Arab religion. Islam would never favor one community over another, one language over another, one region over another, one time over another, or one generation over another except according to their piety. This is in spite of what you see; that the prophet (peace be upon him) was an Arab and that he naturally loved the Arabs, and commended them, and that The Book of God was written in lucid Arabic.

2. ARABIC AND THE RELIGION

The rise of Islam was necessary to establish the truth among other truths of this world, so that a prophet chosen by Almighty God to deliver it unto the people could carry it on behalf of the highest sacredness. And God, may He be exalted, decided to choose His prophet for this calling from among the Arab tribes and no others. He chose the prophet from among the Arabs and from among the sons of Ismail. He chose one from among the sons of Ismail in Kinana and from the Koreish. He chose Koreish from among the Hashemites and then chose Mohammed, son of Abdullah (God's blessing upon him), from among the Hashemites.

God, may He be exalted, has great wisdom in this choice, which we may or may not comprehend.

> Your Lord creates what He wills and chooses. The good is not for them to choose. Too holy and high is God for what they associate with him. Your Lord well knows what they hide in their breasts and what they disclose.[1]

The Quran is an Arabic book and the messenger is Arab, so it is not unnatural that the call of Islam began among the Arabs before it reached others. Likewise, it is not unnatural that the Arabs were the first to hear the call from the bearer of both good news and of warning, and that they were the first whom the messenger urged toward God, and the first whom he tried to gather onto the path of righteousness.

And as such, the prophet of God (peace be upon him) initiated the call among his closest relatives, then among his Arab people, and he hounded them by the aid of God until all the people surrendered to his calling. They eventually came under the political leadership of this prophet, the first to enter into that unity of religion.

3. THE UNITY OF ARABS IN RELIGION
DESPITE THEIR POLITICAL DIFFERENCES

The Arab countries, as we know, contained different kinds of people, different clans and tribes with different dialects, from diverse locations, and they were diversified in their political entities. This includes those who were ruled by the Byzantine Empire and those who were independent. All of this entails, necessarily, a great variance among the Arab peoples as regards types of government, administrative methods, and as regards manners, customs, and many of the faculties of material and economic life.

These [otherwise] heterogeneous communities had gathered in the time of the prophet (peace be upon him) around the call of Islam, and under its banner and became brothers through God's blessing. They were bound with one, tight bond of religion, drawn together behind one fence made up of the leadership of the prophet (peace be upon him) and of his kindness and his mercy. In this way, they formed one community having one leader, who is none other than the prophet (peace be upon him).

That Arab unity that existed in the time of the prophet (peace be upon him) was not a political unity whatsoever. There was not any concept in it related to the concepts of government and state, however, that does not mean that it was a religious unity devoid of political aspects; that is, it was a unity in religion and faith, not a unity of state and types of rule.

4. THE STRUCTURES OF ISLAM
ARE RELIGIOUS NOT POLITICAL

What gives evidence to this is the life story of the prophet (peace be upon him). For we do not know that he ever interfered in the political affairs of these scattered communities, in any of the governments, or in each tribe's administrative and judicial systems, and did not meddle with what already existed between these communities. Neither did he interfere with what were between them and others, as regarded their communal and economic ties. We never heard that he discharged any of the governors, nor appointed any judges, nor created any army, and he did not legislate any rules for their commerce nor their agriculture, nor their industries. Rather, he left them in charge of all of their own affairs and said to them, "You know better about your own affairs." So there remained each community and its holdings in one civil and political unity and what was inherent in that of chaos and order for they were not bound together by him except, as we were told, by Islamic unity and its rules and customs.

Perhaps it is possible to say that these rules, customs and laws, which were brought by the Prophet (peace be upon him) to the Arab communities and the non-Arabs as well, were numerous. Moreover, there were in them that which touched to a great extent most aspects of the lives of those people, for they included regulations, criminal punishment, armed forces, *jihad,* selling, lending, mortgaging, and even manners of sitting, walking, and speaking, and much more. And so, whoever joined the Arabs around these numerous rules, and united as regards their lifestyles, manners, and laws consequently made a civil system and a political unity. Thus, they were one state and the prophet (peace be upon him) was its leader and ruler.

But if you think about it, you will see that all that Islam has made lawful and that the prophet has made the Muslims observe included conduct, manners, and customs that had nothing at all to do with methods of political rule nor anything to do with a civil government. After all, if we put all of these together, they do not amount to more than a very small fraction of what is necessary for a civil state as regards political principles and laws.

Furthermore, all that which had come with Islam, including beliefs, rituals, social obligations, customs, and punitive measures, is pure religious law devoted solely to the Almighty God, for the religious benefit of humanity, and not concealed from us. And it would not matter whether or not it contained civil benefits for human beings; that is neither something considered in the divine law nor something the prophet (peace be upon him) concerned himself with.

5. THE MILDNESS OF POLITICAL
DISSIMILARITY AMONG THE ARABS

The Arabs, even though they were bound together by Islamic law, continued to differ in politics and other aspects of civil, social, economic, and other aspects of life. That is to say, the state was variegated to the extent that Arab life dictated the development of the concept of state and government.

Truthfully, that was the situation of the Arabs the day Mohammed (peace be upon him) joined the Highest Benefactor. A general religious unity exists, but beneath this states are completely different from one another, with the exception of a few. That is the truth and there is no doubt about it.

We had been scared that the issue of that variance, which we say [now] was between the Arab communities even in the time of the prophet (peace be upon him), is not obvious to you, and that the harmonious picture that the historians tried to put forward concerning that period has tricked you. You should know first that in the discipline of history there are many mistakes, and that so often history strays and often enormous discrepancies exist. Second, you should know that in truth many of the traces of the variances and particularities of the Arabs have disappeared through Islam binding their hearts together, collecting them into one religion, and regulating their shared customs. Third, let us not fail to remember the matter that we have previously pointed out, which is the effect of the religious leadership that belonged to the messenger (peace be upon him). It is no surprise then that the variances of the Arab communities lessened his impact, weakened his position, and both lessened its power and sapped its strength.

> And remember when you were one another's foe and He reconciled your hearts, and you turned into brethren through his grace. You had stood on the edge of a pit of fire and he saved you from it.[2]

But despite this, the Arabs are still differentiated communities and variegated states. Differentiated development was natural, but it had lost some of its power and effect. However, it was impossible that it vanish all together. No sooner did the prophet join the Highest Benefactor than the factors for this variance become obvious, plain facts, and eventually each Arab community came to reestablish its distinct character and its independent existence from the others. The Arab unity that was achieved by the messenger (peace be upon him) was about to collapse. Most of the Arabs had regressed in this way except the people of Medina, Mecca, and Taif who did not enter into apostasy.

6. THE DAYS OF THE PROPHET

The Arab unity was, as you know, an Islamic unity and not a political one, and the leadership of the messenger over the Arabs was a religious leadership and not a civil one. The people's submission was a submission to beliefs and faith, not submission to a government or a power, and their society around him was made purely for the sake of the Almighty God. They encountered teachings of the revelation, gifts from heaven, and the commandments and the prohibitions of the Almighty God.

"And he made them to increase in number and he taught them the book and its underlying reason."

This leadership belonged to Mohammed Ibn Abdullah Ibn Abdu-Muttalib al-Hashemi of the Koreish, not because of his character and not because of his descent, but because he was the prophet of God. "Neither does he speak his own will,"[3] but only of Almighty God through his munificent angels. But once he (peace be upon him) was ranked among the angels, there was no one among his peers who could stand in that same position, because he (peace be upon him) was the "seal of the prophets."[4] The message of Almighty God could neither be inherited from the prophet, nor could a gift or authorization to be taken from him.

7. THE END OF THE LEADERSHIP WITH THE DEATH OF THE MESSENGER (PEACE BE UPON HIM) AND
8. THE PROPHET (PEACE BE UPON HIM) DID NOT DESIGNATE A SUCCESSOR AFTER HIMSELF

Mohammad (peace be upon him) had joined the Highest Benefactor without designating anyone as his successor after him, and without reassigning his position to anyone among his people. Moreover, he never hinted at anything that could be called an Islamic or an Arab state any time throughout the length of his entire life.

God forbid that he may have done so. He (peace be upon him) had not joined the Highest Benefactor except after he had completed his entire mission, and after he had revealed to his people all of the foundations free of flashy veneers and ambiguity. So how—if his mission had been to establish a state—could he leave the [continuing] command of that state ambiguous for the Muslims, swiftly leaving them confused and beating each other around the necks? How could he not mention who would be responsible for the command of the state? This is the first thing with which people building an ancient and modern state concern themselves! How could he not leave the Muslims that information that would guide them in this manner?

And how could he have left them subject to that rising black confusion, which overcame them and in whose darkness they almost killed each other while the body of the prophet was still among them and while his preparation and burial were not yet completed?

9. THE SHI'I BELIEF IN THE APPOINTMENT OF 'ALI

You should know that all of the Shi'i agree that the messenger (peace be upon him) had designated Ali (peace be upon him) as his successor (Caliph) over the Muslims after himself. We do not want to engage that topic or even discuss that view, for it has not had its share of academic research and what exists is not worth mentioning.

Ibn Khaldun said: "The texts which they return to again and again and which are necessarily interpreted according to their own doctrine are not known by the great scholars of Sunnah or the transmitters of Shari'ah, most of them are fabricated, or the chains of authority are discredited, or their interpretations are far-fetched and corrupt."

10. THE COMMON BELIEF IN THE
APPOINTMENT OF ABU BAKR

Imam Ibn Hazm al-Dhairi leaned toward the opinion of a group that claimed that the messenger of Almighty God stipulated in plain words the appointment of Abu Bakr after his demise to command the people. Both the Muhajarin and the Ansar of Medina had agreed that he should be assigned Caliph to the messenger of God (peace be upon him); the meaning of "Caliph" in this language is the one who is appointed by the prophet, not the one who appoints himself without it being apportioned for him. It is indisputable and he gives a very long account of this. A different interpretation of this statement is not allowed.

Accepting a different interpretation is to accept an incorrect manner of using the language, for which we cannot find any authority. We reiterated whatever we could find in the books, and we did not discover anything in them to support the words of Imam Ibn Hazm; then we found the consensus agreement of the hadith transmitters had not supported the appointment of Abu Bakr, and that the most esteemed among them had refrained from supporting it. We hear, too, Omar Ibn al-Khatib's (peace be upon him) apology about what he had done on the day of the messenger's (peace be upon him) passing. He said, "Oh, people, even though I told you yesterday something that was nothing other than my opinion; I had not found that in God's book, nor in anything the prophet had expressed to me. Rather, I have thought that the messenger of God (peace be upon him), would manage our affairs until the last of us. God has preserved his book in which He guided his messenger to adhere to that divine gift. He will guide you to what he had already guided the prophet and God has gathered you into a consensus for your own benefit, companions of the prophet, and he is the second of a pair because they were two together in the cave, so rise and acknowledge him as leader."[5]

We found that [saying] and many others and we know from this that the Prophet (peace be upon him) had shown that the question of succession was incorrectly interpreted. The truth is that he (peace be upon him) did not mention anything that had to do with a government after himself. Nor did he bring to the Muslims laws to which they could turn concerning this. He only joined Almighty God after the religion was completed, the grace accomplished, the message of Islam become a firmly established reality. The day he (peace be upon him) died, his prophecy ended, and the special link that was between heaven and his honorable character (peace be upon him) was cut.

NOTES

1. *Al-Quran.* "The Stories," vs. 68–69, trans. Ahmed Ali. Princeton: Princeton University Press, 1988. All translations in this text have been taken from this Ali Ahmed version unless otherwise noted.
2. *Al-Quran.* "The Family of Imran," vs. 103.
3. *Al-Quran.* "The Stars," vs. 3.
4. *Al-Quran.* "The Allied Troops," vs. 40.
5. *Tarikh al-Tabari* [al-Tabari's History], vol. 3. page 203.

CHAPTER 9

AUTHORITY AND THE
PROBLEM OF SUCCESSION

Amir Ali

Excerpt from Sayyid Amir Ali [Ameer Ali]. "The Apostolical Succession."
The Spirit of Islam: A History of the Evolution and Ideals of Islam with a Life of the Prophet. London: Christophers, 1922, pp. 122–33.

THE SPIRITUAL LIFE THE PROPHET HAD INFUSED into his people did not end with his life. From the first it was an article of faith that he was present in spirit, with the worshippers at their prayers, and that his successors in the ministry were his representatives. The immanence of the Master's spirit during the devotions establishes the harmony between the soul of man and the Divine Essence. Amongst all the dynastic rivalries and schismatic strife this mystical conception of his spiritual presence at the prayers has imparted a force to the Faith that cannot be over-estimated.

The two great sects into which Islam became divided at an early stage are agreed that the religious efficacy of the rites and duties prescribed by the Law (the *Shari'at*) depends on the existence of the vice-gerent and representative of the Prophet, who, as such, is the religious Head (Imam) of the Faith and the Faithful.

The adherents of the Apostolical Imams have a development and philosophy of their own quite distinct from "the followers of the traditions." According to them the spiritual heritage bequeathed by the Prophet devolved on Ali and his descendants by Fatima, the Prophet's daughter. They hold that the Imamate descends by Divine appointment in the apostolic line. They do not regard the Pontificate of Abu Bakr, Omar, and Osman as rightful; they consider that Ali, who was indicated by the Prophet as his successor, was the first rightful Caliph and Imam of the Faithful, and that after his assassination the spiritual headship descended in succession to his and Fatima's posterity in " the direct male line" until it came to Imam Hasan al-'Askari, eleventh in descent from Ali, who died in the year

874 C.E. or 260 of the Hegira in the reign of the Abbaside Caliph Mu'tamid. Upon his death the Imamate devolved upon his son Mohammed surnamed *al-Mahdi* (the "Guide"), the last Imam. The story of these Imams of the House of Mohammed is intensely pathetic. The father of Hasan was deported from Medina to Samarra by the tyrant Mutawakkil, and detained there until his death. Similarly, Hasan was kept a prisoner by the jealousy of Mutawakkil's successors. His infant son, barely five years of age, pining for his father, entered in search of him a cavern not far from their house. From that cavern the child never returned. The pathos of this calamity culminated in the hope, the expectation, which fills the hearts of all Shiahs, that the child may return to relieve a sorrowing and sinful world of its burden of sin and oppression. So late as the fourteenth century of the Christian era, when Ibn Khaldun[1] was writing his great work, the Shiahs were wont to assemble at eventide at the entrance of the cavern and supplicate the missing child to return to them. After a long and wistful waiting, they dispersed to their homes, disappointed and sorrowful. This, says Ibn Khaldun, was a daily occurrence. "When they were told it was hardly possible the child could be alive," they answered that, "as the Prophet Khizr[2] was alive why should not their Imam be alive also?" This Imam bears among the Shiahs the titles, the *Muntazar*, the Expected—the *Hujja* or the Proof (of the Truth), and the *Kaim*, the Living.

The philosophical student of religions will not fail to observe the strange similarity of the Shiah and the Sunni beliefs to older ideas. Among the Zoroastrians the persecution of the Seleucide engendered the belief that a divinely appointed Savior, whose name was Sosiosch, would issue from Khorasan to release them from the hated bondage of the foreigner. The same causes gave birth to that burning anticipation among the Jews in the advent of the Messiah. The Jew believes that the Messiah is yet to come; the Sunni, like him, believes that the Savior of Islam is still unborn. The Christian believes that the Messiah has come and gone, and will come again; the Asna-'asharia,[3] like the Christian, awaits the reappearance of the *Mahdi*, the Guide, who is to save the world from evil and oppression. The origin of these conceptions and the reasons of their diversity are traceable to like causes. The phenomena of the age in which the idea of the *Mahdi* took shape in its two distinct forms were similar to those visible in the history of the older faiths. Every eventide the prayer goes up to heaven in Islam, as in Judaism and Christianity, for the advent of the divinely appointed Guide, to redeem the world from sorrow and sin.

The Shiah believes that the Imam, though *ghaib* (absent), is always present in spirit at the devotions of his fold. The expounders of the law and the ministers of religion are his representatives on earth; and even the secular chiefs represent him in the temporal affairs of the world. Another point of difference between them and the Sunnis consists in the qualities required for the Imamate. According to the Shiahs the Imam must be sinless or immaculate (*m'asum*), a quality which their Imams alone possess, and that he must be the most excellent (*afzal*) of mankind. The Sunni doctrines which govern the lives, thoughts, and conduct of the bulk of the Moslem world are diametrically opposed to the Shiah conception. The Sunni religious law insists that the Imam must be actually present in person to impart religious efficacy to the devotions of the Faithful; and that, where it is not possible for him to lead the prayers, he should be represented by persons possessing the necessary qualifications.

These doctrines are enunciated in detail in most works on jurisprudence and scholastic theology. The *Khalifat*, it is explained, is the Vice-gerency of the Prophet; it is ordained by Divine Law for the perpetuation of Islam and the continued observance of its laws and rules. For the existence of Islam, therefore, there must always be a Caliph, an actual and direct representative of the Master. The Imamate is the spiritual leadership; but the two dignities are inseparable; the Vice-gerent of the Prophet is the only person entitled to lead the prayers when he can himself be present. No one else can assume his functions unless directly or indirectly " deputed" by him. Between the Imam and the *mamum*[4] or congregation, there is a spiritual tie which binds the one to the other in the fealty to the Faith. There is no inconsistency between this dogma and the rule that there is no priesthood in Islam. Each man pleads for himself before his Lord, and each soul holds communion with God without the intermediation of any other human being. The Imam is the link between the individual worshipper and the evangel of Islam. This mystical element in the religion of Islam forms the foundation of its remarkable solidarity.

The above remarks serve to emphasize the statement in the *Durr-ul-Mukhtar* that Imamates are of two kinds, the *Imamat al-Kubra* and the *Imamat as-Sughra*, the supreme spiritual Headship and the minor derivative right to officiate at the devotions of the faithful. The *Imam al-Kabir*, the supreme Pontiff, is the Caliph of the Sunni world. He combines in his person the spiritual and temporal authority which devolves on him as the vice-gerent of the Master. Secular affairs are conducted by him in consultation with councilors as under the first four Caliphs, or, as in later times, by delegates, collectively or individually. Similarly with religious and spiritual matters. But in the matter of public prayers, unless physically prostrate, he is bound to conduct the congregational service in person.

Among the Shiahs, even Friday prayers and prayers offered at the well-known festivals may validly be performed individually and in private. According to the Sunni doctrines, congregational prayers, where mosques or other places of public worship are accessible, are obligatory; abstention from attendance without valid reason is a sin, and the defaulters incur even temporal penalties. In Najd, under the rule of the Wahabis, who have been called the Covenanters of Islam, laggards were whipped into the mosque. And today under Ibni S'aud, his followers who designate themselves *Ikhwan*, or "Brothers in faith," pursue the same method for enforcing the observance of religious rites. Prayers *bi'l jama'at* being obligatory (*farz'ain*) naturally made the presence of the Imam absolutely obligatory.[5]

The Sunnis affirm that when stricken by his last illness the Prophet deputed Abu Bakr to lead the prayers. On his death, but before he was consigned to his grave, the Master's nomination was accepted by the "congregation" and Abu Bakr was installed as his vice-gerent by the unanimous suffrage of the Moslems. And this has ever since been the universal practice in all regular lines.

Amongst the qualifications necessary for occupying the pontifical seat, the first and most essential is that he must be a Moslem belonging to the Sunni communion, capable of exercising supreme temporal authority, free of all outside control. The Sunnis do not require that the Imam should be *ma'sum*, or that he should be "the most excellent of mankind," nor do they insist on his descent from the Prophet. According to them, he should be an independent ruler, without any personal defects, a man of good character, possessed of the capacity to conduct the affairs of State, and to lead at prayers. The early doctors, on the authority of a saying of the Prophet, have included a condition which comes at the end of the passage relating to the qualities necessary for the Imamate—viz., that the Caliph-Imam should be a Koreish by birth. The avowed object of inserting this condition, as is stated both in the *Durr-ul-Mukhtar* and the *Radd-ul-Muhtar*, was to nullify the Shiah contention that the Imamate was restricted to the House of Mohammed, the descendants of Ali and Fatima, and to bring in the first three Caliphs, and the Ommeyyade and the Abbaside Caliphs, into the circle of legitimate Imams. The great jurist and historian, Ibn Khaldun,[6] a contemporary of Tamerlane, who died in the year 1406 C.E., long before the House of Othman attained the Caliphate, has dealt at great length with this condition in his *Mukaddamat* (Prolegomena). He does not dispute the genuineness of the saying on which it is based, but explains that it was a mere recommendation, which was due to the circumstances of the times. He points that when the Islamic Dispensation was given to the world the tribes of Koreish were the most advanced and most powerful in Arabia; and in recommending or desiring that the temporal and spiritual guardianship of the Moslems should be confined to a member of his own tribe, the Prophet was thinking of the immediate future rather than of laying down a hard and fast rule of succession. At that time a qualified and capable ruler of Islam could only be found among the Koreish; hence the recommendation that the Caliph and Imam should be chosen from among them. This view, eloquently expressed by one of the most learned of Sunni Jurisconsults is universally accepted by the modern doctors (the *Mutakherin)*, that subject to the fulfillment of all other conditions the law imposes no tribal or racial restriction in the choice of an Imam. Abu Bakr before his death had nominated Omar his successor in the Vice-gerency, and the appointment was accepted by the "universality of the people, including the House of Mohammed." Omar died from the effects of a mortal wound inflicted on him by a Christian or Magian fanatic who considered himself aggrieved by the acts of this great Caliph. To avoid all imputation of favoritism Omar had, before his death, appointed an electoral committee consisting of six eminent members of the Moslem congregation to choose his successor. Their choice fell on Osman, a descendant of Ommeyya, who was installed as Caliph with the suffrage of the people. On Osman's unhappy death, Ali, the son-in-law of the Prophet, who, according to the Shiahs, was entitled by right to the Imamate in direct succession to the Prophet, was proclaimed Caliph and Imam. The husband of Fatima united in his person the hereditary right with that of election. But his endeavor to remedy the evils which had crept into the administration under his aged predecessor raised against him a host of enemies. Mu'awiyah, an Ommeyyade by descent, who held the governorship of Syria under Osman, raised the standard of revolt. Ali proceeded to crush the rebellion but, after an indecisive battle, was struck down by the hand of an assassin whilst at his devotions in the public Mosque of Kufa in Iraq. With Ali ended what is called by the early

Sunni doctors of law and theologians, the *Khilafat-al-Kamila* "the Perfect Caliphate," for in each case their title to the rulership of Islam was perfected by the universal suffrage of the Moslem nation.

On Ali's death Mu'awiyah obtained an assignment of the Caliphate from Hasan, the eldest son of Ali, who had been elected to the office by the unanimous voice of the people of Kufa and its dependencies, and received the suffrage of the people of Syria to his assumption of the high office. This happened in 661 C.E.

It should be noted here that the Ommeyyades and Hashimides were two off-shoots from one common stock, that of Koreish. Bitter rivalry existed between these families, which it was the great aim of the Prophet throughout his ministry to remove or reconcile. The Hashimides owe their designation to Hashim, the great grandfather of the Prophet. His son, Abdul Muttalib, had several sons; one of them, Abbas, was the progenitor of the Abbaside Caliphs. Abu Talib, another son, was the father of Ali the Caliph, whilst the youngest, Abdullah, was the Prophet's father.

Mu'awiyah was the first Caliph of the House of Ommeyya. On the death of Mu'awiyah's grandson, another member of the same family belonging to the Hakamite branch, named Merwan, assumed the Caliphate. Under his son 'abdul Malik and grandson Walid, the Sunni Caliphate attained its widest expansion; it extended from the Atlantic to the Indian Ocean and from the Tagus to the sands of the Sahara and the confines of Abyssinia. In 749 C.E. Abul Abbas, surnamed Saffah, a descendant of Abbas, the uncle of the Prophet, overthrew the Ommeyyade dynasty and was installed as Caliph, in place of Merwan II, the last Pontiff of that House, in the Cathedral Mosque of Kufa, where he received the *Bai'at* of the people. He then ascended the pulpit, recited the public sermon which the Imam or his representative delivers at the public prayers. This notable address, religiously preserved by his successors, is to be found in the pages of the Arab historian Ibn-ul-Athir. It is in effect a long vindication of the rights of the children of Abbas to the Caliphate. Abul Abbas was henceforth the legitimate ruler of the Sunni world and the rightful spiritual Head of the Sunni Church. His first six successors were men of remarkable ability; those who followed were of varying capacity, but a few possessed uncommon talent and learning. Mansur, the brother of Saffah, who succeeded him in the Caliphate, founded Baghdad, which became their capital and seat of Government, and was usually called the *Dar-ul Khilafat* and the *Dar-us-salaam*, "The Abode of the Caliphate" and" The Abode of Peace." Here the house of Abbas exercised undisputed spiritual and temporal authority for centuries. Their great rivals of Cairo became extinct in Saladin's time; the brilliant Ommeyyade dynasty of Cordova disappeared in the first decade of the eleventh century. The Almohades, the Almoravides, and the many Berber and Arab dynasties which, on the decline of the Almoravides, followed each other in succession in Morocco, had no valid title to the headship of the Sunni Church. The right of the Abbasides to the Sunni Imamate stood unchallenged from the Atlantic to the Ganges, from the Black Sea and the Jaxartes to the Indian Ocean. In 493 of the Hegira (1099 C.E.) Yusuf bin Tashfin, the Almohade conqueror after the epoch-making battle of az-Zallaka, where the Christian hordes were decisively beaten, obtained from the Abbaside Caliph al-Muktadi, a formal investiture with the title of *Ameer-ul-Muslimin;* and this was confirmed to him by the Caliph al-Mustazhir. It should be borne in mind that neither the " Caliphs" of Cordova nor any of the Moslem sovereigns in later ages assumed the dignity of the representative of the Prophet *(Khalifat-ar-Rasul)* or arrogated the title of *Ameer-ul-Mominin.*

For five full centuries Baghdad was the center of all intellectual activity in Islam; and here the rules and regulations appertaining to the Caliphate, as also to other matters, secular and religious, were systematized. And the conception that the Caliph-Imam was the divinely appointed Vice-gerent of the Prophet became, as it is today, welded into the religious life of the people. It will thus be seen that, according to the Sunni doctrines, the Caliph is not merely a secular sovereign; he is the religious head of a Church and a commonwealth, the actual representative of Divine government.[7]

The Abbaside Caliphate lasted for five centuries from its first establishment until the destruction of Baghdad by the Mongols in 1258 of the Christian era. At that time Musta'sim b'Illah was the Caliph, and he, together with his sons and the principal members of his family, perished in the general massacre; only those scions of the House of Abbas escaped the slaughter who were absent from the capital, or succeeded in avoiding detection.

For two years after the murder of Musta'sim b'Illah the Sunni world felt acutely the need of an Imam and Caliph; both the poignancy of the grief at the absence of a spiritual Head of the Faith, and the keenness of the necessity for a representative of the Prophet to bring solace and religious merit to the Faithful, are pathetically voiced by the Arab historian of the Caliphs.[8] The devotions of the living were devoid of that religious efficacy which is imparted to them by the presence in the world of an acknowledged Imam; the prayers for the dead were equally without merit. Sultan Baibars felt with the whole Sunni world the need of a Caliph and Imam. The right to the Caliphate had become vested by five centuries of undisputed acknowledgment in the House of Abbas; and a member of this family, Abul Kasim Ahmed, who had succeeded in making his escape from the massacre by the Mongols, was invited to Cairo for installation in the pontifical seat. On his arrival in the environs of Cairo, the Sultan, accompanied by the judges and great officers of State, went forth to greet him. The ceremony of installation is described as imposing and sacred. His descent had to be proved first before the Chief Kazi or Judge. After this was done, he was installed in the chair and acknowledged as Caliph, under the title of al-Mustansir UIllah," Seeking the help of the Lord." The first to take the oath of Bai'at was the Sultan Baibars himself; next came the Chief Kazi Taj-ud-din, the principal sheikhs and the ministers of State, and lastly the nobles, according to their rank. This occurred on May 12, 1261, and the new Caliph's name was impressed on the coinage and recited in the Khutba. On the following Friday he rode to the mosque in procession, wearing the black mantle of the Abbasides,[9] and delivered the pontifical sermon. As his installation as the Caliph of the Faithful was now complete, he proceeded to invest the Sultan with the robe and diploma so essential in the eyes of the Orthodox for legitimate authority.

The Abbaside Caliphate thus established in Cairo lasted for over two centuries and a half. During this period Egypt was ruled by sovereigns who are designated in history as the Mameluke Sultans. Each Sultan on his accession to power received his investiture from the Caliph and" Imam of his time" *(Imam-ul-Wakt)* and he professed to exercise his authority as the lieutenant and delegate of the Pontiff. The appointment of ministers of religion and administrators of justice was subject to the formal sanction of the Caliph. Though shorn of all its temporal powers, the religious prestige of the Caliphate was so great, and the conviction of its necessity as a factor in the life of the people so deep-rooted in the religious sentiments of the Sunni world, that twice after the fall of Baghdad the Musulman sovereigns of India received their investiture from the Abbaside Caliphs. The account of the reception in 1343 C.E. of the Caliph's envoy by Sultan Mohammed Juna Khan Tughlak, the founder of the gigantic unfinished city of Tughlakabad, gives us an idea of the veneration in which the Pontiffs were held even in Hindustan, in those days said to be full six months' journey from Egypt. On the approach of the envoy the King, accompanied by the Sayyid s and the nobles, went out of the capital to greet him; and when the Pontiff's missive was handed to the Sultan he received it with the greatest reverence. The formal diploma of investiture legitimized the authority of the King. The whole of this incident is celebrated in a poem still extant in India by the poet laureate, the famous Badr-ud-din Chach.

About the end of the fifteenth century the star of Selim I., also surnamed Saffah, of the House of Othman, rose on the horizon. His victories over the enemies of Islam had won for him the title of "Champion of the Faith"; and no other Moslem sovereign—not even his great rival Shah Isma'il, the founder of the Sufi dynasty in Persia and the creator of the first orthodox Shiah State—equaled the Osmanli monarch in greatness and power.

The closing decades of that century had witnessed a vast change in the condition of Egypt, and the anarchy that had set in under the later Mameluke Sultans reached its climax some years later. Invited by a section of the Egyptian people to restore order and peace in the distracted country, Selim easily overthrew the incompetent Mamelukes, and incorporated Egypt with his already vast dominions. At this period the Caliph who held the Vice-gerency of the Prophet bore the pontifical name of Al-Mutawakkil 'ala-Allah ("Contented in the grace of the Lord"). According to the Sunni records, he perceived that the only Moslem sovereign who could combine in his own person double functions of Caliph and Imam, restore the Caliphate of Islam in theory and in fact, and discharge effectively the duties attached to that office, was Selim. He, accordingly, in 1517, by a formal deed of assignment, transferred the Caliphate to the Ottoman conqueror, and, with his officials and dignitaries, "made the *Bai'at* on the hand of the Sultan." In the same year Selim received the homage of the Sharif of Mecca, Mohammed Abul Barakat, a descendant of Ali, who was presented by his son Abu Noumy on a silver salver the keys of the Kaaba and took the oath by the same proxy. The combination in Selim of the Abbaside right by assignment and by *Baliat*, and the adhesion of the representative of the Prophet's House who held at the time the guardianship of the Holy Cities, perfected the Ottoman Sultan's title to the Caliphate, "just as the adhesion of (the Caliph) Ali had completed the title of the first three Caliphs." The solemn prayers with the usual Khutbas offered in Mecca and Medina for the Sultan gave the necessary finality to the right of Selim. Henceforth Constantinople, his seat of government, became the *Dar-ul-khilafat*, and began to be called "Istambol," "The City of Islam." Before long envoys arrived in Salim's Court and that of his son, Solyman the Magnificent, from the rulers of the Sunni States to offer their homage; and thus, according to the Sunnis, the Caliphate became the heritage of the House of Othman, which they have enjoyed for four centuries without challenge or dispute.

NOTES

1. See *Post*, p. 126.
2. See Appendix III.
3. See *Post*, p. 344.
4. This is the term used in the *Fatawai-Alamgiri*. The individual follower is usually called the "Muktadi."
5. There is absolute consensus on these points among the different Sunni schools. The jurist Khalil ibn Ishak, the author of the monumental work on Maliki Law, enunciates the rules in the same terms as the Hanafis and the Shafeis.
6. For many years Malikite Chief Kazi of Cairo.
7. Suyuti.
8. Ibid.
9. Black was the color of the Abbasides, white of the Ommeyyades and green of the Fatimides, the descendants of Mohammed.

CHAPTER 10

INTELLECTUAL PLURALISM AND FREEDOM OF OPINION

Sayyid Ahmad Khan

"Azadi Ra'i" (Freedom of Opinion) from Sayyid Ahmad Khan, *Maqalat-i Sir Sayyid*. Edited by Maulana Muhammad Isma'il Pani Pati. Lahaur: Majlis-i Taraqqi-yi Adab, 1962, pp.151–64.

In translating this article by Sayyid Ahmad Khan, (and the other three essays by this author), I have tremendously benefited from an earlier translation, by John Wilder Selected Essays by Sir Sayyid Ahmad Khan from the Journal Tahzib al-Akhlaq. Unpublished M.A. Thesis, Hartford, Connecticut: Hartford Seminary Foundation, 1972 and the help of Kazim Saeed.

WE DERIVE THE THOUGHTS OF THIS ARTICLE FROM A WRITING of one of this age's most worthy and able philosophers.

Everyone is fully entitled to freedom of opinion. Suppose all except one person agrees on something and that one person holds an opposing viewpoint. All those agreed have no more right to call that man's opinion wrong than he has to prove (if he can) the wrongness of the opinion of all others. There is no reason why five people should have the right to hold the opinions of four others to be wrong while one person does not have this right against nine. The wrongness of an opinion does not depend upon numbers of people who oppose it, but rather upon the strength of their arguments. Just as it is possible for the opinion of nine people to be against that of one person, so is it possible for one person's opinion to be correct against nine.

The restriction of opinion is extremely undesirable—it cannot be justified on religious grounds, family and community considerations, fear of personal defamation, or threat of government repression. If an opinion is useful only to the person who holds it, the restriction of that opinion would be considered a loss to one particular person or a limited few. But the restriction of opinions results in the violation of the rights of all people and brings damage to all, not only to the present generation but also to generations to come.

Although customs theory of Gravity were not available for criticism and discussion, the world would not have been able to place firm confidence in its accuracy and truth as it now does. Is there any opposition that people have spared toward that wise philosopher [Sir Isaac Newton]? And what religious taunt has not been made against that wise man and bearer of true views? But we must ponder the result of this opposition: Today all the world, both wise and foolish, both the learned and the prejudiced followers of religion, all acknowledge him, at acts or make statements that damage the very religion they favor. They themselves are the reason why the objections of their opponents remain unknown. They themselves are the reason why the members of their own religion give no attention to providing any answers to the objections, because they are left unresearched and unrefuted. They themselves are the reason why future generations may turn away from religion when they become acquainted with objections that convince due to lack of investigation. Indeed, these foolish people make themselves virtually the means of displaying to the world that the religion they follow is indeed in serious peril from the objections of opponents. If any member of their own religion wishes to bring the issues into the open without caring to conform to the objectives already mentioned, they imagine him to be an objector and in their foolishness hold a friend to be an enemy. How lofty is the opinion of a philosopher:

If the advocates of a point of view object to the dissemination of an opposing viewpoint, they cause more damage to their own viewpoint than to that of their opponents. This is so because if the opposing view is correct, then they would miss the correct idea. And if the opinion is wrong, the refusal to debate it removes the opportunity to compare the false with the true and thus to obtain the excellent benefit of strengthening the correct view and making the influence of its truth greater. Seek to attain this result, which in reality brings very great benefit.

There is no doubt that it is generally very desirable and beneficial for supporting and opposing views to become widely diffused, whether these views are related to religious or worldly affairs. This presents an opportunity to study each opinion separately to see which of the two is better, or to see whether each of them is separately supported by suitable arguments. We can never have perfect confidence that the opinion to whose opposition we are trying to remain committed is really wrong. And even if we are certain it is wrong, to oppose and hinder it has its own damaging consequences.

Suppose that the idea that we desire to restrict is actually a correct opinion, and the people who desire to stop it deny its correctness. But one must consider that the people who desire to restrict it are not infallible. They have no right to decide that matter themselves for all, and to prevent other people from exercising their own opinions. To refuse to give a hearing to an opposing opinion simply by saying that we are convinced it is wrong is to say that our conviction holds a position of infallibility, and to forbid conversation and argument about it is to consider oneself greater than the prophets: incapable of error.

It is a very sad fact about human understanding that although to a large extent humans, theoretically speaking, consider themselves prone to mistakes—on the authority of that famous saying, "Man is compounded of error and forgetfulness"—they do not actually remember their fallibility when it comes to their behavior in expressing particular opinions. Although all admit that they can make mistakes, they seem in their conduct to demonstrate rather little appreciation of the importance of the saying we have quoted. Thus, few admit in practice that any opinion about which they have great certainty may perhaps be an example of the very mistake they understand themselves to be capable of making.

People who become accustomed to unlimited honor and respect on account of their riches, position, authority, or knowledge have complete confidence in the correctness of their opinions in all matters, and they do not suspect themselves capable of making mistakes. More fortunate than these are the people who sometimes hear objections, arguments, and controversies concerning their opinions and are accustomed to abandoning an error once they become aware of it and accepting the correct view. Yet even these people, although they do not have complete confidence in the correctness of their every opinion, still hold to the correctness of the opinions that are accepted by the people who live around them, or those whose opinion they consider worthy of great respect and honor.

It is an accepted fact that, commensurately with the lack of trust in his own opinion, a person usually places his confidence upon the opinion of the world. This opinion of the world is called by some "the opinion of the multitude," or "the creed of the multitude." But one must understand what these people mean by "world" or "multitude." In the mind of every such person the world or the multitude represents the conception of a limited number of people in whom he has confidence or with whom he ordinarily comes in close contact—for example, his particular group of friends—or those who are like-minded, his kin, or people of his own rank or station. Thus, in his thinking, the meaning of the whole "world" and the "multitude" is exhausted by these limited few. Believing this opinion to be that of the world or the collective body of humankind, this person is generally convinced that it is correct.

He has such unshakable confidence and faith in this form of general consensus because he is unaware of the opinions held by people who lived before his age—people of other ages, other countries, other sects, other religions and of the opinions that the people of other countries, sects, and religions presently hold. Such a person is actually disavowing responsibility for answering the question whether in truth he is following the correct way. Instead, he casts this responsibility upon his imagined "world" or "multitude."

So whatever his opinion or position may be, it is not worthy of the slightest reliance or weight. Just as this person, having been born in a Muslim family, is a most pious Muslim, had he been born in a Christian family or country or a pagan family or country, he would have been a good enough Christian or pagan. He totally fails to reflect that just as it is possible for some particular person to fall into a mistake, so it is possible for an entire age or the entire world to fall into mistakes, to say nothing of his imaginary "world" or "multitude."

It is abundantly clear from history and present knowledge that in every age there have been ideas that became established and accepted as true but that in following ages came to be considered not only mistaken but completely absurd. And surely in this age, too, many options must be prevalent that in some later age will likewise be considered unacceptable and rejected, just as many ideas that in the preceding age were commonly accepted have now been rejected.

A word of caution is due here: Those who oppose contrary opinions because they consider them to be wrong and harmful, in doing so do not mean to claim that they themselves are free and immune. Rather, in doing this they mean to perform the duty of acting according to their own faith and belief, notwithstanding their liability to mistake and error.

If people should desist from acting according to their opinions out of fear that perhaps they might be wrong, nobody could function in his normal duties. It is people's duty to establish, as far as possible, their most correct opinions, confirm them with careful deliberation, and when they become perfectly convinced of their rightness, make efforts to put a stop to the opposing opinions. People ought to use their intelligence and ability in the best possible manner. Absolute certainty is not possible in any matter, but a degree of certainty that is sufficient for human purposes is possible. For purposes of carrying on their normal activities, people can consider and ought to consider their own opinion to be correct. And further, under these circumstances, they are not proceeding beyond this legitimate limit when they prohibit bad people from publishing opinions that, in their opinion, are seditious or harmful and by which people are made corrupt, immoral, or irreligious.

But in restricting opposing opinions it is not sufficient that they have acted according to their own faith and belief, while regarding themselves as subject to error. A great deal more is done by those who restrict opposing opinions. There is a world of difference between, on the one hand, the acceptance of an opinion as correct when people have been given a chance to object to it and argue it, and find that it could not be disproved, and, on the other hand, its acceptance when there has been no opportunity given to repudiate it. Surely, then, those who hinder opposing opinions hold their own freedom of opinion to be correct not because it could not be disproved, but because opportunity to disprove it has not been allowed. But, the condition on which we can consider our opinion correct enough for practical purposes is simply this: that people should have full freedom to speak against it and to prove it false. Apart from this there is no other possible way by which man, whose mental and other powers are imperfect, may become certain that he is upon the right path.

Followers of religions, who consider that the true way lies in following the person in whom their personal faith is lodged, cannot be certain that they are following in the right path until they allow their own belief to be discussed and have clarified for them whether their practice or creed is truly the emulation of the person in whom they believe.

It becomes evident after comparing humanity's previous conditions with its present ones that, in every period, out of a hundred people only one has the capability of giving an opinion on an abstruse matter. Ninety-nine are without competence to pronounce an opinion on it. But even the excellence of that one person's opinion is only relative, because among people of previous ages the majority of those who were famous for their understanding held opinions whose error has now come to light. Many ideas that no one now considers correct and right were highly esteemed and practiced by them.

This proves that reasonable and desirable opinions ultimately tend to prevail among people. But there is no other reason why people accepted them except that there is a noble quality in humankind's understanding and wisdom that is very much appreciated. And that quality amounts to the fact that humanity's mistakes themselves contain a capacity for improvement. That is to say that a person has the ability to set right his/her own mistakes by means of discussion and experience.

Thus, the entire weight and value of a person's opinion depends completely on the fact that, when it is wrong, it can be corrected. But it can be trusted only when the means of its correction are kept in use.

We should bear in mind the means by which someone's opinion becomes credible and trustworthy to others. It is because he/she has always disciplined himself/herself to accept criticism. He/she has adopted the method of listening calmly to the adversary's opinion, taken benefit from whatever is true and correct, understood whatever was improper and wrong in it, and, on the right occasion, warned others of any mistake. Such a person testifies through actions, as it were, that the only way one can understand all the varied aspects of some subject is to listen to the conversation of people of every variety of opinion, and consider all the methods by which people of different understanding, methods, and dispositions may look upon the subject.

Wisdom may not be attained in any other method than this. Indeed, the distinctive feature of humankind's intelligence is that it cannot become cultured and reasonable by any other method but this. No other basis can be considered for placing confidence in any matter, but the basis of a permanent habit of comparing one's own opinion with that of others, and then reforming and perfecting it. This is because people who have followed this method will always have listened well to everything that people could say against them; they will have placed their own opinion before all their critics' opinions, and instead of hiding the difficulties and objections, they themselves will have made a search; they will not have shut off any light that might come from any direction. Surely such people have the right to consider that their opinion is superior to that of those who have not carefully confirmed their own opinion.

Anyone who wishes to be able to have any measure of confidence in his opinion, or wishes that ordinary people also may accept it as true, has no other way to do it than to present his opinion for common debate and subject it to the objections of every kind of person. If Newton's wisdom, his astronomy, and his Theory of Gravity were not admissible to criticism and discussion, the world could not have placed such firm confidence in their accuracy and truth as it now does. Is there any opposition that people have spared toward that wise philosopher? And what religious taunt has not been made against that wise man and bearer of true views? But we must ponder over the result of this opposition: Today all the world, both wise and foolish, both the learned and the prejudiced followers of religion, all acknowledge him, all admit him to be right, and his truth has become more firmly established in people's hearts than religious creeds.

Without freedom of opinion, no idea's truth can be inquired into to the fullest possible extent. We can find no certification of or foundation for the admissibility and correctness of those beliefs that we consider the most admissible and correct unless the whole world is allowed to try to prove them to be unfounded. If those concerned do not resolve upon this path, or if, having resolved upon it, they are unsuccessful in carrying it through, we still are not entitled to place full confidence in them. Nevertheless, by giving this permission to test beliefs, we have gained as strong a proof of their correctness as is possible for human understanding in its present condition, because in this condition we have not neglected any effort that would bring the real truth to our knowledge. If discussion is allowed to be continued on a matter under consideration, it is possible for us to hope that if any idea is better or truer, it will come into our grasp when man's understanding becomes capable of finding it out; in the meantime, we can believe that we have reached the truth to the fullest extent that was possible in our age. In short, if the fallible being called human can reach any measure of certainty regarding anything, the only way is the way we have described. And this is my humble commentary on that famous doctrine of the Muslim religion, "Truth is supreme and nothing is superior."

But there is a tremendous deception that inclines humankind and sometimes even good governments to prevent free expression of opinion. It is the conception of Utility, to which the erroneous and false name "The Common Expediency" has been given. As the proverb states, "Contrary to fact, they call kafur the Ethiopian white!" This conception tells us that discussion regarding the correctness and truth of any opinion, doctrine, or creed may be forbidden because public adherence to it is very beneficial and is the cause of the good and the well-being of the people—no matter what the actual truth may be. Nowadays this point of view is very prevalent in India and especially among the Muslims: so much so, in fact, that this sinful attitude is imagined to be noble.

The result is that the throttling of discussion and freedom of opinion regarding some belief or persuasion is usually dependent, not upon its soundness or truthfulness, but upon its general utility. It is a pity that the holders of such opinions do not understand that the very claim that they formerly made and then recanted—that is, of considering themselves incapable of error—has returned and reasserted itself. The only difference is that at first this claim was regarding one thing and now it has shifted to another. Formerly it asserted the truth of some doctrine, and now it asserts its general usefulness. This notwithstanding the fact that the general usefulness of a doctrine stands just as much in need of debate and discussion as the doctrine itself does.

People of this kind commit a second mistake on top of their first when they say that they have only prohibited discussion regarding the truth of the opinion and not regarding its general usefulness, and they fail to understand that the truth of the opinion is itself a part of its being in the general interest. It is not possible to discuss the general usefulness of an opinion without proving its correctness and truth. If we want to know whether some particular idea is beneficial for the people or not, is it poison, will not be called a true opinion; rather, it would be more fitting to call it prejudice and compounded ignorance. But this way of accepting truth does not befit a reasonable creature like the human, nor is this the way of recognizing righteousness and truth. On the contrary, any truth that is accepted in this way is corrupt and vain, and is merely a chance acceptance of things that are imagined to be true.

In fact, to be absolutely truthful, any person who has accepted any opinion or religious teaching is correct and the opposing opinion (which people wish to restrict) is wrong and incorrect. We shall prove that restricting that wrong opinion is also not free from harm and loss.

Everyone should remember, no matter how strong his opinion may be and how unwilling he may be to admit the possibility of his opinion being wrong, that if that opinion cannot be discussed fairly, fearlessly, and boldly, it will be judged a dead and decaying opinion and not a living, true reality, and that it will never be able to find acceptance as one of those truths whose influence permanently affects the outlook of the people.

The study of past and present history shows that sometimes even tyrannous governments have tried to spread some very true and correct ideas, except that their tyrannical nature did not allow for free discussion of it. And many examples also exist of good and civilized governments that have tried to start some very good idea or practice, but the people did not take up the discussion, either because they felt that their discussion and argument had no business meddling with that idea, or because nobody paid attention to them. Or they gave up the discussion because of an imaginary fear, or because of an actual fear of ill-humor on the part of members of the government because they considered it improper at that time to say anything contrary to official opinion, or because they felt that to say anything against the government or anyone else would bespeak ill will. In the end, the idea that the government had been seeking to spread actually did not have an effect on anyone's thinking and found for itself only the place of a lifeless opinion in the hearts of the people.

It is pleasing but fallacious to say that even without debate and the presentation of reasons, a correct opinion will enter and take root in people's minds. Look at the world: so many groups of people stick to opinions that are opposed to one another, and these opposed opinions have taken root in their hearts. Does it follow that both of these opinions are correct? No doubt many ideas take hold of people's minds without being understood, argued, and discussed, but such ideas are not necessarily correct. Truth does not possess any miraculous powers by which it may take possession of the mind by itself. It is only miraculous to the extent that it possesses no fear of discussion.

Even a true opinion, if it captures the mind without arguments and discussion, will not be called a true opinion; rather, it would be more fitting to call it prejudice and compounded ignorance. But this way of accepting truth does not befit a reasonable creature like the human, nor is this the way of recognizing righteousness and truth. On the contrary, any truth that is accepted in this way is corrupt and vain, and is merely a chance acceptance of things that are imagined to be true.

In fact, to be absolutely truthful, any person who has accepted any opinion or religious teaching is answerable; originators of that opinion, or the leaders, teachers, and jurists of that religion, are not in the least responsible. But Muslims have closed their eyes to this fact, which is as clear as day, and have adopted the doctrine of the Roman Catholics (i.e., those Christians who practice idolatry). In the Roman Catholic religion believers are divided into two groups: one that is competent to accept the doctrines of that religion after arguments and proofs; and a second that ought to accept them only by dependence and trust, that is, by conformity. Following the same principle, Muslims, too, have formed two groups in their religion. One group has adopted the accepted tenets after proof, investigation, and prolonged reasoning. They are called, according to their differences in degrees, Independent Mujtahid, Affiliated Mujtahid, and Preferrer. The second group is composed of those who follow them unthinkingly and blindly. They are called Conformists and their action is called Conformity.

Because of this outlook, opposition to conflicting viewpoints has spread very widely among Muslims, and they make a very impressive but befuddling statement concerning it: they say that it is neither necessary nor possible for all men to know all the things that the great doctors, the mystics, and the scholars of religious knowledge know and understand; that it is not possible for every common person to be capable of disputing and refuting all the falsehoods of a clever and intelligent opponent; that it is sufficient for him/her to understand that there will always be someone or other in existence by whose means not a single teaching of an opponent will stand unrefuted; that it is sufficient for people of simple understanding to be taught the truth about such matters, and that for the rest they should rely upon the authority of others; and that when they themselves know that they do not have sufficient knowledge and ability to eliminate all those difficulties, they can rest content with the assurance that whatever difficulties and objections have been raised have already been answered or will be answered by great scholars.

Even if we admit some truth in this line of reasoning, it is not established that the harm caused by obstructing freedom of opinion and stifling opposing opinion is any less. Because according to this argument, too, it is admitted that the people should have sufficient assurance that all objections have been satisfactorily answered, and that this assurance can be there only when there is liberty to discuss and argue, and when the opponents are permitted to explain all their reasons against it without leaving any stone unturned in their refutation.

Nowadays the doctrine of conformity is widely popular, and there is much opposition to free discussion; in fact, it is nonexistent. If the damage and the effects that result from this condition were only in terms of ignorance of reasons validating established opinions (providing that the accepted precepts or settled opinions were sound), then it might be said by some that the harm from this ipso facto ban is only intellectual and not moral. It may also be said that nothing of value is lost through that ignorance.

But this is not the case. There is a great deal more damage than this. The truth is that when discussion and freedom of opinion are absent, people do not forget only the reasons supporting the doctrines or opinions; they also usually forget even the meanings and the purposes of the doctrines. Thus, the words in which a doctrine or opinion has been expressed cease evoking the substantive thought. Or else, very few of the things that were meant by those words in the beginning remain known, and instead of refreshed and living—that is to say, effective—belief in that doctrine, there remain only a few incomplete sayings preserved by memorization. And if some of its purpose and meaning persists, it is only the outermost shell, and the kernel and essence vanish away.

Now Muslims should look at their condition in a fair spirit and see if, because of this very opposition to free opinion because of this Conformity, their entire theological structure, whether derived from the Traditional or Rational disciplines, has actually fallen into this state or not.

The experience that people have obtained up to the present time from all religious beliefs, moral affairs, and scholarly theories proves the correctness of the position I have presented above. So we see that in the time of those who were inventors of some creed, field of learning, or opinion, and in the hearts of their disciples, those beliefs and doctrines were brimming with meanings, purposes, and merit because, between them and those of opposing opinions, argument and discussion centrally aimed at gaining victory over each other's beliefs and doctrines. But when one doctrine attained success and was accepted by the people, the discussions ceased, its development stopped, and its effect upon humankind was that their minds lost their vitality, vigor, and power. At such a stage, a doctrine's own supporters are in such a plight that they are no longer prepared to confront their opponents as before. They do not defend their creed or precept as they did before. Instead, they remain silent and self-satisfied, filled with false pride and improper airs of sufficiency. They do their best not to listen to any argument against their belief or teaching. They seek to prevent the people of their own sect from listening to and discussing questions of doctrine by frightening them with verdicts of blasphemy and false threats of the terrors of hell. They do not understand that the light of knowledge, which spreads like sunlight, and the wind of objections, when they are correct, cannot be stopped by their efforts.

When things reach this state, the creed or doctrine that their leaders established with such great labors begins to decline. Then all the holy people who are counted as leaders in that miserable period complain that they find in the hearts of believers no effects at all of those beliefs, which the latter have accepted in name only. And although the believers outwardly accept those beliefs and doctrines, their conduct, morals, habits, and culture fail to be actually influenced by them. What a woeful fact that those holy people do not even understand that this condition, which they so deplore, comes as a favor of their own kind bestowing! Now I affirm clearly and without any trepidation that what I have set forth here is a completely accurate mirror of the condition of the Muslims of this age!

Now consider the opposite condition, when the concept of Freedom of Opinion reigns, with which free discussion must necessarily and inseparably have free rein; every defender is constantly in argument to establish the reasons for his beliefs and to teach against some other doctrine. At such a time even the common people and those lax in faith understand perfectly well what they are contending for, and what the difference between their tenets and those of others really is. In this situation thousands of people will be found who have thoroughly considered the principles underlying their doctrines, understood them completely by every possible method, and examined and weighed carefully their most noble aspects. This will exert as full an effect upon the morals, habits, and disposition of each person as obtains in the case of people who have thoroughly grasped and believed a tenet or doctrine.

On the other hand, when that creed is an inherited one and people accept the customs of their forefathers or religious preceptors as though they were sacred relics, their credal affirmation is not from the heart. The mind accepts it with a dead spirit, and therefore tends to forget it until the doctrinal tenet retains no connection at all with the humankind's innermost self and remains merely on the surface. All of our morals and habits align contrary to it, and the same conditions are found as we are constantly finding in this age. From them it is clear that such a doctrinal tenet remains far outside the mind, and instead of lodging itself in humankind's heart, it clings to the outside like a worthless thorny shell. Because of this, matters that pertain to humankind's essential nobility and inner integrity are not manifested. Instead, it displays another kind of power, like that exerted by a fence made of thorny brambles: it neither does any good itself to the land it surrounds, nor does it permit anyone else to bring flowers and plant them. It does nothing except allow the good earth of the heart to remain forever vacant, desolate, and worthless.

The follower of every religion, who studies his own situation, can understand perfectly the truth of what has been described here. Each follower supposes some book or other to be holy and feels that confessing it is a requirement of his/her religion. But along with this it is no exaggeration to say that perhaps only one out of thousands actually examines his/her conduct and determines future goodness or badness in accordance with the sacred canonical laws. Actually, whatever authority or rule determines their conduct is nothing more than the customs and traditions of their own clan, sect, or religious community.

In reality we find that, on the one hand, there exists a collection of ethical teachings, which they believe God has revealed for the regulation of their lives, or at least that some very holy sage, who was incapable of error or oversight, has made it; and, on the other hand, there exists a collection of those customs, traditions, and settled beliefs that prevail in that clan, sect, or community. Some things in this latter collection correspond exactly with the former collection, although some correspond only to a certain extent, and others are the complete opposite. Believers no doubt do acknowledge the first collection in word; however, their true allegiance, friendship, and obedience is given to the second collection. They observe it from day to day, and consider it a great shame and disgrace to turn from it or perform any action that contravenes it.

So the disregard of the first body of teaching on the part of those who consider it to be revealed by God springs from the fact that discussion of its doctrines and principles has been closed and therefore it retains no connection with humankind's inner being. Instead of being a living creed it has remained in mankind's hearts only as a dead profession.

The most powerful objection that can appear against this argument might be put this way: "In order to acquire true knowledge and experience, is it really necessary that there should never be agreement between opinions? Must some people remain persistent in error so that discussion may continue and other people may through them be able to acquire the truth? In order that truth may be attained, is it unavoidable for mistakes to exist in the world? When some creed or scholarly doctrine is generally accepted, does its nature change and is its effect lost? Can a doctrine or belief have no influence or people not properly understand it until someone raises persistent doubts about it? When people accept some truth accidentally, does this establish its truth? Up to now it has been thought that the highest purpose and result of progress in knowledge and learning is that all mankind should together agree upon fine and lofty principles, and that this agreement in outlook should gradually increase as time passes. But do knowledge and learning still continue to exist as long as their purpose is not achieved? We have heard it said that the consummation of every matter lies in the attaining of its purpose and result. But we had not heard that the very attainment of the purpose and result constitutes its decay."

But as for me, I will not go along with this objection. I agree that, to the extent that man progresses and is reformed, opinions, doctrines, and beliefs in which there are disagreements will doubtless decrease. In fact, humankind's well-being can be measured especially by the number and quantity of those truths that are not the subject of controversy and have attained the rank of confirmed truths. In order to confirm them, one of the necessary conditions is that mankind's opinions converge and be brought into harmony, and that process of convergence and consensus is just as beneficial to the correct opinion as it is harmful to the wrong one. But when we are apprehensive lest wrong opinions, too, converge and obtain consensus, we ought not fail to use that device by which escape is possible. That device consists precisely in encouraging freedom of opinion and continued discussion. If the possibility of sustaining that device is obviated because of the general acceptance of a creed or doctrine, then we ought to establish some other device. Socrates invented the device of imagined discussions for this very purpose, which Plato has described with great skill in his Dialogues.

But what a great pity it is that the Muslims of this age have not only failed to discover any way to preserve the exercise of intellectual scrutiny, but have even discarded those methods that had been discovered in the past! In acquiring every kind of knowledge the condition of Muslims for a long time has been such that they hardly read in any area of learning in order to find out the reality and truth in it. Their purpose is simply to know all that is written in a given book, regardless of whether it be true or false. This is true, be it the study of books of old stories, or journals of history and past events, or books containing smatterings of primitive geographies of a past age, or that lame and tottering science called Anatomy, or the outdated astronomy of Ptolemy, or ancient mathematics, or well-known religious interpretations that comprise the traditional science of jurisprudence, or the science of the traditions and scriptural exegesis. If discussion occurs, it is not on the question of whether a principle written in a book is true or false, but simply on whether that particular principle is recorded in the book or not.

This method has destroyed freedom of opinion and broken the way of life that used to afford protection against falling into error. All their learning and wisdom has been laid waste. All that their forefathers had accumulated, from which it was expected their descendants would profit, has been destroyed. Now the outstanding scholars, theologians, and learned people who are left are in the position of being without any knowledge about the truth of anything, be it a matter of scholarly teaching or religious belief. Whomever you ask whether something is true or not, even if he/she is a great scholar, can tell you nothing except that such and such a person wrote it. All the relish of learning and all the influence of the articles of belief is gone from the heart! These, then, alas, are the glorious "benefits" of the disappearance of freedom of opinion, and we have seen them with our own eyes!

In order to prove that freedom of opinion is not useful, it is often said that when freedom of opinion and its concomitant discussion prevail, it is not possible to decide conclusively which opinion is true. Each participant becomes even more firm and stubborn in his own opinion. I also admit this point and confess that in actuality all opinions tend to become the opinions of special groups. Even full freedom of discussion and argument cannot remedy this; in fact, it increases it. Truth is subjected to such a treatment that people, instead of understanding and discerning it, indulge in talking about it with an interest only in repudiating the positions taken by those whom they consider adversaries or whom they hate.

But we should clearly understand, too, that although the juxtaposing of ideas and discussing them brings no great benefit to those prejudiced groups who argue with each other, it does bring great benefit to those who observe and hear the discussion, and who do not have in themselves the emotion, passion, selfishness, and partiality that is present in the supporters of those opposing parties. And when, gradually, the passion of the prejudiced people subsides, they, too, begin to confess the truth secretly in their own hearts or to their closest friends, although they may never admit it publicly.

It is not at all harmful or damaging to a true teaching to be exposed to the hottest controversy; it is preventing exposure that seriously harms it. When people are forced to hear arguments on both sides of a matter, there is always hope of justice, but when they hear only one side, falsehoods become obdurate and turn into prejudice. Even truth does not retain the effect of truth because it tends to get more and more exaggerated until it turns into a lie. The virtue of justice, which resides in mankind, comes to useful effect most clearly when, at the time of the public hearing of each case, the contenders and supporters of both sides are present face to face, and both are forceful enough to present their arguments and reasons compellingly to the people. Apart from this procedure there is no way of attaining truth.

Sometimes another thing plays a part in hindering freedom of opinion. People call it authority, or precedent. It often happens that the parties to a debate quote the authority of a statement by some famous person in support of their speeches, although to make one's own opinion depend upon the authority of someone else's opinion goes against freedom of opinion. Then we consider someone's statement correct and true, it does no good to quote it. Instead, we ought to present the arguments that led us to accept the statement's truth. If even Socrates and Hippocrates have said something that is not actually true, their saying it will never make it true; and if some ignorant person has said something that is true, the fact that an ignorant person uttered it will never make it false!

What a noble concept is contained in the following saying! How needful it is that every man practice it! What a pity that it is so little observed! "Look for what is said and do not look for who said it." Blessed be the man who said, "The counsel is written on the wall; would that men would listen!"

III. Islam and Western Civilization

CHAPTER 11

Social Liberalism and Laissez-Faire Capitalism

Anonymous Mu'tazilite Muslim

Anonymous Mu'tazilite Muslim. "The Present Economical Condition of the Musalmans of Bengal," *Aligarh Institute Gazette*, vol. 12, nos. 73, 74, 75, 77, and 79 (1877–1880).

IT IS WELL-KNOWN THAT IN ALL SCHEMES OF EDUCATION greater indulgence is claimed from the State on behalf of the Mahomedans compared with the Hindus. Sometimes more scholarships are wanted and proposed; sometimes smaller schooling fees are proposed and established. The grounds on which this discreditable indulgence is claimed is the poverty of the Mahomedans of India in general.

The evidences of this general poverty are visible on all sides and are too unmistakable to be missed even by the most superficial observers. In banking and monetary transactions as a matter of course the Musalmans are nowhere—the Mabajans are invariably Hindus. In all large towns eminent merchants and wholesale dealers are seldom, if ever, Musalmans; even amongst retail dealing traders the more busy and the more successful are almost always Hindus.

If we turn to observe the condition of landed property amongst us we find that things are not at all better. We know that, within the last 100 years, numerous families of the Musalman gentry have lost their landed property; and the new possessors are generally Hindus. There are few, if any, instances of a Hindu gentleman being succeeded in his property by a Musalman gentleman.

It is not my intention here to adduce facts in support of what is generally admitted by all. My aim is to inquire into the causes of our general poverty and the probable means of improving our economical condition. For it is not necessary that we should continue to be poor; poverty is not an inevitable condition—poverty is not that, do what we may, it must stick to us throughout. Is it right then that, because we are poor, we should make our poverty the ground of a claim for charity from the State? We ought to exert ourselves more energetically and patiently and make ourselves superior to the disgrace of being poor; we ought to make ourselves equal to our Hindu neighbors. But, instead of being ashamed, we are making a parade of our poverty; instead of trying to improve our economical conditions, we are taking steps that are sure to make us even less confident of ourselves than we now are.

The progress of a people is evidenced by the increase and spread of wealth and knowledge. The causes of the progress, however, lie in the greater strength and wider diffusion of habits of energy and patience, self-exertion and self-dependence, prudence and self-responsibility, in other words, in the development of the character of man. The favor, which we ask the State to give us in our education, is calculated to lower our character by rendering weaker the motives for the exercise of our energies and by diminishing our prudence or responsibility to ourselves.

The policy of indulgence is thus a most mischievous policy, as it is injurious to the moral interests of man. Societies improve only by letting individuals feel the consequence of their own acts and omissions; and civilization is almost entirely due to the practice of self-help. For this reason I have always been opposed to the State giving us a free education or even an education less costly than it gives to the Hindus.

What then are the steps that should be taken by us for our education and improvement? We are poor; but for the sake of our own future and permanent interests, no indulgence is desirable from the State. Are we then to continue ignorant and backward forever? Certainly not—and the remedy is in our own hands. It is simply that we should cease to be poor; we should take steps to remove the causes that make us poor.

To trace these causes is the object of this essay,—some of those causes belong to our laws and social institutions. They are almost all more or less connected with our Theology.

First, there is no doubt that the superior classes amongst Hindus are more economical in their domestic habits and less expensive in their social customs. The Musalman gentleman eats better and is clothed better; the furniture in his house is more varied. His servants are more numerous; his amusements are more costly. But he must understand that knowledge is not a thing easily obtained; he must practice great economy, abstinence, and self-denunciation in order to educate his children. He must understand that knowledge must be assiduously sought after; he must learn to value wealth for the sake of knowledge. He must deny himself many comforts in order to educate his children. He must habituate himself to self-denial and self-sacrifice; he must discipline himself to subordinate the claims of self to the claims of the offspring that he has himself brought into existence. He must acquire the habit of self-control; he must try to acquire that highest quality of civilized humanity, the habit of postponing immediate self-gratification to this future welfare of others.

Second, there is less energy and restlessness among the higher Mahomedans than amongst Hindus of the same social rank. The amount of exertion that a Hindu gentleman is capable of undergoing is in general much greater than the amount that a Mahomedan gentleman can undergo. There is a love of repose in the Musalman character and a want of activity which, more than any other thing, have brought about the present decline in the condition of the superior classes of Musalmans and should consequently be regarded with serious anxiety.

To what are these expensive and comparatively inactive habits due?

a. It has never been understood by the great majority of the people that the apparent benefits that the poorer classes get from a rich man's expensive style of living are only temporary and, in the end, wholly illusive. They do not understand that the fund, which goes to the remuneration of labor, is the result only of saving and economy, and that profuse expenditure is therefore in the end injurious to the laboring classes. People are accordingly deceived into giving ready applause to the career of a prodigal gentleman. So that in no country and at no time has extravagance in living been reckoned at its proper worth. And Mahomedan theologians and moralists, while they say nothing against extravagance in expenditure, have invariably held up thrifty and economical habits to contempt and derision. So that, from a desire to deserve and preserve the respect of their neighbors, Mahomedans have, in the course of time, acquired the character of spendthrifts.

b. Besides obtaining wealth by force—which from its very nature could give no inducement to the formation of habits of abstinence—there were two principal sources of wealth open to the Musalmans during their sovereignty. Persons eminent in war or strategy, in the councils of state, or in administrative talents, obtained grants in reward. These grants were always political; but the outlet for the display of such energies has now long been closed. Amongst the talents, politically eminent habits of economy occupy no place; administrative ability is quite different from ability in business and moneymaking.

The grant was always given as a condition of military or civil service; the energy, therefore, which the holder of the grant and his descendants possessed, was always drawn off toward administrative and political results. They desired wealth for the sake of its political privileges—not for the sake of its social advantages, and never for the sake of merely possessing wealth. There was consequently an indifference to economy and a tendency to ineptitude for activity except when directed toward war and politics.

Such was the first source of our wealth. The second source was religious. Men of theological erudition or aesthetic piety were rewarded from superstitious motives, as in all countries, with extensive grants. They were rewarded because they had extinguished in themselves every kind of desire though they might, at the same time, have extinguished every kind of ability. They were indifferent to all worldly prospects; and labor spent in obtaining worldly advantages was to them labor spent in vain.

It is evident therefore that habits of luxury and idleness, which now so decidedly prevail amongst such, are due partly to the contempt with which our theologians and moralists teach us to regard habits of economy and abstinence, and partly to the circumstances under which we first obtained wealth in India. Wherever there is a Musalman family possessing wealth from the time of the Moslem government, the wealth was originally either a religious or a political grant. It was never acquired by habits of economy: in the one case the wealth was acquired by administrative, political, or military activity; in the other, it was gained by selfish piety and pompous asceticism.

c. Our habits of listlessness and inactivity are also partly due to the peculiar belief in predestination that we hold. This doctrine prevails amongst other people and in other countries, but owing to moral and historical causes its hold is not so strong as among Musalmans. When pushed to the extreme this doctrine is sufficient to stop all human progress. But, fortunately, in no age and with no people has this doctrine ever been consistently carried to all its lengths.

I do not know that the activity of our lower classes is inferior to that of the lower classes among Hindus. But this much is certain: that the Hindu is more constant in his labor and the Musalman loses heart sooner when he meets with checks in his pursuit.

Third, one large source of wealth is entirely closed to the Mahomedans—I mean interest on money lent. A considerable portion of every community is placed so as to be able to make savings but not to apply them to any profitable undertaking except lending on interest. When we see how the business of banking facilitates commerce and how it renders possible the creation of new trades and industries, it becomes apparent how, amongst Mahomedans, the connection of religion purely so-called with subjects altogether foreign to it—with criminal law, civil law, laws of inheritance, laws of property, laws of contracts, laws of bequests—has acted most injuriously on their material interests. And as material interests act as well as depend largely upon mental and moral interests, it follows therefore that we have suffered mentally and morally as well as in a worldly point of view from the connection of our Religion with law.

The prohibition against interest prevents a considerable number of people from becoming richer than they are, and consequently from having more mental comforts: in other words, from acquiring more extended knowledge. But what is the more remarkable is that, though this so-called religious prohibition prevents us from lending and thus from becoming richer, it cannot keep us from being obliged to borrow; for to prevent borrowing is physically impossible.

A considerable portion of mankind has been, still is, and will continue to be, poor. A large part of this indigent section of the community will have to borrow the means of subsistence in order to save themselves and their children from starvation. People will borrow whether you like it or not; and if there are borrowers there will necessarily be lenders.

In a society in which matters are allowed to adjust themselves, the number of borrowers, the number of lenders, and the amount of loans will always be in proportion to each other so as to satisfy the wants of the society. But if lending on interest be forbidden, the number of lenders will decline considerably though the number of borrowers will continue almost the same; consequently the amount to be lent will decrease to a much smaller sum.

Suppose that, in a healthy state of society in which there is no interference with the natural operations of trade, there were 100 lenders, 1000 borrowers and 10,000 rupees to be lent. Now if lending money on interest were forbidden many lenders would give up business. I mean those who habitually respect law and opinion—those who do not care to break the one or defy the other. Some lenders, however, will still continue to lend: those who have less respect for law and opinion, those who are audacious enough to disregard the penalties. But the amount of funds to be lent will, as a matter of course, become much smaller.

When there was no interference the borrowers had 10,000 rupees at their disposal. When interest is prohibited the same or almost the same number of borrowers have to divide among themselves a much smaller sum. And there is something still worse. The sum total having diminished while the number of borrowers is about the same, the rate of interest charged is necessarily higher than the rate which was obtained when there was no interference. Moreover, those lenders, who still continue to lend and who act against law or public opinion or both, undergo a certain amount of risk. They therefore, and with justice, charge an additional rate to cover this additional risk. The result then is that the steps taken solely with the view and intention of relieving the poorer classes have altogether a contrary effect, as they inevitably injure instead of helping them.

The diminution of the number of lenders and of the funds to be lent, the rise of the rate of interest and the additional charge for extra risk that the remaining lenders undergo, the decrease of the number of lending officers and therefore of the facilities in borrowing, and the tendency to imposition that the furtive character of transactions produces—all these take place, though in a smaller degree, when interest is not wholly forbidden but the maximum rate is sought to be fixed.

The science of political economy is a sealed book to the Musalman. I must therefore explain why, when a maximum rate is fixed, capitalists should desert the trade of money lending. The profits of all trades consist of three different items. The capitalist or trader must obtain a recompense for his abstinence—for having refrained from spending away the capital on his own gratification. Every trade has some or other risk incidental to it; the capitalist must indemnify himself for this risk. Lastly the capitalist must be recompensed for the labor and inconvenience that he undergoes in conducting and managing the business. Reward of abstinence, insurance against risk, and wages of superintendence make up the profits of a trade.

The lowest rate of profits must afford an adequate equivalent for the abstinence, risk, and exertion implied in the employment of capital. If lending money or any trade offered an exceptionally large remuneration, persons employed in other trades would give up their business and invest their capital in lending money or the trade that was more flourishing at the time.

Similarly, if lending money or any trade offered comparatively inadequate returns to the abstinence, risk, and exertion, persons engaging in it would give up their business and invest their capital in trades that yielded better returns. It is clear then that if the maximum rate of interest were authoritatively fixed, and the ordinary rate of profit were above that maximum, traders would give up their business and resort to other trades—trades in which they could get adequate returns.

But, as the necessary and effective desires of men must be satisfied and any legislative enactment or religious tenet that runs counter to them is sure to be broken, some lenders will continue to lend, and these have the opportunity of exacting extra charges for the smallness of the supply and the greater risk and inconvenience, besides getting the ordinary equivalent for abstinence. So that whether interest be entirely prohibited or only limited in amount the result is the same in kind—viz., that the borrowers will have a lesser accommodation at a greater cost.

Money will be borrowed and interest will be charged. Such is the constitution of human nature and human society. The prohibitions, therefore, which exist in the Quran must be explained away as meaning something entirely different or as applicable only to a particular society in a particular state of development and civilization.

These prohibitions against interest, in conjunction with other matters connected with law, must be separated from those parts of the Quran that strictly refer to Religion. The obligation to believe in what concerns pure Religion—the Unity of God, the Immortality of the Soul, the Inspiration of the Prophet of Arabia, and the various precepts of morality—must be separated from the obligation to believe in what relates to social and political economy—to laws and institutions.

We have seen how the prohibition of interest, instead of relieving those classes for whose benefit it is intended, does actually injure them; but what is much more serious is that it retards the formation of the habit of abstinence and economy and that of postponing immediate gratification to future happiness, and prevents the development of the spirit of self-denial and self-control and that of prudence and self-responsibility. So that the prohibition of interest has decidedly injured the moral, as well as the material, prospects of the entire Mahomedan community; and we may rest assured that no improvement will ever take place in our prospects as a class until and unless we distinguish between the obligation to believe in religious truths and obligation to believe in the propriety of civil and political laws—obligations that we now hopelessly confound together.

Another and a more active cause of our poverty is to be found in our laws of inheritance—both testamentary and intestate. A large estate is under our laws of intestate succession so divided and subdivided that in two or three generations each share comes to represent the barest subsistence. And, what is worse, there is no proper law of testamentary disposition of property to control and modify the operation of this minute subdivision.

The existing laws of inheritance are practically unjust. For when a person dies, some of his children may be old and educated enough to earn a respectable livelihood; others may be too young or inexperienced to be able to earn anything—to give equal shares to both is decidedly an unjust apportionment. Similarly, when a person dies some of his children are already in good and affluent circumstances, while others with a large number of children are living from hand to mouth and in extreme indigence—to give equal shares to both is nothing less than a violation of justice.

The compensatory process by which a law of testamentary disposition of property enables an individual to apportion fair equitable shares to his heirs is entirely wanting among Musalmans. The laws of bequests is limited by so many conditions and surrounded by so many difficulties that it is scarcely, if ever, resorted to. It affects only a limited part of a person's property and is in every respect altogether incomplete and unsatisfactory.

And, what is worse than all, these and all other similar laws have been taken out of the domain of progress by being improperly connected with Religion. They have been made part and parcel of Revealed Religion and are believed on the authority of an ignorant, superstitious, and intolerant priesthood to lie beyond the limits of progress. In truth, however, there is no real connection between Religion and the laws, social, civil, or political, under which a community lives. Religious truths transcend the powers of human understanding, while laws, being phenomenal relations, are amenable to experience. The belief in the fundamental truths of Religion is of universal and permanent obligation, that in the fitness and propriety of laws and institutions is only of local and temporary obligation, and civilization consists in the gradual amelioration and improvement of the laws and institutions of a society.

The laws of interstate succession, however wisely planned, cannot practically act with justice in every case of their application unless supplemented by a liberal and comprehensive law of testaments. But there are some points in the existing laws of inheritance that certainly require improvement. There is no reason why the child of a son or daughter who died during the lifetime of a parent should, contrary to the principles of equity, receive no share of the property of his grandfather. There is no reason why the daughter or son of a son should, and the son or daughter of a daughter should not, receive a share of the property of a deceased person.

With these necessary exceptions, the laws of intestate succession may be allowed to stand as they are; for, if complemented (but not otherwise) by a generous and comprehensive law of bequest, its consequences may be made as just and equitable as is perhaps possible under all the circumstances for human ingenuity to make.

But the law of bequest must be completely altered and remodeled for two reasons: first, in order to compensate for the inequalities due to the practical imperfections of the laws of inheritance, and, second, in order to prevent the frittering away of property by too minute subdivisions and to aid the preservation and continuance of large estates.

As the laws of succession now stand, the children of a rich Musalman parent all expect a share of their father's property and, owing to this feeling of constant expectancy, are all necessarily tainted with a certain amount of indolence; the habits of affluence in which they have been nurtured render them easily liable to encumber and eventually to lose the comparatively small property to which they succeed.

There are three reasons why it is expedient—even necessary—that at least in the present age and in India we should have large estates rather than small properties. An individual possessing a large income is able to give his children a fuller and more liberal education than one commanding a small income. The children of a rich parent, having thus had a liberal education and having been brought up in comparative affluence, will strive to attain the social position of their father and of the brother who has succeeded to the property, and will thus benefit themselves in two ways: by increasing their stock of wealth, and by invigorating their habits of economy and activity and improving their spirit of self-dependence. There are thus three ways in which a larger property acts favorably. First, by strengthening habits of diligence and economy and developing the sense of self-responsibility, in other words by raising the character and elevating the moral nature of man. Second, by increasing the desire for wealth and therefore by increasing wealth and establishing a high standard of comfort and living. And, third, by increasing the resources available for education and therefore by diffusing knowledge and establishing a high standard of education and mental attainment.

I believe it has now been made sufficiently clear that the decline of knowledge amongst the superior classes of Musalmans is owing especially to the decline of wealth; and that the decline of wealth is due to the absence of a law of bequests from our laws of succession, to the prohibition against interest, to the habits of expensiveness and want of economy that have been bequeathed to us by our forefathers as a common inheritance, and to the belief in arbitrarily decreed predestination.

Whoever wishes to ameliorate the condition of the Musalmans of India must strongly and constantly insist on channeling their talents in new directions—though now torpid—that they undoubtedly possess and that under their own sovereigns their forefathers displayed in political and administrative achievements, in subduing nations and winning empires. He must preach to them in lecture rooms and from pulpits that unless they channel their energies and talents into now accessible paths they are sure to lose those energies and talents and must thus permanently accept a subordinate position amongst the units constituting the present and future social organization of Hindustan. He must also devise the best means of entailing and perpetuating landed property and improving the laws of testamentary succession—of removing all moral blame from those who lend money on interest—and of so modifying our belief in predestination so as to prevent it from making us apathetic and listless, careless and improvident.

Habits that have descended to us from preceding generations are not easily altered or modified. But there is no doubt that the present adversity and the prospect of future degeneration have even now aroused us into activity and the practice of forethought, and there is certainly a considerable stir at present among the superior classes of Musalmans likely to produce beneficial results. The attainment of those results, however, which depend on the alteration of substantive juridical laws, is immediately possible. For interest on loans, though held sinful, is taken by many Musalmans both high and low; and if courts of justice were to act according to the received doctrines of Mahomedan law and refuse interest to a Mahomedan suitor, no time would be lost by us in calling upon the Legislature to modify the practice.

The Legislature should now step forward and allow the same latitude to the Musalman in the matter of bequests as it does in that of interest. Though the courts of law without exception decree interest to a Musalman suitor, they will not at present, as things stand, hold valid the bequest—to take effect after his death—of a Mahomedan gentleman, of his entire estate, to a single heir or to a few heirs. There is ample evidence, however, to show that the preservation of family prop-

erty in its integrity by some means or other has become a favorite object of solici-
tude with Musalman gentlemen of property. Some legal excuse or some religious
pretext is generally laid hold of to prevent the division of the property and to secure its possession or management to a single heir.

I know of many such instances. Sometimes the pretext is a deed falsifying
facts, in other cases it is a deed falsifying intentions. In some cases it is a deed ac-
knowledging an indebtedness that is not a fact; at other times it is a deed making
over the entire property to the service of God and thus drawing a veil over the un-
controlled possession of the entire property by the manager or trustee.

These are means liable to frustrate, but they clearly prove that our landed proprietors are now quite alive to the dangers of a too minute subdivision of their estates. A single section added to the Indian Succession Act (X of 1865), allowing
Musalmans to bequeath their properties in the way they choose, would obviate the
necessity of having recourse to excuses liable to frustration and would, by enabling
us to preserve properties from being broken up into mere fragments, be the greatest boon conferred upon us by the Legislature.

The provision is indeed sure to call forth the opposition of those intolerant
and priest-ridden people who look more to the appliances than to the responsibilities, and to the doctrines than to the practical workings of religion; who are
content to see untruthfulness characterize the conduct of men so that the forms
of religion be preserved; who are willing that the duties of religion should be violated and that property intended for the service of God should be devoted to the
benefit of trustees in order that dogmatic teachings of the church may be preserved intact.

But the landed gentry, the class most interested, will hail the permission to bequeath their property in the way they like as their greatest charter. Nor is there
anything in such a measure at all likely to interfere with the Musalman religion,
there being nothing in it of a compulsory nature. The Legislature does not ask any
Musalman lender to take interest from his borrowers; nevertheless, it accedes to
his wishes when he claims the interest. We do not ask the Legislature to compel us
to bequeath our property in any particular way—nor is it likely that it will ever do
so; but if the measure I propose be passed, the Legislature will only have given a
sanction to our testamentary wishes and have put our bequests in the way of being
carried out in accordance with our desires.

The property of a Musalman gentleman is absolutely his own; his heirs have
no right to it whatsoever in his lifetime. A Muhammadan may be on his deathbed,
when he cannot possibly be in full possession of his senses or faculties, when he is
liable to be greatly influenced by the false attentions of interested parties, and
when persons with sinister motives have every facility of successfully urging their
claims on him—a Musalman in such a state of extremity may give away the whole
of his property to a comparative stranger. Why, then, may not a Musalman, when
he is in good health, when he is in full possession of his faculties and knows what
he is about, when he cannot be imposed upon by the false attentions of interested
parties, and when his acts themselves are not irrevocable—why may not a
Muhammadan in such a state of full consciousness make a division of his property
to take place after his death, especially when he is capable of revoking it afterwards

by another division? It is but necessary to put the question in order to see the absurdity of the prevailing law.

The Legislature may and does adjudge to a Musalman interest on money lent; similarly it may and should enable him to dispose of his property by will in the way he chooses. Surely it may do all these without being chargeable in either case with religious interference.

The provisions are only permissive and cannot therefore excite any religious prejudices unless indeed we are, as a class, beyond remedy and past all improvement. We hope, however, that we are still amenable to progress—still capable of advancement; and I am firmly convinced that we are still able to reform our doctrines and practices. This is the faith that alone prevents educated Musalmans from actual secession.

Interest on loans, though forbidden by their laws, is taken by numerous Musalmans, Sunni as well as Shiah. It is time now that a law be enacted enabling us to make testamentary dispositions of our property. And I am certain that when the law should be enacted most, if not all, Musalman gentlemen of property will take advantage of it in order to preserve their property from being frittered away by too much subdivision and thus save themselves from the necessity of planning false excuses and executing false deeds.

With the extension of the practice of moneylending and will-making, habits of luxury and expensiveness will gradually decline, habits of economy and abstinence will by degrees be strengthened, while the love of idle repose will be more and more replaced by the desire for exertion and activity.

But, in order to make the practice of moneylending and executing wills prevail to any large extent, Religion properly called must be entirely dissevered from laws civil or political. It must once and for all be understood that there is no connection whatsoever, either necessary or even contingent, between Religion in its pure sense and civil and juridical laws. Religious truths are transcendental to the understanding and therefore lie beyond the limits of progress. Social and political phenomena are amenable to the experience and the understanding of man; the laws of a society are therefore capable of modification and improvement. And unless thus modified and improved, a society is sure to decline and gradually to disappear and to give way to another whose substantive civil laws are being constantly altered and remodeled in conformity to the increased and increasing knowledge of the laws of living.

This union of Religion with social customs and juridical laws has done the most serious injury to the Muhammadans in every part of the world; and unless soon and timely dissolved there is every probability of the Muhammadan name becoming a by-word and the Muhammadan races a laughing stock among civilized nations. The rapid and general decline of Muhammadan society contemporaneously in Asia, Africa, and Europe is due to this one single but mighty cause; and the gradual and general progress of Christian society in Europe is due to the success with which they have broken through this union between Religion and Civil Laws.

The history of Islam from the time of the Prophet down to the times of the Abbasi dynasty in Egypt and southwest Asia and those of the Omavi dynasty in southern Spain is the history of an uninterrupted success. This general success proves that the social structures that the Arabs overthrew were so rotten to the core that the very first shock of a contest with a nation, in whom the first enthusiasm of a new religion was still high, was sufficient to prostrate it completely, and that the social structure that grew up instead, though imperfect, must have been better suited to the exigencies.

Those numerous schisms of Religion, which occurred in the early history of Islam, and which indicate the existence at least of theological and metaphysical activity, all took place during the ascendancy of the Abbasi dynasty; the mo'tazelahs, who counted among themselves several distinguished Khalifahs, being as regards numbers the largest of the dissenting sects and—what is more important—having as regards doctrine very nearly broken asunder the union between Religious Truths and Civil Laws. But since the downfall of the Abbasi Khalifahs, even religious development has ceased to be perceptible in Musalman countries; and the culture of metaphysics, which formerly gave rise to many systems of philosophy, has now for several hundred years altogether ceased.

The Muhammadans established themselves in India at a much later date, but their Government had neither stability nor freedom—the two essentials of good government. Nor did they in India at the time of their greatest ascendancy materially advance knowledge—abstract or concrete, theoretical or practical—while in a worldly point of view the Hindus have always been much better off than ourselves, and in all the points that go to make up material prosperity we are essentially inferior to the Hindus of the present age.

This general decline of Musalman society must have been due to general causes embracing all the countries that they possessed; and I firmly believe that this decline is due to the connection of Religion with Customs, Laws, and Institutions. To a certain point, no doubt, it aided progress, but the limits were soon reached; from that time it has been a stumbling block to further developments. Not only has it prevented further progress but it has actually reduced the stock of knowledge and taken away from the measure of civilization that we had already acquired.

That this inability to break through the union of Religion and Law is really the cause of our decline may be proved from the history of the Christian Religion. For those nations who were able to assert and maintain the Liberty of Private Judgment have made continued progress in the arts and sciences and in civilization in general; while those nations that were unable to assert the Right of Private Judgment and succumbed to the authority of the Popes, the Bishops, and the Inquisitions have not only made no progress but have on the contrary considerably declined in civilization and power, although they won for themselves, and for a time preserved, extensive empires and almost overpowering political and military prestige among the other nations of Europe.

Such was the glorious condition of Spain; but now it has no voice in European diplomacy and politics and no weight in the councils of European Powers. This decline is due to nothing but the fact that the Spanish Inquisition was too powerful for the disruption of the union of religious ideas and truths with those dogmatic doctrines and laws that the theological and priestly classes are fond of laying down on every subject of human activity and in every department of human life. It seems, however, that the Spaniards have at last come to an understanding of the causes of their decline, and that the example and literature of other European nations are awakening them to new life and vigor.

In Turkey, too, the action of European ideas and modes of thinking has, to some extent, weakened the strength of the connection between Religion and Law, and the juxtaposition of the Christian and Muhammadan populations is a guarantee of its further diminution. Similarly, in India the competition of several religious and legal systems is weakening the connection between Religion and Law; but our hopes of regeneration mainly lie in the influence of English education and the diffusion of European modes of thinking.

This is the point toward which is laboring that much to be revered friend of the Musalmans, Sayyed Ahmed Khan, who has generously taken upon himself the thankless task of trying to improve the Musalmans in spite of themselves. I doubt if, within the memory of Musalmans in India, there has been such an instance of noble self-denial that, for the sake of doing good, has endured so much obloquy and suffered so much ill-will at the hands of his fellows. A striking contrast to the career of those who, possessing considerable influence with the ruling race and holding social position rarely attainable even by men of older and higher lineage or of larger and more durable incomes, devote their powers of tact and energy to the advancement of their own individual reputation amongst their equals and of their own personal importance amongst the governing classes.

CHAPTER 12

ISLAM AND CIVILIZATION

Muhammad Farid Wajdi

Excerpt from Muhammad Farid Wajdi. *Al-Madaniyah wa al-Islam*. Egypt: Matba'at Hindiyah, 1901, pp. 23–47. Translated by Christine Dykgraaf and Kamran Talattof.

RELIGION AND SCIENCE

THE GULF BETWEEN THEISTS AND SCIENTISTS IS NOT a recent development, for history tells us that such a gulf has existed for ages. Furthermore, there have been quarrels and troubles between the two sides in diverse countries the world over. However, the early periods can be distinguished from our present era in the severity of these problems and the harshness of the debate. Many philosophers of science were sentenced to death by poison, the sword, or the yoke for merely defending their call to enlighten their fellow citizens against the delusions that would put down reason and douse its light. As far as our present era is concerned, Mr. Bartlu, a French foreign minister and one of that country's greatest chemists, claims that science, having obtained its absolute freedom, does not fear usurpation at the hands of religion. Mr. Bartlu speaks the truth. When we read the refutations and disparagements put forward by religious leaders, it is clear to us that they were relentlessly shooting arrows of apostasy at their prey. Yet, religious leaders also immediately took a vow to hide their lack of agreement concerning this slyness and disloyalty on behalf of science from the people, thus failing to clarify their qualms concerning the foundations of science.

In his book, *Religion: Its Source, Forms, and Development*, Mr. Benjamin Constant discusses the diseases that weaken the body of human communities by means of false beliefs. He then suggests that the treatment for this disease of society could be achieved through nothing less than the freedom of conscience, freedom of faiths, personal freedom, and, in short, all necessary freedoms. Then he said,

In this way, the religions may become purified from their own disease. But we do not think that this will materialize at all because it is believed that this will render religion baseless. But since the fundamentals of religion contradict science and are indeed opposed to it, the stance that religions are to be exterminated arises.

One may be deeply astonished by the fact that this famous scholar passes this judgment on all religions without exception—that they may be eradicated and ended—because he did not study all of them thoroughly. If he had studied Islam first, even if it were a superficial study, he would have realized before all else that Islam in its foundations does not contradict science, as is the case with other religions.

In this article, we will limit our discussion to the strongest refutations against religion and their weaknesses as based on the sayings of famous European scientists. This is with the intent that our reader understands the direction that European scientific thought has taken and becomes certain, after we cite the basics of Islam, that Islam is truly the destiny of souls and the grace of spirits.

We said that Mr. Constant had warned that all religions are justified through reasoning. He said,

> All principles, no matter how useful they are at any one time, inherently include within themselves the root of that which impedes development in the future. Any principle with the passing of time takes on an immortal form that denies human reasoning its pursuit of discoveries, which advance and purify it each day. When that happens, the religious sense is immediately severed from that principle and another principle is sought after that does not challenge or jeopardize science, and the human intellect remains unsettled until it finds one.

These people [scientists] painstakingly studied mankind and hewed the path that man should take to reach his happiness. They knew that man could only perform the important task assigned to him by divine providence if he utilized all of the faculties and talents given to him and if he did not suppress any of his emotions. Then the scientists looked into the past and saw that what delayed humanity in reaching the noble states available to it was submission to the decrees of religious men who claimed that they were the commanders and the leaders of religions. Scientists challenged and refuted these men and accused their teachings of having led to the backwardness of man, and generally lowering him from an elevated state. Feuerbach expressed this idea sarcastically when he said:

> Religious virtue, more specifically the highest virtue, which is the virtue of the saints, is to abandon civil and political life and to put aside all other acts and material matters as if these were impermissible play (amusements, thoughtlessness). In this way, one pines away for heaven while never pleasing oneself and living with a broken heart. The end result is that one's emotions and natural inclinations are deadened and the Self is abased and finally annihilated (killed).

European scientists saw, since material evidence was in their hands, that the advancement of mankind was dependent upon the development and advancement of science which in turn was dependent upon the intellect's freedom from religion's chains and shackles so that man was controlled by nothing but scientific research. The goal was to eradicate the discord that had existed between scientists and theists in the past as a result of the latter's attempts at control. Mr. Block said,

> The advancement of the mental faculties and having apt judgment on things is dependent upon the advancement of science. We have come to this understanding through the improvement of our information. Once substantiated and through relying on close, detailed investigations into these matters, our new understanding destroyed the foundations of many of our previous errors.

However, because European scientists believe that freedom of the intellect and science is the aim of all material and spiritual happiness, they cannot write the history of their oppression without great irritability and furious desire to see the past avenge those who wish to repeat it. Let us translate a short passage from the sayings of famous Larousse so that we may see the agitation with which Western scholars remember the oppression of those early years. He said,

> If we say that the performance of good deeds demands a belief in rational things they say "No, no!" Then they endeavor to debase the human intellect that claims that it has the right to differentiate between good and evil and between justice and injustice. Once the "eye of their intellect" is blinded and its faculty of mental perception blurred to the extent that miracles are perceived as ordinary things and that which is believed to be evil and vice is considered virtue, religion returns and says "Obey." Obey whom? Should we obey the intellect, natural duties, or emotions, or should we obey the true and beneficial laws to humanity that are a result of these same principles? No. They mean you should blindly obey the one who rules in the name of God even if he orders you to kill your leader or your father or orders you to commit a general mass murder because you do not possess the soul or a conscience. They would have you believe that you are dead: obliterated in God.

The hostility of Europe's scientists to extant religions has reached this degree, even farther, but are we to conclude from this hostility that they have abandoned religiosity altogether and claim that they have dispensed with their knowledge, their humility, and subjectivity to their creator, the creator of all things? No. They admit to theists that they go even farther in deducing with the aid of their own scientific research that religious feelings are instinctive to the human soul, which is no less evident or influential than a human's need for food. Joseph Geyser, the German philosopher, said in his book *The History of Beliefs:* "Religion is as eternal as the feeling that produces it, but religious sciences as all other sciences must be willing to develop in accordance with intellectual development. This is similar to the relation that is always present between inherent rights and legislative science: because rights do not change, legislation should change and be corrected all the time."

Mr. Ernest Ranan wrote in his book, The History of Religions: "It is possible for everything we love and everything we consider pleasurable and blissful in this world to disappear and fade away, and it is possible for freedom to use intellectual ability and science and industry to become untenable, but it is impossible for religiosity to cease or fade away. Rather it will remain through all eternity as conclusive evidence of the falsity of any materialistic ideologies that wish to confine human thought to the lowly defiling ways of the material life."

In short, reliable European scientists agree that it is impossible for the instinct toward religiosity to disappear from the soul just as it is impossible for the soul to lose the instinct of love or hatred. However, they have also established, and their books present evidence of this, that no existing religion is good enough to be the common religion for the entirety of present-day humanity. Why is that? They say it is because the principles of religion are not compatible with the principles of science, and because their texts [religious texts] oppose rudimentary principles of the intellect, and because they limit matters in a way that opposes the freedom that the human intellect must possess. That is why a European philosopher said that religion would have been unsusceptible to a decline and an end had its principles been free from limitations and likewise its foundations void of shackles, for man is inclined to absolute perfection and possesses a readiness to advance that defies description. Yet, you might claim that if any of the present religions can bring together the feelings of religiosity that are implanted in mankind and exist between matter, which are required and incumbent in life and lead the human community to that universal happiness to which scientific research purports to lead us, then it would be incumbent upon us to admit religion's indispensability. Larousse said the following after he found fault in religions that pressure mankind to fulfill its duties:

> Rather it is the intellect in general and one's strong disposition and emotions, which evolve in the shadow of this general knowledge, which itself becomes more pure and refined as civilization and information develop. Therefore, if you define religion to be the sum of thoughts that are good for bringing all human individuals together into a single community that enjoys material benefits and is intellectually enlightened, then you can say that religion is indispensable for the human race.

Moreover, proof that no matter how advanced the human intellect may become it cannot survive without religion is found in the fact that a group of European scientists formulated a religion they called natural religion in which they only included laws and principles that were proven by evidence and sensory perception. In our citation of the principles of Islam we shall mention the most important principles of this new religion so that Muslims can truly see that their religion has left no field unchallenged and nothing unsaid: "Do they seek for other than the Religion of Allah? All creatures in the heavens and on earth have, willing or unwilling, bowed to His Will [Accepted Islam] and to Him shall they all be brought back."[1]

WHAT IS ISLAM?

Which man of eloquence attempts to speak about Islam and does not suffer total and evident failure and an incapacity to give this sublime subject its due right of elucidation? And which man of wisdom embarks upon verifying the wonders of this true religion without finding himself inadequate and inferior? As the saying goes, "Had all the trees of this world become pencils and had the seven seas provided the ink, the words of God would not be exhausted."

One must possess rich knowledge and a noble, universal, and general genius to be able to understand and explain those eternal laws that are subjected to the passing of eras, centuries, and epochs, and yet remain the same. Time makes the laws more youthful and time clothes them with garments of renewal. Generations entrust these laws to future generations. None can understand the laws except those to whom God gives enlightened visions by the light of religious knowledge and reveals the suns of eloquence to the sky of their thoughts: "And such are the parables We set forth for mankind, but only those who have knowledge understand them."[2]

We say with all volition and complete independence—aided by science and supported by the intellect—that Islam is the apex for which man was created and made ready to ascend to and for whose sake instinct was put in man to persevere in searching for it. Rather, Islam is the soul's desire that by its nature seeks and aspires for the greatest goal and the most sublime aim. It continues to develop in all stages and phases of life in persistent search of this precious and difficult goal, which, being attained, frees the soul from confusion and is satisfied in attaining other hopes and desires.

Yes, Islam is the goal of perfection, for which men of wisdom and knowledge have persisted and died to attain. Islam is the straightest law and the greatest canon that God has bestowed upon this weak species so it might provide for its needs, find happiness in this life, and have it as a basis to count on in times of hardship. God bestowed it upon this species as a seal for religions and a crown on the head of time during a period when development of the human intellect had fully grown to be evidence of God. He bestowed upon his subjects that which speaks of truth and speaks out openly for justice and shows us the true path by example so that man has no excuse to refuse Him after he has reached that maturity of the mind.

Islam is a religion that inadvertently benefited from natural science, without the experts realizing it. Its texts have become, in this century, clearer than rays of light and more easily flowing in the mind than rays of light flowing in water. There is no evidence that experiments led to or that theories established by the witness of the senses influenced the advancement of man or the improvement of the construction of civilization. Based on the echo of the sound of a Quranic verse or Prophetic tradition, however, one may feel that any work or activity accompanied by scientists on this earth to elevate the state of humanity is only intended to bring empirical proof to the true principles of Islamic religion. "We will show them Our Signs in the universe and also among their own selves, until it becomes manifest to them that the Quran is the Truth. Is it not enough that thy Lord is Witness over all things?"[3]

Based on what we presented earlier, the course of Islam cannot be stopped in any manner possible, because there is no difference between stopping it and stopping human civilization and the ascensions of the souls, and between erasing the practical and scientific texts and returning mankind to its primitive state. This is a matter that neither all men or *jinn* will be able to do even if they supported each other: "In vain would they extinguish Allah's light with their mouths, but Allah will not allow but that His light should be perfected, even though the Unbelievers may detest (it)."[4]

Let us begin now, with Allah's help, with the affirmation that all that we read of modern civilization is not in accordance with the principles of the Islamic faith except for an occasional ray of the sun or drop from the sea. It would then be easier for us to arrive at our goal if we speak about the bases of present civilization and then we assert some of the basics of the Mohammedan faith in a clear and plain way. So first we say:

WHAT IS RELIGION?

The term "religion" is very old, as old as religion itself and it is common among all human groups present or past, uncivilized or civilized. Men, however, did not comprehend its true meaning, which was delivered by divine righteous ones who speak of the creator's mercy and providence. One who examines history finds that different peoples have seen several stages of development in understanding the meaning of this word according to the development of the capabilities of the human intellect to understand intelligible phenomena.

The ancients knew religion only as a sum of public celebrations in which animals or prisoners of war were sacrificed to please those they worshipped and to calm their anger. When human reasoning and the intellectual instinct grew by means of the sciences and arts, the meanings of religion slowly became clearer and were slowly approached the intended meaning of God, which religions came to command people to understand.

Before we speak of the essence of religion in the meaning intended for Islam here, we must first speak of what European scientists understand of this word after they examined the sciences and amply researched the universe for its laws and principles. In this endeavor, some of the empirical evidence for our theory, that every step the scientist makes to understand truths is evidently an approach toward Islam, becomes clear. We say that, after European scientists went through every single stage, exposing themselves to all kinds of scientific temptations and reading the wonderful history of science from the beginning of Socrates time until now, they realized that peace has become all encompassing and that the sciences are experiencing their golden years. They realize that this universe has a powerful, wise creator who possesses all attributes of perfection and who is above any hint of imperfection, and that God, may He be exalted, created the universe according to a specific order. If one patiently examines this order, one can deduce from it empirically those sublime attributes. One can also learn a few lessons from them which, when followed through, are easily understood, and will sufficiently replace thousands of theorems and guiding principles that were presented to the people who subsequently bowed their heads in submission to them without any understanding of the wisdom behind them or their consequences. Then the scientists saw in their examining of the order and laws of the universe that the Creator, may He be exalted, is too sublime to be in need of a being from this His own creation. Rather, God is sufficient in and of himself. Then they said that this sufficiency of God in Himself did not prevent Him from caring for His creatures in a manner that is evidence of His great mercy and his abundant compassion. A simple examination of this universe provides empirical evidence of this theory.

Look at the different kinds of plants and animals, their lowest to their highest orders: you will see the effects of this Great Mercy made totally manifest to man, which forces man to love the great Creator. God has left none of His creation without providing it with means of sustenance and with defenses against calamity and destruction, except that which occurs due to the order of the workings of the universe on behalf of a higher mercy and more sublime compassion upon the universe at large. Furthermore, a God with such a nature does not force man to worship except in a manner that brings immense wisdom and great benefit to a human being, all human beings, and indeed everything in nature. Because a mere reflection on all kinds of creatures gives us clear evidence that their creator did not create them just so He might turn around and destroy and annihilate them, we can be certain that when he created them, He wanted their well-being and continued existence. God has also put in them the capacity to develop and advance to a level of knowledge He has preordained. Man is related to God in the same manner that all other creatures are related to Him, however man is distinguished above other creatures because he is the highest form of creation. Man is, therefore, more susceptible to the law of development and advancement.

These are the facts, and one who ponders the level of advancement that man has reached from his beginning until now realizes that God, may He be exalted, gave man characteristics to help him continue to develop and advance to a level that the human intellect has not yet fully reached. They said that since the actions of God are devoid of frivolities and contradictions, then the desired worship of God should be consistent with the constant and prevailing laws in the whole universe, and should be suitable to the desires and feelings imbedded in human nature. Based on this scientific given, which cannot be doubted a big group of European scientists founded their natural religion. Listen here to what one of its supporters, philosopher Jules Simon, had to say on the subject: "We perform in this life the duties that God had ordained for us under His protection and providence. When our lives end, God either rewards or punishes us." He then mentioned the reason that necessitates either reward or punishment, saying: "What necessitates good rewards is man's compliance with his own law and doing good deeds. As for man's law, it is man's preservation of himself and his advancement of his own characteristics, his love and service of his brethren, and the love and worship of His Creator. But what is the manner in which man worships God? Performing one's duties and doing good deeds is the center of worship and love and work, and fidelities are in themselves worship and prayer. Being faithful to one's country is in itself a service to God. This is natural religion. This is natural worship. All the principles of our faith are clear and evident. Its principles are the belief in the existence of God who is all powerful and unchanging, the beliefs that He created all universes and made them governed by general laws and canons, and the belief in the existence of another world that gives us the promise of this life and rightly rewards all actions. This is our belief. As for our prayer, it is having our hearts filled with the love of God and love of man, and to have a firm desire to perform our duties and serve God in doing good deeds."

From this, we may deduce that the believers in this new, natural religion do not detest physical worship at all, as it could be understood from the sayings of Jules Simon in another instance. However, they do not lead to good moral benefit. They want their religion to revive their hearts and purify them from impurities. Kant, the famous philosopher, said: "Outward worship is not bad unless it is considered an end, not a means. It can be very beneficial if it is only considered as a means to enliven and strengthen noble sentiments in the human soul."

We deduce four important matters from the above remarks, which constitute the European scientists' belief in religion. These are: 1) the belief that God is sufficient in Himself [independent] from us and our actions, and that the good deeds we perform aim only at our own benefit: 2) that God is compassionate to mankind and wants his well being, and that He does not require worship except that which is for mankind's good: 3) that worship should be consistent with the fixed laws of life, and that it should be suitable to human nature not conflicting with it, which may lead to its destruction: and 4) that physical worship should be considered a means to purify and cleanse the soul, not an end in itself.

We say that these four matters, which the human intellect reached "in earth's old age" and which bewildered and amazed scientists of the nineteenth century, are nothing but a single ray of Islamic religion, a single drop from its wide sea. To convince you more we shall here mention the noble texts that express these four matters in the same order. First, the Almighty said: "And I labor on behalf of those who labor for themselves."

This is our belief in understanding what religion is. I found it in total agreement with the intellect and science, and it is in total agreement with the fixed laws of nature. Since the European scientists' refutations of religion were not generally directed against religion from this basic direction, which is the direction upon which the rest of the foundations of religion are based, it is our prerogative, then, to proclaim loudly that Islam is too high and too noble to be subjected to that disgraceful criticism. It is too great and sublime to be subject to anyone's refutation.

These four principles are considered by the scientists of natural religion as the basis upon which every principle in law is founded which, when acted upon, lead to man's advancement to the point of perfection that this species (although the most advanced) was intended to reach. Since science is generally responsible for finding these principles of advancement for humanity, they consider every principle that is reached through that approach (scientific approach), as a religious principle, that, when followed, will be considered a service to God.

As for the religious principles that came with old tales and myths from thousands of years ago, scientists have found their truths elsewhere, and have therefore abandoned them completely. Kant said: "The only true religion contains nothing but laws or principles that can be applied and that we ourselves feel are absolutely necessary, and that are devoid of myths and the teachings of the clergy." It was as if Kant wanted to implicate the Muslims in God's saying: "That is a nation that has already passed away: there awaits it whatever it has earned, while you will have what you have earned. You will not be questioned about what they have been doing."[5]

NOTES

1. Al-Quran. 3 : 83 trans. Yusuf Ali. Princeton: Princeton University Press.
2. Al-Quran. 29 : 43 trans. Yusuf Ali. Princeton: Princeton University Press.
3. The Quran. trans. Muhammad Zafrulla Khan. 2nd ed. London: Curzon Press, 1974. p.481.
4. Al-Quran. 9 : 32 trans. Yusuf Ali. Princeton: Princeton University Press, 1988.
5. Al-Quran. trans. T. B. Irving. Brattleboro, VT: Amana Books, 1985.

IV. ISLAMIC MODERNISM AND THE ISSUE OF WOMEN

CHAPTER 13

POLYGAMY

Moulavi Chiragh Ali

Moulavi Chiragh Ali. *Proposed Political, Legal, and Social Reforms in the Ottoman Empire and Other Muhammadan States.* Bombay: Education Society's Press, 1883, pp. 118–29.

SOCIAL REFORMS

91. HAVING SHOWN HOW FUTILE AND INSUBSTANTIAL are the grounds on which the Rev. Mr. MacColl argues as to the hopeless task of introducing innovations and improvements in a Mussulman state, I will now test the grounds for the utter despondence he professes to feel for any reasonable reforms being introduced into Moslem society as it now exists, and try to establish that had he been guided by the hallowed tenets of the Quran, of which he seems to be so wholly ignorant, he would have left me no room for this present refutation.

The Reverend gentleman has recorded the following sweeping remark:

Apart from its attitude toward subject races, Mohammedanism carries in its bosom three incurable vices which, being of the essence of the system, bar for ever all possible degradation of woman, and the institution of slavery: the imprisonment of the human intellect within the narrow circle of knowledge possessed by an able and uncultivated Bedouin of the sixth century; the inevitable penalty of death for forsaking Islam.[1]

I will review all these so-called irremediable "vices" in the system of Islam.

THE POSITION OF WOMEN

92. The position of women was ameliorated to a greater degree by the mission of Muhammad than might have been expected by the dispensations of all reformers and prophets prior to him. Before the social amendments introduced by Muhammad throughout Arabia, an unlimited license of polygamy and capricious divorces, together with a revolting system of concubinage, had been prevalent. Some tribes had the nefarious practice of murdering their infant daughters to avoid the disgrace of being fathers-in-law, and those girls who escaped the horrible doom of their fathers never received any inheritance from them at their death. There were also some other tribes whose people were allowed by custom to marry their father's widows, as well as two sisters at one and the same time. The wives of a deceased father were, in the eye of his surviving sons, a sort of goods and chattel or personal possessions, void of life and humanity. They had no respect for the gentle sex, nor showed them any reverence while addressing them; and some, the most savage of them all, went the length of slandering virtuous women with an unbridled and licentious tongue. The dress and demeanor of the females themselves stood in need of improvement. Female orphans, when young, were maltreated by their guardians, who used to marry a great number of them in order to obtain their property, and then to forsake them in an impoverished state, forlorn and friendless. The Quran gradually improved and elevated the degraded condition of women by curtailing, in the first place, the unlimited number of wives to four, and even this latitude was made strictly conditional on the husband feeling confident that he could deal justly—equitably by them all; and, in the second place, declaring it impossible to deal equitably with more than one wife even if men "would fain do so," and thus virtually abolishing polygamy.

93. The new connubial laws imposed by the Prophet of Islam on his followers suppressed the facility of divorce by certain wise, judicious, and discouraging restrictions, reasonable and consonant to the interests of the parties concerned. The Quran advised and exhorted the Arabs to refrain from their evil practices regarding their wives. Muhammad abolished the institution of concubinage by doing away with slavery,[2] and countenancing marriage with the then-existing female slaves otherwise destined to be concubines.[3] But against the murder of infant daughters his invectives were trenchant in the highest degree. He abrogated it by reprimanding this unnatural vice in the Quran, and threatening its perpetrators with the future punishment awaiting their crime.[4] Thus was infanticide exterminated out of Arabia and all parts of the Muhammadan world. The law of inheritance was established for the first time in the Quran in the interest of females throughout Arabia.[5] Marrying a father's widow or two sisters at one and the same time, were terribly denounced by Muhammad as heinous offenses,[6] and widows were no more to be disposed of as a part of their deceased husband's possessions.[7]

Men were enjoined to treat the sex with deference;[8] and perfect reverence was prescribed to be observed in speaking to them. The suppression of slander was the next subject that engaged the Prophet's attention, and he ordained corporeal punishment on those who calumniated virtuous women.[9] Reforms were also introduced in the dress and general deportment of women.[10] Persons entrusted with female orphans during their minority were inhibited from marrying their wards.[11]

All these beneficial measures were fraught with incalculable advantage to the debased condition of women who, by these innovations in their social sphere of life, were greatly relieved from the miseries and insults they had hitherto suffered at the hands of males.

94. Some verses of the Quran bearing on the subjects treated above are given below:

1. O Men! Fear your Lord, who hath created you of one soul, and of him created his wife, and from these twain hath spread abroad so many men and women. And fear ye God, in whose name ye ask mutual favors—and respect women. Verily is God watching you!

3. And if ye are apprehensive that ye shall not deal fairly with orphans, then, of other women who seem good in your eyes, marry but two, or three, or four; and if ye still fear that ye shall not act equitably, then one only: or the slaves whom ye have acquired: this will make justice on your part easier. And give women their dowry as a free gift, but if of their own free will they kindly give up ought thereof to you, then enjoy it as convenient, and profitable.

8. Men ought to have a part of what their parents and kindred leave, and women a part of what their parents and kindred leave: whether it be little or much, let them have a stated portion.

23. O Believers! It is not allowed you to be heirs of your wives against their will; not to hinder them from marrying in order to take from them part of the dowry you had given them, unless they have been guilty of undoubted lewdness; but deal kindly with them; for if ye are estranged from them haply [by extension] ye are estranged from that in which God hath placed abundant good.

24. And if ye be desirous to exchange one wife for another, and have given one of them a talent, make no deduction from it. Would ye take it by slandering her, and with manifest wrong?

25. How, moreover, could ye take it, when one of you hath gone in unto the other, and they have received from you a strict bond of union?

26. And marry not women whom your fathers have married: for this is a shame and hateful, and an evil way: though what is past may be allowed.

29. And whoever of you is not rich enough to marry free believing women, then let him marry such of your believing maidens as have fallen into your hands as slaves; God well knoweth your faith. Ye are sprung the one from the other. Marry them then, with the leave of their masters, and give them a fair dower: but let them be chaste and free from fornication, and not entertainers of lovers.

38. Men are superior to women on account of the qualities with which God hath gifted the one above the other, and on account of the outlay they make from their substance for them. Virtuous women are obedient, careful during the husband's absence, because God hath of them been careful. But chide those for whose

refractoriness ye have cause to fear; remove them into sleeping-chambers apart, and scourge[12] them: but if they are obedient to you, then seek not occasion against them: Verily God is High, Great!

39. And if ye fear a breach between man and wife, then send a judge chosen from his family, and a judge chosen from her family; if they are desirous of agreement, God will effect a reconciliation between them: Verily God is knowing, apprised of all!

126. Moreover, they will consult thee in regard to women: Say: God hath instructed you about them; and His will is rehearsed to you, in the Book, concerning female orphans to who ye give not their legal due, and whom you refuse to marry; also with regard to weak children: and that ye deal with fairness toward orphans. Ye cannot do a good action, but verily God knoweth it.

127. And if a wife fear ill usage or aversion on the part of her husband, then shall it be no fault in them, if they can agree with mutual agreement, for agreement is best. Men's souls are prone to avarice, but if ye act kindly and piously, then verily your actions are not unnoticed by God!

128. And ye May not have it at all in your power to treat your wives with equal justice, even though you fain would do so: but yield not wholly to disinclination, so that ye leave one of them as it were in suspense: if ye come to an understanding, and act in the fear of God, then verily God is Forgiving, Merciful.

129. But if they separate, God can compensate both out of His abundance; for God is vast, Wise.[13]

152. Say: Come, I will rehearse what your Lord hath made binding on you—that ye assign not ought to Him as sharers of His divine honor, and ye be good to your parents; and that ye slay not your children because of poverty—for them and for you will We provide: and that ye come not near to pollutions outward and inward: and that ye slay not any one whom God hath forbidden you, unless for a just cause. This hath He enjoined on you: haply ye will understand.[14]

33. Moreover, kill not your children for fear of want: for them and for you We will provide. Verily, then killing them is a great wickedness.[15]

4. They who defame virtuous women, and bring not four witnesses, scourge them with fourscore stripes, and receive ye not their testimony for ever, for these are impious persons.

23. Verily, they who throw out charges against virtuous but careless women, who yet are believers, are cursed in this world and in the world to come, and a terrible punishment doth await them.

31. And speak to the believing women that they refrain their looks, and observe continence; and that they display not their ornaments, except those which are external; and that they draw their kerchiefs over their bosoms, and display not their ornaments, except to their husbands or their fathers, or their husband's fathers, or their sons or their husband's sons, or their brothers, or their brother's sons, or their sister's sons, or their women, or their slaves, or male domestics who no natural force, or to children who note not women's nakedness. And let them not strike their feet together, so as to discover their hidden ornaments. And be ye wholly turned to God, O ye Believers! haply it shall be well with you.[16]

59. O Prophet! Speak to thy wives and to thy daughters, and to the wives of the faithful, that they let their wrappers fall low. Thus will they more easily be known, and they will not be affronted. God is Indulgent, Merciful![17]

8–9. And . . . the damsel that hath been buried alive shall be asked, For what crime she was put to death.[18]

95. The general tenor of the Quran is to establish a perfect equality between the male and female sex, in their legal, social, and spiritual positions, except in physical strength, and possession of wealth.

228. . . . The same is due to women as it is due from them, but men have precedence over them.[19]

36. . . . The men shall have a portion according to their deserts, and the women a portion according to their deserts.

38. Men are superior to women on account of the qualities with which God hath gifted the one above the other, and on account of the outlay they make from their substance for them.[20]

35. Truly the men who resign themselves to God, and women who resign themselves, and the believing men and the believing women and the devout men and the devout women, and the men of truth and the women of truth, and patient men and the patient women, and humble men and the humble women, and men who give alms and the women give alms, and men who fast and the women who fast, and chaste men and the chaste women, and men and women who oft remember God: for them hath God prepared forgiveness and a rich recompense.[21]

Even these passages do not exhaust what Muhammad did to better the low status of females, for besides his promulgating stringent laws at first against polygamy, and putting restrictions upon the shameful levity of divorce, he stirred up in the minds of his followers the laudable sentiments of love and affection toward women, and inculcated in his Revelations the respect due to them, as well as precepts to secure the mutual comfort and happiness of husband and wife.

20. And one of his signs it is, that He hath created wives for you of your own species, that ye may dwell with them, and hath put love and tenderness between you. Herein truly are signs for those who reflect.[22]

The social equality of both sexes is implied fully in the simile, "husbands are garments to their wives, and wives are garments to their husbands"; and the very word *zoujain, couple,* or *twain,* indicates the propriety of monogamy, and emphasizes the indissolubility of the marriage tie.

96. Compared with Paganism, Judaism, and even Christianity, Islam sanctioned for women a greater stride in civilization and liberty than they had enjoyed prior to the mission of Muhammad. The Mosaic Law fell short of accomplishing any great good for the moral and social elevation of the Hebrew females, and the New Testament did comparatively nothing toward their worldly preferment. It is only the influence of the codes of the Roman Law, and the innate respect felt by the Teutonic nations for the female sex, and centuries of civilization, that have raised women to their proper position in European countries [*Mohammad Anism,* by R. Bosworth Smith, M.A., London: 1876, p. 243]. The condition of Christian women in Eastern Turkey, Syria, and Palestine is as intellectually and socially depressed as that of their Muhammadan and semi-Pagan sisters in the East, or Asiatic countries.

97. The subordination, subjection, inferiority, and degradation of women were generally believed in, and taught by the Jewish and early Christian fathers in conformity with the laws of the Bible. As the introduction of sin into the world was believed to have proceeded through the instrumentality of women, the blame of human vices lay at her door. Therefore she was considered to have brought on her own degradation by her own hands, and her condition of subordination was turned into subjugation. It was also said to her of her husband, "he shall rule over thee" (Gen. iii. 16), a sentence that, regarded as a prediction, has been strikingly fulfilled in the position assigned to women in oriental countries. [The following passages illustrate these points.]

Shortly before the Christian era an important change took place in the views entertained on the question of marriage as affecting the spiritual and intellectual part of man's nature. . . . In the interval that elapsed between Old and New Testament periods, a spirit of asceticism had been evolved. . . . The Essenes were the first to propound any doubts as to the propriety of marriage: some of them avoided it altogether, others availed themselves of it under restrictions (Joseph, B. J. II. 8, § 2, 13). Similar views were adopted by Therapeutae and at a later period by the Gnostics (Burton's Lectures, I. 214), and finally developing into the system of monachism.[23]

Another injurious consequence resulting, in a great measure, from asceticism, was a tendency to depreciate extremely the character and the position of women. In this tendency we may detect in part the influence of the earlier Jewish writings, in which an impartial observer may find evident traces of the common Oriental depreciation of women. The custom of purchase-money to the father of the bride was admitted.[24] Polygamy was authorized and practiced by the wisest man on an enormous scale. A woman was regarded as the origin of human ills. A period of purification was appointed after the birth of every child; but, by a very significant provision, it was twice as long in the case of a female as a male child. "The badness of men," a Jewish writer emphatically declared, "is better than the goodness of women." The types of female excellence exhibited in the early period of Jewish history are in general of a low order, and certainly far inferior to those of Roman history or Greek poetry; and the warmest eulogy of a woman in the Old Testament is probably that which was bestowed upon her who, with circumstances of the most aggravated treachery, had murdered the sleeping fugitive who had taken refuge under her roof.

The combined influence of the Jewish writings, and of that ascetic feeling, which treated women as the chief source of temptation to man, was shown in those fierce invectives, which form so conspicuous and so grotesque a portion of the writings of the Fathers, and which contrast so curiously with the adulation bestowed upon particular members of the sex. Woman was represented as the door of hell, as the mother of all human ills. She should be ashamed at the very thought that she is a woman. She should live in continual penance, on account of the curses she has brought upon this world. She should be ashamed of her dress, for it is memorial of her fall. She should be especially ashamed of her beauty, for it is the most potent instrument of the dæmon. Physical beauty was indeed perpetually the theme of ecclesiastical denunciations, though one singular exception seems to have been made; for it has been observed that in the middle ages the personal beauty of bishops was continually noticed upon their tombs. Women were even forbidden by a provincial Council, in the sixth century, on account of their impurity, to receive the Eucharist into their naked hands. Their essentially subordinate position was continually maintained.

It is probable that this teaching had its part in determining the principles of legislation concerning the sex. The Pagan laws during the Empire had been continually repealing the old disabilities of women, and the legislative movement in their favor continued with unabated force from Constantine to Justinian, and appeared also in some of the early laws of the barbarians. But in the whole feudal legislation women were placed in a much lower legal position than in the Pagan Empire. In addition to the personal restrictions, which grew necessarily out of the Catholic doctrines concerning divorce and the subordination of the weaker sex, we find numerous and stringent enactments that rendered it impossible for women to succeed to any considerable amount of property, and that almost reduced them to the alternatives of marriage or a nunnery. The complete inferiority of the sex was maintained by the law; and that generous public opinion, which in Rome had frequently revolted against the injustice done to girls in depriving them of the greater part of the inheritance of their fathers, totally disappeared. Wherever the canon law has been the basis of legislation, we find laws of succession sacrificing the interests of daughters, and of wives, and a state of public opinion that has been formed and regulated by these laws; nor was any serious attempt made to abolish them till the close of the last century. The French revolutionaries, though rejecting the proposal of Sieyes and Condorcet to accord political emancipation to women, established at least an equal succession of sons and daughters, and thus initiated a great reformation of both law and opinion, which sooner or later must traverse the world.[25]

98. Mr. Bosworth Smith, while admitting and commending the limitation of the unbound license of polygamy, the absolute recklessness of the Eastern divorce imposed by Muhammad, and the strong moral sentiment aroused by his laws afterwards, says:

I do not forget, on the other hand, that Mohammed authorized the corporal punishment of the wife by the husband in extreme cases, provided it was done with moderation; that he allowed or enjoined the seclusion of women; the he relaxed in his own behalf the restriction with regard to polygamy which he imposed on others, and that he allowed concubinage with captives taken in war; and I fully admit that his followers have been far more ready to imitate and obey him in these, the defective part of his teaching and example, than in the more elevated ones; but I say confidently that, compared with Paganism, and even with Judaism, Mohammed gave women a great advance on their previous position, and so has deserved well of them.[26]

I am sorry Mr. Bosworth Smith has been led away by the common and popular notions on these points of defects, as he calls them, and has not judiciously investigated the charges as he has done in other cases.

99. (1) That Muhammad had authorized the corporal punishment of refractory wives by their husbands in extreme cases (Sura iv. 38), is true, but it is also a fact worthy of note that this had been the case only during the early stage of the

patriarchal form of government[27] at Medina, when there were no established tribunals of justice or judges, and the head of the family was the only domestic judge. But as soon as the form was changed, when tribunals were created, and when a systematic administration of justice was carried on, the power given to the husband was abolished, and the contending parties, i.e., husband and wife, were required to appeal to the judges, prohibiting the former from taking the law into his own hands. The very next verse, 39, abolishes the former system of husbands having power of beating their wives. The verse is as follows:

> 39. And if ye fear a breach between man and wife, then send a judge chosen from his family and a judge chosen from her family; if they are desirous of agreement, God will effect a reconciliation between them; verily, God is Knowing, apprised of all![28]

100. (2) Muhammad did not allow or enjoin seclusion[29] of women. He made some improvements in their general dress and demeanor, giving them greater honor and respectability; and he made provisions to save them from the insults of the rude and uncultured common folk, while going out in the streets. The following are the verses of the Quran on the subject:

> 59. O Prophet! Speak to thy wives and to thy daughters, and to the wives of the faithful, that they let their wrappers[30] fall low. Thus will they more easily be known, and they will not be affronted. God is Indulgent, Merciful![31]
> 31. And speak to the believing women that they refrain their looks, and observe continence; and that they display not their ornaments, except those which are external; and that they draw their kerchiefs[32] over their bosoms.[33]

The Muhammadan Common Law[34] also takes particular care as to leave the face and hands of respectable females open and unmasked; for these parts of the body are not called "*Aurah,*" or nakedness. The whole person of a female, except the face and hands, as well as the feet according to some, are "*Aurah,*" and ought to be decently covered.

101. (3) As to the relaxation of the restriction of polygamy by Muhammad in his own behalf, it is simply a wrong and a false idea, and every European author labors under the same mistake. Muhammad did not contract any marriage after he had imposed the limitation of polygamy for the first time[35] or had virtually abolished the same.[36] All his former marriages contracted before the promulgation of the Law were allowed to him to be retained, whilst the other Moslems whose number of wives had exceeded the limit of four (and there were very few) had the option to separate themselves from the rest. This was the special prerogative of the Prophet[37] because when he offered his wives separation on account of the Law restricting polygamy for the first time to four, they preferred to live with him and refused to be separated,[38] and thus he was allowed to retain the former number, but, on the other hand, for this indulgence he was prohibited to marry any more in the place of the then existing wives, even in the cases of their death or separation, or even when the beauty of other women charmed him.[39] He had only to retain what

he already possessed, so there was no relaxation of the law in his favor. He was therefore privileged only so far that he retained the former number, whilst others had the option to put away any in excess of the number to which the new law limited them. But he had the disadvantage that any other woman was prohibited to him except those already possessed, whereas other persons were allowed four wives with every liberty of substituting any woman with lawful marriage in the case of demise or divorce of some of them, within the assigned limit. I think nobody after this will wrongly construe the privilege of Muhammad as a special relaxation of the law in his own favor.

The verse xxxiii. 52, referred to above, is as follows:

> It is not permitted to take other wives hereafter, nor to change thy present wives for other women, though their beauty charm thee, except those women thou already possessest. And God watcheth all things.

102. (4) It is a great mistake on the part of Mr. Bosworth Smith to say that Muhammad allowed concubinage with captives after war. I have fully discussed the subject of concubinage in paragraphs 152–63. I nowhere find in the Quran Muhammad allowing concubinage with captives taken in war. He has everywhere enjoined marriage either with a free woman or a slave. That there was a good deal of slavery combined with concubinage in actual existence at the time, though not sanctioned by law, cannot be doubted, but everywhere marriage was plainly and by implication enjoined in the Quran.

103. Mr. Bosworth Smith, in a footnote to the quotation cited in paragraph 98, writes:

> Sale maintains, and he is supported by many Moslem doctors, and to all appearance, by the words of the Quran (Sura iv. 3), that under no circumstances is a man allowed to take his slaves as concubines, if he has the maximum number of four wives allowed him by the law. Mr. Lane maintains the contrary, and supports his argument by the authority of other Muslim doctors, and by the practice of some of the Companions of the Prophet; but it is surely dangerous to lay stress on this. No Musalman will contend that the Companions are examples to be followed.

Exegetically Mr. Sale[40] is quite right in the interpretation of Sura iv. 3, and Mr. Lane is wrong in his translation of the verse. There is no idea of concubinage expressed or implied in the text of Sura iv. 3. It simply and exclusively confines the union of a man and a woman, either free or slave, to marriage only, and within the limited number. The fact is this, that the verb *"Ankihoo"* of the imperative mood meaning "marry" is mentioned in the first sentence of the verse, and is *understood* in the two other sentences. Thus we are not authorized to place any other verb in these two sentences except what is put down in the first. Mr. Lane has committed the mistake of translating *"Ankihoo"* from *"Nikah"* as *"take"* in the first place instead of *"marry"* and then repeating the same word in parenthesis in the two other places. The verse runs thus:

Marry ("Ankihoo") of the women who please you, two, three, or four, but if ye fear that ye cannot act equitably, [to so many, marry] one; or [marry] those whom your right hands have acquired.

Mr. Lane translates thus:

Take in marriage of the women who please you, two, three, or four: but if ye fear that ye cannot act equitably, [to so many, take] one: or [take] those whom your right hands have acquired.[41]

But supposing Muhammad had allowed concubinage with captives taken in war, as Mr. Bosworth Smith asserts, then when he subsequently abolished slavery, and no captives taken in war were to be made slaves (Sura xlvii. 4 and 5), concubinage was also by implication abolished.

POLYGAMY

104. Polygamy was the indispensable institution of the Arabs before and after the time of Muhammad.[42] It was no invention of the Prophet of Islam. He found it already deeply rooted in the soil of the Arabian society. For a time he availed himself largely of this social institution, but his sagacious mind soon became alive to its dangerous consequences. He had contracted several marriages only during his stay at Medina, that is, during the interval of the seven or eight years of his remaining life. During the greater part of his life, till about the fifty-third year of his age, he had been a monogamist. The early years of his prophetic life were almost taken up with spiritual and moral reforms, at the same time suffering under heavy persecutions at Mecca, and defending himself against the superior numbers of his enemies who were attacking and besieging Medina, the city of his and his followers' refuge. Surrounded as he was with difficulties, the evils of polygamy did not fail to strike his iconoclastic mind, and he set to work to gradually mitigate and finally abolish the institution. This was at first an almost hopeless task, for the reforms he sought were uncongenial to the social constitution of a people he had to deal with. Although it may be pleaded that polygamy was suited to a race like the Arabs in the first stages of their development, and that restricted within certain limits it might be the means of promoting a purer moral and social existence, it must be admitted that the institution is open to serious drawbacks, as Muhammad seems to have been fully aware. This first restriction was no doubt a great step in advance, and for those who could read between the lines, it was tantamount to a mandate in favor of monogamy. But seeing that his followers were not willing to read it in that light, he went a step farther, and in his next commandment on the subject, accentuated what was implied in the first by declaring that it was not in human power to treat a plurality of wives equitably, however much men might wish to do so.

105. The Quranic injunction about this is found in Sura iv. 3 and 128.[43] But the final and effectual step taken by Muhammad toward the abolition of this leading vice of the Arab community was his declaring in the Quran that nobody could

fulfill the condition of dealing *equitably* with more than one woman, though he "fain to do so."

> Certainly you have not in your power to treat your wives with equal justice even though you fain would do so.[44]

This was the virtual abolition of polygamy. But the marriages already contracted by Muhammad and his followers were allowed to be held lawful, as they were performed in compliance with the recognized institution of Arab society. The then existing polygamists were, however, advised not to abandon some of their wives in favor of others in the concluding portion of the above quoted verse:

> But yield not wholly to disinclination, so that ye leave one of them as it were in suspense; if ye come to an understanding, and act in the fear of God, then, verily God is forgiving, Merciful.[45]

106. Those writers are greatly mistaken who think that Muhammad sanctioned the marriage of four wives, or that in curtailing the unrestricted licentiousness that had prevailed in Arabia before him, he partially controlled, but firmly established the practice of polygamy, as if while lightening he riveted the fetter; and that in alleviating the evils of plurality of marriage he adopted it himself on the grounds that he had received a divine privilege to do so. The restriction of the number of simultaneous marriages was only the first step and a temporary measure. The germ of its virtual abrogation lies in the almost impossible condition of dealing equitably with all wives, at the same time declaring men's inability to fulfill it. The practice was so deeply rooted in Arabia and in other oriental countries that all he could venture to do was by imposing obligatory behests in the Quran against it.

> If ye fear ye cannot act equitably with your wives then marry one only.[46]
>   Certainly it is not in your power to deal equitably with your wives, even ye fain would do so.[47]

He could not do more than this. No reformer or legislator can do more.

NOTES

1. *Contemporary Review*, August, 1881, p. 278.
2. Sura xlvii. 5.
3. Sura iv. 29; lxx. 29, 30; xxiii. 5, 6.
4. Sura vi. 152; xvii. 33; lxxxi. 8, 9.
5. Sura iv. 8.
6. Sura iv. 26.
7. Sura iv. 23.
8. Sura iv. 1.
9. Sura xxiv. 4, 6, 23.
10. Sura xxxiii. 59; xxiv. 31.

11. Sura iv. 3, 126.
12. See paragraph 99.
13. Sura iv.
14. Sura vi.
15. Sura xvii.
16. Sura xxiv.
17. Sura xxxiii.
18. Sura lxxxi.
19. Sura ii.
20. Sura iv.
21. Sura xxxiii.
22. Sura xxx.
23. Smith's *Dictionary of the Bible*, vol. II. *Vide* Art. "Marriage," London: 1863, pp. 242–3.
24. The *Quran* abolished this custom.—C. A.
25. Lecky's *History of European Morals from Augustus to Charlemagne*, vol. II. Chapter V, pp. 337–40.
26. "Mohammed and Mohammedanism." Lectures delivered at the Royal Institution of Great Britain in February and March 1874, R. Bosworth Smith, M.A., London: 1876, p. 242.
27. "Aulus Gellius has preserved a passage in which Cato observes, 'that the husband has an absolute authority over his wife; it is for him to condemn and punish her, if she has been guilty of any shameful act, such as drinking wine or committing adultery.'"—*History of European Morals from Augustus to Charlemagne*, W. E. H. Lecky, M.A., vol. II., pp. 93–4.
28. Sura iv.
29. "The wives of the Greeks lived in almost absolute seclusion. They were usually married when very young. Their occupations were to weave, to spin, to embroider, to superintend the household, to care for their sick slaves. They lived in a special and retired part of the house. The most wealthy seldom went abroad, and never, except when accompanied by a female slave; never attended the public spectacles; received no male visitors except in the presence of their husbands, and had not even a seat at their own tables when male guests were there."—Lecky's *History of European Morals*, vol. II., p. 287.
30. The original word is "jalabeeb," plural of "jilbab," which is wrongly translated "veil" by Rodwell. It means women's outer wrapping garment. *Vide* Lane's *Arabic Lexicon*, B. I. pt. II., p. 440. Sale translates it "outer garment" and H. Palmer "outer wrapper."
31. Sura xxxiii.
32. The orginal word is "khomr," plural of "khimar," which means women's head-covering, a piece of cloth with which women cover their heads.—Lane's *Arabic Lexicon*, B. I., pt. II., page 809. Sale and Rodwell are wrong in translating "khomr" as "veils." H. Palmer translates the word as "kerchiefs," which is the true meaning.
33. Sura xxiv.
34. "Book XLIV of Abominations.—A subject which involves a vast variety of frivolous matter, and must be considered chiefly in the light of a treatise upon propriety and decorum. In it is particularly exhibited the scrupulous attention paid to female modesty, and the avoidance of every act which may tend to violate it, even in thought. It is remarkable, however, that this does not amount to that absolute seclusion of women supposed by some writers. In fact, this seclusion is a result of jealousy and

pride, and not of any legal injunction, as appears in this and several other parts of the *Hedaya*. Neither is it a custom universally prevalent in Muhammadan countries."— The *Hedaya* or Guide; trans. by C. Hamilton, vol. I, *Preliminary Discourse*, p. lxxxi.

35. Sura iv. 3.
36. Compare verses 3 and 127, Sura iv.
37. Sura xxxiii. 49, 50.
38. Sura xxxiii. 28, 29, 51.
39. Sura xxxiii. 52.
40. I sought in vain the Rev. Wherry's notes on Sale's translation (*A Comprehensive Commentary on the Quran*, E. M. Wherry, M. A., vol. I., London: Trubner & Co., 1882, p. 206). He is as wrong as Mr. Muir whom he quotes. He writes, "Muir (*Life of Mahomet*, vol. III., p. 303) says, 'There is no limit, as supposed by Sale, to the number of slave-girls, with whom (irrespective of his four wives) a Moslem may, without any antecedent ceremony or any guarantee of continuance, cohabit.' But Sale is exegetically right, and he appeals to the express words of the Quran, it is not a mere supposition of his, as I have shown in the text."
41. *Quran*, ch. IV. v. 3 in *The Modern Egyptians*, Lane, vol. I., London: 1871, p.122.
42. The account that has been handed down to us of Muhammad's contemporaneous marriages cannot be depended upon, as the biographers have only given us the various numbers vouched for by different authorities without coming to any determination as to what the actual number was. But there is no doubt that it exceeded four (compare Sura iii. v. 4, and Sura xxxiii. v. 48). It must be remembered, however, that all the marriages contracted by Muhammad, except one, took place in and after the fifty-fourth year of his age, and were almost all of them contracted with distressed and destitute widows. No less than three were the widows of his followers who, under the pressure of persecution at Mecca, had emigrated with their wives to Abyssinia, and died there. The husbands of two others had died at Medina, in the action fought in defense of Islam. To marry the helpless and homeless widows of friends, who have given their lives in one's cause, and thus to afford them lawful shelter and protection, was and is considered by the Arabs to be an honorable act of generosity and kindness. Lady Duff Gordon writes: "I heard a curious illustration of the Arab manners today. I met Hassan, the Janissary of the American Consulate, a very respectable good man. He told me he had another wife since last year. I asked, What for?" "It [*sic*] was the widow of his brother, who had always lived in the same house as him, like one family, and who died leaving two boys. She is neither young nor handsome, but he considered it his duty to provide for her and the children, and not let her marry a stranger. So you see polygamy is not always a sensual indulgence: and a man may practice greater self-sacrifice than by talking sentiments about deceased wives' sisters." (*Letters from Egypt*; London: 1866, pp. 139–40.)
43. *Vide* paragraphs 93 and 103.
44. Sura iv. 128.a
45. Sura iv. 128.b
46. Sura iv. 3.
47. Sura iv. 128.

CHAPTER 14

THE RIGHTS OF WOMEN

Sayyid Ahmad Khan

"The Rights of Women," from Sayyid Ahmad Khan, *Maqalat-i Sar Sayyid*, edited by Maulana Muhammad Isma'il Pani Pati. Lahaur: Majlis-i Taraqqi-yi Adab, 1962, pp. 201–5. Translated by Kamran Talattof.

DEVELOPED COUNTRIES LOUDLY PROCLAIM THAT MEN and women are created equal and that both hold equal rights. They also proclaim that there is no reason why women should be thought of as less important or less worthy of respect than men. They do not even accept that, by way of illustration, it can be said that a woman is like the left hand and a man the right hand, or that in value a woman adds up to 12 and a man to a dozen. Nevertheless, even today we observe that in no developed country have women been bestowed with the same stature and parity in rights and authority to men as has been bestowed upon them in the religion of Islam. England greatly favors the freedom of women, yet when its laws relating to women are examined, it is obvious that the English consider women quite insignificant, unintelligent, and valueless.

According to English laws, when a woman marries, she is considered to have lost her separate existence, and her distinctive individuality is absorbed into that of her husband. She does not stand in the capacity of a separate member to a contract, and thus she is not able to hold responsibility for any legal instrument she may have signed according to her own will and without the agreement of her husband. The personal possessions, wealth, cash, and property that were hers before marriage all belong to the husband after marriage. That property that comes to a woman by inheritance either before or after marriage is also possessed by the husband for as long as he lives, and he also receives any earnings produced from it. Her status is like that of a feeble-minded incompetent: She cannot bring a lawsuit against anyone, nor can anyone [directly] bring a lawsuit against her. She cannot buy or sell anything without the permission of her husband. Except for the expenses of food, clothing, and living in one house, that is, the basic expenses necessary for daily living, she cannot spend money on anything without her husband's permission.

In 1870 a bill was presented in Parliament regarding the property of married women. Only this much was desired, that the law be rescinded by means of which after marriage a woman's property becomes lost to her. This bill was presented by the Honorable Mr. Russell Gurney, M. P. On this occasion he made some exquisite remarks. He observed that, according to the law then active, whatever a woman had before marriage and received after marriage, and all that she earned by her ability and hard work, left her hands after marriage. Her husband became the owner of it all. Thus the effect of marriage upon a woman was like that of a crime whose prescribed punishment was the confiscation of property! At this, the whole House of Commons burst into laughter and most of the members supported him. Thus, this is the state of English law regarding women, and probably no other law is more deplorable, damaging, and unjust.

MUSLIM LAW CONCERNING WOMEN

Now consider how women are honored in Muslim law, and how their rights and authority have been conceded to be equal to those of men. Before adulthood, just like men, women are considered to be without authority and unqualified to enter into official agreements. But upon reaching adulthood she assumes the same authority as a man and is qualified to enter into a contract. Just like men, women have the authority to marry. Just like a man's, a woman's marriage cannot take place without her consent. She herself is the owner and controller of all her personal property, and has full authority over it. She has the capability, like a man, of executing any kind of contract, and her person and her property stand accountable with respect to any contracts and documents that she may have written. She is the owner of any property that may have come into her possession before or after marriage, and she herself is the claimant to its benefits. Like men, women can file suits or be sued in the courts. She can purchase anything she wants to with her wealth, and can sell anything she wishes. Like a man, she can give, will, or donate any kind of inheritance. In accordance with regular procedures she can inherit from the property of her relatives and her husband. She can gain, then, all the materials a man may gain. All of the pious merits a man may gain, she may gain as well. Likewise, she receives the same rewards or punishments for her behavior in this world on Judgment Day.

There is no special restriction placed upon a woman that is not also placed upon a man, except that which she has taken upon herself in terms of the wedding contract, or the restriction relating to the private parts of her body that differ by nature from man's.

Thus, in truth, in no religion and in no nation's law have women and men been considered as equal as in the religion of Islam. But it is a most astonishing fact that all developed countries strongly criticize the condition of women in Islam. Yet there is no doubt that the condition of the women of developed countries is many levels better than that of Muslim women and women of Muslim countries, although the situation ought to be the reverse.

In admitting the superiority of the state of women in developed countries, we have not considered the matter of their freedom from the veil, because in our opinion, to the same extent as there is excess in this respect in India, there is excess [of another kind] in advanced countries. And as far as man can bring his intellect to bear on this matter, the limit set by the shari&*ah law certainly seems to be perfectly correct.

At this point, what we wish to argue for is simply: good treatment of women by men; good fellowship; courtesy; consideration; love; encouragement; paying attention to their comfort, ease, happiness, and pleasure; keeping them happy in every way. Instead of considering them servants, to consider them as companions, comrades, and partners in both sorrow and happiness and to consider each other the cause of mutual joy and strength is best. Doubtless, as far as we know, considerable progress is being made in areas on these particulars regarding women, in the advanced countries. But in Muslim countries there is no progress in these areas and in India there are perpetrated such unworthy and humiliating events that one can only cry out, "May God have mercy on us!"

People who associate these evils with the religion of Islam are surely mistaken. To the extent that there is deterioration in the condition of women in India, it is due to a failure to observe the regulations of Islam fully. If its principles were brought into practice, no doubt all of these evils would be eliminated.

In addition, there is another important reason for this: Muslims today remain in large part uncivilized. Despite the fact that the laws of the developed nations regarding women were extremely defective and miserable, those nations have elevated the position of their women to an extremely high level while Muslims, despite the fact that the laws of the rest of the world are less generous, on account of being uncivilized have treated women so badly that all the nations laugh at the condition of Muslim women. Because of our inherent evils, and because the whole *ummah* is in a sorry state (with perhaps some minimal exceptions willed by God!), all nations criticize our religion.

Therefore, this is not the time for us to ignore these truths and delay correcting our conduct or to fail to show by the light of our behavior that Islam is an enlightened religion.

CHAPTER 15

THE LIBERATION OF WOMEN

Qasim Amin

Excerpts from Qasim Amin. "The Status of Women in Society: A Reflection of the Nation's Moral Standards." In *The Liberation of Women*, translated by Sarniha Sidhorn Peterson. Cairo: The American University in Cairo Press, 1992, pp. 3–61.

I CALL ON EVERY LOVER OF TRUTH TO EXAMINE WITH ME the status of women in Egyptian society. I am confident that such individuals will arrive independently at the same conclusion I have, namely, the necessity of improving the status of Egyptian women. The truth I am presenting today has preoccupied me for a long time; I have considered it, examined it, and analyzed it. When it was eventually stripped of all confounding errors, it occupied an important place in my thinking, rivaled other ideas, overcame them, and finally reached the point where it became my dominant thought, alerting me to its advantages and reminding me of its necessity. I became aware of the absence of a platform from which this truth could be elevated from reflection to the unlimited space of appeal and attention.

A profound factor that influences human development and ensures its positive future is the strange power that compels a human being to communicate every scientific or literary idea once it crystallizes in the mind, and once it is accompanied by the belief that it will benefit the progress of future generations. Communicating these findings supersedes concern over any negative consequences that may be incurred by the individual in presenting his knowledge. The impact of this power is recognized by anyone who has experienced a trace of it. Such an individual feels that if he fails to use this power toward the goal it is aiming to achieve, and if he does not use whatever strength he has to assist it in reaching that goal, it will eventually overcome him in the struggle, resisting him if he opposes it, coercing him if he tries to force it, and appearing in an unfamiliar form, like a gas that could not be contained through pressure. In fact, the pressure may cause an explosion that would destroy its container.

History offers numerous proofs of this phenomenon. The history of nations is saturated with disputes, arguments, sufferings, and wars that originated with the purpose of establishing the superiority of one idea or ideology over another. During these encounters victory was sometimes for truth and at other times for falsehood. This characterized Islamic countries during the early days and the middle ages, and continues to characterize Western countries. It is reasonable to state that the life of Western countries is a continuous struggle between truth and falsehood, between right and wrong: It is an internal struggle in all branches of education, the arts, and industry; and an external struggle among the various countries. This is especially obvious in this century when distance and isolation have been eliminated by modern inventions, and when the separating borders and forbidding walls have been torn down. These changes are reflected in the increasing number of individuals who have toured the whole world and who presently can be counted by the thousands. Likewise, the ideas of any Western scholar, when formulated in a book, are translated and published simultaneously in five or six languages.

Countries like ours have preferred a less ruffled existence. This is because we have neglected the nurturing of our minds to such an extent that they have become like barren soil, unfit for any growth. Our laziness has caused us to be hostile to every unfamiliar idea, whether a product of the sound principal traditions or of current events. An intellectually lazy person whose arguments are weak is often satisfied, in refuting an apparent truth, to hurl a false remark and declare it a heresy in Islam. He only makes this false remark to avoid the effort of understanding the truth, or to disengage from the labor of research, or to avoid its application. It is as if God created the Muslims from clay especially set aside for them and freed them from obeying natural law, whose power dominates human beings and the rest of living creation.

Some people will say that today I am publishing heresy. To these people I will respond: yes, I have come up with a heresy, but the heresy is not against Islam. It is against our traditions and social dealings, where the demand for perfection is extolled.

Why should a Muslim believe that his traditions cannot be changed or replaced by new ones, and that it is his duty to preserve them forever? Why does he drag this belief along to his work, even though he and his traditions are a part of the universe, falling at all times under the laws of change? Can the Muslim contradict God's laws of creation—God who has made change a prerequisite for life and progress, rather than immobility and inflexibility, which are characteristic of death and backwardness? Is not tradition merely the set of conventions of a country defining the special customs appropriate to its life and behavior at a specific time and place? How can people believe that traditions never change, and at the same time maintain the understanding that traditions are one of the intellectual products of humans, and that human intellect differs according to historical era or geographical location? Does the presence of Muslims in various parts of the world imply a uniformity of traditions or ways of life? Who can pretend that Sudanese preferences are similar to those of the Turks, the Chinese, or the Indians; or believe that the Bedouin tradition is appropriate for an urbanite; or claim that the traditions of any country whatever have remained the same since the creation of that country?

In truth, during a specific historical era every country has peculiar traditions and mores that match its intellectual state. These traditions and mores change continuously in an unobtrusive way so that people living during that era are unaware of the changes. However, the changes are influenced by regional factors, heredity, intercultural exchanges, scientific inventions, ethical ideologies, religious beliefs, political structures, and other factors. Every intellectual movement toward progress is inevitably followed by an appropriate change in the traditions and mores of a society. Therefore, there should be examples of differences between the Sudanese and the Turks comparable to the differences in their intellectual status. This is a well-known, established fact. The differences between Egyptians and Europeans also need to be considered in this context.

We cannot consider traditions (which are merely a way of life for an individual, his family, his countrymen, and the children of his race) to be the same in a civilized nation as in an ignorant, barbaric one, because the behavior of every individual in a society is appropriate to the intellectual abilities of that society and to the method by which its children are brought up.

This total interdependence between the traditions of a nation and its level of civilization and knowledge suggests that the power of tradition controls a country more than any other power, and that tradition is one of the most influential permanent components of a nation, and is least likely to change. Therefore, citizens of a nation cannot but comply with the existing traditions, unless they change or unless their intellectual level increases or decreases. Thus I believe that traditions always overcome other factors in a society and that they even influence the laws of that society. This belief is confirmed through daily observation of the laws and programs of our nation, which are usually intended to improve the state of affairs but are immediately turned around to become new instruments for corruption. It is not difficult to understand this phenomenon, because at times tradition may even supersede the existing religion, destroying or transforming it so that those who are most knowledgeable about religion eventually disown its existing form.

This is the basis of our observations. This evidence of history confirms and demonstrates that the status of women is inseparably tied to the status of a nation. When the status of a nation is low, reflecting an uncivilized condition for that nation, the status of women is also low, and when the status of a nation is elevated, reflecting the progress and civilization of that nation, the status of women in that country is also elevated. We have learned that women in the first human societies were treated as slaves. The ancient Greeks and Romans, for example, considered a woman to be under the power of her father, then her husband, and after him his eldest son. The head of the family had the absolute right of ownership over her life. He could dispose of her through trade, donation, or death, whenever and in whatever way he wished. His heirs eventually inherited her and with her all the rights that were given to the owner. Prior to Islam, it was acceptable for Arab fathers to kill their daughters and for men to gratify themselves with women with no legal bonds or numerical limits. This authority still prevails among uncivilized African and American tribes. Some Asians even believe that a woman has no immortal soul and that she should not live after her husband dies.

Other Asians present her to their guests as a sign of hospitality, just as one would present a guest with the best of his possessions.

These traits are present among emerging societies, which are based on familial and tribal bonds rather than on formal structures. Force is the only law with which such societies are familiar. The use of force is also the medium of control for governments run by autocratic structures.

On the other hand, we find that women in nations with a more advanced civilization have gradually advanced from the low status to which they have been relegated and have started to overcome the gap that has separated them from men. One woman is crawling while the other is taking steps; one is walking while the other is running. These discrepancies reflect the different societies to which these women belong and the level of civilization of these societies. The American woman is in the forefront, followed by the British, the German, the French, the Austrian, the Italian, and the Russian woman, and so on. Women in all these societies have felt that they deserve their independence, and are searching for the means to achieve it. These women believe that they are human beings and that they deserve freedom, and they are therefore striving for freedom and demanding every human right.

Westerners, who like to associate all good things with their religion, believe that the Western woman has advanced because her Christian religion helped her achieve freedom. This belief, however, is inaccurate. Christianity did not set up a system that guarantees the freedom of women; it does not guarantee her rights through either specific or general rules; and it does not prescribe any guiding principles on this topic. In every country where Christianity has been introduced and spread it has left no tangible impact on the normative structure affecting women's status. On the contrary, Christianity has been molded by the traditions and manners of the specific nations in which it was introduced. If there were a religion that could have had power and influence over local traditions, then the Muslim women today should have been at the forefront of free women on earth.

The Islamic legal system, the shari'ah, stipulated the equality of women and men before any other legal system. Islam declared women's freedom and emancipation, and granted women all human rights during a time when women occupied the lowest status in all societies. According to Islamic law, women are considered to possess the same legal capabilities in all civil cases pertaining to buying, donating, trusteeship, and disposal of goods, unhindered by requirements of permission from either their father or their husband. These advantages have not yet been attained by some contemporary Western women, yet they demonstrate that respect for women and for their equality with men were basic to the principles of the liberal shari'ah. In fact, our legal system went so far in its kindness to women that it rid them of the burden of earning a living and freed them from the obligation of participating in household and childrearing expenses. This is unlike some Western laws, which equate men and women only with regard to their duties, giving preference to men with regard to social rights.

Within the shari'ah, the tendency to equate men's and women's rights is obvious, even in the context of divorce. Islam has created for women mechanisms worthy of consideration and contrary to what Westerners and some Muslims imagine or believe. These will be discussed later.

Islamic law favors men in one area only—polygamy. The reason is obvious and is related to the issue of lineage, without which marriage is meaningless. This topic too will be addressed later. In summary, nothing in the laws of Islam or in its intentions can account for the low status of Muslim women. The existing situation is contrary to the law, because originally women in Islam were granted an equal place in human society.

What a pity! Unacceptable customs, traditions, and superstitions inherited from the countries in which Islam spread have been allowed to permeate this beautiful religion. Knowledge in these countries had not developed to the point of giving women the status already given them by the shari'ah.

The most significant factor that accounts for the perpetuation of these traditions, however, is the succession over us of despotic governments. At various times and places Islamic societies have been stripped of the political structures that delineated the rights of the ruler and the ruled, and that granted to the ruled the right to demand that the rulers stop at the limits established for them by the shari'ah. In fact, their governments continually took on a despotic nature, with their sultan and his assistants having total authority. Thus they ruled however they wished, without restraint, counsel, or supervision, and they administered the affairs of their citizens without these having any say.

Yes, rulers, whether important or unimportant, are obliged to follow justice and avoid injustice. Experience demonstrates, however, that unlimited power is a temptation for abuse, especially when it is unaccountable, unchallenged by any other opinion, and unsupervised by any formal structure. This explains why, for so many centuries, absolute and autocratic rule was the norm for Islamic countries. Rulers administered these nations poorly and were excessive in their capricious tampering with the affairs of their subjects; quite often they even tampered with religion. There are a few exceptions to this pattern, but they are insignificant in contrast to the majority of cases.

When despotism prevails in a country, its impact is not limited to individual cases only, since it is central to the ideology of the supreme ruler. Despotism continues to flow from him to those around him, and they in turn influence their subordinates. A despot spits his spirit into every powerful person, who, whenever possible, dominates a weaker one. This attitude pervades the life of all individuals, regardless of the approval or disapproval of the supreme ruler. These despotic systems have also influenced the relationships between men and women-man in his superiority began to despise woman in her weakness. As a result, corrupt morals became the first sign of a country ruled by a despot.

Initially one would assume that a person who experiences injustice would love justice and that he would be inclined toward compassion, having experienced the suffering resulting from the catastrophes that have befallen him. Observation indicates, however, that an oppressed nation does not contain an appropriate and fit environment for the development of desirable virtues. The only plant that grows in an oppressed nation is that of depravity. Every Egyptian who has lived under despotic rule in the not very distant past knows that the village mayor, robbed of ten Egyptian pounds, reclaims 100 pounds from his villagers, and that the village chief, struck with 100 lashes, upon his return to the village takes his revenge upon 100 peasants!

The natural implication of this situation is that human beings respect only force and are deterred only by fear. When women were weak, men crushed their rights, despised them, treated them with contempt, and stomped on their personality. A woman had a very low status, regardless of her position in the family as wife, mother, or daughter. She was of no importance, was ignored, and had no legitimate opinions. She was submissive to a man because he was a man and she a woman. She obliterated herself in the person of the man. She was allowed nothing in the universe except that which she concealed in the corners of her home. She specialized in ignorance and secluded herself with the curtains of darkness. A man used her as an object of delight and pleasure, amused himself with her whenever he wished, and threw her into the road whenever he wished. He had freedom and she had bondage; he had knowledge and she had ignorance; he had a mind and she had simplemindedness; he had light and space and she had darkness and prison; he had absolute authority and she had only obedience and patience. Everything in existence belonged to him, and she was part of that totality of which he took possession.

Despising the woman, a man filled his home with slaves, white or black, or with numerous wives, satisfying himself with any of them whenever his passion and lust drove him. He ignored the prescribed religious obligations, which required good intentions for his actions and justice in his dealings.

Despising the woman, a man divorced her without reason.

Despising the woman, a man sat alone at the dining table, while his mother, sisters, and wife gathered after he was done to eat what was left over.

Despising the woman, a man appointed a guardian to protect her chastity. Thus a eunuch, a legal guardian, or a servant supervised, observed, and accompanied her wherever she went.

Despising the woman, a man imprisoned her in the house and boasted about her permanent restriction, which was lifted only when she was to be carried in her coffin to the grave.

Despising the woman, a man announced that she was unworthy of trust and honesty.

Despising the woman, a man secluded her from public life and kept her from involvement in anything except female or personal issues. A woman had no opinions on business, political movements, the arts, public affairs, or doctrinal issues, and she had no patriotic pride or religious feelings.

I do not exaggerate when I say that this has been the status of women in Egypt until the past few years, when we have witnessed a decrease in the power of men. This change is a consequence of the increased intellectual development of men, and the moderation of their rulers. We have observed that women at present have more freedom to look after their own affairs, that they quite often go to public parks in order to take the fresh air and to see the works of the Sublime Creator, displayed for the eyes of all humans, whether male or female. In fact, many women now accompany their husbands during their business trips to other countries. Likewise, many men have given women a special status within the family structure. This has occurred among men who are confident in their women and have no worries regarding their trustworthiness. This is a new kind of respect for women.

Yet we cannot claim that this change removes the need for criticism. In reality the causes of criticism are not changed, but the conditions surrounding it are. Among the most important of these are the firmly established tradition of veiling among the majority of the population, and the inadequate socialization of women. Were women's socialization effected in accordance with religious and moral principles, and were the use of the veil terminated at limits familiar in most Islamic schools of belief, then these criticisms would be dropped and our country would benefit from the active participation of all its citizens, men and women.

CHAPTER ONE:
THE EDUCATION OF WOMEN

Who do you understand a woman to be? Like a man, she too is a human being. Her body and its functions, her feelings, and her ability to think are the same as a man's. She has all the essential human traits, differing only in gender.

The superior physical and intellectual strength of men can be best explained by considering the past, when for many generations men have been involved in the world of work and in the pursuit of intellectual activities. During those years, women have been deprived of all opportunity and forced into an inferior position. The few variations have been shaped by variations in time and place.

Our people continue to consider it unnecessary to train and educate women; they still question whether teaching women to read and write is acceptable or forbidden according to the shari'ah.

I recall a discussion I had with the father of an attractive and intelligent nine-year-old girl. I was trying to communicate to him the importance of giving his daughter an education. In response to my suggestion he said, "Do you then expect her to have a position in the civil service?" I objected to his response and asked, "Do you believe that we should educate only those who will be employed?" He replied, "I am teaching her all that is necessary for running her household, and I will do nothing else besides that." His answer implied the finality of his opinion. By running a household, this stubborn father meant that his daughter should acquire such skills as sewing, cooking, and ironing—skills I consider important and necessary for every woman. However, what I am trying to communicate—and am not afraid to say—is that this father was in error in thinking that a woman needs only housekeeping skills in order to run her household competently.

In my opinion, a woman cannot run her household well unless she attains a certain amount of intellectual and cultural knowledge. She should learn at least what a man is required to learn up through the primary stage of education. This would ensure her grasp of some introductory principles and allow her to make her own choices. She could master these principles and be involved intellectually whenever she wished.

It is important for a woman to be able to read and write, to be able to examine the basis of scientific information, to be familiar with the history of various countries, and to be able to acquire knowledge of the natural sciences and of politics.

This knowledge needs to be complemented by a thorough understanding of cultural and religious beliefs. Eventually her knowledge will enable her to accept sound ideas and to discard the superstitions and myths that presently destroy the minds of all women.

Whoever assumes the responsibility of educating a woman should accustom her from her earliest childhood to love those qualities that in and of themselves complement the human being. She should be taught to appreciate those qualities that affect the family, maintain the kinship structure, and are needed to support the social structure of our society. She will gradually internalize these values, and they will become a dominant and permanent part of her spirit. This goal can only be achieved through proper guidance and good example.

This is the upbringing I wish for Egyptian women. I have discussed it in a general manner, but it is explained in detail in special studies in all languages. I believe that a woman who lacks this upbringing will be unable to adequately carry out her role in society or in the family.

WOMEN'S ROLE IN SOCIETY

Women comprise at least half the total population of the world. Perpetuating their ignorance denies a country the benefits of the abilities of half its population, with obvious negative consequences.

Ignorance and careless upbringing hinder Egyptian women from working (as Western women do) in the sciences, the humanities, the arts, commerce, and industry. If a woman were led by the hand into the community of the living, if her energy were directed toward active participation in society, and if she were to use her mental and physical abilities, she would produce as much as she consumes, rather than remain as she is now—a burden who lives only through the efforts of others. This change would also benefit her country, since it would increase its public wealth and its total intellectual productivity.

Our present situation resembles that of a very wealthy man who locks up his gold in a chest. This man unlocks his chest daily for the mere pleasure of seeing his treasure. If he knew better, he could invest his gold and double his wealth in a short period of time.

A society is weakened when a majority of its members are dependent on others and not contributing in any significant way to the needs of that society. When, on occasion, some of these people do work, they are like silent machines or dumb beasts of burden, working but not understanding.

A woman needs to be educated so that she can have understanding and a will of her own. The status of women in our country is at a critical stage. At present whenever we think of a woman, we assume that she has a guardian who administers all facets of her life. The assumption is that such a guardian is guaranteed under all circumstances. Facts indicate, however, that many women do not have men to be their guardians. The girl who has lost her relatives and remained single, the divorced woman, the widow and mother with no sons or whose sons are not of age: These are women who need a formal education that would enable them to control their own situations. They would be able to address their own needs and the needs of their children. Depriving these women of an education limits their options for obtaining a livelihood and could lead them to improper occupations or to a parasitic dependence upon generous families.

If we consider what compels a poor woman to sacrifice herself in the dark night to the first pursuer—what a great humiliation this must be for a woman—we find that the most probable cause is her great need for a little gold or silver. Pleasure is rarely behind her actions.

There is hardly an Egyptian family free of the burdensome expense of supporting a number of needy women unable to work or be self-sufficient. This phenomenon is one of the factors that prevent families from following sound economic principles in planning for their financial needs.

This dependency and other relevant factors cause an imbalance in family finances. An Egyptian man who earns a living for himself and his children discovers that a portion of his earnings goes to support some of his relatives, acquaintances, or others with whom he has little contact. His human compassion compels him to give freely of his income in order to prevent their starvation. Although these women are able to work and earn a living, they perceive such a man to be fulfilling his obligations. The gap between men and women in this situation can be attributed to women's deprived upbringing, which leaves them ignorant of their potentialities and abilities.

Assume that a woman does have a husband or guardian to support her financially. If her guardian were poor, would not a proper education be an asset to her? If he were rich, would it not ease the burden of administering the family resources? On the other hand, if a woman were rich—which is rare—would not an education assist her to administer her resources and her personal business?

Every day we come across situations in which women are compelled to hand over the administration of their income to a relative or stranger. We are also familiar with the situation in which trustees care more about their personal concerns than those of their constituents. Eventually we find that the trustees become rich while their constituents become poor.

We also see women use their personal seal for accounts, deeds, and contracts without knowing the content of the documents they are approving, implying that they do not understand the value or importance of the documents. Thus a woman can become stripped of her permanent rights through forgeries, cheating, or embezzlement committed by her husband, one of her relatives, or her trustee. Would this occur if the woman were educated?

Whatever the case may be, education in and of itself is a necessity of human life, one of the primary necessities of every civilized society. Education has become an honored goal, sought by every individual who wishes to achieve economic and spiritual happiness. This is because education is the only medium that elevates the character of human beings from a low and degraded position to the heights of honor and respect. All individuals have the natural right to develop their abilities to their full potential.

Religious teachings and local laws are directed toward both men and women. The arts, industry, inventions, and philosophy demand as much attention from women as from men. What respectable person, in the search for truth and happiness in this world and the next, is not interested in reading about these disciplines and exploring their treasures? How do a man and a woman differ in this desire? We have observed that young men and women have an equal ability to understand that to which they are exposed. Both ask about the causes of whatever they observe; we may even state that this inquisitiveness and curiosity is stronger among women than among men.

What sensitive spirit will accept life in a cage with clipped wings, a drooping head, and closed eyes when the wide-open space before her is endless, the sky is above her, the stars play with her vision, and the spirit of the universe calls and inspires her with the hope and desire to open its treasure of secrets?

The revealed law of God indicates that women were endowed with minds in the same manner as men. Can an objective man assume that God's intellectual gifts to women were an error, or that God gave women feelings and abilities to remain neglected and unused?

Muslims believe that women are the mistresses of their quarters in the home, but that their role ends at the doorstep of the house. These are the beliefs of those who live in a fantasy world, whose shortsightedness has blinded them from seeing beyond those fantasies, setting a veil between them and reality.

Were Muslims to reflect on this situation, they would realize that exempting woman from her first responsibility, namely, her preparation for self-sufficiency, has caused her to lose her rights. Giving a man the responsibility for every aspect of a woman's life has also meant that he has gained control over her rights. Thus a man expects no more of a woman than of a pleasant pet whose needs are provided for by the master in return for his entertainment.

Throughout the generations our women have continued to be subordinate to the rule of the strong and are overcome by the powerful tyranny of men. On the other hand, men have not wished to consider women other than as beings fit only to serve men and be led by men's will! Men have slammed shut the doors of opportunity in women's faces, thus hindering them from earning a living. As a consequence, the only recourse left to a woman was to be a wife or a whore. When women devalued intellectual or useful work, they were left with only the commodity of entertaining and gratifying the physical needs of men according to the men's demands. As a result, women directed all their energy toward inventing ways to attract men and to capture their affection.

History has left the woman behind without nurturing her mind through any sound training and thus awakening her rational and intellectual power. Her feelings have become the primary determinant for differentiating between what is good and evil, useful or harmful, attractive or unattractive. When she loves a person, she is extremely faithful to that person, initiating many desirable actions based primarily on whimsical feelings rather than on sound rational judgment. On the other hand, whenever she has an aversion to someone, she commits the greatest crimes without understanding the consequences of her behavior. Were women given a conscious and systematic training to help them develop their intellectual abilities and natural dispositions, they would develop the ability to control their feelings and would be able to go about their work with wisdom and with the appropriate principles for acceptable behavior.

Women lost their reasoning power during the darkness of past eras. A woman's physical weakness disabled her from acquiring it. She was therefore forced to resort to trickery, and acted toward man—her master and guardian—as a prisoner would toward his prison guard. Her cunning developed into her greatest faculty. Thus she became a skillful performer, an able actor, appearing in contradictory guises and different hues, depending on the situation in which she found herself. This ability is not a consequence of wisdom, but of fox-like trickery.

Women should not be blamed for this state of affairs, because they are not free persons. They lost their freedom because they lost the basis for sound, forceful judgment. The entire blame for this lies with men, those men who preceded us and who neglected the proper education of our women.

CHAPTER TWO:
WOMEN AND THE VEIL

In a book published in French four years ago in reply to the Duc d'Harcourt,[1] I examined the general topic of the veil. I pointed out the most important advantages of this tradition, but I did not address the meaning of the veil, or what the limitations of the veil should be. I intend to address these issues here.

An observer might think that I now maintain the veil should be completely dispensed with—but this is not the case. I still defend the use of the veil and consider it one of the permanent cornerstones of morality. I would recommend, however, that we adhere to its use according to Islamic law, which differs from our present popular traditions. Our people are ostentatious in their caution and in their interpretations of what they believe to be the application of the law, to the extent that they presently exceed the limits of the shari'ah and have harmed the nation's interests.

My observations on this topic also indicate that Westerners have gone too far in the exposure of their women so that it is difficult for a Western woman to guard herself from sensuous desires and unacceptable shameful feelings. We, on the other hand, have gone to extremes in veiling our women and prohibiting them from appearing unveiled before men, to such an extent that we turn women into objects or goods we own. We have deprived them of the mental and cultural advantages that are their natural due as human beings. The legal veil, however, is somewhere between these two extremes.

I sense that a reader who has followed my reasoning thus far and who shares my viewpoint on the upbringing of women may resist with all his strength my proposition for returning to the veil's legal limitations. That person may resort to all the incorrect information he has internalized from the traditions of a society that reflects the ideas of many previous generations. He may therefore defend the status quo. Yet despite his effort to defend this tradition, and his pains to preserve it, it will not continue in its present form much longer.

Why be courageous and firm in preserving a building bound for destruction and desolation, its foundations crumbled, its elements disintegrated, and its condition so deteriorated that each year a section of it collapses all by itself? Is this not what is happening? Is it not true that the seclusion of women during recent years is not the same as it was 20 years ago? Is it not obvious that women in many families go out of the house to accomplish their business, that they work with men in their many concerns, that they seek recreation in a suitable environment where the air is pleasant, and that they accompany their husbands on trips? Have we not also observed that this change has already taken place among families who represent those classes that were most adamant about banning their women from appearing in public?

If we compare our present situation with that of the recent past, we know that a generation ago a woman would have been disgraced had she left her husband's house or been seen by a stranger. When she went on a trip, all necessary measures were taken for her to travel at night so that no one would see her. A man's mother, sister, or daughter was apprehensive about sitting at the same table as him while he was eating. If we compare those times with today, without a doubt we find that these customs are on the wane.

Any person familiar with history knows that the veil played a role in the lives of women of other parts of the world. In his definition of the word "veil," Larousse[2] wrote: "Greek women used the veil when they went out; they hid their faces behind one of its ends as women in the Eastern nations do now." And:

After Christianity was introduced to various countries, it perpetuated the use of the veil. Thus women covered their heads when they went out and during the time of prayer. Women also used the veil in the Middle Ages, especially during the ninth century. The veil at that time was wrapped around a woman's shoulders and almost dragged on the ground. This custom continued up to the thirteenth century, when women began to change its form, until it reached its present state—a thin fabric to protect the face from dust and cold. However, the veil continued to be used in Spain and in those American countries which were colonized by Spain.

This quotation demonstrates that the veil is not a custom peculiar to us. Muslims did not invent it. It was a prevalent custom in many nations, and its disappearance was the result of the societal changes that accompanied the change and progress of civilization. This important topic should also be considered from our religious and social perspectives.

THE RELIGIOUS PERSPECTIVE

Had the shari'ah included specific passages to advocate the use of the veil as it is known now among Muslims, I would not have researched the topic. I would not have written a single letter contrary to those writings, however harmful they might have initially appeared, because heavenly orders should be obeyed without question, research, or discussion. However, the shari'ah does not stipulate the use of the veil in this manner. This custom is a product of the interactions among nations. Muslims were attracted to the use of the veil, approved it, exaggerated its use, and dressed it up in religious raiment, just as other harmful customs have become firmly established in the name of religion, but of which religion is innocent. I therefore find no reason to avoid examining this topic; in fact, I believe that it is our duty to become completely familiar with it, to identify the legal Islamic perspective, and to demonstrate the need for changing the present tradition. The Quran says:

> Tell the believing men to lower their gaze and be modest. That is purer for them. Lo! Allah is Aware of what they do. And tell the believing women to lower their gaze and be modest, and to display of their adornment only that which is apparent, and to draw their veils over their bosoms, and not reveal their adornment save to their own husbands or fathers or husbands' fathers, or their sons or their husbands' sons, or their brothers or their brothers' sons or sisters' sons, or their women, or their slaves, or male attendants who lack vigor, or children who know naught of women's nakedness. And let them not stamp their feet so as to reveal what they hide of their adornment. (XXIV, 30–31)

Through these verses, the shari'ah permits a woman to expose some parts of her body to strangers, even though the specific situations in which this could occur are not spelled out. Scholars have stated that the particularization and understanding of this law needs to be in context of the traditions of the time in which the message was given. Religious leaders assert that the face and palms of the hands are included as exceptions in the verse. But they disagree about other parts of the body, such as the arms and the feet.

Ibn 'abdin[3] has written:

> A free woman's body, including her unbraided, uncovered hair, is not to be seen by strangers. According to reliable opinions, this excludes her face, hands, and feet. Most opinions state that her voice is not prohibited among strangers. A minority opinion also states that her arms are not prohibited. A young woman is forbidden to expose her face because of the fear of temptation, such as being touched. This applies to women even if their ugliness can be considered a deterrent against desire. These reasons explain the lifting of the prohibition within the sanctity of marriage. If a man experiences any passionate feelings, he is forbidden to look at the face of any woman, even if she is ugly. If passionate desire is absent, then a man is allowed to look, even when the face is beautiful.

The Shafi'i[4] doctrine states in the book of *al-Rawd*:[5]

> In the absence of temptation between a man and a woman, a woman's face and palms can be seen. It is also permissible to see a woman's face during business dealings, when she gives testimony in legal situations, and when she is asked to reveal her identity during witnessing.

'Uthman ibn 'Ali al-Zayla'i[6] wrote in his book *Tabiyin al-haqa'iq sharh kanz al-daqa'iq*:

> The body of a free woman is prohibited, except her face, her hands, and her feet, according to the saying of the Most High: "And tell the believing women . . . to

display of their adornment only that which is apparent. . . ." (XXIV, 31)This verse
refers to their clothes (which may be decorated) and the face and the palms (which
are not hidden by their clothes and may be decorated with ornaments). Ibn 'abbas
and Ibn 'Umar[7] have also reiterated this. Even the book *al-Mukhtasir* has excluded
covering the face, the palms, and the feet, because the Prophet, God bless him
and grant him salvation, eliminated the prohibition that implied total covering of
the body, including covering the hands with gloves. If the face and palms had been
considered among the parts of the body that should remain hidden, he would not
have forbidden covering them. Regarding the feet there are two different viewpoints, and the more correct one states that the feet do not need to be hidden.

It is also known that the Malikis and the Hanbalis maintain that the face and
the palms are not sources of temptation. We will not prolong this discussion by
quoting these two doctrines. It is related that the Prophet's wife 'Aisha, may God
be pleased with her, said:

Asma', daughter of Abu Bakr, called upon the Prophet, God bless him and grant
him salvation, wearing a flimsy dress. The Prophet told her, "0 Asma', when a
woman reaches puberty, it is not appropriate for any part of her body to be seen
except this and this," and he pointed to his face and his hands.

Muhammad Siddiq Hasan Khan Bahadir[8] wrote in his book *Husn al-aswa:*

Permission has been given to women on this issue, because a woman needs to use
her hands to do anything; and it is essential for her to expose her face, especially
when testifying, when on trial, and in marriage. It is also essential for her to walk
in the streets; thus her feet will be seen. This is especially the case for poor
women.

Islamic law has given the same fights to women as to men. It makes them responsible for the civil and criminal consequences of their behavior, and gives them
the right to administer their finances and dispose of them. How then is it possible
for a man to conclude business contracts with a woman without seeing her or having proof of her identity?

It is a very peculiar and difficult thing to prove the identity of a woman who is
present but totally covered from head to foot or concealed behind a curtain or
door. The man is told, for instance: Here is the person who wishes to sell her
house, or to appoint you as her proxy for marriage. The woman may state "I have
sold" or "I have appointed," and the man is expected to be satisfied by the testimony of two witnesses, strangers or relatives, that she, as the identified person, has
indeed sold or appointed. In these situations there is no dependable guarantee.
Numerous legal cases demonstrate that cheating and forgery can easily take place
in such circumstances. How often do we learn that a woman has been married
without her knowledge, or that she has leased her property without being aware of
it, or that she may even have been dispossessed of all that she owns and is ignorant
of it? All this can occur because she is veiled and because men have taken charge of
her affairs and come between her and those with whom she is dealing.

How can a poor woman who is veiled take on a business or trade and earn a livelihood? How can a veiled maid render adequate service in a house in which there are men? How can a business woman administer her affairs in the midst of men? How can a veiled peasant woman cultivate her land or reap her crop? How can a veiled worker who has hired herself out as a builder possibly build a house or anything else?

God created this world and gave human beings mastery over it so that they could enjoy the benefits according to what they can achieve. God granted human beings privileges for administering this world, but He also placed limitations on them. Thus God established equality between men and women regarding their obligations and privileges. God did not divide the universe, making one part of it to be enjoyed by women alone and another to be enjoyed by men, working in it segregated from women. In fact, He created the burdens of life to be shared and controlled by both men and women. How can a woman enjoy all the pleasures, feelings, and power that God created for her, and how can she work in the universe if she is banned from the sight of any man except a blood relative or some other man to whom she cannot be married according to Islamic law? Undoubtedly, this is not what the shari'ah meant, and it should not be allowed by either law or reason. Thus we see that necessity has changed the use of the veil among most classes of Muslims. This is apparent among maids, working women, villagers, and even among Bedouin women. All these women are Muslim—indeed they may be more religious than the city-dwellers.

If a woman's presence is required in a legal situation, why allow her to conceal her face? For years, both adversaries and judges paid no attention to this issue— they were lenient and allowed a woman to appear before them veiled. She could be a claimant, a defendant, or a witness, and the judges apparently surrendered to tradition. The danger with this leniency, which I think we cannot tolerate, is quite obvious: there is no positive method by which a veiled person can be identified. This situation lends itself easily to fraud. Every man who opposes a woman in litigation should be concerned about the proof of identity of his adversary, which is especially important in the context of the legal validity of her statements. I find it unacceptable for a judge to give a verdict about a person whose face is veiled. I also consider it unacceptable for a judge to listen to a witness whose face is veiled. In fact, a judge's first responsibility is to verify the identity of the witness and the identity of the adversary, especially in criminal cases. Otherwise, why ask the name, age, occupation, and date of birth, as required by law? What use is it to know all these facts if the person's identity is not verified? The wisdom of the law is obvious when it asks that a woman uncover her face while she is a witness, for it also allows the judge to scrutinize facial expressions, thus enabling him to better evaluate the testimony of the witness.

The disadvantages of veiling are, without a doubt, the reason the shari'ah allows the woman to uncover her face and her palms. I am not asking for more than what the shari'ah allows.

Religious leaders of various schools agree that it is possible for a man who is asking for the hand of a woman in marriage to see the woman he wishes to marry. An instance was quoted about the Prophet, God bless him and grant him salvation.

In conversation with one of his followers who had asked for a woman's hand in marriage, he asked, "Have you seen the woman?" The man answered, "No." The Prophet then responded, "Go and see her. It is appropriate for you to become familiar with one another."

These are the sayings of the Quran, the Prophetic tradition, and our religious leaders. They clearly demonstrate that God has allowed women to uncover their faces and palms for obvious reasons, which can be understood by whoever wishes to understand them.

The judgment of the shari'ah is easy for both men and women to understand and reveals that men and women should not be separated by a veil, for it limits their interaction and hinders them in their work, whether it be authorized by the law or by life's necessities.

Furthermore, I do not believe that the veil is a necessary part of desirable behavior for women. There is no basis for such a claim. What is the relation between desirable behavior and exposing or veiling the face of a woman? What is the basis for discriminating against women? Is not good behavior in reality the same for both men and women? Is it not a product of an individual's intentions and work rather than of external appearances and clothes?

The fear of temptation, addressed by almost every line written on the subject, is a matter close to the hearts of distrustful men. Women should not concern themselves with it nor ask to know anything about it. Whoever fears temptation, whether man or woman, should avert his or her glance. The instructions that appear in the precious verses about averting one's gaze apply to both men and women. This proves clearly that it is no more appropriate for a woman to cover her face than for a man to cover his.

How strange! If men feared that women would be tempted, why were not men ordered to wear the veil and conceal their faces from women? Is a man's will considered weaker than a woman's? Are men to be regarded as weaker than women in controlling their desires? Is a woman considered so much stronger than a man that men have been allowed to show their faces to the eyes of women, regardless of how handsome or attractive they are, while women are forbidden to show their faces to men, from the fear that men's desires may escape the control of their minds, and they may thus be tempted by any woman they see, however ugly or disfigured she be? Any man who claims this viewpoint must then admit that women have a more perfect disposition than men; why then should women always be placed under the protection of men? If, however, this viewpoint is incorrect, what justifies this traditional control over women's lives?

The veil and the gauze face-cover actually increase the risk of temptation. The thin, white, gauze face-cover reveals the good features and hides the blemishes; the veil conceals the tip of the nose, the mouth, and the jaws, and reveals the forehead, temples, eyebrows, eyes, cheeks, and sides of the neck. These two coverings are in reality part of the ornaments worn by women that incite an onlooker's desires. They prompt him to wish to discover more of what is concealed after he has been tempted by the large area exposed. If a woman's face were uncovered, it is possible that her total appearance might turn glances away from her.

Temptation is not provoked by exposing some parts of a woman's body. In fact, the main causes of temptation are the revealing movements of a woman's body as she walks and the actions that reflect what is in her mind. The gauze face-cover and the veil, which hide a woman's identity, allow her to reveal what she wishes to reveal and to act in a manner that incites desire. She need not be concerned that anyone might identify her and report that so-and-so, or the wife of so-and-so, was doing such-and-such. She can accomplish whatever she desires under the protection of her veil. If her face were uncovered, her family status or her own honor would restrain her from initiating any provocative behavior that might attract attention to herself.

In truth, the gauze face-cover and the veil are not part of the shari'ah, in terms either of piety or of morality. They have been handed down to us from ancient traditions that preceded Islam and have continued to survive. The proof is that this tradition is unknown in many other Islamic countries, and it is still a custom in many Eastern countries that do not claim Islam as their religion. Covering the bosom is part of Islamic law, and there are clear admonitions about this—but nothing is mentioned about covering the face.

The discussion up to now has focused on the uncovering of a woman's face and hands. Now we will focus on the question of a woman's confinement to her house and the prohibition on interacting with men. This topic can be discussed from two perspectives: that which pertains to the Prophet's women, God bless him and grant him salvation, and that which pertains to other Muslim women. These are the only two perspectives the shari'ah addresses.

The first perspective is dealt with in the following verses:

> O ye who believe! Enter not the dwellings of the Prophet . . . unless permission be granted you. . . . And when ye ask of them (the wives of the Prophet) anything, ask it of them from behind a curtain. That is purer for your hearts and for their hearts. And it is not for you to cause annoyance to the messenger of Allah, nor that ye should ever marry his wives after him. Lo! that in Allah's sight would be an enormity. (XXXIII, 53)
>
> O ye wives of the Prophet! Ye are not like any other women. If ye keep your duty (to Allah), then be not soft of speech, lest he in whose heart is disease aspire (to you), but utter customary speech. (XXXIII, 32)

All the writings on Islamic jurisprudence agree, whatever the school or the interpretive books, that these passages refer exclusively to the women of the Prophet, God bless him and grant him salvation. God, may He be praised and exalted, ordered them to be secluded, and he clarified the reason for this law: that they were not like other women. These revelations pertained exclusively to the Prophet's women and are not applicable to women in general. Thus this seclusion is not a religious duty required for any other Muslim women.

The second perspective mentioned in the books on Islamic law are the sayings about the Prophet, God bless him and grant him salvation, in which he forbids a woman to be alone with a stranger. "A woman should not be alone with a man except if accompanied by somebody who is in a degree of consanguinity precluding marriage." Ibn 'abdin also states:

Being alone with a woman who is a stranger is unlawful, unless she is being accompanied because she is a debtor escaping her debts in a deserted place, or unless she is old and ugly, or unless there is a partition. It is also said that being alone
with a woman who is a stranger is abhorred to the extent that it is considered a
forbidden action. According to Abu Yusuf[9] it is not forbidden.

He continues:

The prohibition is negated if there is a partition or if there is a man whose degree
of consanguinity to the woman precludes marriage, or if there is a trusted or able
woman. Is it also negated when there is another man? I do not think so.

Some people believe that what God has required of his Prophet's women
should also be desirable for all Muslim women. I respond to this by repeating the
words of God, may he be exalted:

Ye are not like any other women. (XXXIII, 32)

This verse indicates that equality was not expected in regard to the application
of this rule. The verse also brings to our attention the fact that in not secluding our
women lies a wisdom that leads us to give them esteem and respect. At the same
time, it is unacceptable to deny this wisdom by appeasing those who want to follow
the example of the Prophet's women. We should encourage whatever facilitates
the daily needs of people and discourage whatever hinders, obstructs, or limits
people in achieving the necessities of life. The Quran has addressed this. God, may
He be exalted, has said:

Allah desireth for you ease; He desireth not hardship for you. (11, 185)

He has also said:

He . . . hath not laid upon you in religion any hardship. (XXII, 78)

And:

O ye who believe! Ask not of things which, if they were made known unto you,
would trouble you. (V, 101)

Had the example been followed, we would not have seen one of the caliphs,
famous for his piety and devotion to Islamic law, enforce customs in his family
contrary to seclusion. I will demonstrate what I mean by referring to the following
incident. Salma ibn Qais sent one of his relatives to inform 'Umar ibn al-Khattab,[10] may God be pleased with him, about a military situation. The messenger re-
counts his meeting with 'Umar:

After the greetings, I asked permission to see 'Umar. I was given permission and
ushered to where he was. He was sitting on a coarse woolen fabric, leaning on two

fiber-filled pillows. When he saw me he tossed one of the pillows to me, which I used. 'Umar's room was adjacent to a reception room, to which was attached another room with a small curtain drawn over its door. 'Umar said, "Umm Kulthum, bring us lunch." And she brought him bread with oil on which there was some unground salt. 'Umar then said, "Umm Kulthum, why don't you join us and eat with us some of this food?" She said, "I can hear a man's voice with you." 'Umar said, "Yes, and he is not from this town." When she learned that he did not know me, she said, "If you want me to go out where the men are, you should dress me as Ibn Ga'far and al-Zubayr and Talha dress their wives." He said, "Is it not enough to say Umm Kulthum, daughter of 'Ali ibn Abu Talib and wife of 'Umar, Commander of the Faithful?" He then turned to me and said, "Eat, for if she had agreed, your food would have been better than this."

The shari'ah, as we have presented it, does not require women to be secluded. Seclusion is not a constructive activity, and in fact it can be considered harmful.

NOTES

1. The Duc d'Harcourt had published *L'Egypte et les Egyptiens in 1893*, condemning Egypt's backward conditions and in particular the low status of women. Amin responded in 1894 with *Les Egyptiens: Response à M. le duc d'Harcourt*.
2. Pierre Athanase Larousse, French grammarian, lexicographer, and encyclopedist, 1817–75.
3. 1198–1253. Follower of the Hanifi School of law.
4. The four madhahib or schools of law of Sunni Islam are: the Shafi'i (founded by Muhammad ibn Idris al-Shafi'i, 767–820); the Maliki (Malik ibn Uns, 715–795); the Hanbali (Ahmad ibn Muhammad ibn Hanbal, 780–855); and the Hanafi (Abu Hanifa, d. 767).
5. *Rawd al-Talib* by Ibn al-Muqri.
6. d. 713. Hanafi scholar.
7. 'abdallah ibn 'abbas, 619–687, cousin of the Prophet and outstanding authority on the Quran in the generation after the Prophet; and 'abdallah ibn 'Umar, d. 749, son of the caliph 'Umar II.
8. 1248–1307.
9. A follower of the Hanafi school of law, d. 798.
10. 586?–644, Second Caliph.

V. STYLE OF LIVING

CHAPTER 16

THE WAY OF LIFE

Sayyid Ahmad Khan

"Tariqah-I Zandigi" (The Way of Life) from Sayyid Ahmad Khan, *Maqalat-i Sar Sayyid*, edited by Maulana Muhammad Isma'il Pani Pati. Lahaur: Majlis-i Taraqqi-yi Adab, 1962, p. 87–9. Translated by Kamran Talattof.

THE HONOR OR SHAME OF NATIONS IS RELATED to their customs and way of life, and sometimes also to their religion. In all nations, many customs of a barbarous and uncivilized age still persist. But civilized nations have shaped and fashioned such customs to such an extent that barbarity is completely eliminated from them and they have become most pleasant and attractive. Underdeveloped nations still continue to follow customs in a barbarous way and for this reason the developed nations look upon them with insulting and contemptuous gazes.

In ancient days most nations adopted a way of life that was adapted to each country's climate, and the way of life was usually very rough and contemptible. But civilized nations have kept reforming their way of life and raised it to a high level of progress and refinement, while uncivilized nations continued to exist in their ignorance. This is why they are despised and scorned by developed nations.

It has also frequently happened that because of the absence of arts and crafts in a previous age, a nation's way of life was not contemptible then, but through a lack of such things now, it has become contemptible in the present age. Thus to the extent that arts, crafts, and industry have developed, educated nations have embellished their way of life with many tools and accessories, and those who have not done this have remained lowly, despised, and uncivilized.

Nobody can deny that whether a nation receives honor or disgrace in the eyes of others depends on its way of life. But we shall make this even clearer by presenting a few examples. Look at the community of the Kanjars in India who wear only a loincloth and whose bodies are terribly dirty. Their feet and hands are always filthy and they use very dirty and foul-smelling cooking vessels. Their food is also unclean and their way of eating is so bad that to watch it nauseates you. Thus, on account of their base way of living, how contemptible this community appears to us!

Now look at those communities that have gradually progressed beyond their level through reforming their way of living. For example, consider the Chamars whose clothing and way of life are many degrees better than those of the Kanjars. They are not as ignoble in our eyes. Yet compared to the Chamars, the clothing and way of life of the common peasantry are much finer and better still. In our eyes they are not so detestable. Sometimes one might even go to their homes, drink their water with them, eat bread cooked in their homes, and not despise them in the least.

Besides those, there are three other communities in India who consider themselves to be well-bred, civilized, educated, and refined: the Hindus, the Muslims, and the English.

All the people of India are well acquainted with the way of dressing, way of life, manner of eating and drinking, and etiquette of these three communities. But there is no doubt that, of these three groups, the one that has the most refined way of life considers the other two communities to be just as disgraceful, uncivilized, and worthy of contempt as we consider the communities that are inferior to us.

In their own opinion, Muslims dress very well, and when they meet, they conduct themselves with a high level of order and cordiality. They decorate their tables with various kinds of delicious foods and beautiful vessels made of gold, silver, and china. But the community that maintains even greater fastidiousness in clothing, and refinement in ways of eating and drinking, looks at them with the same contempt and disdain as Muslims reserve for less developed communities.

When people who eat with spoon and fork and regularly change their plates, knives, and spoons, see us Muslims eat with our hands, they are filled with great horror or aversion. Although the Turks have changed in this regard, in Egypt to this day women place their food on a low table and eat with their fingers.

Quite recently the Prince of Wales (the official heir to the throne of England) visited Egypt with the Princess of Wales (the wife of the heir). The mother of the Khedive of Egypt invited the Princess of Wales to the ladies' section of the palace for a dinner in her honor. The Honorable Mrs. William Gray was with the Princess of Wales as her lady-in-waiting and was included in the invitation. When she returned from Egypt she wrote an account of the journey. We present here an extract from what she wrote about that meal so that it may become clear what another community, which eats with more refinement than we, thinks of the manner in which we eat. She writes:

> In the dining room a round silver table was set. It stood a foot above the floor and looked like a large tray. Around it cushions were spread. All of us sat down cross-legged on the cushions around the table. The Princess of Wales sat at the right

hand of the mother of the Khedive of Egypt. After her sat all of the women according to their rank.

First of all a large dish of stewed chicken and pilau came, and we received spoons made of shells. But there was neither knife nor fork. After this a large joint of mutton came, and then a score of other dishes one after the other, which were eaten by breaking them off with the fingers of the hands.

I have never before felt such disgust, nor come so close to gagging. I was so filled with repulsion and nausea when I saw fingers immersed in food and eating food broken with one's fingers, that sometimes I refused to take the food which was being offered to me, but the lady sitting next to me thought that I was just shy, and each time she took food with her hand and placed it on my plate. Once she picked an onion out of the stew and placed it before me, and I felt quite sick to my stomach. There was absolutely no alcohol served with the meal.

No doubt the reaction of Mrs. Gray was due mostly to the fact that she was not accustomed to eating in this way. But, to be fair, we must also admit that to eat with knife and spoon and to have a separate dish for every kind of food is better and more refined than to eat with one's bare hands.

It is said that to eat with one's hands is approved in our religion, and to disdain it can even amount to irreligion. We won't enter into the question of whether this view is correct or incorrect, we will simply accept this point. To those who say that to half-follow the elders is disgraceful, I would merely add this: If the Muslims can follow this idea along even further and bear to give up foods cooked in excessive amounts of oil, which soil their hands and faces (for this is what causes the spite and disgust) in exchange for dry barley bread made of unsifted flour with maize cobs and dates—then they will be fully following our elders! Then, nobody will feel any dislike for eating with the hands. But you cannot have the kind of food that Pharaohs eat and then talk of etiquette that emulates the manners of the Prophet.

We should thank God that He has given us His gifts. Let us use them, and show our gratefulness by our acts. When we understand that it is not out of arrogance and pride that we are using knives and forks, but in a spirit of thankfulness to the Provider of all blessings, and that at the same time we are bringing the Muslim community out of a disgrace it suffers in the eyes of non-Muslims—and in doing this there is indeed honor for Islam—then we have every reason to consider eating with knife, fork and spoon a fully laudable and desirable thing to do.

As the Prophet said (may blessings and peace be upon him): "Deeds are known by intentions."

CHAPTER 17

THE WAY TO EAT A MEAL

Sayyid Ahmad Khan

"Tariqah-i Tanawul-i Ta'am" (The Way to Eat a Meal) from Sayyid Ahmad Khan, *Maqalat-i Sar Sayyid*, edited by Maulana Muhammad Isma'il Pani Pati. Lahaur: Majlis-i Taraqqi-yi Adab, 1962, p. 90–2. Translated by Kamran Talattof.

STUBBORNNESS AND SELF-ABSORPTION ARE GREAT enemies of mankind. To refuse to acknowledge something good, and not to ponder its harms and benefits simply on account of stubbornness is not mankind's work. At present, we are neither concerned with eating seated on chairs at a table with knives and forks like the English, nor do we crave to imitate the Turkish. Instead, we want to think very straightforwardly about the way to eat, and discuss to what extent its distasteful aspects can be removed without changing its basic nature.

In the small enclosed area Hindus reserve for cooking and dining, they select and place before the diners small servings of all the different kinds of food, in small cups, saucers, or dishes made of sewn leaves. The diners eat a little from each of the dishes, and what is left over lies uneaten in those same serving dishes until all are finished eating. Then the dishes are taken away.

In India, Muslims eat the same way the Hindus do. The only difference is that Hindus sit in their dining enclosure, whereas Muslims spread large cloths on the floor of a larger room and sit around them. Just as Hindus place all of the different kinds of food before themselves, Muslims lay it out before themselves in serving dishes, small plates, saucers, and small cups, like items laid out in worship of a ancient goddess! There are every kind of bread and all varieties of kabobs and salvers of firni and dishes of eggplant fritters in yogurt sauce and bowls of sour and sweet pickled fruits. While someone is eating firni with his forefinger, another, bless him, is licking it off of all four fingers. Someone is mixing his aruwi curry a little at a time into his pilau as he eats it, while another has finished eating pilau mixed with curry and with fingers still wet and sticky, has begun to dunk bread into the curry and eat it. Someone has put his dish of eggplant fritters to his mouth, taken a noisy sip of the sauce, and exclaimed, "My God, that's hot! Oh! Ah!" All the dirty dishes, half-eaten food, sucked and discarded bones, bits of bread, and the flies picked out of the curry, lay before them. Whoever finishes eating first begins to wash his hands, rinse out his mouth and throat with gargling, rub his teeth with a cleaning powder, and rub his tongue with two fingers to clean it. All this while the others continue to dine nonchalantly!

There is no realization on the part of those washing their hands, of the un-mannerliness of what they are doing so close to those who are still eating. They do not care that those still eating must listen to the disgusting sounds of rinsing and gargling, and see the spectacle of their spitting of saliva yellowed by curry-spice and expelling of blobs of throat-clearings into the basins, where the coagulated globs float around on top of the slopwater like bits of jelly.

The way the English eat is well-known to everyone, and we had better not de-scribe it lest our devout fellow-countrymen, those diligent searchers of the sunnat, stab us with the dagger of this well-known hadith, "Whoever adopts the manners of a people becomes one of them."

Let us tell you how they eat a meal in Arabia. A small cloth is spread over a low table, and one kind of food is brought in a single dish. All the people who are seated around the table begin to eat from the dish. After a few mouthfuls have been eaten, that dish is removed and a second kind of food is brought in on an-other dish. After another few mouthfuls, that dish is also removed. In this way food keeps coming and going regularly. The advantage of eating this way is that used dishes and left-over food do not remain before the diners.

But in no other country is there such slovenliness when people gather to eat as there is among the Muslims of India! In truth, it is a matter of great shame and sorrow that we should continue in such squalidness out of stubbornness and self-absorption and not pay any attention to correcting and reforming this condition.

We do not mean that one must, perforce, sit on a chair at a table and eat with knife and fork, or, like an Arab, spread a cloth on a low table. By all means dine, from your customary tablecloth [because the Prophet did it in that way] even though there are so many [more important] things of the Prophet's example to emulate than this! By all means, sit on the ground and eat your food in accordance with the Holy custom! But for God's sake, give up this slovenliness and in all re-spects be as refined and as clean as you can in your mode of eating. After all, to ob-serve cleanliness and purity is not forbidden in the shari'at!

But we ought to remember that until some method and principle is estab-lished for some procedure and it is carefully followed, the procedure does not en-dure. When the principle is a superior one, it gradually comes into practice by itself, and everybody begins to observe it. After a while it becomes such a habit that it is considered second nature.

Therefore, our objective here is to develop some code of eating and correc-tion in this customary manner of eating that people may be delivered from their slovenliness without being subjected to the taunt in the saying of the prophet, "Whoever adopts the fashion of a people other than his own, becomes one of them." With this in mind, we have examined a few principles in this chapter, and under some later issues we shall write on this further.

CHAPTER 18

CIVIL RIGHTS

Rifa'ah Rifa al-Tahtawi

Raif Khuri, ed. "Selection III: Rifa'a Rafi' al-Tahtawi, 1216–1290 (1801–1873)." In *Modern Arab Thought: Channels from the French Revolution to the Arab East.* Princeton: Kingston Press, 1983, pp. 102–10.

CIVIL RIGHTS ESTABLISHED FOR THE FRENCH[1]

. Article 1: All Frenchmen are equal before the Law.

Article 2: They pay, without distinction, a specified sum of their money to the Treasury, each according to his wealth.

Article 3: Each one is qualified to attain any position or rank.

Article 4: Each one has an independent personality (dhat) whose freedom is guaranteed. Nobody may infringe upon it except in some rights that are stipulated in the Law and in the way the Law is deemed applicable by the judge (hakim).

Article 5: Everyone who lives in France may profess his religion, as required, with no intervention by anybody; he shall be assisted to accomplish that, and anybody who molests him in his worship shall be stopped from doing so.

Article 6: The religion of the state is the Apostolic Roman Catholic faith.

Article 7: The maintenance of Catholic and other Christian churches shall be met by money of the Christians and none of that money shall be allocated for the maintenance of places of worship that belong to other religions.

Article 8: No one in France shall be denied the right to write, print, and publish his opinion provided that it does not contravene the Law. If it does, then it shall be suppressed.

Article 9: All property and possessions are inviolable and nobody shall encroach on the property of another.

Article 10: The state shall have the exclusive prerogative of compelling a man to sell his property for the public welfare, provided that it pay an adequate price before acquisition.

Article 11: All opinions held or riots made prior to this Law shall be forgiven. The same applies to rulings by the courts or actions committed by the people.

Article 12: Recruiting of soldiers shall be arranged, and their number decreased. The posting of soldiers on land and at sea shall be implemented by specific law.

THE RIGHTS OF THE PEOPLE
SECURED BY THE PARLIAMENT

The first article, i.e., "All Frenchmen are equal before the law," means: that all those who live in France, whence high or low, must, without distinction, be subject to the provisions of the Law. Legal proceedings can be initiated even against the king himself and judgment can be passed against him like any one else. Consider this first article: it has great power in establishing justice, in helping the wronged and satisfying the poor by convincing them that they are great as far as legal proceedings are concerned. This criterion has almost become one of the most comprehensive principles among the French. It is clear proof of how highly justice is valued among them and how advanced their cultural program has become. What they hold dear and call liberty is what we call equity and justice, for to rule according to liberty means to establish equality through judgments and laws, so that the ruler cannot wrong anybody, the law being the reference and the guide. This is indeed a country to which the following applies:

> And justice filled it from end to end
> And in it were happiness and sincerity

In general, if justice exists in any country it must be considered as relative and not absolute, for absolute justice as well as perfect faith, complete purity and similar things do not exist anywhere, nowadays. Thus there is no point in limiting impossible things to the ghul (ghouls), the griffin, and the faithful friend, of which the poet says:

> When among the people of my time I found no faithful friend to choose,
> I became certain that the impossible things are three:
> The ghul, the griffin and the faithful friend.

This is not true about the griffin because it is an existing species of birds mentioned by botanists. Al-Thal'labi in his *Stories of the Prophets* (Qisas al-Anbiya) mentions the story of the griffin and King Solomon and how it denied predestination. It is true that the griffin, believed by the common people, Arabs and Franks, to have the head of an eagle and the body of a lion, does not exist; yet it does exist as a bird.

The second article is purely political. It can be stated that had taxes been clearly set in Muslim countries, as they are in that country, this would have been a course of satisfaction, especially when *zakat* (alms tax), fay' (revenue from state lands), and booty cannot meet the needs of the Treasury or are prevented from being levied totally. Taxes might have some roots in Islamic law according to some sayings of the Great Imam (Abu Hanifa). "Kharaj land tax is the pillar of kingship" is an established maxim among ancient wise men. During my stay in Paris, I never heard any complaint against taxes, imposts, and other levies. People do not mind paying, because taxes are levied in a way that does no harm to the payer and at the same time benefits the Treasury, especially in that the wealthy are protected against injustice and bribery.

The third article does not cause any harm at all. One of its merits is that it encourages everyone to learn so that he may be promoted to a higher position. Thus the French could acquire different kinds of knowledge and their civilization is not limited to one condition like that of the Chinese and the Indians, who believe in transmitting arts and crafts from father to son by inheritance. A historian states that the law of the ancient Copts (Egyptians) assigned to everyone his own craft, which had to be inherited by his sons. The reason for such a procedure, according to him, is that all arts and crafts were considered honorable. This procedure was necessitated by circumstances, for it helped them reach the degree of perfection in their arts because the son usually improves on what he witnessed his father doing many times and does not direct his desire to another craft. This method usually cut the roots of covetousness and kept everybody content with his craft. Thus one does not aspire to what is higher but directs his attention to inventing new things that can carry his craft to a higher degree of perfection.

The answer to what this historian claims is that not everyone has the natural aptitude to learn his father's craft. To confine him to it might produce an unsuccessful craftsman, whereas if other crafts were open to him he would prove to be successful and achieve his aim.

The fourth, fifth, sixth, and seventh articles are very useful for both natives and foreigners. Thus the population of this country increased and its culture progressed with the many foreigners who migrated to it.

The eighth article encourages every man to express his opinions, to propagate his knowledge and to say whatever occurs to him if it does not harm others. In this way a man comes to know what his fellow men are thinking, especially on reading the daily sheets called newspapers (jurnalat) and gazettes (kazitat), which publish up-to-date news, both domestic and foreign. Although these abound with innumerable lies, they still contain news that people may wish to know. They may also contain newly established scientific matters, useful notices, or profitable advice, coming from the noble and the vulgar. Sometimes the latter discover what the former miss. It is said: "Do not look down upon a great opinion given to you by a lowborn man, for the pearl does not lose its value because of the mean status of the diver." A poet also said:

When I heard of him I heard of one, and when I
saw him he was to me the whole universe.
Every kind of game is in the belly of the onager
and One man can represent all the good men.

One of the great merits of the newspaper is that if a man does an outstanding deed, whether good or bad, it is reported in the paper, and made known to all people, high and low. Thus the doer of good deeds is encouraged and the doer of evil ones restrained. If a man is wronged by another, he states his case in the newspaper to make it known to high and low, without any alteration in, or deviation from, facts; the case gets to the courts and is dealt with according to established laws, making it thus a good lesson to others.

The ninth article is the heart of justice itself. It is essential to curb the oppression of the weak by the strong. For it to be followed by the tenth article is mere propriety.

Article 15 contains a very interesting point, i.e., that legislation is exercised collectively by three bodies: the first is that of the king and his ministers; the second is that of the Chamber of Peers who side with the King; and the third is the Chamber of the Deputies who represent the subjects and defend them against injustice from anyone. Wherever these deputies speak for the subjects, the subjects seem to be self-ruling. At any rate, this is a safeguard and a security against injustice. The underlying wisdom in the rest of the articles must be clear to you.

THE REVOLUTION OF 1830:
THE CHANGES THAT OCCURRED AND
THE CIVIL WAR THAT RESULTED THEREFROM

In the above mentioned laws about the rights of Frenchmen, the eighth article stipulated that no one in France should be denied the right to write, print and publish his opinion provided that it does not contravene the law. If it does, then it should be suppressed. In 1830, the king issued many decrees in which he prohibited the expression of personal opinions in writing or through publishing except under certain conditions. This was directed especially against the daily newspapers; they were not to appear before submission for censorship by an agent of the state who would not allow the publication of any material he did not want published. The king had no authority to issue such a decree by himself, but only as a law, and law could not be enacted without the agreement of three opinions: those of the king, the Chamber of Peers, and the Chamber of Deputies. Thus the king did by himself what could not be enforced unless done with the consent of others. He also introduced by those decrees some changes in the choice of the members of the Chamber of the Deputies by changing the people who were to choose those deputies and send them to Paris. Furthermore, he inaugurated the Chamber of Deputies before its members convened, although it was the right of that Chamber not to be inaugurated till after its members convened, as had been done the previous time. That was all contrary to the law. When the king issued these decrees it seems that he felt that he was contravening the law, hence he gave military posts to many chiefs who were well-known for their enmity to liberty, the thing which was the sole aim of the French nation. The decrees themselves appeared so suddenly that the French seem not to have been ready for them. And as soon as the decrees appeared, all those well-versed in politics predicted a great crisis, which would generate grave consequences. Or as the poet says:

Underneath the ashes I can see the sparkling of live-coals
and before long it may blaze;
For fire is kindled by rubbing two sticks
and war starts with words.

On the evening of that day, when the decrees appeared in the newspapers, the people started to move restlessly near the Place du Palais-Royal, where the relatives of the king called the Family of Orleans, to which the present king belongs, used to live. At that time, sorrow appeared on all faces. It was the 26th of July. On the next day most of the liberal newspapers did not appear because decrees were not accepted by the journalists. The decrees became known to all the people and great agitation took place, for newspapers did not stop except for very serious matters. Workshops, factories, plants and schools were closed. Some of the liberal newspapers appeared, enumerating the vices of the king and urging the people to disobey him. These papers were distributed free among the people. In this country, and indeed others, words can achieve what arrows cannot. The art of rhetoric here is strong, especially when it appears in eloquent prose, which has a strong, penetrating effect. Truly it has been said that if revelation were to come to men, other than the prophets, it would come to eloquent writers. Also, what the newspapers publish has the deepest effect when it is acceptable by the common people and appeals to the elite. This is the acme of true rhetoric, which is defined as what the common people can understand and what satisfies the elite. When the heads of the Hisba (police) heard of that, they appeared in public places and prevented the people from reading those newspapers, besieged the printing presses, were about to smash the printing machines—they broke some—put the printers whom they accused in jail and insulted many. All those acts showed the great divergence between the king and the subjects, intensified the anger of the French, and made the owners of the newspapers—who were none other than the leaders of the French people, whose opinions were expressed in those papers—write a public protest, print many copies of it and post them on the walls of the city. They ordered the people to prepare for war and assigned the place of battle. The meeting place was to be the Rue de Palais-Royal where, as well as in the adjacent quarters, many people crowded. When the royal troops tried to disperse the crowds, a great tumult arose and the anger of the citizens in all the streets and quarters increased. The soldiers attacked the people and fighting broke out between the two sides. At first, the people fought with stones while the soldiers fought with swords and other weapons. Fighting became fiercer and attack and retreat on both sides became more intense. Then the people started looking for weapons and in the city of Paris the sound of guns was heard on both sides, as though the French seemed to say " . . . so your cousins also have spears." In that fierce fighting, most of those who were killed were from the people. Their anger, therefore, grew stronger and they exposed the dead in public places in order to urge the people to fight and to expose the atrocities of the soldiers.

The people became bitter against their king, for they believed that it was he who had given the orders to fight. Anywhere you went, you would hear the cries, "Weapons! Weapons! Long live the Charte! Down with the cruelty of the king!" From that time on, bloodshed increased. The people bought or grabbed weapons from sword-makers. Most of the laborers and craftsmen, especially the printers, attacked the police-stations and the soldiers' barracks, seized the weapons and gunpowder and killed the soldiers whom they found there. The people removed the royal emblem from the shops and public places—the emblem of the French king was the lily as that of the Muslim Sultan is the crescent, and that of the Russian Emperor the eagle. They broke the lamps in the quarters, pried out the paving stones of the city and gathered them in the main streets to make it difficult for the horsemen to pass. They also plundered the royal depots of gunpowder. When things became very critical and the king learned of what had happened while he was out of the city, he ordered it to be put under a state of siege. He appointed as commander in chief an enemy of the French, well known for his transgression against the principles of liberty. This procedure was contrary to every kind of adroitness, wise policy, and principle of statecraft. It showed the people that the king had no sagacity, for such an attribute would have induced him to show signs of tolerance and forgiveness, and forgiveness from the king renders kingship more lasting. He should not have appointed as leaders any but wise men, friendly to him and to the people, not hated by him and by them, nor enemies to either side. By treating his subjects as enemies, he meant to ruin them, although to conciliate an enemy reveals more judiciousness than to seek his destruction. In this respect, the following verses are much to the point:

> You should stick to clemency, deference,
> Gentleness toward the guilty, and forbearance.
> If you do not forgive the wrong-doer
> You will be attacked by fools.

What the king did produced the opposite of what he desired. He suffered the mischief he had meant for his opponents. Had he given liberty to a people who were worthy of it, he would not have got into such trouble and been forced to abdicate during that last ordeal; particularly so, because the French had become fond of liberty and so used to it that it had become part of their psychological constitution. How admirable is the saying of the poet:

> Men have customs to which they become attached,
> Whose duties and practices they keep.
> He who does not associate with them according to their conventions,
> Is considered by them as boring and odious.

On July 28th, the people captured from the soldiers the Hotel de Ville (the office of the Mayor of Paris) and occupied it. At that moment, there appeared on the scene the National Guard, i.e., the Guards who used previously to protect the people, just as the Royal Guard used to protect the king, before Charles

X disbanded them. They came to defend the people in that civil war. They drew their weapons and expelled all the soldiers from their places, most of which they burnt. Courts, then, were convened and the people were the sole judge. The state had done its best to suppress the rising but failed and now it was helpless. All riflemen and gunners were on the move, as well as 12,000 men of the Royal Guard and 6,000 foot soldiers. The total number of the Royal soldiers was 18,000 not counting the artillerymen and the riflemen. Those who carried weapons among the people were less in number, but those who had no weapons used to fight with stones and help those who were armed. After the occupation of the Hotel de Ville and the seizure of a cannon from the regular soldiers, the defeat of the Royal soldiers in the city became apparent. They moved to a place called the Louvre and to the Tuileries Palace, the residence of the King. Fighting went on in that place, the tri-color flag, which is the symbol of liberty, was raised on churches and large public buildings. Church bells rang to tell the people inside and outside Paris, whether residents of that city or any other, that they were called upon to carry arms and to stand against the soldiers. When the soldiers realized that victory was on the people's side and that by using arms they were killing their compatriots and kinsmen, most of them stopped fighting and many of their officers resigned.

By the morning of the 29th, the citizens had seized control of three-quarters of the city, including the Tuileries Palace and the Louvre, on which the flag of liberty was raised. When the Commander, who was entrusted with reimposing the rule of the King on the people of Paris, heard of that, he retreated, and that sealed the victory of citizens, who were joined by the soldiers themselves. At this time a provisional government was set up and a temporary council chosen to supervise the affairs of the country until a legal ruler could be installed. The head of this provisional government was General Lafayette who had also fought in the first revolution for liberty. This man is well-known as a lover and a defender of liberty. He is held in high esteem like kings because of that and because of his constancy in politics (*bulitiqiyya*). He is not talented in the sciences, the field in which most of the renowned men among the French are known for their marvelous creativity, especially in the military sciences. He occupies the highest rank, though his talents are not the greatest. This is not mentioned to censure his knowledge as much as his worthiness to rule. It is noticeable that, in most countries, attaining high posts is not always dependent on the amount of knowledge acquired, although knowledge should be a prerequisite both by law and nature. It is strange that such a phenomenon occurs also in well-civilized countries. I think this fact conforms with the Prophet's tradition, "Man's intelligence is considered part of the means of livelihood ordained to him." The poet also says:

> Do not wonder if you find a virtuous man suffering poverty.
> The Prophet has truly said, "Man's intelligence is part of the means of his livelihood."

And another poet admirably says:

Had the pouring of the clouds been governed by reason,
It would not have watered both palms and thorns.
Had it been given according to status,
It would have watered the high hills and not the lowlands.

NOTE

1. Selection from Rifa'a al-Tahtawi, *Takhlis al-Ibriz ila Talkhis Baris*, vol. II. Beirut: n. a., 1973, pp. 96–7, 102–4, 205–8.

I. JURISPRUDENCE, BASES OF LAW, AND RATIONAL SCIENCES

CHAPTER 19

ISLAM AS THE FOUNDATION OF KNOWLEDGE

Sayyid Qutb

Sayyid Qutb Shaheed. "Islam and Culture." In *Milestones*, 2nd ed., translated by S. Badrul Hasan, M.A. Karachi, Pakistan: International Islamic Publishers Ltd., 1988, pp. 193–208.

THE FIRST PART OF THE FIRST PILLAR OF ISLAM IS A DEDICATION of prefect servitude to God alone, and witness to this meaning and requirement is given by the recital of "There is no god except God." The second part of this pillar is that for knowing the details of this servitude and its true and correct way one has to refer to the Messenger of God (S.A.W). Witnessing "Muhammed (S.A.W.) is the Messenger of God" refers to this. The practical shape of absolute servitude to God is that Allah alone should be deemed the Lord (the worshipped) in faith, practice, and law.

A Muslim can never hold the belief that anyone else except God can appropriate the position of lordship nor that anyone, being a Muslim, can even imagine that, barring God, any creature can be worshipped or anyone can be assigned the place of sovereignty. In the foregoing pages we have also explained the correct implication and meaning of servitude, faith, and worship. In this chapter under discussion, we shall state the real connotation of sovereignty and its relation to culture.

THE FIELD OF ACTIVITY
OF THE DIVINE CODE

From the point of view of Islamic ideology the meaning of God's sovereignty is not confined to receiving legal orders from God alone and then judgments sought in the light of those commands and delivered accordingly. In Islam the meaning of "Divine Law" itself is not restricted to the sphere of legal orders only, not even to the sphere of fundamental regulations of rulership, its system, and its diverse institutions. This limited and narrow concept of Divine Law does not appropriately explain Islamic law and Islamic ideology. What Islam calls Divine Law, covers the entire scheme that God has devised for regulating human life. It includes within its sphere the regulation of thoughts and views, fundamentals of statecraft, principles of ethics and culture, laws of transactions, and regulations of knowledge and the arts. The Divine code of law circumscribes every angle of human thought and opinion. It discusses all the nooks and corners of human life whether it pertains to the human concept about the Supreme Being or the Universe or the transcendental realities, which are beyond the grasp of human comprehension and senses; whether it is the creative sphere of life or that of legislation, whether it is the question of man's reality and his nature or a discussion relating to his very status in this universe. Similarly the Islamic code does not lose sight of the practical departments of life, for example, politics and sociology, economics and justice, including their fundamental principles and procedures. Rather it desires that the spirit of perfect servitude to one God be infused in them. At the same time it wishes to hold sway over those legal bindings that address and organize those practical departments of life (this is exactly the same thing that is being commonly termed "SHARIAH" now-a-days, although this restricted and narrow sense of Shariah does not absolutely convey the wider and comprehensive meaning that has been adopted in Islam). This Shariah is operative in the regulations of morality and dealings, and it is manifested through those values and standards that are current in society, and that determine the value and worth of men, things, and deeds in social and collective life. Similarly this Shariah dominates all the aspects of knowledge and art, and it reveals itself in all intellectual efforts and artistic activities. We need God's guidance in them just as we require His Divine directives in the legal orders bearing modern and limited senses.

As regards the question of the acceptance of God's sovereignty in respect of Government and law, it should have become clear from our foregoing discussions. Similarly the need of introducing sovereignty of God in morals and dealings, values of the society and standards of acceptance and rejection would have also, it is expected, to have become clear to some extent, for the values that take root in a society, the standards of rejection and acceptance that gain currency, the regulations of morals and dealings that get introduced, are indirectly drawn from those concepts that are dominant over that society, originating as they do from the same source from which the faith, active beneath these concepts, evolves.

But what should be a matter of wonder and marvel for the very revered leaders of Islamic literature, much less the common folk, is that the same Islamic concept and its divine source should be our resort and guide in the intellectual and artistic fields also.

A whole book has since appeared on the subject of art in which discussions have been made on this theme, from this viewpoint, that all artistic efforts are in fact the interpretation of human concepts, its intuitions, and passivity. They reflect the picture of life and existence, as and what it is, in the intuition of man. All these things are such that they are not only controlled by the Islamic concept but also generated by it in the intuition of a faithful Muslim, for the Islamic concept circumscribes the universe, the human self and all aspects of life, and points out all those facets that are related to their Creator. Its particular theme is the reality of man and his position in the universe; the purpose of his creation, his bound obligations, and the real values of his life! All these are essential components of the Islamic concept, for the Islamic concept is not merely an intellectual and abstract structure but is the name of an alive, active, effective, and motivating reality that controls all those feelings, emotions that are engendered within man.

In short the problem of thought and art and the discussion to align them with the Islamic concept and divine source so that the perfect servitude to God may be evidenced in this aspect also, requires a thorough discussion. And just as we have stated before, this discussion would be typical and unique for the educated class of the modern age, rather for Muslims themselves who repose faith in the imperativeness of sovereignty of God and legislation.

BRANCHES OF KNOWLEDGE IN WHICH MAN IS BOUND BY DIVINE REVELATION

A Muslim has not the authority to seek guidance and light from any other source and well-head except the Divine one in any matter that pertains to faith, the general concept of life, rituals, morals and dealings, values and standards, politics, and assembly, principles of economics, or the explanation of human history. Similarly a Muslim is also bound that for seeking this guidance and light he should make such a Muslim instrumental whom he can confide in as regards his religion and piety and there should not be any contradiction and duplicity in his faith and action.

BRANCHES OF KNOWLEDGE IN WHICH MAN IS NOT BOUND BY DIVINE REVELATION

Of course, a Muslim is allowed to imbibe abstract learnings from all the Muslims and non-Muslims alike, for example, Chemistry, Physics, Biology, Astronomy, Medicine, Industry, Agriculture, Administration (to the extent of technical aspects only), Technology, Arts of warfare (from their technical aspect only), and other like learnings, arts, and technology. Although the fundamental principle is that when a Muslim society has come into being it should itself strive to generate these capabilities in all the fields in a big measure, for all these types of knowledge and technology are obligatory for some to acquire special proficiencies and capabilities. If these faculties and capabilities are not developed, nor a congenial atmosphere provided for producing, patronizing, developing, and commissioning them for yielding profitable results, the society as a whole will be deemed guilty. But until all this is available, a Muslim has permission to acquire these knowledges and arts along with their practical explanations from both Muslims and non-Muslims, and benefit from the experiments and strivings of both Muslims and non-Muslims and may consign these duties irrespectively to the Muslims and non-Muslims. These are included in affairs about which the Messenger of God (S.A.W.) has said, "You better understand your worldly affairs." They do not pertain to matters related to Muslim concepts about life and the universe or discuss man's responsibility and the nature of man's relations with the surrounding universe and his relations with the Creator of life. They are also not concerned with those principles and regulations and laws and canons that organize the lives of individuals and community. They are also not connected with morals and manners, customs and traditions, and those values and standards that command supremacy in society and project their impressions onto society, hence the Muslim need not fear that by imbibing these learnings he would be vulnerable to any flaw in his faith or he would revert to Jahiliyyah.

But as regards reason of human struggle, whether it is individual or collective in form—and this struggle is directly connected with human self and concepts of human history—similarly as regards the reason for the beginning of the universe, inception of life and man's own beginning and its interpretation, since all these matters pertain to Metaphysics (and are not related to Chemistry, Physics, Astronomy, and Medicine) they have as such the same position as the principles and regulations, laws and canons organizing the human life and human efforts. They are indirectly related to faith and concept. It is, therefore, not permissible for a Muslim to acquire these learnings from anyone else except a Muslim; rather it should be acquired from only such a Muslim in whose religion and righteousness he may have full confidence. He should have the thorough conviction that he seeks guidance from God alone in all these matters. The real purpose, however, is that this reality should be fully ingrained in the consciousness and feelings of a Muslim that all these affairs pertain to faith and he should be fully cognizant that to imbibe light from the Divine revelation in these matters is a binding demand of God's servitude of the inevitable consequence of the witness wherein it has been proclaimed that there is no god except God and Muhammad (S.A.W.) is the messenger of God.

Of course, there is no harm that a Muslim should thoroughly investigate the Jahili research and all the results of the efforts made in these affairs. However, the point of view should not be to acquire for himself material for conceptualization and comprehension. It should be only for ascertaining the aberrations committed by the Jahiliyyah, and to determine how human misguidance can be eliminated, and converted into a righteous approach embracing man with the right principle under the Islamic concept of life and the Islamic faith.

INFLUENCES OF JAHILIYYAH
ON HUMAN KNOWLEDGE

Philosophy, interpretation of human history, Psychology (with the exception of those observations and disputed opinions that do not investigate the interpretation and explanation), Ethics, Religions and their comparative study, Social Sciences and Humanities (leaving observations, statistics and directly acquired information, and the fundamental concepts that are developed on their basis), the collective aspect and objective of all these learnings, past and present, in every period, had been directly influenced by its Jahili beliefs and fetishes, rather their super-structures were raised on these very jahili beliefs and fetishes. This is the reason why the majority of these branches of knowledge are at loggerheads with religion in their fundamental principles, and nurse an explicit or implicit grudge against the concept of religion ordinarily and the Islamic concept particularly.

These angles of human thought and learning do not bear that importance that is attached to Chemistry, Physics, Astronomy, Biology, and Medicine, provided the latter remain confined to practical experiments and results, and do not extend to philosophical interpretations and explanations (in any shape) by trespassing that limit. For example, just as Darwinism by affirming and arranging its observations in the field of Biology outstepping its limits, without any reason or rhyme, needlessly and merely being overpowered by sentiments, presented this theory that there is absolutely no need of supposing a supernatural power for the beginning of life and its evolution.

Necessary and immutable information has since reached the Muslims in these matters from their Creator. They are so sublime and elevated that human findings and strivings appear trashy and ridiculous compared to them. But notwithstanding, man meddles and interferes within that sphere, which is directly related to faith and servitude to God.

CULTURE AND ZIONISM

The assertion that culture is a human heritage is not bound by any particular country, nor does it have a particular nationality, nor is it related to any particular religion is correct to the extent of scientific and artistic knowledge and their academic explanations, provided we do not outstep their sphere of activity, and begin to metaphysically interpret the results of those learnings, and get involved in the philosophical (explanation) of man, man's struggle, and human history, and give philosophical justification of the phenomena of art and literature and intuitive interpretations. But this concept of culture we have described above is, in fact, one of the many contrivances of world Zionism whose purpose is to demolish all limits and bounds on top of which is the list of the bindings and limitations of religion— so that the position of Jewry may easily pervade within the body of the entire world when it has become lethargic, intoxicated and half-alive, and the Jews should have full liberty to pursue their diabolic activities in the world. Topping the list among these activities are their dealings in usury and moneylending, whose purpose is to channel the hard earnings got out of the sweat and blood of the entire mankind into Jewish institutions run on the basis of usury and interest.

According to Islam two kinds of culture are in vogue in the background of all the scientific and artistic knowledge and their practical experiments. The one Islamic culture, which is established on the Islamic way of life, and second, the Jahili culture, which is apparently raised on multifarious ways. But in fact their basis and foundation is one and the same: that is the urge to confer to human thought the status of god-head so that the matter may not be referred to God for ascertaining its correctness or otherwise. Islamic culture circumscribes the entire intellectual and practical activities of man and it is richly endowed with such principles and regulations, ways and peculiarities which not only guarantee further blossoming of these activities but also impart them eternal life and beauty.

EUROPE'S EMPIRICAL SCIENCES ARE
THE PRODUCT OF THE ISLAMIC PERIOD

One should not be unaware of this fact that the empirical sciences, which in the modern age are permeating vitals of the industrial civilization of Europe, were not born in Europe. Their birthplaces were the Islamic Universities of Cardova (Spain) and other Muslim countries of the Orient. The fundamental principles of these sciences were drawn from the teachings and instructions of Islam in which clear indications are present about the universe and its nature, which the diverse deposits and treasures hidden within its bosom make clear. Subsequently on the same pattern a permanent literary movement was launched in Europe and it went on traversing stages of progress and perfection gradually. During the same period the Islamic world came to such an impass that it drifted away from Islam. Consequently this (literary) movement, in the world of Islam, first of all, fell prey to indolence and inertia and then gradually exhausted away. Various factors contributed to its end. Some of them were inherent in the internal set up of the then Islamic society, and some pertained to the incessant attacks aimed at the Islamic world by the Christian and Zionist powers at that time. The method of experimental sciences was imbibed by Europe from the Islamic world. But it snapped its relation with the Islamic foundation and the Islamic concept. Ultimately when Europe cut asunder its relation with the Church, which was tyrannizing human beings under the garb of "The Heavenly Kingdom," it deprived, during this upheaval, the Islamic method of experimental sciences of the guidance of God. Thus the intellectual treasure of Europe, on the whole, became a purely new thing like the Jahili thought of every period and place, which was not only alien to the Islamic concept, but also wholly at loggerheads with it. It is, therefore, obligatory for a Muslim that he should revert to the principle and regulations of the Islamic concept of life and acquire enlightenment only from the teachings of God. If he has got the ability to directly imbibe these teachings, so far so good. If he does not possess this capability then he should acquire it from such a God-worshipping Muslim upon whose religion and piety he may have confidence and whom he can make the source of his learning with full equanimity of heart.

SEPARATION BETWEEN KNOWLEDGE
AND ITS SOURCE NOT DESIRABLE

That "Knowledge is one thing and the source of knowledge a different thing," Islam does not subscribe to this theory in relation to the learnings that are connected to those details of faith that influence man's outlook about life and existence, morals and values, habits and customs, human self and human struggle. Undoubtedly, Islam shows this much magnanimity; that a Muslim may reveal the source of his information to a non-Muslim or a non-God-fearing Muslim about Chemistry, Physics, Astronomy, Medicine, Industry, Agriculture, Administration, and other like sciences, and that too under circumstances when a God-worshipping Muslim may not be available for imparting them. The exact same situation has developed because Muslims have drifted away from their religion and way of life and have forgotten that concept of Islam that it has presented for discharging the requisites of the vicegerency of God and about those learnings and experiments and the multifarious capabilities that are indispensable for performing the affairs of vicegerency according to Divine purpose. However, Islam allows a Muslim to make a non-Muslim his source as regards abstract learnings. But certainly it does not permit him to acquire, from un-Islamic sources or a Muslim source whose religion may not be dependable and may be devoid of piety and righteousness, the principles of his faith, the foundations of his concept of life, commentary on the Holy Quran, explanations of the sayings of the life of the Holy Prophet (S.A.W.), philosophy of history, philosophical interpretation of movement, ways and habits of his society, his system of government, the manner of his politics, and motivations of his art and craft.

This assertion is being made to you by a person who has spent full 40 years in the study of books, whose sole job over this span has been to study as much as possible the results provided by human knowledge and research, were those in which he was specializing and in certain other aspects he toiled under his natural aptitude and temperamental affinity. When he referred this stock of knowledge and information to the fountainhead of his real faith and concept and studied them, he came to the conclusion that whatever he had read so far was quite inconsequential and utter trash compared to those unfathomable treasures. (In fact it should be rightly so). He is not ashamed of that pursuit in which he passed 40 years, for during this period he has acquired but thread-bare information about the Jahiliyyah. He has witnessed its aberrations with his own physical eyes. He has observed the paucity and penury of the Jahiliyyah, has fathomed its depravity and has seen its clap-trap and fictitious rowdyism. He has thoroughly tested its pride, haughtiness, and claims, and he has been fully convinced that a Muslim cannot simultaneously benefit from both these contradictory sources, i.e., the Divine source and the Jahiliyyah.

Notwithstanding, this is not my personal view for the matter is too high that a decision be taken on the basis of personal opinion. The weight this matter carries on the Divine scales leaves no question of confidence or non-confidence on the opinion of a Muslim in comparison to it. This is the verdict of God and His Messenger (S.A.W.) and we deem this verdict to be the judge and adjudicator in this matter. We refer to God and His prophet (S.A.W.) for decision in their mutual differences. Exposing the vicious designs the Jews and Christians harbor about Muslims in general, God, Most High, states:

> Many of the people of the scripture long to make you disbelievers after your belief, through envy on their own account, after the truth has become manifest to them. Forgive and be indulgent (toward them) until Allah give command. Verily Allah is able to do all things. (2: 109)
>
> And the Jews will not be pleased with you, nor will the Christians till you follow their creed, Say: "Verily the guidance of Allah (Himself) is guidance." And if you should follow their desires after the knowledge which has come to you then would you have from Allah no protecting friend nor helper. (2: 120)
>
> O, you who believe! If you obey a party of those who have received the scripture they will make you disbelievers after your belief. (3: 100)

The saying of the Messenger of God (S.A.W), which Hafiz Abu Yali has quoted on the authority of Hazrat Jabir (R.A.A) Hammad and Shaabi, further explains the statements of the Quran. The Holy Prophet (S.A.W.) is reported to have said,

> Inquire not from the people of the Book regarding anything. They will not lead you to the right path. They themselves are misguided. If you followed them, you would either corroborate a falsehood or falsify a truth. By God, had Moses been alive amongst you it would not have been permissible for him to adopt any other course except following me.

When God, Most High, has explicitly and categorically stated this hazardous determination of the Jews and the Christians about the Muslims, it would be a peak of foolishness and short-sightedness to nurse this good-will even for a moment that the discussions made by them about Islamic faith or Islamic history or proposals offered about the system of Muslim society or Muslim politics or Muslim economics could be based on any good intention, or they have Muslim's well-being in view, or in fact they are sincerely in search of guidance and light. Those who entertain this good opinion about them after the clear declaration and categorical verdict of God, their reason and intellect are worth lamenting.

Similarly God, Most High, has also decided this:

> Say! the guidance of God is in fact the real guidance. (2: 120)

This statement has also determined the fact that the instruction of God, Most High, is the only source toward which a Muslim should refer all his matters. After deviation from Divine guidance nothing shall accrue except misguidance and aberration. Rather there does not exist any other source except God, from when guidance and light could be obtained. This statement, made in the verse above, inferred in restrictive terms that "the guidance of God is in fact the real guidance" goes to prove that what remains after the Divine revelation is only deviation, aberration, misguidance, deflection, and misfortune. This meaning and import of the verse is so significant that it does not admit to any doubt and discourse.

This absolute command also lies in the Quran, that no link should be had with a person who turns his face from the remembrance of God and world-seeking alone is his objective and outlook. The Quran has further elaborated about such a person that he is a worshipper of surmise and suspicion; knowledge and faith have not even touched him. The Quran forbids man from following suspicion. Such a person whose eyes get stuck upon the outward glitterings of the world, according to the Quran, is devoid of both the essence of knowledge and correctness of sight. God says:

> Then withdraw (O Mohammed) who flees from Our remembrance, and desires but the life of the world. Such is their sum of knowledge. Verily your Lord is well aware of him who strays, and He is best aware of him who goes right. (53: 29–30)
>
> They know only some appearance of the life of the world, and are heedless of the Hereafter. (30:7)

This superficial, appearance-loving person unaware of the real knowledge can only be one who is oblivious of the remembrance of God and fond of the transient worldly life. This is equally true of all of the scientists and expert artists of the modern age. The knowledge whose standard-bearers they are, is not the one a Muslim may trust its holder to single-mindedly and go on imbibing and benefiting from unhesitatingly. As regards this knowledge, a Muslim is allowed to reap its fruits to the extent of purely academic information. But he should not pay any heed to the interpretation and explanation offered by it in regard to life, human self, and its conceptual ramifications. This, however, is not the knowledge about which the Quran has time and again praised and complimented. It is stated:

> Are those who know equal with those who know not?

Those who quote such verses, detached from their context for misplaced argumentation, are totally on the wrong. The verse which contains this categorical and distinguishing line about knowledge is cited here below.

> Is he who pays adoration in the watches of the night, prostrate and standing, bewaring of the Hereafter and hoping for the mercy of his Lord (to be accounted equal with a disbeliever?) Say (to them, O! Muhammad): Are those who know equal with those who know not? But only men of understanding pay heed. (39:9)

This servant of God who in solitary nights prostrates himself before Almighty Allah remains absorbed in whisperings and solicitudes with his Creator, while standing and prostrating he quivers and trembles with the fear of the Hereafter; keeps his heart and eyes brightened up in the hope of his Sustainer's mercy, in fact such is the fortunate person who, in the right sense has shared the wealth of knowledge, and this is the very knowledge to which the afore-cited verse refers. That is a knowledge that guides man toward God; that enables him to embrace the blessings of piety and truth. This is not the knowledge that distorts the human nature, and directs him on the wrong meandering path of apostasy and refusal of God.

The sphere of knowledge is not confined to faith, religious obligations and duties, commandments and jurisprudence only. It is very wide. It is as much concerned with these laws of nature and also subjugation of those laws under the interest and purpose of the vicegerency of God, as it is with the faith and obligations and Divine laws. Of course a knowledge that has no basis in faith is outside the definition of that knowledge, to which reference has been made in the Quran and whose possessors have been praised therein. A very strong link exists between foundation of faith and all those sciences that pertain to the charters of the universe and laws of the nature (e.g., Astronomy, Biology, Physics, Chemistry, and Geology). All these sciences provide open proof of the existence of God, provided they do not come under the influence of deviated human desires, and render them bereft of God's concept, just as this deplorable state of affairs has actually happened during the renaissance in Europe. In fact a period came in the history of Europe when extremely painful and hateful differences grew between the scholars and the tyrannical and cruel Church, as a result of which the entire literary movement of Europe proceeded on an anti-God path. This movement cast its far-reaching effect on all aspects of life in Europe. In fact it changed Europe's entire attitude of thought. These venomous influences not only provoked the fire of anger and enmity against the Church and its concepts and faiths but also the very concept of religion as a whole came under the fire of hatred and grudge, so much that the contribution of thought that Europe made in the field of knowledge and wisdom was inundated with enmity of religion, whether it was transcendental philosophy or pure academic and artistic research, which apparently do not have any concern with religion.

This you have known, that the foundation and basis on which the West's attitude of thought and its contribution in all fields of knowledge was erected had those venomous influences active beneath them, which were engendered by the enmity of religion. It is not, therefore, difficult to understand why feelings of extreme animosity are found against Islam as a whole in the intellectual contributions of the West and its attitude. This expression of hatred against Islam is deliberate and is done knowingly, and under most circumstances thorough effort is made under a pre-planned scheme to shake the pure building of Islamic faith and concepts and gradually demolish those foundations that distinguish the Muslim society from other societies. Even after knowing this nefarious conspiracy if we continue to bank upon Western thought and its intellectual contribution in imparting Islamic sciences, there cannot be a more shameful indolence and inexcusable apathy than this. Rather it is obligatory on us that we should be cautious even while receiving education in pure scientific knowledge and technology, which we are, under present circumstances, compelled to acquire from Western sources. We should keep these sciences aloof from the shadows of philosophy, for basically these happen to be the travesty and contradiction of religion in general and Islam in particular. Even its slightest influence is enough to defile the pure and clear stream of Islam.

CHAPTER 20

FALLACY OF RATIONALISM

Sayyid Abul A'la Maududi

Sayyid Abul A'la Maududi. "Fallacy of Rationalism I and II." In *West Versus Islam*, translated by S. Waqar Ahmad Gardezi and Abdul Waheed Khan. New Delhi, India: International Islamic Publishers, 1992, pp. 110–41.

FALLACY OF RATIONALISM I[1]

INFLUENCE OF THE WESTERN EDUCATION AND CIVILIZATION on the religious views of our youth, raw in Islamic grooming, can be judged from their writings and utterances. A Muslim graduate from U.P. (India) wrote an article giving an account of a tour of China and Japan undertaken by him. He wrote:

Our Chinese co-travelers are extremely voracious eaters and liquor boozers. They die for pork. It is now that I have come to know the secret of Christianity's popularity. Modern education has made the Chinese ashamed of their age old religion. He could have embraced Islam without any hesitation had he understood it in letter and spirit. But, Islam deprives him of his favorite food. Therefore, willingly or unwillingly, he becomes Christian. No wonder if Christianity becomes China's official religion in the near future. I am a bit lenient toward the European and Chinese Muslim converts in the matter of pork. Moreover, I doubt the Quran has explicitly forbidden it. I feel pork was forbidden for the Arabs for some special reason. I see no harm in permitting it in the countries where it is but a physical need without any intention of flouting divine injunction. Any how I must admit this is the only Quranic injunction or general prohibition which is beyond my comprehension, as to me the motivation and incentive for good and evil has nothing to do with the stomach. If we concede such a relationship and let religion determine even our menu, then why should it not teach us the principles of the job of blacksmith, goldsmith and tailor. I feel the main reason Islam is making no headway, is that it snatches all discretion from human beings reducing them to a body deprived of all life and action or a child devoid of all senses and urges for material betterment. Religion in my opinion should be as permissive and liberal as Christians consider their religion.

Talking of Shanghai he writes:

One refuses to believe that this multitude of happy and smiling prosperous people are all destined to be the fuel of hell after a given time as if the very purpose of their creation was just that. All of them except a few, are nonbelievers and idolaters; are they condemned to hell only because they committed the mistake of populating the earth? They neither waylay and kill the pilgrims to Mecca, nor are they sodomites, nor do they usurp others belongings and then try to justify it. They are leading a calm and quite life, yet they deserve hell as their final resort, why? No doubt pantheism is nonsense, but if one concedes to the fact that there is a Being who is the sole authority to kill and to revive him, then why do you become his enemy and consider him your enemy, simply because he fails to conceive the Being in the same way as you fail to comprehend Him exactly, or that he does not acknowledge Arabic as the Divine language. But no, all this does not matter the least to you. What you consider important is that one should wear trousers of a particular cut and shirt of a particular type, eat such and such food, keep a beard or a particular size and should never dare to go to school because religion and the religious language are not taught there.

About the Japanese port of Kobe, he says:

I went around Kobe for two hours and did not find any beggar or any destitute in tattered clothes. Such is the development of a people who neither know religion nor God.

Then he delivers a sermon and advises the people:

Mind it that fair dealing is the real religion, and doing good deeds, not art or language. The innate objective of religion is to convince us that we are and we shall be answerable for our deeds in this life or in the life hereafter. This is real Islam. Whatever is demanded beyond it in the name of religion is nothing but self-delusion or mental derangement. The day religion is confined to these two realities and the shackles of *Shariah* broken, you too will attain the heights or progress like other nations. You will awaken the world's conscience and those, who do not lose the world, shall not be losers in the kingdom of Heaven as well. In fact you are no nation, but a reformer of nations. For God's sake do not let others say that while other nations are at the zenith of progress the Muslims are only backward and the cause of their backwardness is their religion.

This article is a self-explanatory example of the mind and thinking of our new generation with modern education. They were born into a Muslim family and brought up in a Muslim society, with strong social and cultural ties with the Muslims. Love for Islam, sympathy for the Muslims, and the desire to remain Muslim has become their second nature and rooted deep in their hearts without any intention and without any contribution whatsoever of their heart and mind in it. Before developing their involuntary and unconscious attachment with Islam into voluntary and conscious conviction through education and proper grooming to enable them to fully understand and follow Islamic teachings and experience the change Islamic teachings and experience the change Islamic injunctions bring to practical life and approach, they were admitted to English schools and colleges. Their intellectual and ideological upbringing was done there on a pattern quite alien to Islam. Western thought and western civilization influenced them so deeply that they started looking at everything from the western angle, and pondered on every issue with a western mind. It became impossible for them to think and to observe independently keeping their approach free of western domination. They learnt rationalism from the west, without any reasoning of their own but that acquired from the west. Thus it was no independent rationalism of their own but entirely a rationalism lent from the west. They learnt the art of critical appreciation from the west. Naturally it was not an objective and independent criticism. It was just a training and grooming to measure everything with a western yardstick and consider western standards as over and above all criticism. When our new generation completed their studies in western-oriented educational institutions they came out fully trained and groomed in the western way of thinking and with their minds totally changed. Their hearts were no doubt Muslim, but their minds had turned secular. They lived among the Muslims, had dealings with the Muslims, were tied to the Muslims in innumerable social and cultural bonds, had relations of love and sympathy with them and watched the cultural and religious activities of Muslims in their day to day life. But all their faculties of thinking, understanding and opinion-forming had turned Western, having nothing to do with Islamic values and Muslim mannerism. They started criticizing Islam and Muslims in every matter by western standards, declaring obsolete and amenable whatever they found incompatible with the western standards, be it some fundamental matter, or any detail of Islam, or just a practice in Muslim society. Some of them also tried to know Islam to some extent and to ascertain the truth, but the yardstick of their criticism and research was the same western approach. How could the plain truth of Islam adjust so as to fit into the crooked frame of their west-oriented mind?

Whenever these gentlemen speak on religious issues they are mostly irrelevant and do not even know what they are talking about. Neither are their premises correct, nor do they argue in any logical sequence or try to draw correct conclusions, so much so that they can not even determine their own standpoint while arguing. They take divergent stands in a single breath. Speaking from one pedestal they shift all of a sudden to a quite contradictory viewpoint. Loose-thinking is the glaring feature of their commentaries on religion. They are very alert and cautious while speaking on issues other than religion. They fully realize that any slip on their part might condemn them in the intellectual circles. Religion carries no weight or importance for them. Hence they do not care in the least to apply their mind to it. They take it very lightly, just as if they are gossiping after their meals in a very relaxing mood, talking just for the sake of fun and feeling no need to observe any limits.

Another thing that is very obvious in their writings is shallowness of mind and paucity of proper knowledge. They dare not speak on any issue other than religion with such poor knowledge and without any serious thinking. They know they lose face and credibility if they pass any illogical or unreasonable remark or comment, but speaking on religion they see no need of any research, study, contemplation, and serious thinking. They form their opinion on off-hand information and give it out without any second thought. It is so because they have no fear of any check or criticism. Any confrontation or criticism, if it comes at all, would be from the orthodox religious leaders who are already labeled as a rigid, backward and narrow-minded class.

The article of the learned writer under discussion bears both these features. Firstly, the article does not indicate whether the writer is speaking as a Muslim or a non-Muslim. Speaking on Islam, one is either a Muslim or a non-Muslim. If he speaks as a Muslim, may he be orthodox, a liberal thinker, or a reformer, whatever be the case, he is expected to talk within the orbit of Islam with the Quran as the final authority and within the fundamentals of religion and the laws of Shari'ah as enunciated in the holy Quran. Whoever does not believe in the holy Quran as the final authority, and considers its injunctions as open to discussion, automatically goes out of the pale of Islam and thus loses every right to speak as a Muslim. If one speaks as a non-Muslim, he will have every right to criticize the principles and injunctions enunciated by the Quran in whatever manner he likes, because he does not believe in the holy Quran as the final word of Allah. But, speaking as a non-Muslim, he will have no right to pose himself as a Muslim and try to explain to the Muslims the meanings of Islam and the ways and means to promote Islam. Any sensible person talking about Islam with sense and reason will have to decide whether he is going to speak as a Muslim or a non-Muslim and, while giving his opinion, will fully observe the logical requirements of the position he has chosen.

But it is against all cannons of justice and reason to call oneself a Muslim, and yet use the right to criticize the principles and laws given by the Quran, question the Quran's authority, and yet try to advise and guide Muslims. It is nothing but an attempt to use antonyms as synonyms. Paradoxically, it means that a person can be a Muslim as well as a non-Muslim at the same time and remain within the pale of Islam and outside its fold simultaneously.

We do not expect the learned writer, with all his wisdom and learning, to juxtapose two diametrically opposed positions for himself while speaking on any issue other than Islam. We can never expect him to criticize British laws sitting in the chair at a British Court of law. Nor do we expect him to be so daring as to profess adherence to any school of thought, and yet to criticize the fundamentals on which that school is based. Ironically he has taken up two diametrically opposed positions in relation to Islam without the least pricking of conscience that he is shifting his position time and again. On one hand, he claims to be a Muslim, carries a Muslim name, shows deep concern for the Muslim's miserable plight, wishes the progress of Islam, and delivers a sermon to the Muslims on *Ehsaan* (beautifying their deeds), which is to him the real Islam. On the other hand, he severely criticizes the fundamental tenets and teachings of Islam, which must be believed as final authority by a Muslim.

The Quran has specifically forbidden pork in four places,[2] but you like to grant relaxation in this matter, and that, too, ironically, in the name of and for the cause of Islam. In other words, you pose to be more concerned than even the Quran itself for the welfare of Islam, or there is some other Islam, besides that presented by the Quran, for which you are so much worried. The Quran no doubt lays down the menu for human beings and sorts out the eatables as lawful and unlawful,[3] foul and chaste, and unequivocally declares that you have no authority to declare any thing lawful or unlawful. You insist that it is your right, and you are not ready to concede this right to the Quran and allow the religion to have any say in what one should eat or drink. In fact, the Quran does not confine Islam within the limitation like that which the followers of Saint Paul (not the followers of Jesus Christ) had imposed on their religion.

Islam formulates laws for dress, eating and drinking, marriage and divorce, inheritance, trade, politics, justice and punishment for crimes etc., but you are against these divine injunctions and consider them a hurdle in the path of progress of Islam. You accuse Islam of turning human beings into lifeless bodies and helpless children and propose that religion should be accepted in the same sense and to the same extent as Christians (truly speaking, followers of Saint Paul) believe in Christianity.

The Quran has itself framed laws and ordained their compliance as the Divine limits. You consider these limits of the *Shariah* as fetters and want to break these fetters like Saint Paul did, and even see this move as imperative for the promotion and expansion of Islam. According to the Quran, belief is the first and foremost condition for salvation of man. It warns in clear words that those who do not believe in Allah shall be thrown into the hell,[4] may they be countable or countless and prosperous or destitute. But to you it is unbelievable that such a vast multitude of bouncing and prosperous people could go down to hell as its fuel after a given period. You cannot understand their fault save that they have inhabited the earth. Now the question is, how can one remain a Muslim having such an obvious disagreement with the holy Quran?

A Muslim who believes in the Quran as the word of Allah cannot dare to differ with the Quran. If you do not see eye to eye with the Divine book, you are free to differ but only after denouncing faith in Islam. Whoever feels dissatisfied with the teachings and injunctions of a religion and doubts its veracity, fails to understand its logic and needs, and considers its views and concepts objectionable, has only two options. Either he may clearly denounce and disown it and then criticize its tenets and teachings as bitterly as he likes or, if he does not want to say good-bye to his religion in spite of his doubts and apprehensions, he must avoid projection of his disagreement. He should try to solve his differences and clear his doubts as a seeker of truth instead of trying to demolish the foundations and structure under the garb of renaissance.

Reason and wisdom show only two courses open in such a situation, and a sensible person shall take to any one of the courses when confronted with such a situation. But the difficulty with our learned writer and the like, brought up in west-oriented institutions, is that they do not have the courage to adopt the first course and feel ashamed of taking to the second course. They have, therefore, taken to a middle course, which is quite illogical. They insist on being accepted as Muslims, claim to be desirous of the name and fame of Islam, and express great concern for Islam and the Muslims, yet they speak and work against Islam in the same way as a non-Muslim may say or do. Not to speak of the traditions (*hadith*) of the holy Prophet or Islamic jurisprudence (*fiqh*), they do not spare even the holy Quran from their criticism, and hit at the very foundations of Islam.

These gentlemen claim to be rationalists and boast of rejecting all that is irrational. Their most common charges against so called *Mullas*, a misnomer for the Ulema, is that they do not use their brain while they themselves are quite contradictory in their utterances and impressions about religion, and contradictory in their behavior. What they say in one breath, they contradict in the next breath. What sort of rationalism is invented by these so-called enlightened scholars?

Now let us have a look at the depth and extent of their knowledge. They consider it necessary to remove all the limitations imposed by *Shariah* and shrink it to just a mere dogma and faith like Christianity. The secret of the progress of Christianity, according to them, is that it does not impose any restrictions of lawful and unlawful and no moral regulations. It does not reduce man to a lifeless body or a helpless child usurping his human rights. On the contrary, it grants free license to anybody who claims belief in Jesus Christ to do what he likes. But little do they think that Islam is nothing but all that is mentioned in the holy Quran.

According to Quran, Islam is a composite whole of beliefs and good deeds along with its limitations, its rules and regulations, and a complete working system for all individual and social activities without which Islam cannot stay as a system of life and a civilization. No Muslim has any authority to revoke these limits, because to revoke these limits is to revoke the Quran and to revoke Quran is the revocation of Islam. When Islam itself is revoked, where does its progress lie? You can invent a new religion of your own and propagate it, but you have no right to dub anything against the teachings of the Quran as Islam and claim its propagation as the progress of Islam. You call this dogma as Islam that "we are and shall be answerable for our actions in the life hereafter or even in this world." You thus hope to make Islam more easy and acceptable by confining it to each individual as his private matter. But going a little deep in the meanings and implications of this belief, you would know that Islam cannot conform to your desires even if confined to private life.

The first requirement of faith in Islam is to believe in the life Hereafter. Then there are three requisites of the concept of answerability. Firstly, to determine to whom one is answerable and to accept him as supreme. Secondly, to determine the nature of answerability and that what sort of deeds in this life can lead to success and what actions could be condemned in the life hereafter. Thirdly, what difference would it make if certain actions and deeds are condemned, because if it makes no difference whether any action or deed is accepted or condemned, then the concept of answerability loses all its sense and meanings.

These are quite logical and rational requisites of the belief you call the real religion. Now if Islam is confined and reduced to what you consider the real concept of belief in Islam, even then the problem you want to avoid would still remain. You will have to believe in Allah, the converse of what you believe is the secret of Japan's phenomenal progress. You will have to abide by the limits of *Shariah* and Islamic ethics, which you wish to override and which, in your view, are the real hurdle in the progress of Islam. The issue of punishment and recompense in the life hereafter shall also crop up, and you will again wonder how these countless people leading a happy and prosperous life without believing in Allah and accountability before Him could all be destined to go through the agony of Hell just after a few years of this mundane life.

Would it not be better if such people bring out a new edition of Islam of their own choice to relieve them of all restrictions and leave it to their sweet will to adhere or not to adhere to it without it being detrimental to their welfare in the life hereafter, and which may guarantee success in this world as well as in the life hereafter on the ground that they were kind enough to inhabit the earth, and you may rest assured that all the non-believers would be accommodated in paradise because they lived a very happy and prosperous life in this world.

You doubt there is a total and explicit prohibition of pork in the holy Quran. You interpret the prohibition of pork as meant only for the Arabs, for some reasons exclusive to them. This suspicion could be removed, had you just taken the trouble of going through the holy Quran before expressing this suspicion. It is vividly written in the holy Book that:

> Say: I find not that which is revealed to me, ought prohibited to an eater what he eats thereof except it be carrion, or blood poured forth, or pork for that verily is foul, or the abomination which was immolated to the name of other than Allah. But whoso is compelled (there to) neither craving, nor transgressing, (for him) lo your Lord is Forgiving, Merciful (6:146).

This Quranic verse has forbidden pork for every one, without exception, on the ground that it is foul. Does the eater here means Arab eater alone? And whether any thing can be foul for the Arabs and fair for non-Arabs. Shall you, in the same away, allow some relaxation for the carrion eater too? If you want to allow relaxation in the case of pork, do it on your own, but you have no right to say that its explicit prohibition in the Quran is doubtful despite its clear verdict.

One of the principles that our modern casuists have framed for themselves is that any injunction of Islam they wish to violate, they declare it, without any hesitation, exclusive for Arabs even if there is not the slightest indication of such exclusiveness in the holy Quran and even if they may not be able to put forward any reason or quote any instance in support of their notion. Such practice, if allowed, may result in confining the Quran and its teachings exclusively to the Arabs.

And to argue on the basis of the Quranic injunction *"but whoso is compelled (thereto) without any intention of disobedience or transgression"* is so interesting that one cannot but stand confounded. He has perhaps translated this verse to the effect that "take pork when you feel irresistible desire to have it, but never take it in a garden, and do not make it a habit."[5]

Nobody, except one who is quite ignorant of the meanings of conditions beyond one's control or intention of disobedience, can dare interpret it in terms of relaxation for the people of China and Europe. Anybody who knows the meanings of the verse would never dare interpret the verse in that sense. This verse does not in any way refer to those who are habitual carrion eaters or blood suckers or have a craze for pork and eat all that is slaughtered in any name other than Allah as a matter of routine. Such an interpretation would practically negate the Quranic injunction.

If the prohibition was meant for those who were used to all the prohibited things, then such exception would have granted them a free license. If they say the prohibition was meant for those who already avoided such things, then what was the need for such prohibition for them. In fact the condition of a situation beyond control with no intention of transgression is meant for one who is dying of hunger, and nothing except the prohibited is available to save his life: he is permitted to eat from the prohibited thing only that much that is inevitable to save his life without the least intention of transgressing the Divine limits. The same is repeated at another place prohibiting pork and the carrion as follows:

> However one (lying or hunger, can eat of any of these forbidden things without any inclination to sin. (5:3).

There is a world of difference between this exemption and the contention that the pork be permitted for the Europeans and Chinese, because they have a craze for it, under the cover of exemption given in the verse:

> (Whoso is left with no option, with no inclination and no intention of transgression)

and that too to lure them into the fold of Islam. If permissiveness and relaxation is made just to accommodate various nation's likings and desire, then liquor, gambling, adultery, usury and so many other things shall have to be permitted one after the other. The question is what is the fun in proselytizing to Islam the people who are not prepared to accept the injunctions, limits, and prohibitions ordained by Allah? Islam is in no need of such people, then why should Islam strike such a bargain with them?

To start with, you could not appreciate the logic of prohibition of pork. Pondering over it further you found that the stomach and moral incentives are poles apart, hence you arrived at the conclusion that religion has no right to impose any restrictions of lawful and unlawful in the matter of food and drinks. It unfolded the secret that your knowledge about physical science is no more than your knowledge about the holy Quran. It is no shame for an "enlightened and educated person" to be ignorant of Quran but so much ignorance of the science is no doubt very shameful. You are still ignorant of the relationship between your physical build and your inner self and between your physique and your diet.

It is by no means surprising that the diet restores the body's spent up constituents and builds its tissues and nerves, rejuvenating an entirely old body into a new physique within a few years. What is surprising is that diet has nothing to do with the inner self. The world of science was generally unaware of this fact before, but the recent scientific research on dietetics disclosed the fact that diet has an unmistakable effect on one's morals and intellectual faculties. Hence our scientists are busy exploring the effects of different foods on our hearts and minds. It appears our graduate friend is not up to date in scientific information, otherwise he would not dare to assert that the stomach and the faculties of mind are, as a matter of principle, poles apart.

FALLACY OF RATIONALISM II

Rationalism and naturalism are being projected with great humdrum by the West for the last two centuries. And who can deny the power of publicity. One cannot shield his heart and mind from the influence of a thing being constantly and frequently brought before his eyes and drummed into his ears. Thanks to the force of propaganda, the world has at last conceded that western sciences and culture are based entirely on rationalism and naturalism. Although a critical study of western civilization shows, beyond doubt, that it is based on neither rationalism nor naturalism. On the contrary, its entire structure stands on feelings, lust, and urges. The western renaissance was nothing but a revolt against reason and nature. Discarding logic and reason, it turned toward whims and feelings and material urges. It relied on moods instead of reason, rejected rational guidance, logical reasoning, and innate intuition, and made perceptible material results its real criterion. Rejecting nature's guidance, it preferred to be guided by desires and urges, regarded everything as baseless that cannot be measured and weighed, condemned everything as negligible and worthless that did not produce any perceptible material gain.

In the beginning even the West was unaware of this fact. Hence despite going against reason and nature, they remained under the illusion that the new era of enlightenment, ushered in by them, was based on rationalism and naturalism. Later the truth dawned on them, but they had not the courage to confess it. Hypocrisy, materialism, and submission to the urges of body and instincts were given the cover of rationalism and naturalism. But now the cat is out of the bag. Irrationality and violation of nature is so obvious that it cannot be concealed under any cover now. Hence there is an open revolt against reason and nature. The banner of revolt has been raised. Everywhere, right from the sacred precincts of learning and thought to the social, economic, and political fields, this revolt can be noted. With the exception of a section of conservative hypocrites all the leading personalities of the modern world confess that urges and desires now rule their civilization.

However, the orientalists and the westernized of the East are still a few steps behind their leaders. The education, the intellectual atmosphere, and the factors of culture and civilization responsible for their intellectual evolution demand unconditional submission to physical desires and urges and devotion to materialism on their part, and they are submitting to it. But the stage when the cat comes out of the bag has yet to arrive. They are still insisting in their writings and speeches that they would accept nothing but reason and nature, hence they call for logical reasoning. They refuse to accept anything not proved by cogent arguments and the evidence of nature.

But all this bragging is motivated by the same mentality, which is neither rationalism nor naturalism. An analysis of their articles shall reveal to you that they are unable even to grasp the implications of logic and intuition. What they call pragmatism comes out to be empiricism, when probed. Empiricism is something that is solid and weighty, and that can be measured and enumerated. Anything that cannot be assessed by measurement, counting, or weighing in the balance is of no use to them.

They consider it illogical to believe or to follow anything until and unless its utility is established in that particular sense. Even their claim of following nature's guidance cannot stand scrutiny. By nature they do not mean human nature but animal nature, which is devoid of intuition and conscience and has only passions and the animal appetites of sex and stomach. They consider worthy of acknowledgment only that which can be materially felt, which can satisfy desires and fulfill physical and sensual urges, and whose return is instantaneous and visible, and whose harm is either invisible or apparently less than its gain. But the requisites of human nature, which are important intuitively, whose harms or benefits are not material and sensuous but psychological and spiritual, are superstitions labeled by them as nonsense, worthless, and negligible. It is obscurantism, superstition, and conservatism in their view to acknowledge or to give any importance to such thinking. With such digression from reason and nature, they still claim to be rationalist and naturalist. Yet their intellectual bankruptcy does not let them realize this contradiction at all.

Education and refinement of thought should at least serve to remove confusion in the views, enabling a person to adopt a clear and straight thinking, draw correct conclusions by putting their propositions in proper order, and avoid contradictions and the confusing of issues. But barring a few exceptions we generally find our educated people deprived of even preliminary benefits of intellectual evolution. They cannot even determine their exact stand, understand its logical requirements and, keeping it in view, adopt a way of arguing that is relevant to their stand. Going through their writings or discussing with them any issue, the first impression one gets is that they are badly confused in their views. They start a discussion with a certain standpoint and then go on shifting it on each step. They can neither choose propositions intelligently enough to establish their point of view, nor arrange them in logical sequence. One cannot follow, from the beginning to the end, what is exactly the issue and what they want to prove and establish. It is so because modern civilization and the education under its influence are mostly inclined toward feelings and material realities. They stir desires, develop an awareness of demands and requirements, impress the importance of feelings and perception, but do not duly regulate the intellect and the mind. Modern civilization no doubt creates vanity as a lust, rather a vanity of criticism and reasoning and this vanity exhorts them to criticize each and everything in the name of rationalism and to reject anything that they are unable to grasp. But truly speaking, their minds are bereft of rationalism and the ability to solve any issue or to form a considered opinion in any matter.

This irrational rationalism is displayed in matters relating to religion mostly, as these are the matters that come in fundamental conflict on each and every point with the western concepts in spiritual, moral, social, and collective fields of life.

Talk to any modern educated person on any religious issue, but first get an affirmation from him of his being a Muslim to test his state of mind, and then put before him an injunction of the Shariah along with its authority. He will just shrug his shoulder and comment, in a very philosophic style: "It is all mullaism. Bring me some rational argument. If you have only some sayings to quote and no logic and reason, I am not going to accept it." Just these cursory remarks are enough to disclose the secret that such a person is poles apart from rationalism. Even after years of education and academic grooming he is still ignorant of the rational requisites of argumentation and the proper stand of the seeker of argument.

Rationally, there can be only two positions of a person with relevance to Islam. Either he is a Muslim or a non-Muslim. If he is a Muslim, it means that he has conceded that Allah is the Supreme Authority and the holy Prophet is the authentic Messenger of Allah. He has also committed that he will surrender unconditionally to all the injunctions conveyed to him by the authentic Messenger of Allah. He has thus surrendered his right to demand any rational proof of argument for each and every injunction.

Being a Muslim he is expected only to ascertain whether a particular injunction has been issued by the authentic Messenger of Allah or not. And, as soon as it is proved that any injunction is authoritative, he must obey it. He may ask for rational justification just for his own satisfaction and knowledge only after compliance with the injunction. But subjecting compliance to rational justification of any injunction and refusal to obey any injunction on the grounds of dissatisfaction after committing to obey prophetic injunctions unconditionally, amounts to denial of the authority and authenticity of the holy Prophet (S.A.W.).

Such a denial is nothing less than infidelity although he had started his discussion with an affirmation of Islam. Now if he prefers for himself the position of an infidel, his proper place is not inside but outside the pale of Islam. He must first show at least this much moral courage to disown faith in Islam, then only would he deserve to ask for and get rational justification for any Islamic injunction.

This is what common sense demands as a rule, and no system and no regulation can stay without it. No government can stay even for a moment if every person starts demanding rational justification for its orders and refuses to submit to any order without getting its satisfactory justification. No army can be called an army if every soldier starts seeking the reason for his commander's orders and demanding his satisfaction before compliance. No school, no college, no association, in short no system can work on the basis of satisfying each and every individual prior to the compliance of its order.

Anybody who joins a system or organization does so only when he accepts and believes in the authority of that system as supreme authority, and as long as he is a part of that system, he is duty bound to obey its supreme authority, may he be convinced and satisfied with any order or not. To violate any order is no doubt a crime but it is a different matter. One can remain a part and parcel of a system even if he commits any violation of any part of it.

But to subject obedience to personal satisfaction, even in the smallest issue, is to refuse to submit to its final and supreme authority, which is a clear revolt. If such is the attitude against a government established by law, the culprit shall be tried for rebellion. In the case of the army, such a person would face court martial. In the case of an educational institution, he would be expelled from the school or college within no time, and in the case of religion he would be declared an apostate. This is all so, because no system can afford such a questioning of its justification within its rank and file. The proper place of such a seeker of justification is not within but outside a system. He may challenge any order in a system, but he must first denounce his faith and belief in that system.

Unconditional faith is the first and foremost requirement of Islam. It calls people to believe in Allah and His Prophet first, instead of issuing injunctions. All arguments and justifications have been exhausted to establish Allah and His prophet as the final and supreme authority. Every possible rational justification and evidence from Nature is meant to convince man that Allah is the only authority in the universe and Muhammad (peace be upon him) is His authentic messenger and prophet.

Scrutiny and rational justification should be sought on this fundamental issue as conclusively as necessary for satisfaction and conviction. If you are not satisfied, by any reason and logic, you will not at all be forced to embrace Islam, nor shall any Islamic injunction be imposed on you. But the moment you embrace Islam, you become a "Muslim," that is you have committed yourself to the unconditional obedience of Allah and His prophet. Now you are not expected to call for argument and justification for each and every order, and now compliance and obedience is not at all subject to your satisfaction. The first and foremost duty after embracing Islam is to submit to the orders given to you by Allah through His prophet without any ifs, ands, or buts.

> The saying of all (true) believers when they appeal unto Allah and His Messenger to judge between them, is only that they say, "We hear, and we obey." (24:51)

It is not at all compatible with faith to argue and to seek justification as a condition for obedience and submission. This juxtaposition of opposites is clearly against common sense. A believer would never seek arguments and justification and whoever seeks arguments and justification cannot be a true believer.

> And it becometh not of a believing man or believing woman when Allah and His Messenger have decided a matter for them that they should (after that) claim any say. (33:36)

The magnificent task of reform and organization performed by Islam is all due to this rule alone. Once the belief was instilled deep in hearts and minds, the believers halted where they were asked to stop. And whatever was enjoined millions and millions of people adopted it forthwith. Reform of human morals and regulation of social activities by the holy prophet, in a short span of 23 years, could never be possible, had submission to these imaginations depended on rational justification for each and every order and explaining the wisdom of all dos and don'ts.

But it does not at all mean that the Islamic injunctions are irrational, or any of its part is devoid of wisdom and prudence. Nor does it mean that Islam demands blind faith and puts any bar on its followers on their search of the logical and natural base or probe into the wisdom of its injunctions. In fact it is just the reverse. Insight and prudence is indispensable for the proper following of Islam. The more one understands the wisdom and prudence of Islamic injunctions, the more he will be able to follow it properly.

Islam is not against such comprehension and enlightenment, rather it encourages it. However, there is a world of difference between this intellectual probing and scrutiny, which is governed by an urge to obey, and that rational test, which instead of being governed by an urge to obey is in itself a requisite for submission. A Muslim is he who is fully convinced and offers unqualified submission first and then strives to probe into the wisdom of injunctions.

It is not necessary that he must succeed in finding out the prudence of each and every injunction. He is fully convinced that Allah Almighty is the supreme and ultimate authority and the Prophet is His authentic messenger and spokesman. What he needs is the attainment of complete enlightenment and getting as much evidence as possible to substantiate his belief. If he succeeds in getting what he is striving for he thanks God for it, but if he does not succeed he goes on obeying the injunctions without the slightest hesitation because of his conviction and faith in Allah.

This seeking of more and more evidence can by no means be compared with the attitude where submission and obedience is subjected to satisfaction in each and every matter.

Recently a statement issued by a Muslim organization has come to our notice. This organization is comprised of well educated persons who do not shun religion. This organization is doing, according to them, "meritorious" service to Islam. What they preach in the name of religious "reform" is that they are advising Muslims to refrain from ritual sacrifice on Eidul Azha and to donate that money to charitable institutions, help the widows and the orphans, and provide employment to the jobless. Somebody perhaps objected to this campaign, details of which we do not know. What has been said in rebuttal of the objection is as follows:

> Nobody has so far cared to explain the wisdom and benefits of the ritual sacrifice on Eid-ul-Adha except blindly advocating and following an age-old practice. We shall be grateful to anybody who enlightens us about the wisdom of this ritual sacrifice.

This is just a sample of the intellectual approach of those who call themselves educated and enlightened. On one side is their loud claim of "rationalism" and on the other side is such a rigid show of "irrationalism." The two sentences quoted from them above are enough to show that they have not yet determined their position. If they are speaking as a Muslim then they are bound to concede to the commandments of the Quran and Sunnah first and then ask for any reason and justification, and that too for the sake of enlightenment and satisfaction and not as a condition for submission and obedience. But if you ask for reason and rational justification as a prerequisite for submission and obedience then you have no right at all to speak as a Muslim. Such a seeker of rationality and wisdom should first accept the position of a non-believer, and then and then only shall he be entitled to raise an objection on any Islamic teachings. But he will have no right to give a verdict on any Islamic issue as an authority on Islam.

Both of these are quite contradictory to each other and it is irrational to take both the positions at the same time and fail to fulfill requisites of even one position. On the one hand, they pose themselves not only as a "Muslim" but as a juristic authority on Islam as well, while on the other hand, they give no importance to traditions and commandments of the Quran and Sunnah and refuse to submit even if it is proved beyond a doubt that a certain commandment is from the ultimate Authority, and ask for the rational justification and pragmatic benefits of the divine injunction before compliance.

In other words, they are not ready to submit to any injunction proved to be a Divine and Prophetic injunction until and unless they are themselves duly convinced of its wisdom and pragmatic benefits. They will reject any injunction forthwith, if they are not convinced of its benefits, or feel such benefits are not substantial enough. They will propagate against it, prove it irrelevant, meaningless, and useless, rather a harmful and extravagant ritual and try their best to prevent Muslims from following it. Is there any wisdom that would allow mixing up of such conflicting attitudes and contradictory positions? No doubt, anybody can ask for justification and rationality but first his own attitude and approach should be rational.

Rational pragmatic benefit is nothing very specific, but relative and proportionate. One may consider a particular thing beneficial while the other may declare it damaging, yet another may admit some benefit, but consider it immaterial as compared to some other more beneficial thing. There is much to differ in pragmatic benefits. Every one has his own concept of benefit, and decides according to his concept as to which of his own experience or others is beneficial or not. One may be after immediate gain and avoid immediate loss. His choice shall definitely differ from the other one who has his eye on the ultimate end.

There are so many things that are beneficial in one way and harmful in some other way. One adopts them because he is ready to bear harms for the sake of benefit. The other one avoids it as he considers it more harmful than beneficial. There is also a difference in pragmatic and rational benefits. One thing is pragmatically harmful, but prudence advises to face harm for a bigger rational benefit. There is some other thing, which is pragmatically beneficial, but prudence gives its verdict against it to avoid its rational harm. It is not possible to elaborate the pragmatic and rational benefits of something in such a way as to convince everybody of its utility leaving no room for refusal.

Such an elaboration has never been possible of rational and pragmatic advantages of not only ritual sacrifice, but Salat, Fasting, Hajj, Zakat, and all the other commands and prohibitions of *Shariah* making its utility crystal clear to all and sundry and convincing them to submit and obey. Had it been so, not a single person in the world would have avoided Salat, Fasting, and refused to pay Zakat or go for Hajj pilgrimage. This is why the injunctions of Islam do not depend on everybody's understanding and experience but solely on faith and submission. A Muslim has faith in Allah and His Prophet and not in pragmatic or rational benefits. He does not call for any rational or practical proof of the utility and benefit of a certain thing to make it acceptable for him, or establishment of its harm to reject it. He concedes only that which is established as an injunction from Allah and His prophet, and refuses all that does not come from Allah and His prophet.

Hence the main question is whether one believes in wisdom and experience or in Allah and His prophet. In the first case, he has nothing to do with Islam and he has no right to speak as a Muslim and to advise Muslims to keep away from the "so called Sunnah" (i.e., ritual sacrifice of animals) of the unproductive land (Arabia). In the other case, the point of discussion should not be pragmatic and rational benefits but the question whether animal sacrifice is just a ritual innovated by the Muslims or whether it is a submission to Allah, who is pleased with it, and a sacred practice introduced to his *Ummah* by the holy Prophet (S.A.W.).

NOTES

1. Article published in the monthly *Tarjumanul Quran* in its issue of December 1934, Sha'aban 1353 A.H.
2. The Quran (2: 173, 5:3, 6:145, 16:115).
3. And do not say what your tongues falsely utter, "This is lawful, and that is prohibited"(16:116).
4. Surely you, and those whom you consider sharing the authority of Allah are fuel of Hell and you are destined to go down to it. (22: 98).
5. Here it is noted that the Arabic words *Idtarra, Baghin,* and *Aadin* mean conditions beyond control, garden, and habit in Urdu respectively, and the learned writer Sayyed Maududi has satirically referred to their Urdu meanings.

II. ISLAM AND POLITICS

CHAPTER 21

WAR, PEACE, AND
ISLAMIC JIHAD

Sayyid Qutb

Sayyid Qutb. "Jihad in the Cause of Allah." In *Milestones*, 2nd ed., translated by S. Badrul Hasan, M.A. Karachi, Pakistan: International Islamic Publishers Ltd, 1988, pp. 107–42.

STAGES OF THE MOVEMENT OF JIHAD

THE GREAT SCHOLAR IBN QAYYIM IN HIS BOOK *Zad-al-Ma'ad* has introduced a chapter entitled "The Prophet's treatment of the unbelievers and hypocrites from the beginning of Messengership until his death." In fact the learned scholar has summed up therein the nature of the Islamic concept of Jihad. He writes:

> The first revelation made to the Holy Prophet was *"Iqra bisme rabbikal lazee khalaq."*
> (Read in the name of your Sustainer who created).

This was the beginning of the Messengership. Allah, Most High, ordained him to recite this revelation in his heart. He was not commanded to preach it to others. Then Allah revealed:

> *"Ya ayyuhal-Muddassir, Qum Fa-anzir"*
> (O' you who are wrapped in your mantle arise and warn).

Thus with the revelation of *"Iqra"* Prophethood was conferred upon him, while with *"Ya ayyuhal-Muddassir"* he was commissioned to Messengership. Subsequently, he was commanded to warn his relations. Therefore, first of all he warned his people, then the Arabs surrounding him, then all the Arabs residing in Arabia, and finally he warned all the people of the world. Thus since the inception of his Messengership for about 13 years he kept on warning the people and inculcating the fear of God through preaching. During this period he neither waged war nor levied *Jizyah*. Rather he was ordered to restrain himself, practice patience and forbearance, and take recourse to forgiveness. Then he was commanded to migrate and was also given permission to fight. Then he was ordered to fight those who came to fight him and restrain himself from those who did not make war with him. Later on he was ordered to fight the polytheists so that Allah's religion was established fully. The non-believers were divided into three categories after the command of Jihad came. Firstly, those who were at peace, secondly, those with whom Muslims were at war, and, thirdly, the zimmies (non-Muslims residing under Muslim rule). Those unbelievers with whom the Holy Prophet (S.A.W.) had entered a treaty and was at peace with them, he was ordered to keep up the treaty, and so long as they abided by the treaty, its terms should be honored. And if any breach of the terms of the treaty was apprehended, they should be paid back in the same coins, and no war should be waged against them until they were notified of having broken it. It was ordered that he should fight with those who had committed breach of the treaty. When the chapter captioned *"Bara'at"* was revealed, details of the treatment to be meted out of these three types of people were given. It was made clear that wars should be declared against those from amongst "the people of the Book" who were enemies of Allah and His prophet, until they agreed to pay *"Jizyah"* (a tax levied on non-Muslims in lieu of military service by a Muslim state) or embrace Islam. About the unbelievers and the hypocrites, it was ordered in this chapter that Jihad should be declared against them and they should be treated harshly. The Holy Prophet (S.A.W.) therefore waged Jihad against the polytheists with sword, and against the hypocrites with arguments and preaching. It was also announced in this chapter that all the treaties entered into with the polytheists should be brought to an end and they shall no more be binding. In this regard, treaties were divided into three categories. The first related to people who broke the treaty and did not honor its terms. He was ordered to fight against them. He fought with them and was victorious. The second category pertained to those people with whom the treaty was made for a definite period, and they neither infringed the terms thereof nor helped any one against the Holy Prophet (S.A.W.). Concerning them Allah ordered that the term of the treaty be completed. The third kind related to such people with whom there was neither any treaty nor war with the Holy Prophet (S.A.W.) or with whom the treaty was for an indefinite period, no term having been stated therein. For all such people command was given that a notice period of four months be given to them for the expiration of the term, whereafter they should be fought with. Accordingly, those who had committed infringement were put to sword and a grace period of four months was given to all such people with whom there was either no treaty, or it was for an indefinite period. Order was given for the fulfillment of the term of treaty to those whose treaty was about to expire. All such people embraced Islam even before the expiration of the grace period, and Jizyah was imposed on the zimmies (non-Muslims).

In short, with the revelation of the chapter *Bara'at*, the treatment of the Holy Prophet (S.A.W.) with the believers took three definite shapes:

1. Adversaries in war
2. People with treaties
3. Zimmies

Ultimately, people who had entered into treaties also embraced Islam. Thus only two categories were left: 1) Adversaries and 2) Zimmies.

Firstly, the Muslims who had reported faith and belief in him, secondly, those at peace with him who enjoyed protection from him and, thirdly, those who opposed him and kept on fighting. As regards behavior with the hypocrites, he was ordered to accept their outward appearance, and leave their inward state and intentions to God, and carry on Jihad with them by arguments and persuasive means, to shun them and treat them with harshness and to influence their hearts by the deep penetrating words of God. He was forbidden from offering funeral prayers for them and from praying at their graves and he was told that Allah shall not forgive them even if he sought forgiveness for them. So this was the practice of the Holy Prophet (S.A.W) concerning his enemies amongst the unbelievers and hypocrites. In this discourse, all the stages of the Islamic Jihad have been summarized. In this summary we find glimpses of the distinctive and far-reaching characteristics of the dynamic movement of the true religion. They are worthy of deep and penetrating study. But we can here at best only afford to make a few concise explanatory remarks.

FIRST DISTINCTIVE CHARACTERISTIC
OF THE DYNAMIC JIHAD

The first distinguishing characteristic of this true Religion is that the entire practical system of this religion is realistic. Its movement addresses human beings as they exist in actuality, and mobilizes the resources and means that are in accordance with practical conditions. Since this movement has to confront such Jahiliyyah, which prevails over ideas and beliefs and on the basis of which a practical system of life is established duly backed by political and material authority, the Islamic movement has, therefore, to produce parallel resources to countenance the Jahiliyyah. This movement resorts to the method of preaching and persuasion for reforming the ideas and beliefs. It harnesses material power and invokes Jihad for eliminating the Jahili order and its supporting authority for they interfere with and prevent the efforts to reform the beliefs and ideas of humanity at large, and by dint of its resources and aberrant methods forces them to obey it and makes them bow before human lords instead of the Almighty Lord. This movement does not confine itself to mere preaching and persuasion while confronting the physical power, nor does it deem it proper to utilize force and coercion for converting the ideas and thoughts of the common man. Both these principles are of equal importance in the application of the method of this religion. The very purpose of this movement is to set human beings free from the yoke of human enslavement and make them serve the One and Only God.

SECOND DISTINCTIVE QUALITY

Its second distinguishing characteristic is that it is a practical movement, which progresses stage by stage and at every stage provides parallel and proper resources according to its practical needs and requirements. Every stage prepares the ground for the subsequent one. In fact this religion does not confront the problems of practical life with abstract theories, nor does it traverse the various stages of life with static and unchangeable means. Those who, while talking about the system of Jihad in religion, quote Quranic verses in support of their argument, do not keep under consideration this distinctive aspect nor are they aware of the nature and reality of the various stages through which the movement of Jihad has passed, nor are they cognizant of the fact that the various verses are correlated with each stage. Thus such people, while speaking about the system of Islamic Jihad, do so in a clumsy way, mixing up the various stages, thereby distorting the very concept of Jihad. They try to extract final principles and derive generalities from the verses of the Holy Quran for which there is no justification whatsoever. The root of their mistake is that they presume that every verse of the Quran is the final and last verse on the subject in which the final order of the religion has been stated. This group of thinkers, in fact, under the pressure of pessimistic conditions under which the present Muslim generation is laboring, has nothing left except the label of Islam, laid down arms spiritually and intellectually. It is the result of this defeatist mentality that these people maintain that "Islam only believes in defensive war." On top of that, they are laboring under the misconception that they have rendered some good to the religion by this discovery, although by this incorrect deduction they want religion to surrender its distinctive method. In other words, religion should relinquish its ideal of destroying all the Satanic forces from the face of the earth and making human beings bow down their heads before one God, relieving them from the servitude of the servants and making them enter the servitude of the Lord and Creator of the servants. But Islam, in order to translate this ideal into reality, does not forcibly compel people to accept its faith but provides them with a free atmosphere to exercise their choice of faith. It either completely dynamites the reigning political systems or, subjugating them, forces them into submission to and acceptance of Jizyah. Thus it does not allow any impediment to remain in the way of accepting the belief. Thereafter it allows complete freedom to people to accept or reject belief.

THIRD DISTINCTIVE CHARACTERISTIC

The third distinguishing characteristic is that this arduous and progressive movement of religion and its fresh and new resources did not alienate religion from its very inception, but rather accosted and addressed people—whether they were near relations of the Holy Prophet (S.A.W.) or they were Quraish or the Arabs as a whole or all the people of the world—regarding one single fundamental, that is that they could become single-minded in the servitude of One Lord only by coming out of the servitude of human beings. It brooks no compromise on this principle nor tolerates any flexibility. Then it embarks upon a set plan in order to realize and achieve this sole purpose. This plan consists of certain definite and defined stages and for every stage new and corresponding resources are harnessed, as we have already explained in the foregoing pages.

FOURTH DISTINCTIVE CHARACTERISTIC

The fourth characteristic is that this religion regulates the mutual relationship between the Muslim society and other societies by giving it a legal shape, as is evident from the quotation of 'Zad al-Maad' referred to above. The basis of this legal regulation is that "Islam" (submission to God) is a universal truth, acceptance of which is binding on the entire humanity. If it does not incline toward Islam or accepts the same, it should then adopt an attitude of total compromise and should not impose any impediment in the shape of a political system or material power forestalling the way of Islam's message and persuasion. It should leave everybody to his free will to accept or reject it. If he does not wish to accept the same he should not, at the same time, oppose it or hinder the way of others. If anyone adopts the attitude of resistance, it would then be obligatory on Islam to fight against his until he is killed or he declares his loyalty and submission. Scholars of defeatist and apologetic mentalities, while expressing their views on the subject of "Jihad" in Islam, trying to wash this "blot," intermingle two things and thus confuse the issue: first, this religion forbids imposition of belief by force, as is clear from the verse, "There is no compulsion in religion"(2: 256), while on the other hand, it annihilates all those political and material powers that stand between the people and Islam, which make one people bow before another and prevent them from the servitude of Allah—these two principles are quite apart and have no mutual relevance nor is there any room for intermixing them. Despite this, these people with defeatist mentalities confound these two aspects and endeavor to confine the meaning of Jihad to what is today called "defensive war." The Islamic Jihad is a different reality, and has no relationship whatsoever with the modern warfare, neither in respect of the causes of war, nor the obvious manner in which it is conducted. The causes of Islamic Jihad should be linked with the very temperament of Islam and its real role in the world, and in its high principles which God has laid down for it and for whose fulfillment the Holy Prophet of Allah was commissioned to the high office of prophethood and was made the last Prophet and Messenger.

ISLAM IS A GENERAL DECLARATION
OF MAN'S FREEDOM

The true religion is in fact a universal declaration of man's freedom from the servitude to other men and to his own desires, which, too, are a form of human servitude.

This declaration is, in fact, a natural corollary to the declaration that sovereignty rests with God alone and that He is the Lord and Cherisher of the entire universe. This means that religion is an all-embracing and total revolution against the sovereignty of man in all its types, shapes, systems, and states, and completely revolts against every system in which authority may be in the hands of man in any form or in other words, where he may have usurped sovereignty under any shape. Any system of governance in which the final decision is referred to human beings and they happen to be the source of all authority, in fact defies them by designating "others than God," as lords over men. But once this declaration has been made that sovereignty and authority were exclusively meant for God alone, it is tantamount to restoring God's usurped authority again to Allah, from the usurpers who by their home-made legislations and devised law wanted to rule over others, thus elevating themselves to the status of lords and reducing others to the position of slaves. In short, proclamation of the sovereignty of Allah and the declaration of His authority connotes the wiping out of human kingship from the face of the earth and establishing thereon the rule of the Sustainer of the world. In the words of the Holy Quran:

> He alone is God in the heavens and in the earth. (43:84)
> The command belongs to God alone. He commands you not to worship anyone except Him. This is the right way of life.
> Say: O' People of the Book, come to what is common between us: that we shall not worship anyone except Allah, and will not associate anything with Him, and will not take lord from among ourselves besides Allah; and if they turn away, then tell them to bear witness that we are those who have submitted to Allah. (2:64)

HOW CAN GOD'S RULE BE
ESTABLISHED ON EARTH?

It is not the way of establishing Allah's rule in the world that a few "consecrated persons," i.e., priests or religious leaders, should occupy the seat of authority as was the case with the Papal regime (or church rule). Nor is it worthwhile that some representatives of the deities assumed power as was current in the system known as a theocracy (government by a spokesman of God). The establishment of God's rule means that the laws of God should reign supreme and all the affairs should finally be decided accordingly. But one has to keep in mind that the establishment of God's domain in the world, the elimination of human kingship, the reversion of authority from the hands of the usurpers toward God, the faithful enforcement of the Divine laws and the annulment and revocation of the human laws—all these campaigns cannot be realized merely by the help of persuasion and propagation of the message. Those who are ruling over the people by usurping the authority of God cannot be made to abdicate their authority by mere persuasion and appeal. Had it been so, the job of establishing the true religion would have been a very pleasant and easy affair for the messengers of God (peace be upon them). But what transpires from the history of the Prophets and the episode of the true religion, spanning over generations, is totally different. Such an important proclamation that Sovereignty and Lordship are exclusively meant for God of the universe, and in consequence thereof man will enjoy freedom from all authority except that of God, was not a mere theoretical, philosophical, and passive declaration but was a positive, practical, and dynamic message, which aimed at establishing a way of life that should rule upon the people in accordance with the Divine laws and forcibly rescue them from the servitude of men, make them enter the fold of servitude of One God, who has no associates. Obviously for accomplishing such an important mission, it was inevitable that this announcement should not remain confined to mere propagation of the message but should side by side also take the form of a movement so that every aspect of the practical eventualities should be confronted with practical and corresponding resources.

Man has in every period of history in the past, in the modern times, and perhaps in the future also, tried to confront the true religion with diverse tactical feats to subdue it, because this religion sets human beings free from the lordship of others than Allah. That is why men placed all sorts of impediments and obstacles—political, social, and economic—in the way of this religion. They resorted to racial and class shibboleths. Along with the above factors, their corrupt and distorted beliefs and fallacious concepts also worked and, as a result of the alliance of both, an extremely complicated situation developed.

If "preaching" sets right the beliefs and concepts, "movement" removes from the path other material obstacles, foremost of which is the political power that is established on intricate and complex but interrelated ideological, racial, class, social, and economic foundations. And these two -preaching and movement—jointly collaborate in influencing the established system from all four directions, and are conducive to bringing about the new system along with their elements and factors, and for this purpose countenance every adverse factor with a corresponding one. For accomplishing the stupendous mission of realizing the real freedom of man on this earth rather than the entire humanity inhabiting the whole world, both of these (i.e., preaching and movement) have to work side by side. This is a very important point, which has to be kept in mind time and again.

THE REAL NATURE OF WORSHIP

This religion is not for the freedom of Arab people only, nor its message confined to the Arabs alone. The subject of this religion is "Man"—the whole human species—and its sphere of activity is earth—the whole of it. Allah, Most High, is not the Sustainer of Arabs only, nor is His providence confined to those people who have embraced the faith of Islam. Allah, Most High, is the Sustainer of all the people of the world. This religion wishes to revert all the people to their Creator and Nourisher. It wants them to be free from the worship of others than God. The real servitude according to Islam is that man should follow the laws made by his own fellow men and this is the "worship" about which this religion has ordained that it should be exclusively confined to God. Anyone performing this "worship" for others than God, howsoever he may boast and trumpet about his religiosity, in fact becomes a renegade. The Prophet of God (S.A.W.) has stated in very clear words that obedience to the current laws and government is synonymous to "worship" when the Jews and Christians refused to worship One God. According to this meaning of the word, they were classed with "polytheists."

Tirmizi has narrated on the authority of Adi bin Hatim (R.A.A.) that when the message of the Prophet of God (S.A.W.) reached him, he fled away to Syria, for he had embraced Christianity before the advent of Islam. But his sister and a few other persons of his tribe were taken prisoners of war. The Prophet (S.A.W.) showed mercy and gratitude to her (and released her without ransom) and arranged for her to return with some gifts. She came to her brother and persuaded him to embrace Islam and advised him to visit the Holy Prophet (S.A.W.). Adi, therefore, got ready. People in Madina talked about his arrival. When he got in the presence of the Holy Prophet of Allah (S.A.W.) he had a silver cross dangling round his neck. The Prophet of Allah (S.A.W.) was at that time reciting verses from the Holy Quran.

> They (the people of the Book) have taken their rabbis and priests as lords other than God. (9:31)

Adi reports, "I submitted, 'They do not worship their priests.'" The Prophet (S.A.W.) replied, "Whatsoever their priests and rabbis call permissible, they accept as permissible, whatever they declare forbidden, they consider as forbidden, and thus they worship them." This explanation of the above verse by the Holy Prophet (S.A.W.) is the final and indisputable verdict that obedience to other than Divine law and government is tantamount to worshipping it, and a Muslim after committing the same falls outside the pale of religion. This verdict further elucidates that worshipping other than God means taking some people as lords, which practice of the true religion has come to banish and obliterate. It proclaims that the people inhabiting this earth should be free from the servitude of others than Allah.

ISLAM WAS ESTABLISHED THROUGH BOTH PREACHING AND MOVEMENT

If the practical life of human beings is found contrary to the above referred proclamation of freedom, then it becomes incumbent upon Islam to enter the field, simultaneously armed with preaching and movement for redressing this state of affairs. It should strike hard against those political powers that force people to bow at the threshold of others than God, and rule over them unmindful of the Divine laws, restricting the message of Islam from reaching the people. Consequently, even if the people wish to choose the faith of Islam, they do not have the freedom to exercise their volition undeterred and independent of the ruling power. It is, therefore, all the more necessary for Islam to assert itself in both respects—preaching and movement—so that it may, by wiping off the tyrannical powers from the face of the earth—whether they may be of a purely political nature cloaked in the form of racism or class distinctions within a race—establish a new social, economic, and political system, which may impart a practical shape to the freedom movement of man and be helpful in popularizing the same in the world.

THE MEANING OF MAN'S FREEDOM
ACCORDING TO ISLAM

It is not the intention of Islam to thrust its faith upon people. But it is also not a mere "belief." As we have stated above, Islam is a universal proclamation of emancipation of man from the servitude of other men. Its message starts with the ideal that it strives to annihilate all such systems and governments that establish the hegemony of human beings over their fellow beings and relegate them to their servitude. When it releases people from the political pressure of human sovereignty, and presents before them the message that enlightens the soul and reason, it allows them freedom to accept any belief or concept according to their free-will. But this freedom does not mean that they can make their desire their god or may themselves decide to remain under the servitude of other men, making some men lords over others. Whatever system of governance may be established in the world, it should be based on the worship of God, and the source of authority for the laws of life should be God alone, so that under the shade of this universal system every one may be free to embrace any faith one likes. This is the only way under which religion, that is, laws, submission, obedience, and servitude could be purified for God alone. The meaning of religion is more exhaustive and profound than the meaning of belief. Religion means the system and way of life that brings under its fold human life with all its details. In Islam this system wholly depends on faith. But its hold is far more comprehensive than faith. Under the Islamic system of government there is the possibility of many such habitations, which may be loyal to the country's Islamic laws but many have not accepted Islam.

IS ISLAM A DEFENSIVE MOVEMENT?

Anyone who fully understands this peculiar character of the religion, which we have explained above, will automatically arrive at the conclusion that it was indispensable that the Islamic movement should start under both circumstances, that is Jihad—*bis-saif*, i.e., striving through fighting and striving through preaching. This fact would also be evident to him that Islam is not a defensive movement in the narrow and limited sense that transpires from the technical term of "defensive war" current in the modern age. In fact, this narrow and wrong meaning has been attached to and suggested by those who, vanquished under the pressure of circumstances and wily attacks of the orientalists, have presented this picture of the Islamic government of Jihad. Islam was a deluge which swept away tyranny and brought real freedom to man. It challenged each and every aspect of the practical life of man and, for redressing the same, utilized resources that were aptly needed for them. Its movement of Jihad passed through definite stages and harnessed new and effectual resources for each stage.

Supposedly if it is admitted that the Islamic movement of Jihad is a defensive movement, then we shall have to alter the very meaning of the word "defense" and apply the word to mean "defense of man" against all those factors and motives that demolish the freedom of man or serve as impediments in the way of his real freedom. Just as these elements are found in the shape of faith and concepts, similarly they exist in the form of political systems based on economic, class, and racial distinctions. When Islam ushered into the world, these elements were rampant on the earth, and even in the new Jahiliyyah of the modern age they are current in some form or another. Appropriating this broad sense of the word "defense" we can easily apprehend those motives that created the Islamic movement in the world in the wake of Jihad. Thus the true nature of Islam will also be amply reflected before us and we shall have no difficulty in understanding what Islam stands for: Freedom of man from servitude to man, submission before the teachings of God, the establishment of His Sovereignty, an end of man's arrogance and selfishness, and implementation of the Divine Shariah in human affairs.

As regards the efforts that are being made in concocting arguments and reasons to justify the narrow and limited sense of Islamic Jihad which is found in the current phraseology of 'defensive war' and the painstaking researches made in excavating traditions and authorities to prove that battle fought in Islamic Jihad were for the defense of the homeland of Islam (some considering the Arabian peninsula to be the homeland of Islam) against the aggression of the neighboring powers, they, in fact, betray that these "benefactors" either did not understand the character of Islam and its role in the world, or have, in view of the difficult conditions and circumstances, laid down arms before the wily and treacherous attacks of the orientalists.

Can anyone say if Abu Bakr, Umar, Othman (R.A.A.), had they been satisfied that the Roman and Persian powers would not attack the Arabian peninsula, would not have striven to spread the message of Islam throughout the length and breadth of the world? Obviously the reply is in the negative, for without it the message of Islam could not have progressively expanded, because of the several material difficulties interrupting it, for example, the political system of the State, racial and class distinctions of the society, the economic system emanating from these racial and class concepts, and the material resources of the State shielding and defending them. All these factors were stumbling blocks along the way.

It would be the height of naiveté to imagine that a message that proclaims the freedom of the entire human species inhabiting the earth would confront the aforementioned impediments merely with the Jihad of expression and exposition. Undoubtedly this message does strive through tongue and speech. But when? Only then when people are free to accept this message. Therefore, this message, after redeeming the human beings from all influences and obstacles, appeals to them in an atmosphere of freedom and observes the regulation, "There is no compulsion in religion." But when the above mentioned material influences and impediments may be ruling, there is no recourse but to remove them with force, so that when this message may appeal to the heart and reason of man, they should be free from all such shackles and bonds to pronounce their verdict open-heartedly in response to the said appeal.

If the ideal of the Islamic message is the decisive proclamation of man's freedom, which is not confined to philosophical and ideological explanations only, but
wishes to tackle practical situations by confronting every aspect with corresponding resources, aptly suited and effective to counter them, then for such a revolutionary message, the path of Jihad is one of the fundamental requirements,
whether the homeland of Islam—more correctly in the Islamic terminology
Daras-Salam—is in a state of peace, or threatened by neighboring powers. When
Islam strives for peace, it does not visualize the superficial peace by safeguarding
from the hazards of only the votaries of Islam residing in a particular area of land.
The peace Islam desires is that the religion should be established in its entirety in
the world. All the people should bow in submission before One God, and should
not take their fellow men as lords in place of God. After the period of the Holy
Prophet (S.A.W.) only the final stages of the Islamic movement of Jihad have to be
followed. The initial or intermediary stages are no more applicable as the same
have since ended. As the great scholar Ibne Qayyim has stated, "Thus after the
revelation of the chapter Bara'at the Holy Prophet (S.A.W.) treated the unbelievers into three categories—first, adversaries in war; second, those with treaties; and
third, zimmies. When the people with treaties embraced Islam only two kinds
were left in the confrontation with the Prophet of Allah (S.A.W.); people at war
and zimmies. The people at war were always afraid of him (hence it was a perpetual state of war with them). Thus the entire people of the world stood classified
under three categories: first, the Muslims who had reposed belief in him; second,
those peace-loving who had been granted peace by the Holy Prophet (S.A.W.)
(and they are zimmies as is evident from the above sentence); and third, the opponents who were afraid of him.

The attitude of the Islamic message toward unbelievers as delineated in the
above discussion is the logical position consonant with the character and aims of
this religion. Explanations given by people defeated by circumstances and upset by
the attacks of the orientalists, when weighed on the scale of logic and reason, have
no relevance with the temperament of this religion.

PROGRESSIVE COMMANDMENTS OF JIHAD

In the beginning when Muslims migrated to Madina, God, Most High, restrained
them from fighting and told them:

> Restrain your hands and establish regular prayers and pay Zakat. (3: 77)

Subsequently they were permitted to fight.

> Permission to fight is given to those against whom war is made, because they
> are oppressed, and God is able to help them. These are the people who are ex-
> pelled from their homes without cause because they said 'Our lord is Allah,' for
> had it not been that Allah repels some men by means of others, synagogues;
> churches; oratories and mosques, wherein the name of Allah is oft mentioned,

would assuredly have been pulled down. Verily Allah helps one who helps Him. Allah is Strong and Almighty. Those who, if we give them power in the land, shall establish prayer and pay Zakat and enjoin right and forbid wrong and the end of all his affairs is with God. (22:39–41)

The Next stage came when Muslims were commanded to fight those who fight them.

Fight in the cause of God against those who fight you. (1:190)

And finally, war was declared against all polytheists.

Fight against those among the people of the Book who do not believe in God and the Last Day, Who do not forbid what God and His Messenger have forbidden, and who do not consider the true religion as their religion, until they are subdued and pay Jizyah. (9: 29)

Thus according to the explanation by Imam Ibne Qayyim, first all Muslims were restrained from fighting against the polytheists and unbelievers, then permission was accorded them to fight, then they were commanded to fight against the aggressors and, ultimately, they were commanded to fight all the polytheists and the unbelievers. These clear verses of the Holy Quran, the traditions of the Holy Prophet (S.A.W.) prompting and inciting to Jihad, the Islamic wars of the early period, rather the entire Islamic history replete with the description of Jihad, are eloquent testimonies in the presence of which every Muslim's heart will abhor to accept the commentary about Jihad conceived by minds having been defeated by the pressure of unfavorable conditions and the treacherous propaganda or the orientalists. Can such a person claim to be an intellectual who may have listened to the clear commandments of God, pursued the distinct sayings of the Prophet of God (S.A.W.) and seen the historical records full of Islamic victories, but still labors under the misconception that the scheme of Jihad is a temporary injunction, related to changing conditions and transient circumstances and only that aspect of the scheme has a perpetual effect which is concerned with the defense of the borders.

In the initial commandment regarding permission for fighting, God, Most High, informed the believers that this perpetual and permanent principle of God is operative in the worldly life that He counters one group of people with the other so that corruption may be banished from God's earth.

Permission to fight is given to those against whom war is made, because they are oppressed, and God is able to help them. These are the people who are expelled from their homes without cause because they said 'Our lord is God.' Had God not checked one people by another, then surely synagogues and churches and oratories and mosques would have been pulled down, where the name of God is remembered often. (22: 39–40)

Thus this struggle is not a temporary phase but a perpetual and permanent war. This war is the natural corollary to this eternal verdict that Truth and Falsehood cannot co-exist on the face of the earth. Whenever Islam proclaimed to establish in this world a system based on the lordship of God, and launched a movement to emancipate man from the bond of servitude to other men, the powers of usurping the authority of God, struck out against it fiercely and were not prepared to tolerate its existence at any cost. Islam, too, was alert in wiping out these insurgents and kept on effacing the system of Taghoot astride the necks of human beings. The struggle between Truth and Falsehood, Light and Darkness, continues from the beginning of the universe and the surging tide of the Jihad for freedom cannot cease until the satanic forces are put to an end and the religion is purified for God in toto.

WHY JIHAD WITH A SWORD WAS NOT PERMITTED IN THE MECCAN PERIOD

The command restraining the use of force during the Meccan period was only a temporary phase of the long-term plan. The same policy continued during the initial phase of the Hijra. But, subsequently, when the Muslim community stood up for Jihad the motivating force was not merely the defense of Madina. Undoubtedly its defense too was indispensable as an initial purpose or pretext but was not the ultimate aim. The spirit working behind Jihad was to safeguard the center of the movement from the dangers threatening it, so that the caravan of the movement could keep on marching ahead toward the realization of the mission of man's freedom, and to demolish all those obstacles impeding the way of the freedom of mankind.

THE FIRST REASON

The reason for restraining Muslims from fighting during the Meccan period is quite understandable and appeals to reason. Freedom of preaching was assured in Mecca. The Messenger (S.A.W.) was under the protection of Banu Hashim and had, therefore, the opportunity of openly proclaiming his message. He could make people listen to his message and appeal to their hearts and minds, and could address them collectively as well as individually. No organized political power existed that could place hurdles in the way of the propagation of the message and completely deprive people from hearing it. As such, there was no need for the movement at that stage to resort to force. Besides, there were certain other reasons which necessitated in this phase the continuation of preaching without this application of force. I have briefly summed up all those causes in my commentary "fi zilal al-Quran" (In the Shade of the Quran) while explaining the verse "Have you seen the people to whom it is said, 'Restrain your hands and establish regular prayers and pay Zakat?'" (3:7). It may be useful here to reproduce certain portions of this commentary.

THE SECOND REASON FOR RESTRAINING FROM JIHAD WITH THE SWORD IN THIS STAGE

The prohibition of the use of force in this stage may yet be for the reason that this phase of the Islamic message was that of training and developing the potentialities in a particular environment for a particular nation under particular conditions. Amidst the multifarious purposes of this training and the preparation necessary in this atmosphere, one was to train the individual Arab to tolerate things to which he was not accustomed. For example, to patiently bear the excesses and oppressions allowed to be placed upon himself or those under his protection, so that he should be free from the pride of his personality and dictates of his unbridled self. The purpose of his life should not be confined to the defense of himself or those under his protection. He should practice forbearance so that he may not lose his temper on listening to anything unpalatable to him or get infuriated and enraged on confronting a provocative situation, if this was his prior temperament. He should evince sobriety and be temperate in his temper and actions. He should also abide by the party's discipline having top organization under the patronage of a supreme leader. He should refer to that leader in every affair of his life. Every action of his should reflect the command of the leader, irrespective of the consideration whether that order was against his habit and taste or favorable to it. During the Meccan period these things were the foundation-stone for the character-building and reformation of an Arab. The purpose was to establish a Muslim society comprised of persons with sublime characters, who should move at the beck and call of the leader, be progressive and civilized and free from wild habits and tribal delinquencies.

THE THIRD REASON

Another reason for the prohibition of Jihad with the sword in this period was that the environment surrounding the Quraish was brimming with the feeling of pride and superiority of lineage. Under such circumstances peaceful means of propagating the message could be more effective. Resorting to force at this stage could, therefore, further provoke vengeance and inflame enmity. It could generate fresh feelings of revenge and motivate blood-feuds. Tribal warfare based on blood-feuds was already rife among the Arabs, such as the wars of the Dahis, Gaba, and Basus, which continued for years and years and annihilated tribe after tribe. If new feelings of blood-feuds would have entered their hearts and minds associated with Islam, then they would have never been attenuated and appeased. Islam, instead of being a call toward the true religion, would have turned into an unending sequence of blood-feuds and its basic teachings would have been forgotten in its preliminary stage with no hope of its revival ever in the future.

THE FOURTH REASON

It may also have been a reason that avoidance of civil war on a massive scale was envisaged. At that time no organized government existed that could persecute and torture the believers, rather the duty of chastisement and chastening was being discharged by the relations and guardians of the believers. In such an atmosphere, the use of force could only mean turning each and every household into a battlefield and a long and unending civil war would have ensued. People would have got an opportunity to say: "so this is Islam." In fact it was said so about Islam even though fighting had not been permitted. People of the Quraish during the Hajj season would go to the camps of Arab tribes coming from far and wide for pilgrimage and commerce and tell them "Muhammad (S.A.W.) is not only dividing his nation and his tribe; he is even dividing sons from fathers." The Quraish were leveling these charges under the circumstances that Believers were not permitted to resort to force. But had this front been opened in every house and every locality and the son factually allowed to behead his father, a slave to kill his master, then what would objectors have said and what situation would have in fact developed?

THE FIFTH REASON

Another reason may have been that Allah, Most High, knew that the majority of the opponents of Islam, who had at the outset put the Muslims to various religious trials, heart-rending tortures, and subjected them to all kinds of tyrannies and cruelties, would at a later stage turn out to be sincere and loyal soldiers of Islam, one even its great leader! Was Umar Ibn al-Khattab not amongst them? The position he acquired after embracing Islam needs no elucidation.

THE SIXTH REASON

Another reason may have been that the sense of pride of the Arabs, particularly in the tribal environment, could naturally be prone to supporting a persecuted person, who perseveres through oppression and torment, and does not yield or surrender. This feeling of pride gets further excited if the target of the oppression and tyranny happens to be their elites and gentry. Many incidents of this nature took place in Mecca, which corroborate this thesis. For example, when Abu Bakr, an extremely gentle and generous person, left Mecca with the intent of migrating to some other place, Ibn al-Doghna could not bear it and restrained him from migration for he considered such a step a disgrace for the Arabs. He, therefore, offered his own protection to Abu Bakr. The best example of such an incident is the tearing up of the contract under which those of Banu Hashim were confined to the valley of Abu Talib. When the period of their hunger and deprivation had been unreasonably prolonged to an unbearable extent, the Arab youth tore it to pieces. This chivalry was a peculiar trait of the Arabs, whereas ancient civilizations that have been accustomed to disgracing people depict a contrary picture: Those who suffered and were persecuted were derided and mocked while the oppressors and the tyrants were shown respect.

THE SEVENTH REASON

It may also have been a reason that the number of Muslims at that time was very limited, and confined to Mecca only. The Islamic message had not reached other parts of the Arabian peninsula or, if at all, it was by way of hearsay. Other tribes considering it to be an internal strife of the Quraish simply watched and awaited the final outcome, hitherto maintaining neutrality. Under the circumstances, if fighting had been made obligatory on the Muslims, this limited warfare would have ended with the complete annihilation of this small community. Even if the Muslims had killed a number of their adversaries many times larger than their own, they would have eventually been wiped out of existence, root and branch. Idolatry and polytheism would have ruled as usual and the mourning of Islamic order would have never dawned, nor would its practical implementation have yielded its blessings, although it was revealed solely for the purpose of fashioning human life according to its pattern.

WHY WAS JIHAD FORBIDDEN
IN THE EARLY MADINITE PERIOD?

Fighting was also prohibited in the early period of Madinite life. The reason being that the Holy Prophet (S.A.W.) had entered into a no-war pact with the Jews of Madina and the unbelieving Arabs living in and around Madina. This was the natural demand of the new situation and an appropriate action of the Holy Prophet (S.A.W.) in the following perspective.

Firstly: open opportunities for preaching and persuasion were available. There was no political power to impose sanctions and restrict the people. The entire population had acknowledged the new Muslim state and agreed upon the leadership of the Holy Prophet (S.A.W.) for settling the political matters. It had, therefore, been stipulated in the above treaty that no person was authorized to conclude a pact of peace, declare war, or establish foreign relations without the permission of the Prophet of God (S.A.W.). This fact had become clear as daylight; that the real political power of Madina rested within the Muslim leadership. As such, doors were open for the expansion and promotion of the Islamic message: freedom of faith was existent, and people were free to embrace, without let or hindrance, any faith or creed according to their liking.

Secondly: at this juncture, the Prophet of God (S.A.W.) wanted to settle all scores with the Quraish with a singleness of purpose, for their opposition was posing a great hindrance to the spreading of the message among other tribes, who were waiting for the final outcome of the domestic strife going on between the Quraish and their progeny. As such, the Holy Prophet (S.A.W.), without losing the opportunity, hastened to send scouting parties in various directions. The first such party arranged by him was headed by Hamza bin-Abdul Mutallib. It left in the month of Ramazan, hardly six months after the immigration. Many more scouting parties were dispatched after this: one in the thirteenth month, the third at the outset of the sixteenth month and when the seventeenth month after Hijra commenced an expedition was sent under the command of Abdullah bin Jahash. This party made the first encounter in which blood was also shed. This incident took place in the month of Rajab, which was considered a sacred month. The following verse of the chapter Al-Baqara refers to this:

They ask thee about fighting in the sacred months. Say: "Fighting in them is a great sin, but to prevent people from the way of God, and to reject God and to stop people from visiting the sacred mosque and to expel people from their homes are a much greater sin, and oppression is worse than killing." (2: 217)

During the second year of the Hijra, the Battle of Badr took place, and in the chapter al-Anfal this battle was reviewed.

This stand of the Islamic movement, if viewed in its true perspective, leaves no room for the assertion that its basic aim, in the limited sense, was its own defense. This explanation is tantamount to the one offered by the so-called thinkers over-awed by the society and discomfited by the mischievous attacks of the orientalists. Those calling the matchless movement for the hegemony of Islam a result of de-fensive factors in fact stand defeated by the aggressive campaign of the orientalists, who have started an incessant attack at a time when Muslims are bereft of worldly glory and their attachment with Islam is also not enviable. Of course a small group by the Grace of God, is secure from their machinations, firmly as it does believe that Islam is a universal declaration of the freedom of man on the earth from every authority except God's Authority, and that religion should be purified for God, and it is striving for Islam's supremacy. Other thinkers are in search of moral grounds for the Islamic Jihad to satisfy those objecting to it. But the reasons justifying the Islamic movement presented in the Quran are enough, leaving no moral authority to be further desired.

The Holy Quran says:

They ought to fight in the way of God who have sold the life of this world for the life of the Hereafter, and whoever fights in the way of God and is killed or be-comes victorious, to him shall we give a great reward. Why should you not fight in the way of God for those men, women, and children who have been oppressed because they are weak and who call, "Our Lord, take us out of this place whose people are oppressors, and raise for us an ally, and send for us a helper." Those who believe fight in the cause of God, while those who do not believe fight in the cause of tyranny. Then fight against the friends of Satan. Indeed, the strategy of Satan is weak. (3: 74–76)

Say to the unbelievers that if they refrain, then whatever they have done be-fore will be forgiven them; but if they turn back, then they know what happened to earlier nations. and fight against them until there is no oppression and the reli-gion is wholly for God. But if they refrain then God is watching over their ac-tions. But if they do not, then know that God is your Ally and He is the best Ally and the best Helper. (8: 38–40)

Fight against those among the people of the Book who do not believe in God and the Last Day, who do not forbid what God and His Messenger have forbid-den, and who do not consider the true religion as their way of life, until they are subdued and pay Jizyah. The Jews say: "Ezra is the son of God" and the Christians say, "The Messiah is the son of God." These are mere sayings from their mouths, following those who proceeded them and disbelieved. God will assail them, how they are perverted! They have taken their rabbis and priests as lords, other than God, and the Messiah, son of Mary, and they were commanded to worship none but One God. There is no god but He, glory be to Him above what they associate with Him. They desire to extinguish God's light with their mouths, and God intends to perfect His light, although the unbelievers may be averse. (9: 29–33)

The reasons for Jihad, which have been described in the above verses, are these: To establish the Sovereignty and Authority of God on earth, to establish the true system revealed by God for addressing the human life; to exterminate all the Satanic forces and their ways of life, to abolish the lordship of man over other human beings. Since all men are creatures of One God only, no other slave has the right or authority to make them his servants or make arbitrary laws for them. These reasons and factors are enough to declare Jihad. Besides, this principle should also be observed that "there is no compulsion in religion." After deliverance from the authority of creatures and supremacy of the principle that Sovereignty would rest with God alone or, in other words, religion will be all in all for God alone, nobody will be forced to change his belief and to accept the creed of Islam. If one deliberates on these causes of Jihad, one will arrive at this conclusion that the purpose for which Islam stands for Jihad is to secure the real and complete freedom of man on this earth. This freedom can only then be consummate when man is delivered from servitude to other men and allowed to breathe in the limitless atmosphere of God's servitude Who is One and without any partner. Does this great purpose alone not sufficiently justify the declaration of Jihad?

The reasons and purposes enumerated by the Quran were always kept in view by the Muslim warriors. There is not a single instance where a Muslim warrior may have been questioned about the purpose of Jihad, and he may have replied: "Our country is in danger. We are up for its defense" or "We have come out to checkmate the aggressive designs of the Persians and the Romans against the Muslims" or "We want the expansion of our country and wish to amass more and more spoils of war." Conversely their reply was the same that Rabi' bin Aamir, Huzaifa bin Mohsin, Mughira bin Shuba gave to the Persian general Rustam when he asked them, one by one, separately for three days continuously before commencement of the battle of Qadisiyyah, "For what purpose have you come here?" But the reply of them all was the same:

> God sent us so that we should take out, whom He likes, from the servitude of men into submission of One God alone, from the narrowness of the world into the vastness of this world; and from the tyranny of religions into the justice of Islam. For this purpose, God Most High has sent His Messenger (S.A.W.) with His religion toward His creatures. Hence who accepts our religion, we shall acknowledge his submission, and turn back leaving the country to him, and fight against those who will rebel until we are martyred or become victorious.

ONE MORE NATURAL REASON FOR JIHAD

Besides the external factors of Jihad there is also one inherent reason, which is hidden in the nature of this religion and its all embracing demand of human freedom. Just as this religion confronts the practical human conditions with corresponding resources and resorts to new means at each and every front within the specific stages, this realistic procedure itself points to the natural cause of Jihad. This is engendered right from the very inception of the message, and endures irrespective of any danger (of external aggression) to the Islamic lands or its Muslim population residing therein. The factors responsible for bringing this reason into existence are neither the demands of defense of a limited nature nor temporary conditions. But, on the one hand, the practical difficulties and obstacles for the propagation of the Islamic message in a Godless society and, on the other, Islam's own specific way of life and its struggle in the practical life conjointly contribute to its existence. Hence this in itself is a vital argument in favor of Jihad that a Muslim strives in the path of Allah with his life and wealth, for the supremacy of those values in which neither his personal gain is envisaged nor any greed motivates him. When a Muslim embarks upon Jihad and enters the battlefield, he has already won a great encounter of the Jihad. This consists of his adversary Satan, his own self, his own desires and longings, his alluring ambitions and yearnings, his personal interests and inclinations, and the interests of his family and nation. In short, he is confronted with every slogan that is against Islam, against every feeling that is in conflict with the worshipping of God, against every impediment in the way of establishing the Divine rule in the world and the extermination of the usurpers of God's Authority.

THE REAL MOTIVE OF THE COUNTRY'S DEFENSE IN THE EYES OF ISLAM

Those who justify the Islamic Jihad by confining it to the defense of Islam's homeland, in fact degrade the greatness of the Islamic way of life. This pure way of life, in their view, does not carry even as much importance and weight as the "homeland." Islam does not hold that view about country and other similar factors which these people try to present. This point of view held by them is a creation of the modern age. It is totally alien to the Islamic consciousness and Islamic education. From the Islamic point of view, the real justification for declaring Jihad is the defense of the Islamic faith, or the defense of that way of life that presents the practical exposition of that faith or the defense of that society in which that way of life is operative. As regards the soil of the country, it is itself of no significance in the eyes of Islam nor does it hold any weight. If anything can impart respectability and greatness to the soil of the country under the Islamic concept, it is exclusively the establishment of God's rule there and the implementation of the way of life revealed by God. In this context, the country becomes the citadel and fortress of Islam, the glimmering spot of the Islamic system of life, the Home of Islam (Dar ul-Islam) and center and source of the movement for complete freedom of mankind. Undoubtedly the protection and defense of Dar ul-Islam (Home of Islam) is the defense of the Islamic faith, and the defense of the representative society of Islam and the Islamic way of life. But defense cannot be regarded as the real and ultimate purpose nor is the protection of Dar ul-Islam the real purpose of the Islamic movement of Jihad, rather the protection of Dar ul-Islam is one of the means of establishing God's government, and secondly its purpose is to make Dar ul-Islam a central and pivotal place from where the world-illuminating sun of Islam should enlighten every nook and corner of the world and where mankind should benefit from its proclamation of freedom. We have already explained that the subject matter of this religion is "Mankind" and its sphere of activity is the entire universe.

JIHAD IS AN INHERENT NECESSITY OF ISLAM

As we have already stated before, there are many material obstacles that hinder the establishment of God's rule in the world. The inexorable might of the state, the system and traditions of the society, and the entire human environment are all stumbling blocks in the way of Islam. In order to remove all these hindrances, Islam resorts to force so that there may remain no curtain between Islam and human beings and so it may appeal to the human soul and reason in a free and unfettered atmosphere. Emancipating human beings from the shackles of false and fabricated masters, it provides them freedom of choice and volition so that they may accept or reject a thing of their own free-will.

We should neither be deceived nor put to any consternation due to the despicable attacks of the orientalists against the Islamic theory of Jihad. Nor should this fact be a source of despondency and despair to us that the tide of circumstances is surging against us and the big powers of the world are opposing us. These are not such things that we should get impressed with them and try to search the justification of Islamic Jihad outside the nature and reality of the religion and come to regard Jihad as the result of defensive needs and transient causes and conditions. Jihad is continuing and shall continue whether defensive needs or temporary factors and conditions persist or not. While reviewing the vicissitudes of history, let us never forget those real motives and demands that are inherent in the nature of this religion, its universal proclamation of freedom, and its realistic procedures. It would not be appropriate to confuse the discussion between real motives and demands and defensive needs and causal emotions. Undoubtedly this religion will have to make thorough arrangements for its defense from external invaders. The advent of religion in this shape is, in fact, the proclamation of the universal lordship of God and a message for the deliverance of humans from the servitude of others than Allah. Again it's shaping itself into an organized movement, rebellious of Jahili leadership, and regenerating a typical and permanent society challenging the human sovereignty on the basis of the indivisible right of One God only; this introduction of religion to the world is enough cause for all the surrounding Jahili societies and classes founded on the servitude to human beings to rise up for its annihilation and come out for the protection and defense of their existence. Obviously, under the circumstances, the Islamic society shall have to make arrangements for its own defense and safety. Such a situation will inevitably follow. No sooner shall Islam make its appearance than this is bound to develop. There is no question of Islam's choice or otherwise for initiating this struggle, for this is foisted on Islam. This is a natural struggle, which is bound to take place between two such systems that cannot live together for long on the principle of co-existence. This is a fundamental reality which is undeniable, indubitable. And in view of this, it becomes obligatory for Islam to manage its defense. There is no way out for it but to fight out the defensive war imposed on it.

NO CEASE-FIRE BY ISLAM AGAINST JAHILIYYAH

Besides, this fundamental reality, one more immutable fact should be kept in view, which is more important and clearer than the previous one. It is the inevitable demand of the nature of Islam that it takes strides from the very beginning to pull mankind out from the servitude to others than God. Hence it is impossible for it to abide by geographical boundaries and bind itself within racial limitations. It cannot be brooked to leave the entire sprawling mankind from East to West to be devoured by vice and corruption and servitude to others than God, and, leaving it, take to seclusion.

It may happen with the opponents of Islam that, deeming it expedient, they may not commit aggression against Islam provided it allows them to continue the leadership of human beings over others within their geographical limits, leaves them to their lot and does not force them to follow its message and its declaration of freedom. But Islam cannot declare a "cease-fire" with them unless they surrender before the authority of Islam and they will no more place impediments in its way by virtue of any political power. Exactly this is the nature of this religion and, being a declaration of the universal lordship of God and a message of deliverance from the servitude to others than God for the people living in the East and West, it is also the inevitable duty of Islam. The difference between this concept of Islam and that which confines it to the racial and geographical limitations, withholding permission to take necessary steps until threatened by any external aggression, is obvious. In the first instance, Islam is a live and dynamic force while in the latter case stands totally deprived of all inherent and natural motivations.

In order to understand the justifiable reasons for the dynamism and initiative of Islam more vividly and effectively it is necessary to remember that Islam is the Divine system for human life. It is neither man-made nor a self-devised way of any human organization of a particular human race. The need for searching external causes of the Islamic movement of Jihad only then arises when we lose sight of this vital fact that the real problem of religion is to banish all the fabricated gods through the establishment of the rule of God, Most High. It is impossible that man should always keep this vital and decisive fact fresh in his mind and still strive to search an external reason justifying Islamic Jihad.

TWO CONCEPTS ABOUT ISLAM
AND THEIR DIFFERENCE

The difference between the two concepts of Islam cannot be fully evaluated in the initial stage of the journey. The one concept is that Islam was unwillingly forced to fight against Jahiliyyah. It was the natural demand of its existence that the Jahili society should attack it, and Islam should compulsorily rise up for its defense. The other concept is that Islam will, in its own right, take the initiative and ultimately enter the battlefield. The relative difference between the two aspects cannot be vividly apparent in the beginning for, under both circumstances, Islam is bound to enter the arena of war, but on reaching the final stage it would be quite evident that there is a world of difference between the two concepts. There is a fundamental and delicate difference between the feelings and emotions, and thoughts and concepts of both about Islam.

There is a very great and extraordinary difference between the concept that Islam is a Divine way of life and the concept that it is a regional system. According to the first mentioned concept, Islam has come into the world to proclaim the rule of God on God's earth, and invite all people toward the servitude to One God. It should transform its proclamation and message into a practical mold and prepare a society in which people are free from the servitude to other people and converge on the servitude to One God. Only the Divine law, which represents the Supreme Authority of God, should hold sway over them. Only such an Islam has the right to remove all the obstacles that hinder its path, so that it may freely appeal to the reason and conscience of the people by demolishing the walls of the political system of the state and self-made social traditions. According to the second mentioned concept, Islam is only a system for the country, and it has only this much right that when any power invades its territorial limits it may manage its defense. Both the concepts are before you. Undoubtedly, Islam raises the banner of Jihad under both circumstances. But the two practical pictures yielded by the motives, purposes, and consequences of Jihad under the two conditions are totally different from each other, both from the point of view of thought and view, and plan and aptitude.

Of course, Islam has the right to start with initiative. Islam is not the inheritance of any single nation or country. It is the religion of God and is for the whole world. It must have the right to shatter all those impediments that are found in the form of traditions and systems, and that fetter the freedom of choice of human beings. It neither invades persons nor does it forcibly impose its creed on them. It only deals with conditions and concepts in order to save humanity from the putrid and poisonous effects that have tarnished their nature and trampled upon their freedom of choice.

Islam is not prepared to abdicate this right at any cost. Islam directs people toward the servitude to One God by delivering them from the lordship of other people so that the movement of lordship of God, Most High, and complete freedom of human beings may be pushed to its culmination. From the point of view of Islamic concept, as well as the matter of fact, the servitude to God can only be attained in its full bloom under the shade of the Islamic order. The Islamic system alone is the singular order in which all people, whether the ruler of the ruled, black or white, poor or rich, near or far, have God, Most High, as their Sole Law-giver and all are equal before His laws and all human beings submit before Him equally. As regards other systems of life, people live in the servitude to other like human beings and follow the laws made by like men. Framing of laws is one of the characteristics of sovereignty. A person who claims that he has the authority to frame laws for the people, of his own accord, in other words is claiming sovereignty, whether he proclaims the same as such or not. Whosoever acknowledges the right of such an impostor to freely frame laws, in fact submits to his right to sovereignty, whether he names it or coins some other technical term for it.

Islam does not connote a mere faith or concept so that it may confine itself to communicating its message to the people through preachings or statements. Islam is a way of life, which takes practical steps for the freedom of human beings in the form of an organized movement. Anti-Islamic societies and ways of life do not afford it the opportunity to organize its votaries according to its own procedure. As such it becomes obligatory for Islam to put an end to all such systems that serve as obstacles in the way of complete freedom of mankind. Religion can be established for God in all its fullness only in this way. Thereafter neither the power and authority or any human being will last nor the question of servitude to any human person arise, as is the case with other systems of life that prosper on the lordship of human beings and servitude to them.

CHAPTER 22

THE PILLARS OF
AN ISLAMIC STATE

Imam Ruhullah Khomeini

Imam Ruhullah Khomeini. "The Nature of the Islamic State and the Qualifications of the Head of State." In *Khumeini [Khomeini] Speaks Revolution*,
compiled by Mohiuddin Ayyubi, translated by N. M. Shaikh. Karachi, Pakistan: International Islamic Publishers, 1981, pp. 14–19.

THE COMMON MISUNDERSTANDING

IT IS A COMMON MISTAKE THAT ANY ONE OF THE PRESENT systems of Government is considered an Islamic State. And having its good and bad qualities in
mind, discussions begin on the topic of the Islamic State. In fact, the label of the Islamic State cannot be affixed to any prevalent form of government in the whole
world. The Islamic State is neither a despotic nor a dictatorial one that plays with
the lives of the people according to the whims of despots or dictators. The dictatorial government slaughters its opponents and rewards its favorite ones. Such powers
have been generally used by dictators and kings. Even the Holy Prophet (S.A.W.)
and his Caliphs and Hazrat Ameer (Ali) did not enjoy such powers. An Islamic State
has neither the parliamentary form of government in which the people elect a group
of people who enact laws and impose them upon the people, nor is an Islamic State
a presidential form of government in which the people elect a president who, along
with his other colleagues, makes laws and imposes them upon the people.

THE GOVERNMENT OF THE LAWS OF ALLAH

If the nomenclature of Islamic State could be labeled, it would be known as the
"government of Law" and that law is neither made by a man nor by a group of

men, but it is made by their creator, Almighty Allah. This law is equally applicable to the head of State; members of parliament, the executive branch, the judiciary branch; and the people.

In the Islamic form of Government, the Holy Prophet (S.A.W.), the Holy Caliphs, and all others were under the control of the law of Allah, and this process will continue until the Day of Judgment. This Law of Allah has been revealed in the language of the Holy Quran through the Holy Prophet (S.A.W.) who became the Head of the Islamic State through the direct Commandment of Allah. He (S.A.W.) was the Head of State neither for himself nor the self-styled head appointed for the sake of forming a Government.

Similarly, since it was probable that after him (S.A.W.) there would be differences in the Muslim nation, it was considered necessary to determine the Caliphate. Thus Islam demands a Government at every stage that is obedient to the Law of Allah. In fact, that Law is the real sovereign of human society. And whatever authority was assigned to the Holy Prophet (S.A.W.) or to the Caliphs, it was from Allah.

Whenever the Holy Prophet (S.A.W.) explained anything or issued any order, it was always in accordance with the Law of Allah. Hence Islam is the name of the Law that it is incumbent upon the whole of mankind to follow. In an Islamic State, the head of the State and the subjects both are to follow without exception and practice the Law of Allah. In fact the obedience due to the Holy Prophet (S.A.W.) is due to the Commandment of Allah. Because the Holy Quran says, "Obey the Holy Prophet (S.A.W.)." The individuals who run the affairs of the people according to the Law of Allah and who obey the judiciary, which in common terminology means Government, do so because of Allah's order. As it is said in the Holy Quran, "And obey them who are in authority amongst you." There is no place for an opinion of any individual in it. All are necessarily under the control of the Will of Allah.

THE ESSENTIAL CHARACTERISTICS
OF THE ISLAMIC HEAD OF STATE

The Government in which the real sovereign is the Law logically demands that the head of the Islamic State must know the Law thoroughly. There has been no difference of opinion on this issue among the Muslim Nation, even after the passing away of the Holy Prophet (S.A.W.). An acquaintance with Law is incumbent upon him. If there was any difference among leaders, it was on the question of who knew more. Our religious leaders also followed the same principle that the Imam should be learned, the difference among them being only who was more learned.

Another characteristic of the Islamic Head of State is that he must be just. In other words, he must be the upholder of justice and not unjust and wicked. It is the logical necessity of the Islamic State that the man who is authorized to enforce the laws, manage the vast affairs of Bait ul-Mal (the Government Treasury), and look after the affairs of the Muslims must not be an embodiment of evil. "My promise shall not reach the tyrants" says Allah. Hence it is a Shiite belief that during the period of absence the Imam must be learned. He must know the laws of Islam thoroughly and enforce them justly.

THE ORDER OF THE PERIOD OF ABSENCE

According to Shiite belief, the Caliph is to be appointed by the Holy Prophet (S.A.W.). Under the plea of this belief, certain opponents have maligned the minds of the people that, as there is a visible Imam after the invisible Imam, so there is no need of establishing an Islamic government and that the Muslims can have a Government of their own choice. This is an absolutely incorrect notion. Undoubtedly in the absence of the Imam of the time, no one is appointed by Allah to run the Government, but does it mean that the necessity of Islam no longer remains? Was Islam meant to last for only 200 years? According to this logic, the orders of Islam now, its social laws, and its economic order are no longer required to be established and enforced; so have these things become harmful for mankind instead of useful?

If the injunctions of Islam are destroyed, and the frontiers of the Muslims are lost, let them be, but we Muslims should be sitting idle as it is going on now. The enemies of Islam are doing what they like to, but we should not even defend Islamic laws if we cannot enforce them.

If this happens during the period of the absence of the Imam, or if it is necessary to have the Islamic state that can enforce an Islamic character, Islamic prayers, and an Islamic penal code so that Muslims can remain as Muslims and their next generations also, then so be it. If this necessity still remains as it was before the invisibility of the Imam of the age, then it is also necessary to establish such a state whose head should have the knowledge of Islamic law and the ability to enforce it justly. This Ummah was never devoid of such a man and even now, if the people endeavor, they can surely find him to run the Islamic Government.

THE POWERS OF LEARNED AND JUST HEAD OF STATE

If a Government whose head possesses the knowledge of Islamic laws and the capability to enforce them comes into existence, then the Government shall be entitled to get the same rights from the people which the Government of the Holy Prophet (S.A.W.) had and it will be incumbent upon all the people to obey it.

No whim should be created here that (May Allah forbid) we are trying to interfere with the glorious status of the Holy Prophet (S.A.W.) or the Ameer, as is commonly claimed by our enemies and unfaithful Muslims to Malign the minds of the people on such occasions. The affairs of the Government have nothing to do with personal glory. But, as the Holy Prophet (S.A.W.) and, after him, the Holy Caliphs had managed the collective affairs of the people, the succeeding heads of the Islamic States who followed their footsteps also have the same rights. They have to organize an army, appoint staff, collect revenues, and work for the general welfare of the people as they (the Holy Prophet [S.A.W.] and the Holy Caliphs) did. The condition is the same that they (heads of the Islamic State) must be learned and just.

To sum up, the argument is that, at present, no one is appointed on the basis of the revelation but the object is determined and its necessity has become all the more essential in recent times. It is probable that the Imam of the age may not reappear for a long time. We do not know the Will of Allah and it may be that he may reappear at the time of Doomsday as is apparent from the traditions. Does that mean that the injunctions of Islam will remain suspended until then? Can the intellect accept the ruination of the Islamic character, Islamic prayers, Islamic laws, and Islamic punishments at the connivance of Allah, the Holy Prophet (S.A.W.), the Caliphs, and the Imam? Is it possible that we keep quiet at the disappearance of Islamic Laws? Hence it is essential to have an Islamic Government for the enforcement of Islamic laws and to prevent anti-Islamic forces from penetrating into Muslim countries with a view to mislead the Muslims. This objective cannot be achieved without the establishment of a Government based on Islamic law. However, those who would run the Islamic Government must be earnest, virtuous, and just Muslims. Those rulers are useless who are tyrants and do not possess the power to enforce Islamic Law.

CHAPTER 23

THE NECESSITY OF ISLAMIC GOVERNMENT

Imam Ruhullah Khomeini

Imam Ruhullah Khomeini. "The Necessity for Islamic Government." In *Islam and Revolution: Writings and Declarations of Imam Khomeini*, translated and annotated by Hamid Algar Berkeley: Mizan Press, 1981, pp. 40–54.

A BODY OF LAWS IS NOT SUFFICIENT FOR A SOCIETY TO BE reformed. In order for law to ensure the reform and happiness of man, there must be an executive power and an executor. For this reason, God Almighty, in addition to revealing a body of law (i.e., the ordinances of the *shari'ah*), has laid down a particular form of government, together with executive and administrative institutions.

The Most Noble Messenger (peace and blessings be upon him) headed the executive and administrative institutions of Muslim society. In addition to conveying the revelation and expounding and interpreting the articles of faith and the ordinances and institutions of Islam, he undertook the implementation of law and the establishment of the ordinances of Islam, thereby bringing into being the Islamic state. He did not content himself with the promulgation of law; rather, he implemented it at the same time, cutting off hands and administering lashings and stonings. After the Most Noble Messenger, his successor had the same duty and function. When the Prophet appointed a successor, it was not for the purpose of expounding articles of faith and law; it was for the implementation of law and the execution of God's ordinances. It was this function—the execution of law and the establishment of Islamic institutions—that made the appointment of a successor such an important matter that the Prophet would have failed to fulfill his mission if he had neglected it. For after the Prophet, the Muslims still needed someone to execute laws and establish the institutions of Islam in society, so that they might attain happiness in this world and the hereafter.

By their very nature, in fact, law and social institutions require the existence of an executor. It has always and everywhere been the case that legislation alone has little benefit: legislation by itself cannot assure the well-being of man. After the establishment of legislation, an executive power must come into being, a power that implements the laws and the verdicts given by the courts, thus allowing people to benefit from the laws and the just sentences the courts deliver. Islam has therefore established an executive power in the same way that it has brought laws into being. The person who holds this executive power is known as the *vali amr*.[1]

The Sunna[2] and path of the Prophet constitute a proof of the necessity for establishing government. First, he himself established a government, as history testifies. He engaged in the implementation of laws, the establishment of the ordinances of Islam, and the administration of society. He sent out governors to different regions; both sat in judgment himself and appointed judges; dispatched emissaries to foreign states, tribal chieftains, and kings; concluded treaties and pacts; and took command in battle. In short, he fulfilled all the functions of government. Second, he designated a ruler to succeed him, in accordance with divine command. If God Almighty, through the Prophet, designated a man who was to rule over Muslim society after him, this is in itself an indication that government remains a necessity after the departure of the Prophet from this world. Again, since the Most Noble Messenger promulgated the divine command through his act of appointing a successor, he also implicitly stated the necessity for establishing a government.

It is self-evident that the necessity for enactment of the law, which necessitated the formation of a government by the Prophet (upon whom be peace), was not confined or restricted to his time, but continues after his departure from this world. According to one of the noble verses of the Quran, the ordinances of Islam are not limited with respect to time or place; they are permanent and must be enacted until the end of time. They were not revealed merely for the time of the Prophet, only to be abandoned thereafter, with retribution and the penal code of Islam no longer to be enacted, or the taxes prescribed by Islam no longer collected, and the defense of the lands and people of Islam suspended. The claim that the laws of Islam may remain in abeyance, or are restricted to a particular time or place, is contrary to the essential credal bases of Islam. Since the enactment of laws, then, is necessary after the departure of the Prophet from this world and, indeed, will remain so until the end of time, the formation of a government and the establishment of executive and administrative organs are also necessary. Without the formation of a government and the establishment of such organs to ensure that through enactment of the law, all activities of the individual take place in the framework of a just system, chaos and anarchy will prevail and social, intellectual, and moral corruption will arise. The only way to prevent the emergence of anarchy and disorder and to protect society from corruption is to form a government and thus impart order to all the affairs of the country.

Both reason and divine law, then, demonstrate the necessity in our time for what was necessary during the lifetime of the Prophet and the age of the Commander of the Faithful, 'Ali ibn Abi Talib (peace be upon them)—namely the formation of a government and the establishment of executive and administrative organs.

In order to clarify the matter further, let us pose the following questions: From the time of the Lesser Occultation[3] down to the present (a period of more than 12 centuries that may continue for hundreds of millennia if it is not appropriate for the Occulted Imam to manifest himself), is it proper that the laws of Islam be cast aside and remain unexecuted, so that everyone acts as he pleases and anarchy prevails? Were the laws that the Prophet of Islam labored so hard for 23 years to set forth, promulgate, and execute valid only for a limited period of time? Did God limit the validity of His laws to 200 years? Was everything pertaining to Islam meant to be abandoned after the Lesser Occultation? Anyone who believes so, or voices such a belief, is worse situated than the person who believes and proclaims that Islam has been superseded or abrogated by another supposed revelation.[4]

No one can say it is no longer necessary to defend the frontiers and the territorial integrity of the Islamic homeland; that taxes such as the jizya, kharaj, khums, and zakat[5] should no longer be collected; that the penal code of Islam, with its provisions for the payment of blood money and the exacting of requital, should be suspended. Any person who claims that the formation of an Islamic government is not necessary implicitly denies the necessity for the implementation of Islamic law, the universality and comprehensiveness of that law, and the eternal validity of the faith itself.

After the death of the Most Noble Messenger (peace and blessings be upon him), none of the Muslims doubted the necessity for government. No one said: "We no longer need a government." No one was heard to say anything of the kind. There was unanimous agreement concerning the necessity for government. There was disagreement only as to which person should assume responsibility for the government and become the head of the state. Government, therefore, was established after the Prophet (upon whom be peace and blessings), both in the time of the caliphs and in that of the Commander of the Faithful (peace be upon him); an apparatus of government came into existence with administrative and executive organs.

The nature and character of Islamic law and the divine ordinances of the shari'ah furnish additional proof of the necessity for establishing government, for they indicate that the laws were laid down for the purpose of creating a state and administering the political, economic, and cultural affairs of society.

First, the laws of the shari'ah embrace a diverse body of laws and regulations, which amounts to a complete social system. In this system of laws, all the needs of man have been met: his dealings with his neighbors, fellow citizens, and clan, as well as children and relatives; the concerns of private and marital life; regulations concerning war and peace and intercourse with other nations; penal and commercial law; and regulations pertaining to trade and agriculture. Islamic law contains provisions relating to the preliminaries of marriage and the form in which it should be contracted, and others relating to the development of the embryo in the womb and what food the parents should eat at the time of conception. It further stipulates the duties that are incumbent upon them while the infant is being suckled, and specifies how the child should be reared, and how the husband and the wife should relate to each other and to their children. Islam provides laws and instructions for all of these matters, aiming, as it does, to produce integrated and virtuous human beings who are walking embodiments of the law, or to put it differently, the law's voluntary and instinctive executors. It is obvious, then, how much care Islam devotes to government and the political and economic relations of society, with the goal of creating conditions conducive to the production of morally upright and virtuous human beings.

The Glorious Quran and the Sunna contain all the laws and ordinances man needs in order to attain happiness and the perfection of his state. The book *al-Kafi* [6] has a chapter entitled, "All the Needs of Men are Set Out in the Book and the Sunna," the "Book" meaning the Quran, which is, in its own words, "an exposition of all things."[7] According to certain traditions, the Imam[8] also swears that the Book and the Sunna contain without a doubt all that men need.

Second, if we examine closely the nature and character of the provisions of the law, we realize that their execution and implementation depend upon the formation of a government, and that it is impossible to fulfill the duty of executing God's commands without there being established properly comprehensive administrative and executive organs. Let us now mention certain types of provisions in order to illustrate this point; the others you can examine yourselves.

The taxes Islam levies and the form of budget it has established are not merely for the sake of providing subsistence to the poor or feeding the indigent among the descendants of the Prophet (peace and blessings be upon him); they are also intended to make possible the establishment of a great government and to assure its essential expenditures.

For example, *khums* is a huge source of income that accrues to the treasury and represents one item in the budget. According to our Shi'i school of thought, *khums* is to be levied in an equitable manner on all agricultural and commercial profits and all natural resources whether above or below the ground—in short, on all forms of wealth and income. It applies equally to the greengrocer with his stall outside this mosque and to the shipping or mining magnate. They must all pay one-fifth of their surplus income, after customary expenses are deducted, to the Islamic ruler so that it enters the treasury. it is obvious that such a huge income serves the purpose of administering the Islamic state and meeting all its financial needs. If we were to calculate one-fifth of the surplus income of all the Muslim countries (or of the whole world, should it enter the fold of Islam), it would become fully apparent that the purpose for the imposition of such a tax is not merely the upkeep of the *sayyids*[9] or the religious scholars but, on the contrary, something far more significant, namely, meeting the financial needs of the great organs and institutions of government. If an Islamic government is achieved, it will have to be administered on the basis of the taxes that Islam has established—*khums*, *zakat* (this, of course, would not represent an appreciable sum),[10] jizya, and *kharaj*.

How could the *sayyids* ever need so vast a budget? The *khums* of the bazaar of Baghdad would be enough for the needs of the *sayyids* and the upkeep of the religious teaching institution, as well as all the poor of the Islamic world, quite apart from the *khums* of the bazaars of Tehran, Istanbul, Cairo, and other cities. The provision of such a huge budget must obviously be for the purpose of forming a government and administering all the Islamic lands. It was established with the aim of providing for the needs of the people, for public services relating to health, education, defense, and economic development. Further, in accordance with the procedures laid down by Islam for the collection, preservation, and expenditure of this income, all forms of usurpation and embezzlement of public wealth have been forbidden, so that the head of state and all those entrusted with responsibility for conducting public affairs (i.e., members of the government) have no privileges over the ordinary citizen in benefiting from the public income and wealth; all have an equal share.

Now, should we cast this huge treasury into the ocean, or bury it until the Imam returns, or just spend it on 50 *sayyids* a day until they have all eaten their fill? Let us suppose we give all this money to 500,000 *sayyids;* they would not know what to do with it. We all know that the *sayyids* and the poor have a claim on the public treasury only to the extent required for subsistence. The budget of the Islamic state is constructed in such a way that every source of income is allocated to specific types of expenditures.

Zakat, voluntary contributions and charitable donations, and *khums* are all levied and spent separately. There is a *hadith* to the effect that at the end of the year, *sayyids* must return any surplus from what they have received to the Islamic ruler, just as the ruler must aid them if they are in need.

The *jizya,* which is imposed on the *ahl adh-dhimma,*[11] and the *kharaj,* which is levied on agricultural land, represent two additional sources of considerable income. The establishment of these taxes also proves that the existence of a ruler and a government is necessary. It is the duty of a ruler or governor to assess the poll-tax to be levied on the *ahl adh-dhimma* in accordance with their income and financial capacity, and to fix appropriate taxes on their arable lands and livestock. He must also collect the *kharaj* on those broad lands that are the "property of God" and in the possession of the Islamic state. This task requires the existence of orderly institutions, rules and regulations, and administrative processes and policies; it cannot be fulfilled in the absence of order. It is the responsibility of those in charge of the Islamic state, first, to assess the taxes in due and appropriate measure and in accordance with the public good; then, to collect them; and, finally, to spend them in a manner conducive to the welfare of the Muslims.

Thus, you see that the fiscal provisions of Islam also point to the necessity for establishing a government, for they cannot be fulfilled without the establishment of the appropriate Islamic institutions.

The ordinances pertaining to preservation of the Islamic order and defense of the territorial integrity and the independence of the Islamic *umma*[12] also demanded the formation of a government. An example is the command: "Prepare against them whatever force you can muster and horses tethered" (8:60), which enjoins the preparation of as much armed defensive force as possible and orders the Muslims to be always on the alert and at the ready, even in time of peace.

If the Muslims had acted in accordance with this command and, after forming a government, made the necessary extensive preparations to be in a state of full readiness for war, a handful of Jews would never have dared to occupy our lands, and to burn and destroy the Masjid al-Aqsa[13] without the people being capable of making an immediate response. All this has resulted from the failure of the Muslims to fulfill their duty of executing God's law and setting up a righteous and respectable government. If the rulers of the Muslim countries truly represented the believers and enacted God's ordinances, they would set aside their petty differences, abandon their subversive and divisive activities, and join together like the fingers of one hand. Then a handful of wretched Jews (the agents of America, Britain, and other foreign powers) would never have been able to accomplish what they have, no matter how much support they enjoyed from America and Britain. All this has happened because of the incompetence of those who rule over the Muslims.

The verse: "Prepare against them whatever force you can muster" commands you to be as strong and well-prepared as possible, so that your enemies will be unable to oppress you and transgress against you. It is because we have been lacking in unity, strength, and preparedness that we suffer oppression and are at the mercy of foreign aggressors.

There are numerous provisions of the law that can't be implemented without the establishment of a governmental apparatus; for example, blood money, which must be exacted and delivered to those deserving it, or the corporeal penalties imposed by the law, which must be carried out under the supervision of the Islamic ruler. All of these laws refer back to the institutions of government, for it is governmental power alone that is capable of fulfilling this function.

After the death of the Most Noble Messenger (peace and blessings be upon him), the obstinate enemies of the faith, the Umayyads[14] (God's curses be upon them) did not permit the Islamic state to attain stability with the rule of 'Ali ibn Abi Talib (upon whom be peace). They did not allow a form of government to exist that was pleasing to God, Exalted and Almighty, or to his Most Noble Messenger. They transformed the entire basis of government, and their policies were, for the most part, contradictory to Islam. The form of government of the Umayyads and the Abbasids,[15] and the political and administrative policies they pursued, were anti-Islamic. The form of government was thoroughly perverted by being transformed into a monarchy, like those of the kings of Iran, the emperors of Rome, and the pharoahs of Egypt. For the most part, this non-Islamic form of government has persisted to the present day, as we can see.

Both law and reason require that we not permit governments to retain this non-Islamic or anti-Islamic character. The proofs are clear. First, the existence of a non-Islamic political order necessarily results in the non-implementation of the Islamic political order. Then, all non-Islamic systems of government are the systems of *kufr*,[16] since the ruler in each case is an instance of *taghut*,[17] and it is our duty to remove from the life of Muslim society all traces of *kufr* and destroy them. It is also our duty to create a favorable social environment for the education of believing and virtuous individuals, an environment that is in total contradiction with that produced by the rule of *taghut* and illegitimate power. The social environment created by *taghut* and *shirk*[18] invariably brings about corruption such as you can now observe in Iran, the corruption termed "corruption on earth."[19] This corruption must be swept away, and its instigators punished for their deeds. It is the same corruption that the Pharaoh generated in Egypt with his policies, so that the Quran says of him, "Truly he was among the corrupters" (28:4). A believing, pious, and just individual cannot possibly exist in a socio-political environment of this nature and still maintain his faith and righteous conduct. He is faced with two choices: either he commits acts that amount to *kufr* and contradicts righteousness, or in order not to commit such acts and not to submit to the orders and commands of the *taghut*, the just individual opposes him and struggles against him in order to destroy the environment of corruption. We have in reality, then, no choice but to destroy those systems of government that are corrupt in themselves and also entail the corruption of others, and to overthrow all treacherous, corrupt, oppressive, and criminal regimes.

This is a duty that all Muslims must fulfill, in every one of the Muslim countries, in order to achieve the triumphant political revolution of Islam.

We see, too, that together, the imperialists and the tyrannical self-seeking rulers have divided the Islamic homeland. They have separated the various segments of the Islamic *umma* from each other and artificially created separate nations. There once existed the great Ottoman State, and that, too, the imperialists divided. Russia, Britain, Austria, and other imperialist powers united, and through wars against the Ottomans, each came to occupy or absorb into its sphere of influence part of the Ottoman realm. It is true that most of the Ottoman rulers were incompetent, that some of them were corrupt, and that they followed a monarchical system. Nonetheless, the existence of the Ottoman State represented a threat to the imperialists. It was always possible that righteous individuals might rise up among the people and, with their assistance, seize control of the state, thus putting an end to imperialism by mobilizing the unified resources of the nation. Therefore, after numerous prior wars, the imperialists at the end of World War I divided the Ottoman State, creating in its territories about 10 or 15 petty states.[20] Then each of these was entrusted to one of their servants or a group of their servants, although certain countries were later able to escape the grasp of the agents of imperialism.

In order to assure the unity of the Islamic *umma*, in order to liberate the Islamic homeland from occupation and penetration by the imperialists and their puppet governments, it is imperative that we establish a government. In order to attain the unity and freedom of the Muslim peoples, we must overthrow the oppressive governments installed by the imperialists and bring into existence an Islamic government of justice that will be in the service of the people. The formation of such a government will serve to preserve the disciplined unity of the Muslims; just as Fatimat az Zahra[21] (upon whom be peace) said in her address: "The Imamate exists for the sake of preserving order among the Muslims and replacing their disunity with unity."

Through the political agents they have placed in power over the people, the imperialists have also imposed on us an unjust economic order, and thereby divided our people into two groups: oppressors and oppressed. Hundreds of millions of Muslims are hungry and deprived of all forms of health care and education, while minorities comprised of the wealthy and powerful live a life of indulgence, licentiousness, and corruption. The hungry and deprived have constantly struggled to free themselves from the oppression of their plundering overlords, and their struggle continues to this day. But their way is blocked by the ruling minorities and the oppressive governmental structures they head. It is our duty to save the oppressed and deprived. It is our duty to be a helper to the oppressed and an enemy to the oppressor. This is nothing other than the duty that the Commander of the Faithful (upon whom be peace) entrusted to his two great offspring[22] in his celebrated testament: "Be an enemy to the oppressor and a helper to the oppressed."

The scholars of Islam have a duty to struggle against all attempts by the oppressors to establish a monopoly over the sources of wealth or to make illicit use of them. They must not allow the masses to remain hungry and deprived while plundering oppressors usurp the sources of wealth and live in opulence. The Commander of the Faithful (upon whom be peace) says: "I have accepted the task of government because God, Exalted and Almighty, has exacted from the scholars of Islam a pledge not to sit silent and idle in the face of the gluttony and plundering of the oppressors, on the one hand, and the hunger and deprivation of the oppressed, on the other." Here is the full text of the passage we refer to:

> I swear by Him Who causes the seed to open and creates the souls of all living things that were it not for the presence of those who have come to swear allegiance to me, were it not for the obligation of rulership now imposed upon me by the availability of aid and support, and were it not for the pledge that God has taken from the scholars of Islam not to remain silent in the face of the gluttony and plundering of the oppressors, on the one hand, and the harrowing hunger and deprivation of the oppressed, on the other hand—were it not for all of this, then I would abandon the reins of government and in no way seek it. You would see that this world of yours, with all of its position and rank, is less in my eyes than the moisture that comes from the sneeze of a goat.[23]

How can we stay silent and idle today when we see that a band of traitors and usurpers, the agents of foreign powers, have appropriated the wealth and the fruits of labor of hundreds of millions of Muslims—thanks to the support of their masters and through the power of the bayonet—granting the Muslims not the least right to prosperity? It is the duty of Islamic scholars and all Muslims to put an end to this system of oppression and, for the sake of the well-being of hundreds of millions of human beings, to overthrow these oppressive governments and form an Islamic government.

Reason, the law of Islam, the practice of the Prophet (upon whom be peace and blessings) and that of the Commander of the Faithful (upon whom be peace), the purport of various Quranic verses and Prophetic traditions—all indicate the necessity of forming a government. As an example of the traditions of the Imams, I now quote the following tradition of Imam Riza[24] (upon whom be peace):

> 'abd al-Wahid ibn Muhammad ibn 'abdus an-Nisaburi al-'Attar said, "I was told by Abul-Hasan 'Ali ibn Muhammad ibn Qutayba al-Naysaburi that he was told by Abu Muhammad al-Fadl ibn Shadhan at-Naysaburi this tradition. If someone asks, 'Why has God, the All Wise, appointed the holders of authority and commanded us to obey them?' then we answer, 'For numerous reasons. One reason is this: Men are commanded to observe certain limits and not to transgress them in order to avoid the corruption that would result. This cannot be attained or established without there being appointed over them a trustee who will ensure that

they remain within the limits of the licit and prevent them from casting themselves into the danger of transgression. Were it not for such a trustee, no one would abandon his own pleasure and benefit because of the corruption it might entail for another. Another reason is that we find no group or nation of men that ever existed without a ruler and leader, since it is required by both religion and worldly interest. It would not be compatible with divine wisdom to leave mankind to its own devices, for He, the All-Wise, knows that men need a ruler for their survival. It is through the leadership he provides that men make war against their enemies, divide among themselves the spoils of war, and preserve their communal solidarity, preventing the oppression of the oppressed by the oppressor.

'A further reason is this: were God not to appoint over men a solicitous, trustworthy, protecting, reliable leader, the community would decline, religion would depart, and the norms and ordinances that have been revealed would undergo change. Innovators would increase and deniers would erode religion, inducing doubt in the Muslims. For we see that men are needy and defective, judging by their differences of opinion and inclination and their diversity of state. Were a trustee, then, not appointed to preserve what has been revealed through the Prophet, corruption would ensue in the manner we have described. Revealed laws, norms, ordinances, and faith would be altogether changed, and therein would lie the corruption of all mankind.'"[25]

We have omitted the first part of the *hadith*, which pertains to prophethood, a topic not germane to our present discussion. What interests us at present is the second half, which I will now paraphrase for you.

If someone should ask you, "Why has God, the All-Wise, pointed holders of authority and commanded you to obey them you should answer him as follows: "He has done so for various causes and reasons. One is that men have been set upon certain well-defined path and commanded not to stray from it, nor to transgress against the established limits and norms, for if they were to stray, they would fall prey to corruption. Now men would not be able to keep to their ordained path and to enact God's laws unless a trustworthy and protective individual (or power) were appointed over them with responsibility for this matter, to prevent them from stepping outside the sphere of the licit and transgressing against the rights of others. If no such restraining individual or power were appointed, nobody would voluntarily abandon any pleasure or interest of his own that might result in harm or corruption to others; everybody would engage in oppressing and harming others for the sake of their own pleasures and interests.

Another reason and cause is this: we do not see a single group, nation, or religious community that has ever been able to exist without an individual entrusted with the maintenance of laws and institutions—in short, a head or a leader; for such a person is essential for fulfilling the affairs of religion and the world. It is not permissible, therefore, according to divine wisdom, that God should leave men, His creatures, without a leader and guide, for He knows well that they depend on the existence of such a person for their own survival and perpetuation. It is under his leadership that they fight against their enemies, divide the public income among themselves, perform Friday and congregational prayer, and foreshorten the arms of the transgressors who would encroach on the rights of the oppressed.

"Another proof and cause is this: were God not to appoint an Imam over men to maintain law and order, to serve the people faithfully as a vigilant trustee, religion would fall victim to obsolescence and decay. Its rites and institutions would vanish; the customs and ordinances of Islam would be transformed or even deformed. Heretical innovators would add things to religion and atheists and unbelievers would subtract things from it, presenting it to the Muslims in an inaccurate manner. For we see that men are prey to defects; they are not perfect and must needs strive after perfection. Moreover, they disagree with each other, having varying inclinations and discordant states. If God, therefore, had not appointed over men one who would maintain order and law and protect the revelation brought by the Prophet, in the manner we have described, men would fall prey to corruption; the institutions, laws, customs, and ordinances of Islam would be transformed; and faith and its content would be completely changed, resulting in the corruption of all humanity."

As you can deduce from the words of the Imam (upon whom be peace), there are numerous proofs and causes that necessitate the formation of a government and the establishment of an authority. These proofs, causes, and arguments are not temporary in their validity or limited to a particular time. The necessity for the formation of a government, therefore, is perpetual. For example, it will always happen that men overstep the limits laid down by Islam and transgress against the rights of others for the sake of their personal pleasure and benefit. It cannot be asserted that such was the case only in the time of the Commander of the Faithful (upon whom be peace) and that afterwards, men became angels. The wisdom of the Creator has decreed that men should live in accordance with justice and act within the limits set by divine law. This wisdom is eternal and immutable, and constitutes one of the norms of God Almighty. Today and always, therefore, the existence of a holder of authority, a ruler who acts as trustee and maintains the institutions and laws of Islam, is by necessity a ruler who prevents cruelty, oppression, and violation of the rights of others; who is a trustworthy and vigilant guardian of God's creatures; who guides men to the teachings, doctrines, laws, and institutions of Islam; and who prevents the undesirable changes that atheists and the enemies of religion wish to introduce in the laws and institutions of Islam. Did not the caliphate of the Commander of the Faithful serve this purpose? The same factors of necessity that led him to become the Imam still exist; the only difference is that no single individual has been designated for the task.[26] The principle of the necessity of government has been made a general one, so that it will always remain in effect.

If the ordinances of Islam are to remain in effect, then, if encroachment by oppressive ruling classes on the rights of the weak is to be prevented, if ruling minorities are not to be permitted to plunder and corrupt the people for the sake of pleasure and material interest, if the Islamic order is to be preserved and all individuals are to pursue the just path of Islam without any deviation, if innovation and the approval of anti-Islamic laws by sham parliaments[27] are to be prevented, if the influence of foreign powers in the Islamic lands is to be destroyed—government is necessary. None of these aims can be achieved without government and the organs of the state. It is a righteous government, of course, that is needed, one presided over by a ruler who will be a trustworthy and righteous trustee. Those who presently govern us are of no use at all for they are tyrannical, corrupt, and highly incompetent.

In the past we did not act in concert and unanimity in order to establish proper government and overthrow treacherous and corrupt rulers. Some people were apathetic and reluctant even to discuss the theory of Islamic government, and some went so far as to praise oppressive rulers. It is for this reason that we find ourselves in our present state. The influence and sovereignty of Islam in society have declined; the nation of Islam has fallen victim to division and weakness; the laws of Islam have remained in abeyance and been subjected to change and modification; and the imperialists have propagated foreign laws and alien culture among the Muslims through their agents for the sake of their evil purposes, causing people to be infatuated with the West. It was our lack of a leader, a guardian, and our lack of institutions of leadership that made all this possible. We need righteous and proper organs of government; that much is self-evident.

NOTES

1. Vali amr: "the one who holds authority," a term derived from Quran, 4:59: "0 you who believe! Obey God, and obey the Messenger and the holders of authority (uli' l-amr) from among you."
2. Sunna: the practice of the Prophet, accepted by Muslims as the norm and ideal for all human behavior.
3. Lesser Occultation: ghaybat-i sughra, the period of about 70 years (260 A.H./872 C.E.–329 A.H./939 C.E.) when, according to Shi'i belief, Muhammad al-Mahdi, the Twelfth Imam, absented himself from the physical plane but remained in communication with his followers through a succession of four appointed deputies. At the death of the fourth deputy no successor was named, and the Greater Occultation (ghaybat-i kubra) began, and continues to this day.
4. The allusion is probably to the Baha'is, who claim to have received a succession of post-Quranic revelations.
5. Jizya: a tax levied on non-Muslim citizens of the Muslim state in exchange for the protection they receive and in lieu of the taxes, such as zakat, that only Muslims pay. Kharaj: a tax levied on certain categories of land. Khums: a tax consisting of one-fifth of agricultural and commercial profits (see p. 44). Zakat: the tax levied on various categories of wealth and spent on the purposes specified in Quran, 9:60.
6. al-Kafi: one of the most important collections of Shi'i hadith, compiled by Shaykh Abu Ja'far al-Kulayni (329 A.H./941 C.E.). Two fascicules have recently been translated into English by Sayyid Muhammad Hasan Rizvi and published in Tehran.
7. The Quran, 16:89.
8. The reference is probably to Imam Ja'far as-Sadiq, whose sayings on this subject are quoted by 'Allama Tabataba'i in al-Alizan fi Tafsir al-Quran (Beirut, 1390/1979), XII, pp. 327–28.
9. Sayyids: the descendants of the Prophet through his daughter Fatima and son-in-law 'Ali, the first of the Twelve Imams.
10. Zakat would not represent an appreciable sum presumably because it is levied on surplus wealth, the accumulation of which is inhibited by the economic system of Islam.

11. Ahl adh-dhimma: non-Muslim citizens of the Muslim state, whose rights and obligations are contractually determined.

12. Umma: the entire Islamic Community, without territorial or ethnic distinction.

13. Masjid al-Aqsa: the site in Jerusalem where the Prophet ascended to heaven in the eleventh year of his mission (Quran, 17: 1); also the complex of mosques and buildings erected on the site. The chief of these was extensively damaged by arson in 1969, two years after the Zionist usurpation of Jerusalem.

14. Umayyads: members of the dynasty that ruled at Damascus from 41/632 until 132/750 and transformed the caliphate into a hereditary institution. Mu'awiyah, frequently mentioned in these pages, was the first of the Umayyad line.

15. Abbasids: the dynasty that replaced the Umayyads and established a new caliphal capital in Baghdad. With the rise of various local rulers, generally of military origin, the power of the Abbasids began to decline from the fourth/tenth century and it was brought to an end by the Mongol conquest in 656 A.H./1258 C.E.

16. Kufr: the rejection of divine guidance; the antithesis of Islam.

17. Anyone who claims the prerogatives of divinity for himself, whether explicitly or implicitly. See also p. 92.

18. Shirk: the assignment of partners to God, either by believing in a multiplicity of gods, or by assigning divine attributes and prerogatives to other-than-God.

19. "Corruption on earth": a broad term including not only moral corruption, but also subversion of the public good, embezzlement and usurpation of public wealth, conspiring with the enemies of the community against its security, and working in general for the overthrow of the Islamic order. See the commentary on Quran, 5:33 in Tabataba'i, *al-Mizan*, V, pp. 330–2.

20. It may be apposite to quote here the following passage from a secret report drawn up in January 1916 by T.E. Lawrence, the British organizer of the so-called Arab revolt led by Sharif Husayn of Mecca: "Husayn's activity seems beneficial to us, because it marches with our immediate aims, the breakup of the Islamic bloc and the defeat and disruption of the Ottoman Empire.... The Arabs are even less stable than the Turks. If properly handled they would remain in a state of political mosaic, a tissue of small jealous principalities incapable of political cohesion." See Philip Knightley and Colin Simpson, *The Secret Lives of Lawrence of Arabia* (New York: McGraw Hill, 1970), p. 55.

21. Fatimat az-Zahra: Fatima, the daughter of the Prophet and wife of Imam 'Ali.

22. I.e., Hasan and Husayn.

23. See *Nahj al-Balagha*, ed. Subhi as-Salih (Beirut, 1397 A.H./1967 C.E.).

24. Imam Riza: eighth of the Twelve Imams, born in 148 A.H./765 C.E. and died in 203 A.H./817 C.E. in Tus (Mashhad). According to Shi'i belief, he was poisoned by the Abbasid caliph Ma'mun, who had appointed him as his successor at first, but then grew fearful of the wide following he commanded (see p.148). His shrine in Mashhad is one of the principal centers of pilgrimage and religious learning in Iran.

25. The text of this tradition is to be found in Shaykh Sadduq, *'Ilal ash-Shara'i* (Qum, 1378/1958), Vol. 1, p. 183.

26. That is, in the absence of the Imam or an individual deputy named by him (as was the case during the Lesser Occultation), the task devolves upon the fuqaha as a class. See argument on pp. 62–125.

27. Here the allusion may be in particular to the so-called Family Protection Law of 1967, which Imam Khomeini denounced as contrary to n.p., n.d., pp. 462–3, par. 2836, and p. 441.

CHAPTER 24

THE POLITICAL
THEORY OF ISLAM

Sayyid Abul A'la Maududi

Sayyid [Sayed] Abul A'la Maududi. *Political Theory of Islam*. Lahore: Islamic
Publications Limited, 1976, pp. 4–22.

FUNDAMENTALS OF ISLAM

IT SHOULD BE CLEARLY UNDERSTOOD IN THE VERY BEGINNING that Islam
is not a jumble of unrelated ideas and incoherent modes of conduct. It is rather a
well-ordered system, a consistent whole, resting on a definite set of clear-cut postulates. Its major tenets, as well as detailed rules of conduct, are all derived from a logical connection with its basic principles. All the rules and regulations that Islam has
laid down for the different spheres of human life are in their essence and spirit a reflection, an extension and corollary of its first principles. The various phases of Islamic life and activity flow from these fundamental postulates exactly as the plant
sprouts forth from its seed. And just as even though the tree may spread in all directions, all its leaves and branches remain firmly attached to the roots and derive sustenance from them and it is always the seed and the root that determine the nature and
form of the tree, similar is the case with Islam. Its entire scheme of life also flows
from its basic postulates. Therefore whatever aspect of the Islamic ideology one may
like to study, he must first go to the roots and look to the fundamental principles.
Then and then alone he can have a really correct and satisfactory understanding of
the ideology and its specific injunctions and a real appreciation of its spirit and nature.

THE MISSION OF THE PROPHETS

The mission of a prophet is to propagate Islam, disseminate the teachings of Allah,
and establish the Divine guidance in this world of flesh and bones. This was the

mission of all the divinely inspired prophets who appeared in succession ever since the man's habitation on earth up to the advent of Muhammad (peace be upon him). In fact, the mission of the prophets was one and the same—the preaching of Islam. And Prophet Muhammad (peace be upon him) was the last of their line. With him, prophethood came to an end and to him was revealed the final code of human guidance, in all its completeness. All the prophets conveyed to mankind the guidance that was revealed to them and asked it to acknowledge the absolute sovereignty of God and to render unalloyed obedience to Him. This was the mission, which each one of the prophets was assigned to perform.

At first sight, this mission appears to be very simple and innocuous. But if you probe a little deeper and examine the full significance and the logical and practical implications of Divine Sovereignty and the concept of *Tawheed* (the Unity of Godhead), you will soon realize that the matter is not so simple as it appears on the surface, and that there must be something revolutionary in a doctrine that roused such bitter opposition and sustained hostility on the part of the non-believers. What strikes us most in the long history of the prophets is that whenever these servants of God proclaimed that "there is no ilah (object of worship) except Allah," all the forces of evil made common cause to challenge them. If it were merely a call to bow down in the places of worship before one God with perfect freedom outside these sacred precincts to owe allegiance to and carry out the will of the powers that be, it would have been the height of folly on the part of the ruling classes to suppress the religious liberties of its loyal subjects for a minor matter which had no bearing on their attitude toward the established government. Let us, therefore, try to explore the real point of dispute between the prophets and their opponents.

There are many verses of the Quran that make it absolutely clear that the non-believers and polytheists too, who opposed the prophets, did not deny the existence of God, nor that He was the sole Creator of heavens and earth and man, nor that the whole mechanism of nature operated in accordance with His commands, nor that it is He Who pours down the rain, drives the winds and controls the sun, the moon, the earth, and everything else. Says the Quran:

> Say: unto whom (belongeth) the earth and whosoever is therein, if ye have knowledge? They will say, unto Allah. Say: Will ye not then remember? Say: Who is Lord of the seven heavens, and Lord of the Tremendous Throne? They will say, unto Allah (all that belongeth). Say Will ye not then keep duty (unto Him)? Say: In whose hands is the dominion over all things and He protecteth, while against Him there is no protection, if ye have knowledge? They will say: unto Allah (all that belongeth). Say: How then are ye bewitched?[1]
>   And if you were to ask them: who created the heavens and the earth, and constrained the sun and the moon (to their appointed task)? they would say: Allah. How then are they turned away? . . . And if thou wert to ask them; who causeth water to come down from the sky, and therewith reviveth the earth after its death? they verily would say: Allah."[2] "And if thou asked them who created them, they will surely say: Allah. How then are they turned away.[3]

These verses make it abundantly clear that the dispute was not about the existence of God or His being the Creator and Lord of heavens and earth. All men acknowledged these truths. Hence, there was no question of there being any dispute about what was already admitted on all hands. The question arises, then, what was it that gave rise to the tremendous opposition that every prophet without any exception had to face when he made this call! The Quran states that the whole dispute centered round the uncompromising demand of the prophets that the non-believers should recognize as their *rabb* (Lord) and *ilah* (Master and Lawgiver) also the very being whom they acknowledged as their Creator and that they should assign this position to none else. But the people were not prepared to accept this demand of the prophets.

Let us now try to find out the real cause of this refusal and what the terms *ilah* and *rabb* mean. Furthermore, why did the prophets insist Allah alone should be recognized and acknowledged as *ilah* and *rabb* and why did the whole world arrange itself against them upon this apparently simple demand?

The Arabic word *ilah* stands for *ma'bud* (i.e., the object of worship) which in itself is derived from the word *'abd*, meaning a servant or slave. The relationship that exists between man and God is that of "the worshipper" and "the worshipped." Man is to offer *'ibadat* to God and is to live like His *'abd*.

And *'ibadat* does not merely mean ritual or any specific form of prayer. It means a life of continuous service and unremitting obedience like the life of a slave in relation to his Lord. To wait upon a person in service, to fold one's hands in reverence to him, to bow down one's head in acknowledgment of his elevated position, to exert oneself in obedience to his commands, to carry out his orders and cheerfully submit to all the toil and discipline involved therein, to humble oneself in the presence of the master, to offer what he demands, to obey what he commands, to set one's face steadily against the causes of his displeasure, and to sacrifice even one's life when such is his pleasure—these are the real implications of the term *'ibadat* (worship or service) and a man's true *ma'bud* (object of worship) is he whom he worships in this manner.

And what is the meaning of the word *rabb?* In Arabic, it literally means "one who nourishes and sustains, and regulates and perfects." Since the moral consciousness of man requires that one who nourishes, sustains, and provides for us has a superior claim on our allegiance, the word *rabb* is also used in the sense of master or owner. For this reason, the Arabic equivalent for the owner of property is *rabb al-mal* and for the owner of a house, *rabb al-dar.* A person's *rabb* is one whom he looks upon as his nourished and patron; from whom he expects favors and obligations; to whom he looks for honor, advancement, and peace; whose displeasure he considers to be prejudicial to his life and happiness; whom he declares to be his lord and master; and, lastly, whom he follows and obeys.[4]

Keeping in view the real meaning of these two words, *ilah* and *rabb*, it can be easily found who is it that may rightfully claim to be man's *Ilah* and *Rabb* and who can, therefore, demand that he should be served, obeyed, and worshipped. Trees, stones, rivers, animals, the sun, the moon, and the stars, none of them can venture to lay claim to this position in relation to man. It is only man who can, and does, claim godhood in relation to his fellow-beings. The desire for godhood can take root only in man's mind. It is only man's excessive lust for power and desire for exploitation that prompts him to project himself on other people as a god and extract their obedience; force them to bow down before him in reverential awe, and make them instruments of his self-aggrandizement. The pleasure of posing as a god is more enchanting and appealing than anything else that man has yet been able to discover. Whoever possesses power or wealth or cleverness or any other superior faculty, develops a strong inclination to outstep his natural and proper limits, to extend his area of influence and thrust his godhood upon such of his fellow-men as are comparatively feeble, poor, weak-minded, or deficient in any manner.

Such aspirants to godhood are of two kinds and accordingly they adopt two different lines of action. There is a type of people who are comparatively bold or who possess adequate means of forcing their claim on those over whom they wield power and consequently make a direct claim to godhood. For instance, there was, Pharaoh who was intoxicated with power and so proud of his empire that he proclaimed to the inhabitants of Egypt: *"Ana rabbokum al-a'la"* (I am your highest Lord) and *"Ma 'alimto lakum min ilahin ghairi"* (I do not know of any other *ilah* for you but myself). When the Prophet Moses approached him with a demand for the liberation of his people and told him that he too should surrender himself to the Lord of the Universe, the Pharaoh replied that since he had the power to cast him into the prison-house, Moses should rather acknowledge him as *ilah!*[5] Similarly, there was another king who had an argument with the Prophet Abraham. Ponder carefully over the words in which the Quran has narrated this episode. It says:

> Bethink thee of him who had an argument with Abraham about his Lord because Allah had given him the kingdom; how, when Abraham said: My Lord is He Who giveth life and causes death, he answered: I give life and cause death. Abraham said : Lo! Allah causeth the sun to rise in the East, so do thou cause it to come up from the West. Thus was the disbeliever flabbergasted.[6]

Why was the unbelieving king flabbergasted? Not because he denied the existence of God. He did believe that God was the ruler of the universe and that He alone made the sun rise and set. The question at issue was not the dominion over the sun and the moon and the universe but that of *the allegiance of people;* not that who should be regarded as controlling the forces of nature, but that *who should have the right to claim the obedience of men.* He did not put forth the claim that he was *Allah:* what he actually demanded was that no objection should be cast over the absoluteness of his authority over his subjects.

His authority as the ruler should not be challenged. The claim was based on the fact that he held the reins of government: he could do whatever he liked with the property or the lives of his people; he had absolute power to punish his subjects with death or to spare them. He, therefore, demanded from Abraham that the latter should recognize him as his master, serve him, and do his bidding. But when Abraham declared that he would obey, serve, and accept no one but the Lord of the Universe, the king was bewildered and shocked and did not know how to bring such a person under his control.

This claim to godhood, which the Pharaoh and Nimrod had put forth, was by no means peculiar to them. Rulers all over the world in ages past and present have advanced such claims. In Iran the words *Khuda* (Master) and *Khudawand* (Lord) were commonly employed in relation to the king, and all the ceremonies indicative of servility were performed before him, in spite of the fact that no Iranian looked upon the king as the lord of the universe, that is to say God, nor did the king represent himself as such. Similarly, the ruling dynasties in India claimed descent from the gods; the solar and lunar dynasties are well-known down to this day. The *raja* was called *an-data* (the provider of sustenance) and people prostrated themselves before him although he made no pretense of being God and his subjects never recognized him as such. Much the same was, and still is, the state of affairs in other countries.

Words synonymous with *ilah* and *rabb* are still used in direct reference to rulers of many places. Even where this is not customary, the attitude of the people toward their ruler is similar to what is implied by these two words. It is not necessary for a man who claims godhood that he should openly declare himself to be an *ilah* or *rabb*. All persons who exercise unqualified dominion over a group of men, who impose their will upon others, who make them their Instruments and seek to control their destinies in the same manner as Pharaoh and Nimrod did in the heyday of their power, are essentially claimants to godhood, though the claim may be tacit, veiled, and unexpressed. And those who serve and obey them, admit their godhood even if they do not say so by word of mouth.

In contrast to these people who directly seek recognition of their godhood there is another type of men who do not possess the necessary means or strength to get themselves accepted as *ilah* or *rabb*. But they are resourceful and cunning enough to cast a spell over the minds and hearts of common people. By the use of sinister methods, they invest some spirit, god, idol, tomb, plant, or tree with the character of *ilah* and dupe the common people successfully into believing that these objects are capable of doing them harm and bringing them good; that they can provide for their needs, answer their prayers, and afford them shelter and protection from evils which beset them all around. They tell them in effect: "If you do not seek their pleasure and approval, they will involve you in famines, epidemics, and afflictions. But if you approach them in the proper way and solicit their help they will come to your aid. We know the methods by which they can be propitiated and their pleasure can be secured. We alone can show you the means of access to these deities. Therefore, acknowledge our superiority, seek our pleasure and I entrust to our charge your life, wealth, and honor." Many stupid persons are caught in this trap and thus, under cover of false gods, is established the godhood and supremacy of priests and shrine-keepers.

There are some others belonging to the same category who employ the arts of soothsaying, astrology, fortune-telling, charms, incantations, etc. There are yet others who, while owing allegiance to God, also assert that one cannot gain direct access to God. They claim that they are the intermediaries through whom one should approach His threshold; that all ceremonials should be performed through their mediation; and that all religious rites from one's birth to death can be performed only at their hands. There are still others who proclaim themselves to be the bearers of the Book of God and yet they deliberately keep the common people ignorant of its meaning and contents. Constituting themselves into mouthpieces of God, they start dictating to others what is lawful (*halal*) and what is unlawful (*haram*). In this way their word becomes law and they force people to obey their own commands instead of those of God. This is the source of Brahmanism and Papacy which has appeared under various names and in diverse forms in all parts of the world from times immemorial down to the present day, and in consequence of which certain families, races, and classes, have imposed their will and authority over large masses of men and women.

If you were to look at the matter from this angle, you will find that *the root-cause of all evil and mischief* in the world is *the domination of man over man*, be it direct or indirect. This was the origin of all the troubles of mankind and even to this day it remains the main cause of all the misfortunes and vices which have brought untold misery on the teeming humanity. God, of course, knows all the secrets of human nature. But the truth of this observation has also been confirmed and brought home to humanity by the experiences of thousands of years that man cannot help setting up someone or other as his god, *ilah*, and *rabb*, and looking up to him for help and guidance in the complex and baffling affairs of his life and obeying his commands. This fact has been established beyond question by the historical experience of mankind that if you do not believe in God, some artificial god will take His place in your thinking and behavior. It is even possible that instead of one real God, a number of false gods, *ilhas*, and *rabbs* may impose themselves upon you.

Even today man is enchained in the slavery of many a false god. May he be in Russia or America, Italy or Yugoslavia, England or China, he is generally under the spell of some party, some ruler, some leader or group, some money-magnate or the like in such a manner that man's surveillance of man continues unabated. Modern man has discarded nature-worship, but man-worship he still does. In fact, wherever you turn your eyes, you will find that one nation dominates another, one class holds another in subjection, or a political party having gained complete ascendancy, constitutes itself as the arbiter of men's destiny; or again in some places a dictator concentrates in his hands all power and influence setting himself up as the lord and master of the people. Nowhere has man been able to do without an *ilah*.

What are the consequences of this domination of man by man, of this attempt by man to play the role of divinity? The same that would follow from a mean and incompetent person being appointed a police commissioner or some ignorant and narrow-minded politician being exalted to the rank of a prime minister. For one thing, the effect of godhood is so intoxicating that one who tastes this powerful drink can never keep himself under control. Even assuming that such self-control is possible, the vast knowledge, the keen insight, the unquestioned impartiality and perfect disinterestedness, which are required for carrying out the duties of godhood, will always remain out of the reach of man. That is why tyranny, despotism, intemperance, unlawful exploitation, and inequality reign supreme, whenever man's overlordship and domination (*uluhiyyat* and *rabubiyyal*) over man are established. The human soul is inevitably deprived of its natural freedom and man's mind and heart and his inborn faculties and aptitudes are subjected to such vexatious restrictions that the proper growth and development of his personality is arrested. How truly did the Holy Prophet observe:

God, the Almighty, says: "I created men with a pliable nature; then the devils came and contrived to lead them astray from their faith and prohibited for them what I had made lawful for them."[7]

As I have indicated above, this is the sole cause of all the miseries and conflicts from which man has suffered during the long course of human history. This is the real impediment to his progress. This is the canker, which has eaten into the vitals of his moral, intellectual, political, and economic life, destroying all the values that alone make him human and mark him off from animals. So it was in the remote past and so it is today. The only remedy for this dreadful malady lies in the repudiation and renunciation by man of all masters and in the explicit recognition by him God Almighty as his sole master and lord (*ilah* and *rabb*). There is no way to salvation except this; for even if he were to become an atheist and he would not be able to shake himself free of all these masters (*ilahs* and *rabbs*).

This was the radical reformation effected from time to time by the prophets in the life of humanity. They aimed at the demolition of man's supremacy over man. Their real mission was to deliver man from this injustice, this slavery of false gods, this tyranny of man over man, and this exploitation of the weak by the strong. Their object was to thrust back into their proper limits those who had overstepped them and to rise to the proper level those who had been forced down from it. They endeavored to evolve a social organization based on human equality in which man should be neither the salve nor the master of his fellow beings and in which all men should become the servants of one real Lord. The message of all the Prophets that came into the world was the same, namely, "O my people, worship Allah. There is no *ilah* whatever for you except He."[8]

This was precisely what Noah said; this is exactly what Hud declared; Salih affirmed the same truth; Shoaib gave the same message, and the same doctrine was repeated and confirmed by Moses, Christ, and by the Prophet Muhammad (peace be upon them all). The last of the Prophets, Muhammad (God's blessings and peace be upon him), said:

I am only a warner, and there is no god save Allah, the One, the Absolute Lord of the heavens and the earth and all that is between them.[9]

Lo! Your Lord is Allah Who created the heavens and the earth in six days, then mounted He the Throne. He covereth the night with the day, which is in haste to follow and hath made the sun and the moon and the stars subservient by His command. His verily is all creation and (His verily is the) commandment.[10]

Such is Allah, your Lord. There is no god save Him, the Creator of all things, so worship Him. And He taketh alone care of all things.[11]

And they are not enjoined anything except that they should serve Allah, keeping religion pure for Him, as men by nature upright.[12]

Come to a word common between us and between you, that we shall worship none but Allah, and that we shall ascribe no partner unto Him and that none of us shall take others for lords beside Allah.[13]

This was the proclamation that released the human soul from its fetters and set man's intellectual and material powers free from the bonds of slavery that held them in subjection. It relieved them of the burden that weighed heavily upon them and was breaking their backs. It gave them a real charter of liberty and freedom. The Holy Quran refers to this marvelous achievement of the Prophet of Islam when it says, "And he (the Prophet) relieves them of their burden and the chains that were around them."[14]

CHAPTER THREE: PRINCIPLES OF ISLAMIC POLITICAL THEORY (EXCERPT)

The belief in the Unity and the Sovereignty of Allah is the foundation of the social and moral system propounded by the prophets. It is the very starting-point of the Islamic political philosophy. The basic principle of Islam is that human beings must, individually and collectively, surrender all rights of overlordship, legislation, and exercising of authority over others. No one should be allowed to pass orders or make commands *on his own right* and no one ought to accept the obligation to carry out such commands and obey such orders. None is entitled to make laws on his own authority and none is obliged to abide by them. This right vests in Allah alone:

> The Authority rests with none but Allah. He commands you not to surrender to any one save Him. This is the right way (of life).[15]
> They ask: "Have we also got some authority?" Say: "All authority belongs to God alone."[16]
> Do not say wrongly with your tongues that this is lawful and that is unlawful.[17]
> Whoso does not establish and decide by that which Allah hath revealed, such are disbelievers.[18]

According to this theory, sovereignty belongs to Allah. He alone is the lawgiver. No man, even if he be a prophet, has the right to order others *in his own right* to do or not to do certain things. The Prophet himself is subject to God's commands: "I do not follow anything except what is revealed to me."[19]

Other people are required to obey the Prophet because he enunciates not his own but God's commands:

> We sent no messenger save that he should be obeyed *by Allah's leave.*[20]
> They are the people unto whom We gave the Scripture and Command and Prophethood.[21]
> It is not (possible) for any human being unto whom Allah has given the Scripture and the Wisdom and the Prophethood that he should have thereafter said unto mankind: Become slaves of *me instead of Allah;* but (what he said was) be ye faithful servants of the Lord.[22]

Thus the main characteristics of an Islamic state that can be deduced from these express statements of the Holy Quran are as follows:

1. No person, class, or group, not even the entire population of the state as a whole, can lay claim to sovereignty. God alone is the real sovereign; all others are merely His subjects;

2. God is the real law-giver and the authority, of absolute legislation vests in Him. The believers cannot resort to totally independent legislation nor can they modify any law that God had laid down, even if the desire to effect such legislation or change in Divine laws is unanimous;[23] and

3. An Islamic state must in all respects, be founded upon the law laid down by God through His Prophet. The government that runs such a state will be entitled to obedience in its capacity as a political agency set up to enforce the laws of God and only insofar as it acts in that capacity. If it disregards the law revealed by God, its commands will not be binding on the believers.

NOTES

1. Al-Quran, 23: 84–89.
2. Ibid., 29: 61,63.
3. Ibid., 43: 87.
4. For a detailed discussion over the meaning and concept of *ilah* and *rabb* see: Abul A'la Maududi, *Quran Ki Char Bunyadi Istilahen*. (Four Basic Terms of the Quran), Islamic Publications Ltd., Lahore.
5. Al-Quran, 26: 29, 28:38, 79:24.
6. Ibid., 2: 85.
7. Al-Madani, *At-Ittehafat al-Saryya fi al-Ahad Qudsiyya*, Hadith No. 343, Daira't al-Ma'arif, (Deccan) 1323 A.H.
8. Al-Quran, 7: 59, 65, 73, 86; also 11: 50, 61, 84.
9. Ibid., 38: 65–66.
10. Ibid., 7: 54.
11. Ibid., 6: 102.
12. Ibid., 98:5.
13. Ibid., 3: 64.
14. Ibid., 7:157.
15. Ibid., 12: 40.
16. Ibid., 3: 154.
17. Ibid., 16: 116.
18. Ibid., 5: 44.
19. Ibid., 6 50.
20. Ibid., 4: 64.
21. Ibid., 6: 90.
22. Ibid., 3: 79.
23. Here the absolute right of legislation is being discussed. In the Islamic political theory this right vests in Allah alone. As to the scope and extent of human legislation provided by the Shari'ah itself please see Maududi, *Islamic Law and Constitution*, chapter II: "Legislation and Ijtihad in Islam" and chapter VI: "First Principles of Islamic State," Islamic Publications Ltd., Lahore.

CHAPTER 25

ALL-ENCOMPASSING PROGRAM
OF AN ISLAMIC STATE

The Islamic Salvation Front of Algeria

FIS. "Encart Central: Front Islamic du Salut: Le Programme." *La Tribune*, no. 11, July 25, 1989. Translated by Nicky Peters.

ISLAMIC SALVATION FRONT
IN THE NAME OF GOD, THE
COMPASSIONATE AND THE MERCIFUL

AT A TIME WHEN THE RULING POWER IS PROVING ITSELF to be incapable of managing the multidimensional crisis that is shaking the country to its depths, the Algerian people are questioning themselves as to the solutions that are most likely to bring about a process of renewal within a resolutely civilizational approach and which would lead, through a democratic and pluralist confrontation, to the setting up of an authentic Islamic society.

The failure of different Western and Eastern ideologies makes it our obligation to implement our religion so as to safeguard our historical and civilizational accomplishments and our human and natural resources against internal and external influences.

The consolidation of the ideals of justice, liberty, and democracy cannot take place without an organization that will take charge of all demands and needs (material, moral, and spiritual) in order to strengthen resolve according to the demands of renewal and the requirements of the moment.

The birth of the Islamic Salvation Front (F.I.S.) answers the need to channel the Islamic calling and the organization of believers. The specifications of the F.I.S. can be summarized in seven points.

1. The Front works for the unity of Islam and the Oumma in accordance with the verse: "This is your Oumma and I am your Lord, adore me," and

    according to the hadith: "Every believer for his fellow believer; like a solid construction, one supports the other."

2. It presents a global and general substitute for all ideological, economic, and social problems within the framework of Islam in accordance with the precepts of the Quran and the Sunna and whilst taking into account psychological, social, and civilizational conditions. Allah said: "For Allah, religion means Islam. Whoever adopts a religion other than Islam will be refused and will be in the beyond amongst the lost." He also said: "Yes, the Quran guides toward what is most right." Allah also said: "Today I perfected your religion for you and gave my blessing to you and it pleased me that Islam be your religion." The prophet said: "I have left you two things and if you follow them closely after I have left your midst, you will never stray: The Book of Allah and my Sunna."

3. Amongst the methodological characteristics of the Front, there are moderation, the golden mean, and universality, according to the verse: "And it is thus that an Oumma of the middle way has been given to you." And according to the hadith: "Facilitate and do not complicate, preach and do not rebuke, accommodate and do not oppose."

4. Complementarity and balance between demand and pacifistic pressure, without fanaticism or negligence, constitutes one of the characteristics of the Front's approach. Allah said: " If it wasn't, corruption would have won over the earth." And according to the hadith: "There will always remain a community of my Oumma that will demonstrate the truth and that neither opponents nor cowards will be able to mislead."

    Equally the Front makes claims that highlight the legality of the cause, according to the verse: "God does not allow those that He has enlightened to turn back to error until He has shown them what they have to fear."

    It also uses a convincing argument in the aim of safeguarding the interests of the Oumma, conserving and protecting its acquisitions according to the words of Omar Ibn-El-Khattab: "Since when do you enslave people who were born free?"

5. One of the characteristics of the scientific methods of the Front is the exercising of the will of the Oumma through collective work and general effort, which means that individualism, improvisation, favoritism, personal interest, and self-reliance can be avoided.

    Allah said: "Help each other for charity and pity, do not help each other for sin and transgression." He also said: "Oh Daoud, We have designated you as the successor on earth to judge with justice between people. Do not succumb to passion which will lead you from the way of Allah." The prophet, may God's Salvation be upon him, said: "Religion is council. For whom did his companions ask? He responded: For Allah, His Book, His prophet, the chief Muslims, and all Muslims." He also said: "Control it (the soul) and count on Him (Allah)."

6. Missions of the F.I.S.: Encourage initiative and the exploitation of intelligence and talent as well as goodwill in political, economic, social, cultural, and civilizational edification.

7. From these specifications, historical and civilizational prophetic salvation will come by taking the prophet, the Savior of mankind as a model; may God be with him, in accordance with the verse: "And you were on the brink of Hell's abyss and he saved you from it."

In order to consolidate all that went before it, the Front adopts an approach within a global plan that is succinct and concise (political program) in its main lines and that it hands over, for the Oumma to decide upon, within the context of Islamic resolution.

God be with us.

Alger, le 29 Radjab 1409
le 7 mars 1989 (March 7, 1989)

PLAN OF THE POLITICAL PROGRAM OF THE ISLAMIC SALVATION FRONT

Praise be to God of whom we plead help and pardon, that he may be our guide. We search His protection against the evil that is in us and against the sin that we may have committed. Whoever is guided by God will not go astray, whilst he who God has cast aside will never again find guidance. There is no other God but Him, the Unique, nothing can be associated with Him; Mohammed is His servant and His prophet. "Oh you who believe, have fear that God may not fulfill His promises. Die only being submissive to Him: Oh you men, fear your Lord who created you from a sole being, then from that created many men and women. Fear God! Ponder these things and respect the wombs that carried you—God is watching you."

Oh you, who believe, fear God! Speak with honesty so that He reforms your behavior and He pardons your sins. Whoever obeys God and His prophet enjoys happiness without limit.

The most truthful word is the Book; the best guide is the tradition of Mohammed.

The worst of things are deceptive "callings." Every calling is a *bid'a* (reprehensible break from tradition) and every *bid'a* is an aberration and every aberration leads to Hell.

INTRODUCTION

Seriousness is one of the essential characteristics of active Islamic engagement. To acquire this seriousness it is necessary to conform to the Shari'ah, to reason, to interest, and to the Real. It is necessary to trust human nature, which is the object of our action.

So as to avoid any aberration and deviation and so that our action is neither excessive nor fainthearted we have set out the main lines of the political activity of the Islamic Salvation Front according to the following principles:

- Keep to the Islamic Shari'ah and its fair, moderate, and exhaustive method, which alone allows the treatment of all questions, whatever their importance; and this, conforming to the divine word: "We have placed you then on a way proceeding from order. Follow it then and do not follow the passions of those that know nothing."
- Use all scientific resources in a methodical way for a healthy approach to questions in abeyance and in order to better define problems, to analyze and then resolve them; take advantage of diverse techniques to put into practice the essentials of our activity as it is true that competence and experience are the necessary conditions for any healthy, beneficial, and committed enterprise. Thus will we consolidate the words of the Almighty: "He to whom wisdom has been given benefits from a great good Say: My Lord advances my science!"
- Conform to the aspirations of the Muslim people of Algeria who wish to advance and break free from the shackles of colonialism for good and get rid of the multifaceted burden of underdevelopment, armed with their faith, strong in their Muslim convictions and confident in God the Almighty. Only faith in God lets us leave the viscous circle of underdevelopment and the various forms of neo-colonialism. The core of what we propose to put into practice will know nothing other than popular will in action; it is inspired by the genius and the experience of our people and aims to perpetuate the message that is carried with it.

To realize these objectives it is necessary to methodically determine the successive steps that need to be taken, taking into account the spirit of the times. Thus will we avoid setbacks and the resentment of the people due to hasty action. We must appreciate what reality and the imperatives of efficiency have to offer.

In a word, we must, with help from God, respect the feelings and the aspirations of our people. Our political plan will go unheeded if it is not accompanied by practical modalities for the putting into practice of models and solutions, in brief, a political plan of action. All this so that the Islamic Salvation Front, with the help of God, can begin upon conscious action at the same time as supplying adequate effort to consolidate the will of all generations of people and accomplish their ends.

One of the characteristics of the Islamic Salvation Front is its intimate relationship with the people.

All concrete initiatives are done in phase with the people and all acquisitions are due to the effort of the popular Jihad. In that, we follow the way of the companions of the prophet who told him: "Even if you asked us to launch an attack on the ocean we would be present."

THE PLAN

1. Elements of method
2. Prelude
3. The framework of Islamic ideology

4. The political axis
5. The economic axis
6. The social axis
7. The cultural and civilizational axis
8. Information policy
9. The Army
10. Foreign policy

ELEMENTS OF METHOD

The methodological criteria for the elaboration of a scientific political plan.

1. The Shari'ah
2. Science
3. The transitory state of mind of the Algerian people
4. Conditions for the implementation of the plan
5. The parameters allowing action in the political field in harmony with the aforementioned criteria

In conformance with these criteria, the Islamic Salvation Front will establish relations and decide on its positions, without equivocation, with regards to associations and institutions that are already in place in accordance with their ideological, political, social, and cultural options. Our supreme reference being Islam and the major interests of the Algerian people and their constant worries. We reject all improvisation, personalization of decisions, and all attitudes that are not thought-out or are devoid of political lucidity. Method and legitimacy are the cement of our enterprise.

Thus the Islamic Salvation Front will be able to guarantee political action carried out in fairness and moderation, that is, at once both rigorous and exhaustive, and that we propose to organize as follows:

IDEOLOGICAL FRAMEWORK

The Algerian people are a Muslim people; its Islamic nature is as ancient as it is true. It constitutes their historical and civilizational vocation. In consequence, Islam is the framework and ideological reference for political action that embraces all aspects of life. Whilst the world is prey to a crisis shaking all civilizations and one that is exposing the ideological incapacity that is assailing nations, Islam is proving itself to be the most reliable ideology on which to found a political plan equal to the crisis.

The Almighty said: "Who therefore can profess to a better religion than that of he who submits to God, he who does good?" He said again: "The true religion in the eyes of God is Islam; the cult of he who seeks another religion outside Islam is not accepted. That man will in his future life be among the number of those that have lost everything." The Almighty also said: "God has chosen a religion for you: Die only being submissive to Him." And again: "Judge between them in accordance with what God has revealed to you: do not conform to their desires: take care that they do not try to draw you away from what God has revealed to you."

THE POLITICAL AXIS

Politics, according to the Islamic Salvation Front, is politics of the Shari'ah allied to practical wisdom, harmony in action, a sense of prevention, and suppleness of dialogue. Everything is in the quest of what is just and true, of what is fair and moderate. This policy is synonymous with sincerity: it is founded on the effort to convince and not to conquer. Say: "Bring your decisive proof if you are truthful"; "Let the call be heard! You are but he who makes the call heard and you are not charged with watching over them." It advocates free choice and not constraint, following the words of the Almighty. "Truth emanates from your Lord. Be it that he who wants to believe may do so and he who wants to be incredulous may do so: If your Lord had wanted it thus, all the earth would have believed. Is it up to you to constrain all men to be believers?" This policy is that of the choura and not that of despotism. The Almighty praises "those that deliberate amongst themselves," and orders His prophet to: "Consult them on all things."

So as to go beyond the contradictions that undermine the policies inspired by imported ideologies, the political program of the Islamic Salvation Front is working to realize the following:

1. To put an end to despotism, the Front adopts the choura and to put an end to political monolithism and to the monopoly on economy and society, it calls for the equality of political, economic, and social opportunity. With a view to preventing the stifling of public liberties, the Front is working to enlarge the field of these liberties and to pave the way for the exercising of genius and of the collective will of the Umma in all aspects of life. People should be able to enjoy these liberties on an equal footing. To shatter the perverse dialectic of nepotism-frustration the Front is working to codify responsibility and to offer guarantees for the accomplishment of duty to the people; it encourages the spirit of collective work, the best antidote against egotism, corruption, and individualism.

To guard against these faults, the Front guarantees freedom of expression, encourages self-criticism and sets out the accountability of all institutions and organizations of administrative, political, or economic character. It works to enlighten the people, to make them aware of their responsibilities, to rehabilitate them into the Islamic regime of the *"hisba"* and the principle of the transparency of revenues within the limits fixed by the Shari'ah.

2. To achieve these objectives the Front owes it to itself to work to reform the political regime, starting with the following areas.

A. Legislation should be submitted to the imperatives of the Shari'ah (Are there divinities that would have established religious laws for them that God would not have sanctioned?" Do they seek the judgement of ignorance? Who then is a better judge than God for the people who firmly believe?")

New data created by the multiparty system ought to be taken into account so that all parties may participate in the reform of institutions of the National Assembly of the council of Wilayas or municipalities and confer on them the legitimacy desired by the Muslim people of Algeria in conformance with their convictions.

B. All executive bodies must also be reformed—the presidency, the government, the Wilaya, the Da'ra, the municipality.

C. The military institution calls for a reform that would make it the instrument of protection of the country and the people from any threat to the sovereignty, liberty, rights, duties, and interests of the Umma as a whole.

D. Reform security policy to banish abuse and oppression and to make the security system a guarantor of the interests of the Umma, respectful of its message and its liberties recognized by the Shari'ah. All security services and institutions must have clearly defined tasks that guarantee equity, stability, and peace.

E. Reform the system of information. The institutions of this system must be redefined according to their cultural and educational vocations and must be equipped with the means for a renaissance of civilization and of political and cultural consciousness in order to avoid the country's cultural dependence and to preserve it from the cultural conquests of which it is often the object.

F. Reform the economic system by a redistribution of political, economic, and civilizational duties allowing for new policies on energy, hydrocarbons, and the export of mineral resources and other riches of the country.

G. Reform the policy on internal and external trade to bring an end to monopoly, usury, corruption and waste.

H. Reform the administrative system in the simplification of tasks and the correct functioning of services so as to preserve the rights of the administrated and to cut down on superfluous bureaucracy.

I. Reexamine agricultural policy and take charge of the means to intensify agriculture, implement a true complementarity between the primary sector and transformation industries so as to obtain self-sufficiency and develop the export market, therefore responding to internal and external market needs respectively.

J. Reform of the education system to put an end to the scholastic deficit which will take into account all ages and a longer schooling for the majority, plus rights to instruction and education responding to their needs. Thereby our successive generations will be real guardians of civilization and will be able to guarantee the continuation of the message and aspire to the best. This global reform of all structures and institutions is equivalent to a restructuring of the whole of the political regime. This is the change advocated by the policies chosen by the Islamic Salvation Front.

K. Reform of the judicial system by the restoration of the independence of justice and the judge's immunity as prescribed in the Muslim Shari'ah. The basis of Shari'ah politics is a climate of divinely inspired justice that suffers from no form of oppression, as minimal as it may be; it is the reason for power and the supreme goal of the political regime.

L. It is necessary to reassess the electoral code in order to guarantee the free arbiter of the Umma and safeguard its rights to express its will legitimately and according to the Shari'ah. Apart from those who are too young and those who have shown themselves unworthy in the eyes of the Shari'ah and have had their civil rights revoked, the vote is a right for everyone, to be freely exercised. On the other hand, no one must be constrained by it such as those on military service or those carrying out security or administrative duties, etc. Ballot boxes must be legally protected and placed under the supervision of just witnesses whose integrity is not contested by anyone. The counting of votes and the transmission of results to the national and international public will be carried out under legal guarantees to dissipate all suspicion as to the regularity of the operation. It is assured that there will be witnesses present that are representative of the parties concerned and the right to justice in the case of dispute. Moreover, it is necessary to put together conditions of candidature that are fairly distributed and truly representative of the Umma and that emerge from the efficient participation of all legitimate representatives of the people in the management of national affairs in all legislative, executive, and political proceedings.

THE ECONOMIC AXIS

The economic doctrine of the Islamic Salvation Front is founded on the search for balance between demand for consumption and conditions of production, on the necessary complementarity between quality and quantity in relation to demographic growth and the evolution of civilization. To this preoccupation with harmony and complementarity is added the major imperative of economic independence. Only equilibrium in the balance of trade will lead to avoidance of the specters of inflation and debt. These two curses are contradictions that urgently need to be resolved if we want to ensure a decent life for our people and avoid economic, political, and civilizational dependence.

For more than a century our country has suffered the pillage of colonialism, its economy has gone adrift under former regimes and has entered into economic crisis, which is characterized by the rupture of the balance between supply and demand and the worsening of the shortage in basic essentials such as medicine and housing. This is where the infernal spiral begins: consumption continues to increase while production cannot keep up, therefore there is recourse to the importation of goods for consumption and the worsening of economic dependence.

The imperative of planning has become the pretext for the stifling of liberties and the necessity to catch up with development plans has become the argument used to justify oppression. This can only cause the discouragement of the spirit of initiative and marginalize vital energy to the "advantage" of mediocrity and incompetence. Result: productive projects are blocked and small businesses penalized. That can only diminish employment and increase unemployment and inactivity and their two consequences: inflation and economic imbalance. The current regime is, in fact, unable to control an economy that is on the road to ruin.

The economic policy followed until now gives priority to large industrial complexes, to factories that consume a lot of raw materials, imported equipment, and experts that need to be "borrowed" from abroad. This choice, which ensures neither the quality nor quantity of production, has led the country into economic bankruptcy. An industry that does not aim for self-sufficiency, employment, and industrialization brings about more poverty and dependence. Presently, industry is a parasite on the economy of our country. How, then, can the discourse for the justification of industrial choice invoke self-sufficiency, the employment of young and competent people?

Is it necessary to further remind ourselves of the bad management and loss of market share? In a country such as ours, investment is one of the most important ways of putting a plan of global development into action. Demographic growth is such that two-thirds of the population is under 30 years old. This proves that the financial effort of the State is crucial in that it facilitates the absorption of the growing demand for employment. An economic policy that does not offer aid structures to the young runs the risk of marginalizing entire generations, sending them into the unknown, and condemning them to a future of unemployment and poverty, in short casting them to the margins of society.

For all these reasons our economic policy revolves around the following axes:

1. The implementation of a judicious agricultural policy.
2. A reexamination of current industrial policy to find a level of profitability in line with the demands of the country.
3. A reexamination of commercial structures and the strategies of consumption of the marketing and distribution system.
4. A reexamination of financial and monetary policy with a view to ensuring the independence of decision-making within the internal as well as the external sphere.

The Islamic Salvation Front, which has an Islamic plan whose goal is the salvation of man and civilization, sees the economic dimension as being in the service of man. Be it a question of production or consumption, investment to overcome shortages or civilizational projects, the final goal remains the elevation of man and his happiness here or in the after-life. This is our starting point, our economic credo on the basis of which we have developed the axes of our Islamic economic model which embraces all aspects of life: agriculture as well as industry, commerce as well as monetary policy, or more generally a plan for global development.

1. Agriculture

Agriculture is one of the most important resources of the country as Algeria is blessed with an enormous territory, a temperate climate, and varied countryside, without mentioning the natural propensity of the Algerians to the land, which makes them some of the most accomplished, productive, and quality-conscious land workers. Not long ago this was of great benefit to the country. It exported enormously and supplied the most demanding markets. This wealth is a tribute to the only cultivated land in the northern fringe and to the interior of the high plateau. As for the high plateau themselves and the cultivable fringes of the Sahara, they are still not used due to the absence of an adequate irrigation policy that is capable of taking advantage of the good rain that God in his great kindness lavishes on the country, or the groundwater from the wadi and rivers that split in the shaat at the heart of the Sahara and on the northern coast.

The agricultural policy that has prevailed during the last few years has caused the depopulation of the countryside and has caused the Umma to lose precious time because it neglected the construction of barrages and the channeling of water resources to places in need; this policy pushed the country into an agricultural under-development that it had never before seen in its recent or distant past. The exploitation of the riches mentioned above depends upon a lucid agricultural policy, a policy of hydraulic development allowing for great plans and a better exploitation of the land thanks to techniques and science that could allow the Sahara to benefit from the water in northern zones and transform it into a veritable garden of fruit that could feed the markets of the North.

Natural diversity in Algeria is potential wealth and it is merely waiting for an adequate policy for its potential to be revealed and for a flood of agricultural produce to make its way onto the national market and for our exports to become some of the most competitive on the international market.

The policy proposals of the Islamic Salvation Front on agriculture are summarized as follows:

a. In conformance with Shari'ah politics, agricultural policy must first put a stop to abusive expropriation and feudal redistribution of land. The Prophet said: "Whoever abuses of the smallest plot of land will know the wrath of God," as reported by Bukhari and Muslim quoting Acha.

b. To seriously undertake the exploitation of the land, the most advanced technology must not be spared. Neither can it be done before land has been distributed, without any kind of nepotism or other form of corruption, to those who deserve it. This distribution should, above all, conform to the precepts of the Shari'ah.

c. There must be particular attention given to breeding; it is urgent that our country move away from the ruinous importation of meat, milk, and its products.

d. It is necessary to re-assess the policy of internal and external marketing from top to bottom.

e. The consolidation of agriculture and the farm-produce industry through the encouragement of small and medium-sized production units in accordance with agricultural needs and the most acute concern for economy.

f. The construction of silos and depots for the stockpiling of agricultural products in case of crisis, war, or other ills.

g. The elaboration of a balanced agricultural plan whose only concern is common interest and which does not sacrifice long-term needs for those of the short-term and vice-versa.

   Any policy that allows itself to be carried away by a good harvest so as to forget about provision for possible future crises, is a short-sighted policy. Does the Almighty not say: "As usual you will sow for seven years. Keep aside what you reap, except the small quantity that you will consume."

h. The creation of agronomic research centers in pilot farms in order to develop the science of agronomy and agricultural techniques.

i. Raise the level of means and structures for the teaching of agriculture in accordance with the needs of the country so as to advance to the highest level of knowledge in agricultural matters. In this way the self-confidence of the Algerians will be restored and their thirst for knowledge and apprenticeship developed. Whenever the structures show themselves to be insufficient, they must be developed and consolidated.

j. Look to the elaboration of an agro-industrial plan to develop the agricultural mechanism and hoist our agriculture up to the technological level of our competitors on the international markets. The quality of production is linked to the quality of the techniques used and to their high competitiveness. It is, of course, understood that priority must be given to the satisfaction of local needs. It is out of the question that trade take priority over agriculture.

In enumerating the negative or positive elements of the agricultural melting pot, The Islamic Salvation Front is getting back to basics. It is aware that God the Almighty will recompense the infatuation of the Algerian people for the Islamic faith, which comes from deep within the Algerian conscience. He can lavish His goodness upon us. Does He not say: "I only created the Jinn and men that they may adore me. I do not expect any gift from them. I do not want them to feed me. God is the giver of all gifts; He is the unshakeable Master of strength"?

2. Industry

A country whose people, guided by religion, are aspiring to put an end to dependence is preparing itself for a fight on a planetary scale, in which the stake is civilization itself: "Prepare all your force to fight against them."

In a country such as ours, industry is one of the necessary conditions for renaissance.

But the Islamic Salvation Front hastens to make it clear that industry, crucial sector as it is, must not infringe in any way on agriculture as was the case in the past. Complementarity and mutual reinforcement between these two sectors must be the rule. The Muslim man must not be subordinated to industry. As opposed to what happens in capitalist countries, America or elsewhere, or in communist countries, such as Russia and countries like it, human values and dignity must not be sacrificed to the machine. Industry must serve man and planetary civilization, create wealth, serve peace but equally be efficient in procuring the military material necessary to defend "the Umma of the One and only God and of the message of his Prophet" and to preserve rights and liberties in the world.

1. Realization of a real integration between productive industrial forces and other sectors.

2. In order to reduce unemployment, we must encourage small and medium-sized industries so as to create jobs. This must, at the same time, respond to the needs of the country without depending on raw materials from abroad, which would be synonymous with economic dependence. In other

words, it means the promotion of industry that ensures both integration and quality.

3. Encouragement of the diversification of structures and industrial enterprises with the aim of self-sufficiency thanks to an interdependent, harmonious, balanced, and highly productive industrial chain. In short, finely organized industry capable of doing without foreign help.

4. Development of our technological potential by the improvement of teaching in schools, universities, and research centers. Only thus can we aspire to the industrial renaissance of which the country is so much in need.

5. Keep in mind the fact that the natural wealth of the country requires industry adapted to technological evolution and capable of withstanding acute industrial competition, in the field of armaments as well as in marketing and buying.

6. Creation of pilot factories dedicated to scientific and technological research which will be breeding grounds for highly qualified experts and highly specialized technicians in domains as diverse as theoretical science, applied technology, physics, chemistry, architecture, and spatial engineering. It is necessary to stimulate intelligence and work for the birth of new talent and vocations in all creative areas.

7. The management of businesses is a decisive factor in industrial prosperity. In consideration of this, Islam advocates the collegiate spirit, management founded on the choura, mutual respect, and a sense of responsibility that all workers of a business must share in applying the directives of the Prophet: "You are all guides and all guides must be responsible for their charges."

8. The rehabilitation of dignity and rights to the worker in ensuring good mental and physical health and social conditions and ensuring his prosperity by guaranteeing him security, transport, promotion, indemnities, bonuses, housing, in short all the conditions of a dignified life conforming to what our Prophet said: "Give what is owed to the worker even before his sweat is dry." Mohammed also said, "God forgives he who is troubled by work."

9. Reassessment of the customs policy in the Great Maghreb and the creation of an Arab and Islamic common market. We must break the shackles of the traditional customs system which hinders the exchange of agricultural or industrial produce and services between Islamic countries, and stops all economic, demographic and natural reciprocation between them. Only daring in customs policy will free us from the dictates of rich countries who have acted, for example against Libya, because they dared to brave the United States, or against the Turkish part of Cyprus or against the Iran of Mossadegh. The complementarity of supply and demand is a vital necessity at the Maghreb, Arabic, and Islamic levels. It is equally necessary to open up to our African nations in order to consolidate African unity.

10. Creation of public organizations equipped with sufficient budgets and charged with the protection of all initiatives: research and inventions, renovation of all that is to be developed in the industrial sectors. These organ-

isms must be able to act internally as well as externally by the partial or total raising of customs barriers.

11. Reexamination of the legislation on public priority, in a move toward better protection against foreign ascendancy and that of local potentates. Speaking about money, the Almighty warns "that it is not attributed to those amongst you that are rich."

12. Fixing of precise parameters to delimit State intervention in industrial property and to protect the private sector whilst making sure that the latter does not turn into a monopoly and encroach upon public interest, for that would be opening the door to economic, political, and social parasitism.

Fixing standards would guarantee the quality of products and consumer rights.

Having said this, in the light of this policy and with help from God, the Islamic Salvation Front commits itself to adapting its orientations according to the development of production and consumption; to check that progress conforms to the spirit of the Shari'ah which guides us in our global Islamic policies. The Front is concerned with the realization of harmony and balance between the economic axis and the other axes which make up its political program. Putting them into practice will give rise to obstacles and difficulties, which will call for amendments and corrections necessary for the judicious implementation of a global development plan inspired by the Shari'ah.

3. Commerce

Commerce, as it is envisaged by the Islamic Salvation Front, constitutes the nervous system of the economy, which channels the production of wealth, co-ordinates various interests and maintains equilibrium. Thus it allows material values to be determined, checking their conformity with the Islamic Shari'ah! Interest should be equally divided up; the producer should not exploit the consumer, the seller must not bully the buyer and vice-versa: " Do not do wrong to man and his goods," says the Almighty. This law is echoed by the Prophet who repeated: "neither prejudice nor constraint."

The following principles underlie the choices of the Islamic Salvation Front in commercial matters:

1. Reform the commercial system by the abolition of monopolies and usury, through the suppression of intermediaries and the criminalization of all forms of economic parasitism like fraud and voluntary bankruptcy. This accomplished, we would be faithful to the word of the Prophet: "The cheat is not one of us."

2. Reorganize the circuits of distribution and work for the decentralization of businesses.

3. Modify marketing policy to move toward decentralization and the elimination of the black market. Encourage competition that brings abundance. Facilitate consumers' access to their needs and give priority to the internal, over the external, market for the distribution of national wealth.

4. Reassess pricing policy to curb the rise of inflation in conformance with the rule: "neither prejudice nor constraint." The regime of the hisba (market police) allows us to deal with prejudice and re-establish equity.

5. Operations of buying and selling will be organized according to the conciliating directives of the Islamic Shari'ah, and of course the interests of everyone and of moral values.

6. Rejuvenate shareholding and encourage private commercial societies to bring dynamism to the economy, make the circuits of distribution more flexible and ensure the abundance of products on the market.

7. Renew standards in line with the Shari'ah and the procedures of the fiqh in commercial contracts and reintroduce these same standards in the organization of businesses and in relations between partners at all levels, this in order to guarantee the rights and duties that ensue.

8. Create organizations of economic and commercial information to help traders, producers, and consumers to be familiar with the merchandise, the centers of distribution and the means to access them. This should encourage the fluidity of exchange between producer and consumer who would both benefit according to their contribution and need.

9. Implement an administrative, technical, and economic reception structure to supervise the aforementioned organisms.

10. An external trade policy responding to the imperative of independence and protection of the economy and founded on the following principles:

a. External trade relations must respond to needs and bring a solution to the shortage of products consumed internally. In no instance should external trade be at the expense of the internal market, of the producer or of the consumer.

b. Trade monopolies should be banned apart from when the State is obliged to intercede to safeguard major political or economic interests.

c. Free trade must be implemented progressively to prevent any imbalance between imports and exports. At first, great care must be taken with industrialized products of a sanitary or scientific nature so as to liberate national will and ingenuity and contribute to the effort of civilization. Armed with the Message that is ours we will thus be able to fulfill our duty toward humanity through the propagation of peace in the Islamic sense, of justice, and by the support of oppressed peoples and nations that are victims of colonial policy. We can thus help to restrain the effects of dependence, under-development, poverty, hunger, illness, ignorance, and distraction, although it may mean having to resort to autarky.

d. The balance of trade must be submitted to the objectives of a long-term plan of civilizational development. It is necessary to avoid turning raw materials strategic to industry into resources for immediate consumption. This would be signing away the future. That is why its vision of economic and civilizational renaissance is a vision in the long-term, which is casting its gaze far into the future.

e. Equally the balance of imports and exports must protect local production whilst at the same time guaranteeing quality. The State must watch over this even if it means subsidizing local products.

f. Exportation is an activity that crystallizes the will of the Algerian people and their determination to make, thanks to their tenacious efforts, a place in the world market where competition is at its height. The quality of export products and moderate prices will be our asset for gaining confidence from our importers.

g. It is essential to reassess relations with the I.M.F. and different financial and commercial organizations that are responsible for the current world crisis. The question of debt must be raised without beating around the bush in the light of the new political, economic, and social course proposed by the Islamic Salvation Front.

Finally, the trade policy of the Front has just been completed and is articulated around its agricultural and industrial proposals. It places itself in the framework of an economic vision whose goals are independence, abundance, and growth; all in harmony with the necessities of social, cultural, and civilizational development.

4. Finance

Monetary policy constitutes one of the levers of the economy and an efficient way to avoid the dilapidation of wealth; it therefore insures development and prosperity, two of the primary objectives of the economic policy of the Islamic Salvation Front. That is why our monetary policy revolves around the following points:

A. Revaluation of currency making the internal monetary value conform to the external, taking into consideration financial conditions and those relative to import-export that make up the real stimulants for production. However, it is necessary to make sure that there is conformity on monetary matters between monetary choices and Islamic laws.

B. Reassessment of the purchasing power of the internal national currency and its parity outside the country, not only for the benefit of the Algerian citizen and when he goes abroad, but also to stimulate the productive effort and to protect the economy.

In order to seat decisions of internal policy or external policy on solid foundations, the State budget must draw on the following resources:

1. Natural wealth.
2. Agricultural, industrial, and commercial products that must ensure self-sufficiency and break with dependence at the same time as guaranteeing equity.

These premises allow:

a. The reassessment of fiscal and customs policy.
b. The consideration of the Zakat and the waqfs as legal resources of the State as long as they keep to the policies of the Shari'ah.
c. The creation of a social solidarity and credit fund conforming to the Shari'ah, in case of economic and social crisis. A State that borrows from its citizens is worth infinitely more than one that usurps their riches or one that fortifies its vaults by resorting to inflation and foreign debt.
d. The encouragement of prosperous Algerians and Muslims abroad, including emigrants, to invest in Algeria and thus give life to the national economy and allow it to achieve self-sufficiency. This is where a sort of "Financial Jihad" is fought in the form of loans, subscription, or direct investment. The State commits itself, in all cases, to protect the good of the people.
e. The reassessment of banking policy and the banking system to better insure the resources of the State and to protect the assets of the citizens and all the depositors and facilitate their participation in the enrichment of the country through investment. This mobilization of internal energies applies to autonomous policy decisions nationally as well as internationally.
f. The creation of Islamic banks and credit and savings funds where all forms of usury will be forbidden and where individual interests will be guaranteed. These banks will be as much schools of solidarity, co-operation and social progress as economic development.

Therefore the annual State budget will be fixed in accordance with short-term and long-term needs in order to allow a progressive improvement of the economic situation and a rhythm supported by and adapted to national as well as international political and historical avatars. Budgetary policy must respect the range of financial priorities, except for the Zakat whose unchanging management is determined by supreme Legislation, and by that alone.

Social Policy

The basic principle of the Islamic Salvation Front is the promotion of man, which the Almighty exhorts us to consider as our chief preoccupation: "We have ennobled the sons of Adam. We have carried them over solid ground and over the sea. We have given them excellent food. We have preferred them over many that we created." Promoting the dignity of man is above all guaranteeing him the rights and duties prescribed in the Shari'ah in its infinite wisdom. Thus will we be faithful to the Quranic model of "the best community created for men," which presupposes equality between all men and which is the model of social solidarity excluding class and clan struggle.

In consequence, the social policy of the Front hinges on the following points:

A. The right to existence. God has honored man by making a blessing of earthly existence and by making the earthly mission of man their reason for being. "I only created the jinn and men that they may adore me. I do not expect any gift from them. I do not want them to feed me. God is the giver of all gifts; He is the unshakeable Master of strength," affirms the Almighty; We see that God justifies human existence by the adoration that is owed to him and not by the profit that modern theories, from Malthus to Marx, recognize to be a handicap to the economy and a parasitic element to the world economy. The elevation of man desired by God is obvious in this verse: "In the opinion of God, the noblest amongst you, are the most pious of you," which bases man's nobility on his relationship with God and not with the cosmic environment that the latter has created for him.

Thus favored, man becomes the pivotal point of the universe. His engagement in the universe is not purely bestial for he is not only concerned with passive consumption. Man transcends his immediate individual and collective needs to attain a civilizational dimension. Far from being a passive product, a dead weight, on civilization, man is the creator of civilization. As a result, slogans that call for birth control constitute an attack on the dignity of man, a negation of his value and the central position that he occupies in the universe. God has told us: "do not kill your children for fear of poverty. We will support you as well as them." The community must, for its part, guarantee the protection of all newborn children and equal opportunities for everyone. Any dispensation of these rules is tantamount to an attack on the supreme value of existence.

B. The right to protection and care. This right must be guaranteed to the citizen from the fetal stage until full maturity. Existence must be taken as a religious, historical, and civilizational value, which is why the right to education is so sacred. It is the responsibility of the mother to place the accent on the notion of duty in the education of her children. Education is therefore concerned, at the same time, with both right and duty. God commands us: " Read in the Name of your Lord the Creator! He created man from a clot of blood."

1. Education Policy
a. Education is an integral part of the general policy choices of the State. The Islamic Front bases its choices on the Shari'ah; the educational policy that it prescribes must be a vehicle for the precepts of the Shari'ah and above all must ensure the right to education of all the children in the country regardless of race, clan, religion, or any other factor.
b. As well as being an individual right, education is a duty toward the community whose interests must be taken into account.
c. The education budget must aim to combine conditions for equality with quality teaching.

2. The Education Budget
The budget must be balanced between need and investment, it being understood that education is one of the primary areas of investment.

3. Educational Orientation
It is conditioned by the following principles:

   a. The need to develop skills in order to obtain better qualifications.

   b. The respect of Islamic values like segregation of the sexes and good morals inspired by the Shari'ah.

   c. The need for a greater appreciation of the state official with a view to re-assessing his income and refining his role as Muslim instructor and "civilizer," in short his role as teacher of the next generation; to arm them better against unemployment and equip them with the knowledge necessary for the most complex and technical jobs.

   d. Examination policy must conform to all these imperatives at once so as to lower the education "deficit" and to put an end to graduate unemployment. Equally a second chance should be given to those who have failed academically and found themselves in the street. To integrate them into the economic, religious, and civilizational plan, universities and secondary learning centers should be provided so that they can catch up and be reinserted into society.

4. Educational Content and Methods
   a. Educational content must be reassessed according to the needs of the country and with the aim of a global renaissance whilst ensuring the quality of education that is required at all levels and in all fields of specialty.

   b. A reassessment of educational content to remove any ideologies and concepts that have contrary values to those of Islam; this is to preserve our personality, realize authenticity, and stimulate creativity.

   c. Reformation of the educational methods that are currently in practice in our country, those that favor blind mimicry and that make our university a place where knowledge is consumed rather than produced and that turn out poorly educated graduates instead of wise men. Technological specialty must be marked with the seal of Islam at the same time as aiming for the highest levels of technological qualification; this is the only way for us to get by without competence from abroad.

5. Teacher Training
It is necessary to reform educational institutions starting with the training of teachers on all rungs of the educational ladder, so as to ensure the highest qualifications and the most exemplary behavior, because the teacher is also an instructor. He must be an example, not only to his pupils but also to the community as a whole. In other words we need to reform the task of teaching as well as its value and the consideration that it deserves in the Islamic Umma. To this end the example of the Prophet Mohammed must remain our supreme reference. It is also necessary to re-evaluate the material condition of the teacher. This would only be just considering the particulars duties that he is responsible for in this decisive stage of the history of the Umma. Let us not forget that right underlies duty.

It is self-evident that the better the quality of the education provided, the more material and moral recompense the teacher will receive.

6. Social Organization in Educational Institutions
   a. Social organization at the heart of the educational establishment is one of the most important conditions in the development of the personality of the pupil and the student, so that the educational microcosm is the best example for the Umma as a whole.
   b. All the necessary psychological, material and social conditions of school life must be provided at the heart of the institution so that there is a global progression of the Islamic personality on a physical, psychological, rational, cultural, and moral level.

7. The Educational System from Primary School to Post-graduate Study
It is necessary to reassess the education system from school to university in accordance with new political, economic, and social data and make it so that the passage from one cycle to another is submitted only to educational criteria and no other. At the same time, all university programs that are not Arabic should be made to be so.

8. Compulsory Education
It is important to extend the compulsory period to secondary education.

9. Educational Methods
School manuals must be reassessed in the light of the precepts of the Shari'ah and the requirements of Islamic education.

10. The System of Sports Education
The policy of sports education must be reformed to make it a way to bodily, spiritual, and moral development conforming to the laws of the Islamic Shari'ah.

11. Educational (pedagogical) Information
All programs and objectives must be reassessed to prevent intellectual and cultural invasion and so that the programs serve to deepen the Law, expand technical abilities, and liberate the talent of generations and their capacity to create and excel themselves.

12. The Policy of Internal and External Grants
The only criteria for the attribution of grants will be merit or need.

13. The Management Systems of the Various Authorities
Administrative management must be reformed to create a balance between centralization and decentralization and in order to generalize the collective spirit and conciliate educational and administrative objectives. This will facilitate the job of the teacher and the disciple and will be beneficial to the whole country.

14. Organization in the Educational Field
The attribution of posts in the educational field must be re-examined on a management level as well as on a practical teaching or research level; the goal being quality above all else.

C. Man must have the right to vote and be eligible for election and participation in management. Islam is the religion of liberty, the latter being based on responsibility, the expression of the conscious will to do good inasmuch as the law, morality, and spiritual integrity remain the foundations of liberty. Does the Almighty not say: " Acquit yourselves of the obligations of religion, through true belief and in accordance with the nature that God gave to man when creating him. God's creation is unchanging." In turn the Prophet said: "Every newborn baby comes to the world in his natural state." For his part, Omar Ibn al-Khattab said: "With what right do you reduce to slavery men that were born free."

This Islamic conception of man makes of him a responsible being worthy of the following rights:

1. The right to vote and the choice of his leaders.
2. The right to vote also permits him to be eligible for election when he fulfills the following conditions: belief in justice; being of exemplary behavior; talent and ability; the ability to appreciate psychological predispositions and new objective data.
3. The right to lead is to take charge of administrative and professional responsibilities that rely on compassion, competence, and rectitude, and on nothing else. In virtue of this, the state servant, or he who has been designated this charge, is responsible before God and before the whole community; he is responsible before the department in his charge or of which he is a managing member. As he is held in trust by the whole community he owes it to himself to be responsible: "God orders you to return what has been entrusted to you," as it is said in the sacred Quran. The Prophet also said: "You are all guides and all guides must be responsible for their charges."
4. The reliability of any person in responsibility is not possible unless they have all of the above qualities. The idea of reliability is meant in the sense of the Shari'ah and in the ethical, professional, and political sense.

D. Liberation of initiative. So that the community is capable of facing political, economic, and civilizational requirements, it is absolutely necessary to break the shackles that are stifling the initiative spirit of our self-taught people and that have almost completely reduced them to a most dangerous state of passivity. We must pave the way for productive and creative initiative in all aspects of life for therein lies the psychological condition necessary at the present time for future generations to be prepared for the religious, civilizational, and historical tasks that await them.

E. Assurance of the protection of religion, the person, reason, honor, and goods. The Islamic Shari'ah guarantees the inherent interests of the five imperatives that make up humanity:

Protection   of religion
             of person
             of reason
             of honor
             of goods.

Together these make up the guarantees of psychological stability.

F. Reformation of the Algerian family in the framework of Islamic legality. The interest that Islam accords to the family has no equal in any other religion, philosophy, or system (modern or ancient): It occupies a central place at the heart of the community. It assures: the protection and charge of the child until the age of reason; the assurance of social solidarity to the point of abnegation; the assurance of social solidarity through family solidarity.

Thanks to the attention given to it in the Shari'ah, the family has been able to blossom through the ages, especially in the time of the Prophet. And if the Islamic family has had to suffer the negative effect of colonialism under its ancient and current forms it has not, for all that, resigned itself to decline. And it is thanks to this that the Algerian people have been able to face the enemy in the absence of a State. The family unit has long been the victim of attempts at destruction; it has suffered many forms of decadence, misery, or ignorance. The restoration of the family constitutes one of the greatest preoccupations of the Islamic Salvation Front who proposes to:

a. Guarantee work for the father of the family so as to stop the hemorrhage of emigration that has become the dislocating factor of the Algerian family.
b. Reassess the housing policy to ensure decent housing for couples and avoid vagrancy and the other various ills that are due to a lack of decent buildings that conform with future and present needs.
c. Home in on the question of emigrants in order to facilitate their return by providing them with the things that forced them into exile where they have suffered bitterly and painfully and have pined for their homeland.
d. Take care of the mother who is raising children. She must be supported in cases of necessity, by adequate aid and must be given maternity allowance as her work at home must be legitimately considered as a social and educational function giving her the right to the same allowance as a salaried worker in a factory or in the fields. Of course it is necessary to take into consideration her level of experience and competence in family education. For this end, an organization of social solidarity must be set up and charged with looking after the conditions of security, morality, and development of the family.

e. Take care of the woman. The Muslim woman enjoyed a certain prestige in the time of the Prophet. She took her example from "the mother of believers" and particularly Acha (God bless her) who won renown through her great culture: the written tradition owes more than 2000 hadith to her. The women in early Islam took part in the conquests of the Prophet: We know of the heroism of Oum Salama Huda biya, which is proof of the great political consciousness of women. The feminine genius was also deployed in the spheres of thought, literature, fiqh, politics, and medicine during the course of the golden age of Muslim civilization. The heroic contribution of the Muslim woman in the Jihad in Morocco, Andalusia, and in Algeria during the war against colonialism must also be remembered: the revolution of November was also a time when the faith and devotion of the fighters recalled the female heroism of early times. At the stage we are at, and when two-thirds of our students are female, the Islamic Salvation Front considers the role of the woman to be more crucial than ever. The Muslim woman is an irreplaceable force on a psychological, social, and cultural scale. It is a case of knowing how to channel this force and employ its potential in the most judicious manner for the development of our civilization. To do this our attention must be turned to the following!

Re-enforce the faith and good morals of the woman.
Raise her level of political, educational, and civilizational consciousness.
Restore the consideration of women in Islam by guarding her from all repression and by fighting against the slackening of morals and blind imitation.
Enlighten society as to the importance of the role and mission of the woman. In fact, Islam was and remains the religion that makes no distinction between the woman and the man, her brother. She enjoys the same distinction and the same honors with which God has gratified man. The Prophet taught us that "women are the sisters of men" and urges us to "treat women gently."

f. Re-examine the family allowance policy. Particular attention must be given to workers and those whose revenues are not sufficient to supply them with basic essentials.

g. Increase retirement pensions, which have been kept at too low a level in relation to inflation, the cancer of our economy. War widows must be given the same treatment as other widows.

h. Take better care of the elderly and the handicapped by allowing them the income from social security that they deserve and that will safeguard their dignity and shelter them from abandonment or need. Thus will they feel the warmth and tenderness that society and the community devotes to them. It is important to point out that this particular care is not affected by sex, race, confession, or clan, etc.

I. Reassess prison policy and the treatment of prisoners so that their dignity, physical and psychological integrity are assured: help them to deepen their Islamic faith, their professional knowledge and aptitudes; and thus prepare them for reinsertion into social, economic, and cultural life after their release.
j. More generally, establish a balance between remuneration, effort, experience, and spending power, responding to needs.
k. Global social reform. In Islam the method of "hisba" is considered as the best legal method for the organization of relations between people in the following domains:
1. The street
2. The market
3. The factory
4. The field
5. Administration
6. The mosque

With the supervision of the system of "hisba" through justice, these domains are stabilized and conditions of harmony and understanding are established, the factory is maintained, high standards and customs are respected, and the nation evolves toward the objectives of the Islamic Shari'ah.

Health Policy

It is indispensable and necessary to take charge of health in order to arm the nation against diseases and handicaps that ensue from a lack of hygiene, in accordance with the following verses:

> "Be harsh with infidels, mild amongst yourselves."
> "God has chosen amongst you and has added to him skill in science and the ways of the body."
> "The best man to take on is he who is strongest and the most faithful."

The Prophet illustrates these verses with a hadith: "The strong believer is better and is preferred by God to the weak believer and both of them are charitable."

For effective care of the sick, the F.I.S. proposes the following recommendations:

1. Raise health and education consciousness in all establishments (schools, institutes, universities, mosques) and in all of the mass media, which will give the nation the chance to be informed of illnesses that arise and the ways of curing them. It is also necessary to bring together all healthcare resources, human and material, such as specialists, centers of admission, resuscitators and first-aiders, means of transport and even, if necessary, a fleet of helicopters.

2. Combat the depraved and the libertines who are considered by religion and confirmed by science as being high-risk groups for the transmission of venereal diseases such as syphilis and AIDS.
3. Organize rigorous sanitary control in health establishments (hospitals, care centers)
4. Implement links between free medicine and private medicine, allowing for complementarity between the two at the heart of an equitable health system that does not forfeit the poor, marginalize experts, nor exploit taxpayers.
5. Provide medicines in sufficient quantities and subsidize them to make them accessible to people of low income.
6. Provide technological equipment adapted to the development of medical science; increase the number of university hospital centers and centers of scientific research. Self-sufficiency in health matters cannot be achieved if certain specialties or paramedical sectors are neglected. New centers will create new jobs without putting a strain on the economy or hindering social and civilizational development.
7. Develop the means for pharmaceutical production and research laboratories with a view to self-sufficiency, autonomy, and to put an end to dependence.
8. Increase the number of dispensaries so that they can be found in all districts.

The Cultural and Civilizational Axis

The cultural and civilizational program of the Islamic Salvation Front consists of the protection of the community against all cultural invasion and against the maneuvers of adverse civilizations; in a word, the preparation of the renaissance of Muslim culture and civilization, through action in the following areas:

a. Religion and the Shari'ah
b. Islamic ethics and values
c. The development of talent in Muslim thought
d. Freedom of initiative and the liberation of scientific and juridical resources

Our culture conciliates reason with the Shari'ah, morality with art and science, theory with practice. This culture is the synthesis of the historical experience of a whole community and its combined wisdom. It is made up of the sum of historical treasures and the psychological mechanism that is set toward future goals that will bring about an immense space where the genius of future generations will prosper. Our culture is the secret of the longevity of our community, "the best created for man," the Community of the Message and of civilization.

To summarize, no psychological and historical objectives can be clearly realized without the following conditions:

1. The need to take into consideration the psychology of the nation and its right to a glorious life where it will effectively contribute to the civilizing effort thus giving free course to general initiatives.

2. The pressing need to restore Islam as a way of life and a source of happiness in both worlds and as guarantor of the objectives of honor already mentioned.
3. Rehabilitate science and its techniques so that they reclaim their place in society and so that the Quran and the Sunna are assured. This rehabilitation will take place firstly through the reconsideration of men of science as decision-makers, given that no decision will be taken without their prior consultation. These decisions are a function of their position as long as they submit to God and the Prophet and demonstrate the goodness of their works.
4. Encourage the generalization of the national language, the language of the Quran and the Sunna, over the whole of the territory, with the aim of unifying the language and the country without condemning other languages that facilitate exchange and cultural relations. Because of what has come before it, culture will be one of the protectors of our unity and a guarantor of cultural and civilizational acquisitions and one of the sources of richness of moral, artistic, scientific, and technological faith. This will allow the country to guarantee a better life for its future generations, where the brilliance of their authenticity and their genius will dominate and they will be inheritors of the Message and constructors of civilization.

So as to achieve this, the following points will be revised:

1. Radio and television programming and the organization of libraries, exhibition rooms, cultural centers, theaters.
2. Sport and art complexes and cinemas.
3. Encouragement of specialized and general scientific reviews.
4. Supply Islamic, scientific, and technical books, thereby ensuring through libraries, supply to institutes, universities, research centers.

For the Islamic Salvation Front, the field of information is where freedom of expression and the rights of the community to a breath of fresh air are consolidated, for information is an open window on the world. It allows us to access news, follow events, and be on top of recent scientific and technological discoveries. Unfortunately, this window has long been closed and the air confined inside. The community, itself deprived of expression, could neither put to use its cognitive, scientific, and technological experience, be up-to-date with the evolution of human civilization, nor in consequence resolve the problems that face humanity today. One of the most infuriating consequences of this "black-out" is that the Algerian community finds itself unable to respond to the denigrators of Islam who malign our religion with the most vile slander, nor can it defend the community and the Islamic people who are victims of the worst attacks against their interests.

This is why the current stage is so decisive, precisely because freedom of expression is one of the most precious acquisitions. We will use this freedom to defend Islamic identity. Information, which is found at the heart of political, economic and cultural activity and since it is the vector of them, is of strategic importance.

Information conditions our relations with the world. It is up to us to make sure that the exchange with others is enriching. We must give the best of ourselves by referring ourselves to the Message of the Lord; and we must gather the quintessence of scientific and technical knowledge and all that can serve our current and future needs. This exchange must serve us in the fight that is taking place on a planetary scale and of which the stake is of a civilizational dimension, our principal asset being our cultural independence. In consideration of this, the media must be the filter that allows the good seed to be separated from the rye among the data that circulates in the world, on technical, and other kinds of information. The media also allows the transmission of the word of God.

For the media to achieve this status, the Islamic Salvation Front proposes the following reforms:

1. Encourage periodical publications: daily, weekly, monthly, or others. The role of the press is to "track down" objective data and search for truth, to keep a finger on the pulse of what is happening in the country. It allows us to follow the evolution of the local and world situation in all areas. The Front wants to go further by encouraging the Algerian press to be more audacious in the face of foreign media and to get rid of the inferiority complex that is paralyzing it. Only thus will our press be able to recover the confidence of the people and regain its cultural role. Only thus will the journalist be rehabilitated and receive the consideration that is due to him for the immense task that he undertakes.

2. Encourage specialization in all areas: political, economic, social, and cultural, both internally an externally. The journalistic production of our country is often made up of commonplace material. Accuracy is rare and cultural mediocrity is standard. Political consciousness is lacking, as is the sense of what is at stake on a civilizational level. From colonial times everything has been done to deny the Islamic nature of the Algerian people and to keep them in ignorance of what constitutes their glory, everything has been attempted: the falsification of the divine message, the deformation of the image of Islam. What is most serious is that this policy continues to the present day. To put an end to this state of affairs, the Front signals to the Algerian people attached to their religion, the importance of the creation of newspapers and periodicals in the service of the Islamic message, which is currently being devalued. Through them, the awakening of the people can only be more rational and more convincing and the truth will be able to win through. The vocation of Islam is the salvation of our Umma and of humanity as a whole; an Islamic press will allow us to face up to the denigrators of our religion and to the maneuvers that aim to mislead and intoxicate public opinion and to set them against Islam and the Muslims. Up until now the absence of a free Islamic press has constituted a breach, which cultural invasion has rushed to fill. The aim of the invasion is to hinder the Islamic renaissance, which has mobilized many people under the

banner of the Message. A whole community raised itself up to sweep away the aftermath of colonialism and its dark maneuverings and has launched an assault on the future.

Today fans of music or film are well provided for, whilst those who are looking to know more about their religion and its teachings are left hungry. The fact is that access to the media is forbidden to partisans of the Right and the True. Their only concern is the promotion of Islam and the Shari'ah as well as science and technology. To be rid of this degradation, the choice of the Islamic Salvation Front is to rectify the situation in the interests of society and in an educational way that will see the full blossoming of faith and thought, art and literature. Beauty will not be to the detriment of goodness; nor information to the detriment of truth, and direction can not replace objectivity.

3. The consolidation and diversification of our national press agency (APS) through association with the most qualified people and by devoting the most advanced techniques to it.

The Army

Throughout history the Algerian army has forged a reputation for itself that many armies of the world envy. Its fleet guarded the Mediterranean and its troops guarded the "Dar al-Islam." In addition to this, the whole of the Algerian army has always been an army of Jihad, always ready to defend the religion, unity, and the glorious, invincible community of Islam. In a word, the Algerian army was dreaded and its voice was heard afar.

After the colonial invasion, our army suffered a serious turn of fortune but the armed people never gave in and the popular, organized resistance bore witness to the tenacity and courage of our faithful people. The fight was crowned by the victory over colonialism and we were able to recover our independence and our sovereignty thanks to help from God. The successive revolutions all over our country, and particularly that of the liberation, have shown that our army is the people and our people are the army. The will of the Islamic Salvation Front is that it remains so and that our army regains its reputation and its skill for combat. To this end we estimate that we must:

1. Reform the programs of military training starting with religious and moral instruction. Faith must be the first virtue of a soldier.
2. A sense of ethics is a source of courage, pride, and devotion to the soldier in the exercise of his duties.
3. Improve the scientific and technological skills of the army.
4. Improve logistics and ensure serious training to improve weapon skills.
5. Create high-level military academies to enable former high-level officers to master the technology that is evolving within the fields of land, sea, air, and space.
6. Construct a military industry capable of taking up the challenge of civilization that awaits us.

7. Encourage research and discovery in the military domain.
8. The army must not be involved in questions of politics so that it remains the army of the Message, the community, and the country as a whole. In this way, the reputation of the army can do nothing but grow over time as it proves its competence, morality, and ability to defend the country.
9. To avoid military service being of detriment to economic development and social cohesion, the length of military service will be fixed to six months and will be dedicated to military training giving the young Algerian the physical and technical capabilities to defend his country.
10. Military service must be combined with a professional qualification. This qualification will be renewed each time military service is undertaken and young generations will succeed each other, making military service a right for each Algerian ready to defend his country at any moment. The word of God confirms this rule: "Prepare them with all the strength you have." The newly created Algerian army, deeply rooted in its history and glory, needs to undergo great efforts of training and experience to regain its fighting ability and recover its place along with the strategic level required.

Foreign Policy

The foreign policy of the F.I.S. is defined according to the following framework:

1. The prestige of Algeria and its renown across the world;
2. Moderation in its position, equity in its study of international problems and economic, social, historic, and civilizational emancipation;
3. Its economic and political relations are determined within the framework of the Islamic Shari'ah. Thus Algeria supports any just cause and will bring help to any destitute nation. It is also ready to reinforce links of friendship and salvation in its Islamic expression toward other countries and reinforce stability in the world, which will allow civilization to overcome its crises and prosper.

Islam represents the most significant mastiff in the world, the catalyst of human consciousness and its checkpoint, the greatest divine message for the conversion of humanity, the richest reservoir of goodness, the most ambitious hope in respect of mankind, and the most just law for the protection of his rights. Because of this, the F.I.S. considers the rights of man, as it is noted in the Quran and the Sunna, as one of its major preoccupations, and works with ardor for their propagation and application, thus protecting man from humiliations such as social segregation, torture, the horrors of detention, and the stifling of his freedom of expression as well as unfair treatment, which lowers his dignity and humanity. God said: "Only through pity were you sent into the two worlds."

CHAPTER 26

BOYCOTTING THE 1997 ELECTION IN JORDAN

Society of the Muslim Brothers

Muslim Brotherhood. "Why does the Muslim Brotherhood Boycott the 1997 Parliamentary Elections?: A Statement to the People" (pamphlet). Muslim Brotherhood Headquarters, Amman, Jordan. 13 July 1997.

In the name of Allah, the Compassionate, the Merciful

God doth command you to tender back your trusts to those to whom they are due; and when ye judge between man and man, that ye judge with justice. Verily how excellent is the teaching which He giveth you! For God is He who heareth and seeth all things.

—Translation of the meaning of the Holy Quran (Sura IV: 58).

IN 1989 THE GRAND HOPE FOR DEMOCRATIC transformation that could foster development and prosperity for Jordan (the society and the state) was revived. The Muslim Brotherhood (MB) responded positively to the new political developments which formed a part of their comprehensive project of building the country and serving the society through a moderate methodology. Through this project, the MB has realized, over several decades, significant achievements for the society in the charitable, social, cultural, educational, public service, and health fields in addition to its ongoing ethical guidance. It had interacted positively with the requirements of these transformations and participated in the 11th parliamentary session, in the laying down of the National Convention in cooperation with other intellectual trends and political powers, and in the formation of the 1991 cabinet amidst critical local and regional circumstances. The MB responded positively and honestly to political pluralism. The MB participated in the 1993 elections despite the dissolution of parliament before the end of its legal mandate and the issuance of the temporary law of "One Man One Vote" in 1993 which, according to many local, Arab, and international leaders of public opinion and public work, aimed to diminish and contain the Islamic movement. This law has torn the social fabric and paralyzed the popular political forces from developing the political and social life of Jordan. It has also aborted the possibility of any real exchange of power and any influence on political and legislative decisions.

The MB participated in the 1993 elections because it was understood that this was a new experiment and that it needed a natural environment, convenient opportunities, and true efforts in which it could become established in order to enhance and maintain the solidity of the state and society in order to make Jordan the most advanced and civilized society in the Arab world.

But the obstructions and deformations to the democratic process caused by this law were deepened by time. This was evident in the coming of a parliament that did not represent the people's conscience of the different social categories. It was a parliament run by the government and through which it succeeded to pass all legislations, laws, and decisions the government wanted.

Despite the fact that this law was rejected by the different social and popular activists and trends, it was passed by the parliament as a permanent law of elections that overruled all popular powers and the institutions of the civil society as well as the political activists in the country.

THE STATUS QUO . . .
CONTINUOUS DETERIORATION

During the period from 1989 to 1993, the 11th parliamentary session witnessed a democratic awakening which became evident by the issuance of a host of laws that established grounds for a more advanced political life, such as the law of parties, the 1992 press law, the law of the state security court, the law of municipalities, and the abolition of martial law. However, the serious measures of following up corruption cases, the attempts to issue a law forcing government officials to declare their assets, and the united official and popular stand against the Western-Zionist aggression on Iraq, were all issues that were either ignored or were not addressed with much democratic aggressiveness.

The period between 1993 and 1997 witnessed significant and critical deterioration in the following areas.

1. Parliamentary and Legislative Work

The deterioration of democracy began with the holding of parliamentary elections utilizing the "One Man One Vote" law (rejected by the public and by a large percentage of the official sector) as well as the government intervention in the results of these elections in several constituencies against the Islamic Movement's candidates in favor of the government's candidates. The successive governments have tightened their grasp on the parliament by restricting the movement of the Opposition deputies; they have restricted the number of these deputies by falsifying the elections and preventing them from providing services to the citizens in their constituencies. By limiting or even preventing the efforts of the deputies to provide services to their electors, the government was able to pass all the laws and political decisions it wanted as well as control the parliament because it possessed all the facilities in the public services field.

The government began distributing these facilities to the deputies based on their responses and whether or not the government was satisfied with their performance. It also stopped issuing law to establish teachers' and students' unions; it avoided issuing the law that obliges public officials to declare their assets; it amended the law of the state security court; it passed legislation and laws that allow the Zionist Enemy to enter the country, devastate it, and implement its aggressive and expansionate plan; it also approved the Wadi Araba treaty, canceled a law that was prohibiting the selling of real estate to the Israeli Enemy, and issued the law of companies and the law of investment encouragement, which allows the foreign capitals, including the Zionists, to possess companies or buy their shares without limitation in a period in which the national capital is not able to purchase the States' portions in the largest economic establishments, which are the mainstay of the Jordanian economy such as companies producing potash, phosphate, and cement. The "One Man One Vote" law was approved even after its negative consequences and its role in corrupting the parliamentary and political life became clear. The deterioration of democracy became evident upon the issuance of a temporary law of the press, which slaughtered press democracy and the freedom of expression. This law, together with the "One Man One Vote" law, demolished two democratic bases.

2. Public Freedoms, Democracy, and Parties

There was a marked increase in arbitrary and unjustified arrests, especially those members of the MB and those who sympathized with the Islamic Resistance Movement (Hamas). Some of those political prisoners were subject to different types of unprecedented physical and psychological torture in this country. A large number of citizens were arrested following the increase of bread prices, and many others were pursued on charges of slander and received severe sentences. The government prevented the majority of the peaceful activities of the parties in which they wanted to express their stands. The Opposition parties were dealt with as if they were illegal parties. Several measures taken by the government made these parties live in fear and obsession over an expected collapse of democracy. The continuous abuse of public freedoms versus enhancing and developing the democratic process and the achievement of the national comprehensive development, or social peace and security, is a thing that might destroy the third base of democracy, which is political pluralism and parties. This abuse did not save the charitable social establishments that were founded by the citizen's initiatives. These people did great services through these establishments regarding the social development amidst the increasing rates of unemployment and poverty. Add to this the intervention of the security services in the arbitrary transfers and promotions of many public servants, in denying the rights of some of them, or depriving them or their children of scholarships.

3. Administration and Corruption Control

It was acknowledged that administrative and financial corruption does exist and at the highest levels. Committees and departments were created for administrative development, follow-up, and inspection. However, the administrative corruption and the embezzlement of public funds became aggravated. The election of a parliament through a just legal system, a free and honest election, and the use of correct procedures is the real guarantee to fight the administrative and financial corruption because reformation cannot be achieved without a reforming manner or honest and efficient men. As long as the administrative policies and the basis of selection of the senior state officials remain as they are, no positive change can be expected.

4. Politics

The Wadi Araba treaty and its addendums form the most dangerous threats to Jordan. They endanger its existence, identity, sovereignty, independence, and power. The present practices confirm this vision day after day. The treaty also stresses the falsity of the promises of the so-called peace. The citizens are now rejecting it more than any time before. They also understand its dangers and fear the future more than at any other time. Moreover, the government policies pertaining to the refugee question and the relevant provisions stated in the treaty arouse suspicion. Together this proves the true view of the political opposition and supports its attitude toward the treaty. While Jordan's relations with the Arab states were disturbed, its relations with the Zionist State had been fostered. The Zionist State treated the Arab parties that signed agreements with it according to the rule "sign, implement, and then demand," using the methods of blackmail and humiliation. Moreover, Jordan's entry in a Zionist-American-Atlantic alliance to carry out any role dictated by this alliance against any of the Arab brothers or others is rejected. The entry of a country like Jordan in size and abilities in such an alliance means a functional role against the interests of the country and the Nation. It is against its religion, interests, sovereignty, existence, future, and expectations. On the internal level, the political practice goes on in marginalizing the role of the parliament and all of the opposition parties and the civil society establishments. In the meantime, the government adopts a political party and provides it with the state's abilities to serve and support it. The definite results of such conduct is the formation of the one-party government and the maintaining of a symbolic representation of other parties to deceive the people into thinking that there is a democratic party life.

5. Economy

This field was not safe from sharp deterioration. The citizen's content with the deception of the fruits of peace and a prosperous economy has become more established. In fact, poverty has spread, the unemployment rate and the prices of commodities and the cost of living has increased sharply. The citizen is made to bear all the costs of his living alone and the state has abandoned its role of helping him without any increase in his income. Moreover, the laws that prohibit selling real estate to the Israeli enemies were abolished, and new laws and decisions were issued to facilitate their ownership of economic establishments, whether partially or totally. The local markets were also opened for their products, and they were allowed to establish factories to compete with the national industries, which began suffering from recession in production, marketing, and competition. Under the new law of investment, fears arise because of the possibility of the creation of nucleuses for colonies that can be fattened with time. The consequences of signing agreements to release international trade, the "Medpartenariat," and the domination of the multinational companies are not less dangerous because our limited and weak economy would transform them from production to services. In this case, the majority of the people become mere cheap manpower. The focus will be on tourism, which in turn will horribly contribute in corrupting the society and public morals under the pretext of the tourist industry and the building of hundreds of hotels and night clubs.

6. Judiciary

The judiciary authority is not safe from the domination of the executive authority, which caused many judges known for their long experience, efficiency, and honesty to resign in recent years. This disturbed the judicial authority and made the citizen worry. There cannot be a democratic model in the absence of a reliable and assuring judiciary.

7. Culture and Information

The information programs, especially those related to television, are continuously falling. The rapid downward steps had followed the signing of the Wadi Araba treaty. These programs spoil the Arab and Islamic morals in the society and undermine the identity of the generations. The educational curriculum is being formed in a way that complies with the cultural normalization process with the Zionist Enemy. There is an intentional and very real weakening of the Islamic religious guidance taking place by making sure that the mosques are without efficient scholars and preachers. Education is also deteriorating; the teacher, who is the most important element in the educational process, is being overworked and kept busy with his own livelihood and obsessed by the regression of his social status in view of the absence of a social organization that can guard his affairs and protect his rights. Education is also in a continuous process of regression, which is evident in the prosperity of private education at the expense of public education. In the age of the exciting developments in communications with the use of satellites and electronics, all means of siege and suppression will not be useful. The solution is to immunize the generations on the basis of Arab and Islamic identity and in cooperation with all loyal individuals and groups to develop the society educationally and culturally. The MB is still exerting efforts in this field and it is willing to exert more efforts if the chance becomes available.

CONCLUSION

The society's potential should be released and individuals and popular establishments should be allowed to contribute. The pursuit of the civil society's bodies such as the professional associations, parties, societies, and activists under the pretext of "professionalization" should be stopped. United popular and official efforts are needed in accordance with a deliberate approach to be agreed upon by the parties concerned to develop the society and the state. While the world tends to allow popular participation in managing the state and building and fortifying the society, the government in our country tends to siege the popular efforts, to deform the people's participation, and to paralyze their powers as if we are in the beginning of this century when in fact it is about to finish.

THE POSITION

All that has been mentioned proves that what is going on is a kind of total reformation of the society and the state in a way that does not achieve justice, stability, or freedom. This reformation is being done without the participation of the citizens in making decisions or setting the trends and policies. The deliberate readying of the political process solely by the government establishes a conviction that the deterioration of freedoms and democracy as well as the effectiveness of the establishments of the civil society will continue; parliament's role will continue to be of less importance, making the Opposition a mere symbol in parliament thus leading to a political structure that does not have any impact regarding the issuance of decisions and legislation.

The Muslim Brotherhood are aware of the critical state of the local, regional, and international politics and understand their responsibility toward the country and the nation's causes, especially at this critical stage, and they believe that their decision of boycotting the 1997 parliamentary elections is necessary to establish democracy and protect the homeland just as their decision came after deliberate and responsible dialogues and considerations at all the internal levels. If the MB refrained from taking this position in previous important political occasions, this was for the purpose of giving reform a chance and with the hope to activate its role in parliament as well as to fulfill important achievements to confront the reconciliation agreements with the Israelis and their consequences. The MB was also hoping to stop the deterioration of democracy. However, the accumulation of events and pressures continued because of the progressive regression in various areas which obliged the Movement to stop and reconsider the situation.

The decision to boycott the coming parliamentary elections, both voting and running for them, is not a form of political isolation nor is it an abandonment of the public work. It also should not be understood as an abandonment of the Movement's approach to openness and peaceful work. But it is a reconsideration of the political process and of our position in our country, an attempt to stop the deterioration of democracy and to protect the remains or to restore what was usurped.

Therefore, the Islamic Movement, which is keen on national interests and which does not know of political opportunism, must feel jealous of the country and nation and of its freedoms and rights. It sees that it should willingly take any stand it deems convenient.

The Muslim Brotherhood believes that the approach to rectifying the present situation could start by the following steps:

1. Making constitutional reforms that establish the separation between authorities and give the legislative authority its full right and role in legislation, supervision, and accountability.
2. Canceling the "One Man One Vote" law and replacing it with a civilized law that can achieve impartiality and justice in order to allow the citizens to elect the deputies who represent them honestly.
3. Canceling the temporary press law in order to maintain the freedom of expression and the democracy of the press and media.
4. Ceasing all arbitrary measures against parties and other establishments of the civil society and allowing the activities of the peaceful Opposition.
5. Treating the different economic situations through serious action by resisting all forms and instruments of corruption and rejecting the implementation of dictation by the International Monetary Fund and the policies of the New World Order.
6. Releasing freedoms and ceasing the abuse and violations against these freedoms in a way that fosters the popular partnership in decision-making and in forging the trends that affect the present and future of the people.
7. Ceasing the normalization of relations with the Zionist State and closing the door to prevent its penetration into our society.

The Muslim Brotherhood will remain, as it is well-known by all, loyal to the interests of its country and nation, and will continue to contribute to its building and development. It will continue doing its best to achieve these goals.

I only desire [your] betterment to the best of my power; and my success [in my task] can only come from God. In Him I trust, and unto Him I look."
—Translation of the meaning of the Holy Quran (Sura XI: 88).

Muslim Brotherhood
Jordan
Amman—13 July 1997

CHAPTER 27

ISLAMIC ACTION
FRONT PARTY

Interview with Dr. Ishaq A. Farhan

Interview with Ishaq A. Farhan, the Leader of Islamic Action Front Party (Hizb Jibhih al-Amal al-Islami). By Mansoor Moaddel in Amman, Jordan, spring 1997.

THE HISTORY OF THE ISLAMIC MOVEMENT IN JORDAN displays a glaring contrast with that of other Middle Eastern countries like Algeria, Egypt, pre-Revolutionary Iran, and Syria. In the latter cases, the relationship between the state and Islamic opposition has been characterized by a sequence of bloody confrontations. In Jordan, on the other hand, the Islamic movement, with the exception of some minor trends, has not only been predominantly peaceful and nonviolent but also defended the state vis-à-vis the challenges of radical ideologies. Following the democratization process launched by King Hussein and the emergence of political openness, the Muslim Brothers embraced the democratic rule of the game and began to participate in the 1989 elections and thereafter. What is more, to reconcile their belief in the sovereignty of the Shari&*ah and the secular framework established by the state, the Brothers made a keen political move by forming the Islamic Action Front Party (IAFP). The latter's sole objective was to participate in the elections within the framework of the political parties law. This proactive move also provided additional political space for the pragmatic and moderate Islamic activists who otherwise might have left the Brothers for a more rewarding political career. The formation of IAFP has thus far hindered a split in the rank of the Brothers, even though the movement has become diversified and politically heterogeneous in recent years. This phenomenon is remarkable because the Jordanian Brothers have considerable ideological and organizational affinities with their counterparts in Egypt and Syria. They have also enjoyed a social basis of support similar to their counterparts in Egypt, Iran, and Syria.

INTERVIEW WITH DR. ISHAQ A. FARHAN, THE LEADER OF ISLAMIC ACTION FRONT PARTY (HIZB JIBHIH AL-AMAL AL-ISLAMI)

BY MANSOOR MOADDEL

M: Since the second part of the nineteenth century, five important issues have been crystallized as the points of contention between Islamic thinkers and theologians, on the one hand, and secular intellectuals and Westernizers, on the other. These are (i) Islamic jurisprudence and conception of knowledge versus Western science and the validity of any learning that is not rooted in Islamic cosmological doctrine; (ii) the relationship between religion and politics; (iii) the dar ul-Islam versus dar al-harb duality and the issue of jihad; (iv) Western civilized order and the relationship between Islam and civilization; and (v) women and polygamy. Muslim thinkers from diverse backgrounds have addressed these issues. Those who were more intellectually sophisticated naturally tended to address all these issues and provide more comprehensive expositions. As a leader of an important Islamic movement in Jordan, I would like to know your views and reflections on these issues.

Let us begin with the first issue. The Islamic orthodoxy has specified four sources of jurisprudence: the Quran, the hadith or the dicta attributed to Prophet Muhammad, qiyas or juristic reasoning by analogy, and ijma or consensus among the ulama. These principles constituted the core methodology and framework of Islamic jurisprudence that dictate the rule of reasoning in Islam. All Muslim thinkers were to follow these rules. Outside this framework, no rational speculation and independent ruling is allowed. The gate of ijtihad is thus considered closed. What is your position on this? How do you reconcile this notion with the Western conception of scientific methods?

F: Let me begin with my understanding of Islam's cosmological doctrine. Islam is a well-integrated system of beliefs (aqidah). In its center is the belief in the unity of divine principle (towhid). God is the creator of the universe. There is a balance or equilibrium in the universe, and every created being has a purpose and role to play. Islam is a universal creed, not a local or tribal phenomenon. It is a comprehensive belief system constitutive of all the domains of life. Islamic movement should thus be understood within this overall context.

Islam has established the general principles to guide mankind. The more specific details of how to go about building a proper social order should be worked out within the specific historical context of the Islamic movement itself. Take the movement of the Muslim Brothers, for example. In response to the challenges of the secular and Westernized leaders who wanted to abandon Islam, our movement started with *da&**wah*, calling the public to join Islam and understand its teachings. That was the early phase of the Brothers' activities. In the second phase, we emphasized education and charity work. Now, we are in the phase of political participation. The Islamic movement is therefore not restricted to this or that aspect of life but is comprehensive of all domains.

Islamic views on the detailed aspects of social and political interaction will be developed as a result of practice. The interaction between theory and practice will enable us to develop Islamic guidelines on the emerging problems of social life. Our political fiqh, for example, is not mature enough. We should work on it and develop it. Therefore, the gate of ijtihad is not closed. No one can close the gate of independent reasoning within the general Islamic framework.

The findings of the natural sciences conform to the teachings of Islam. The laws of nature discovered by Western sciences do not contradict Islam.

M: Do I understand you correctly that your position conforms to that of the Islamic modernist writers who argued that since nature is God's deed and the Quran is God's word, then the two cannot contradict each other, and that, therefore, you also believe in natural theology?

F: Yes. And as we have natural laws, we have social laws, sort of, that are discovered by social scientists.

M: If this is the case, what of economists who may argue that usury is good for the economy because it contributes to investment, and hence to the expansion of industry and employment?

F: Well, Islam is against usury. But the Islamic Bank has found a way around this problem. Say, for example, you want to borrow money to buy a car. The bank, instead of lending you the money and charging you interest, would buy the car, say, for $1,000 and sell it to you for something like $1200. And you pay this amount to the bank in installments. I am not playing with words, of course, but this arrangement works in the Muslim countries. And if the borrower does not pay the periodic installments to the bank, it will be reflected on his credit record.

M: Let us move to the next issue: the relationship between religion and politics. Islam does not accept the separation of religion from politics, and the person who is in the position of spiritual authority is also occupying the position of political leadership. How does this notion fit in today's political reality?

F: Before talking about the more general Islamic conception of politics, let me begin by emphasizing that our movement does not believe in violence as a means to achieve political ends. We believe that Islam offers general guidelines on how political decisions are to be made. It instructs Muslims to consult with each other. But the form or mechanism of consultation has not been specified in the Quran. It is left to the believers to design such a form within its proper historical context. We believe that democracy is the proper form, and Islam is wholly compatible with parliamentary democracy.

For sure, the Quran and the Sunna are sacred to us, but past understandings of them are not mandatory to us. We make laws according to social context and exigencies. Fatwas are not obligatory. We make decisions not based on this or that fatwa, but based on the consensus of our shura. This consensus should be respected. A general consensus such as that in the parliament is more important than the views of the ulama. I hesitate to consider those who disagree with us as being out of the bound of Islam. I even hesitate to apply the term *jahiliyya* to the conditions of non-Muslims.

M: How relevant to your movement is the Islamic division of the world into dar ul-Islam and dar ul-harb, and how do you describe the issue of jihad? What is the relevance of these concepts to the reality of contemporary world politics?

F: This distinction is historical because in the past Muslims were living in one place and non-Muslims in another. Back then, it made sense to think of a place as being exclusively the abode of Islam. But now it does not make much sense to divide the world in terms of this duality. There are many Muslims who live in America. They are American citizens. It makes little sense to call America dar al-harb. Moreover, technological development and inventions in the means of communication and transportation have transformed the entire world into a small village. And like a village, everybody needs everybody else. This terminology, in my view, is obsolete, and putting it away is not in contradiction with Islam. Everybody has the right to exist, and we should concentrate on the right of Muslim minorities living in Western countries. By the way, that which used to be the dar al-harb are more developed than us, and we can learn a lot from them. I myself have benefited from the United States educational system. I am a graduate of Columbia University.

The real challenge is how to live together while being different. We must accept the rights of different people and their right to be different.

As for jihad, the term does not mean aggression. Our movement does not believe in violence. It basically means that you exert your effort to fulfill your goal. Working hard is a form of jihad; writing a book to defend a rightful idea is a jihad. Jihad also means defense. But, I must say, if engaging in the act of defense may lead to more troubles, this kind of jihad is not constructive and should be avoided. Any act that aggravates the problem is not appropriate. Violence is different from jihad. You defend yourself for your rights. If someone takes your land you should defend yourself. Resisting the Israelis is a jihad. But we are against violence.

Islam has spread through convincing people of the rightful nature of its message, not through force and compulsion.

M: The fourth issue is what appears to be the contradiction between Islam and Western civilization. As a Muslim, you naturally believe that Islam is the best belief system and, if it is observed, it would produce the best society. Yet Islamic countries are quite backward vis-à-vis the West. Western societies, on the other hand, are based on the cultural codes and laws, perhaps to be discovered by sociologists, that are responsible for their progress and advanced level of civilization. How could such cultural codes and laws be inferior to those of Islam? If you believe that Islam is a far superior belief system, how do you reconcile the presence of the best belief system in a backward social environment, yet not so superior Western belief system being located in an advanced social environment?

F: Every civilization would contribute to international civilization. The Western civilization itself is based on Greek, Roman, Christian, and even Islamic civilizations. In fact, historical Islam contributed a lot to Western civilization. There is no doubt that Western civilization has advanced. I myself, being a Columbia graduate, benefited from it. We appreciate the materialistic aspects of Western civilization. We have a duty to cooperate with and learn from it. But we should not borrow all its values. I do not believe that the West has advanced because of Christianity. Nor do I believe that Muslims are backward because of Islam. Certainly, there are objective reasons for our backwardness such as, for example, colonialization and the plundering of our resources by the West. In addition, we have a tendency of spending our resources on such wrong things as the military.

M: Is it really the West that should be blamed for the backwardness of the Muslim countries? How about the current and past leaders of Islamic countries. Take Saddam Hussein, for example. He started the war with Iran (and of course Iran was also responsible for giving him the excuse and for continuing the war for eight years). Over one million people were killed, and many more were wounded and became physically impaired. And billions of dollars worth of property were destroyed. Then he invaded Kuwait. Saddam has killed many of his own people. He has dropped chemical bombs on Iraqi Kurds. He is a dictator. Yet when the Western democracies were mobilized to defend Kuwait and Saudi Arabia, you took the side of Saddam Hussein. Is the West that bad?

F: The Islamic Action Front was against Saddam in its war with Iran. We believe that the war was an American plot. The Front was against Saddam invading Kuwait because we believed that it was an American plot also. America gave the green light to Saddam, encouraging him to go into Kuwait. But when America and European countries came to the Gulf and to our sacred places such as Mecca, we could not remain indifferent. We were against American intervention. We were never for Saddam. Frankly, we are simply against Western intervention in the internal affairs of the Muslim people.

M: How do you view gender relations, the issue of women and polygamy?

F: Islam addresses men and women alike. Adam and Eve were created together, they were in paradise together, and then came to the earth together. There is no real difference between men and women. Women have the right to education and work. But Islam gives men the leadership role in the family.

   Polygamy is a touchy issue. The Quran gives the man the right to have up to four wives. Polygamy is more of an exception than a rule, like a war situation where there is a shortage of men. In Jordan, however, it is a rare phenomenon, and out of so many men I know, only four or five are polygamous. The rate of polygamy is very low in Jordan.

M: If the parliament passes a law that makes polygamy illegal, what would be your reaction?

F: We will oppose this law on Islamic ground.

M: How come? Some Islamic thinkers in the past, notably in India and Egypt, developed an Islamic exegesis of the Quran that rendered the institution of polygamy practically illegal, arguing that it is against the spirit of Islam. For them, a man cannot implement justice equally in a love relationship. That is, a man cannot love two women equally. Since he cannot be just, polygamy is illegal in Islam. What do you think?

F: Well, it is a matter of one's interpretation.

III. ISLAM AND WESTERN CIVILIZATION

CHAPTER 28

CRITICAL ATTITUDE TOWARD THE WEST AND THE IDEA OF WESTERN DECADENCE

Ali Shariati

Ali Shariati. "Modern Calamities." In *Marxism and Other Western Fallacies: An Islamic Critique*. Translated by R. Campbell. Berkeley: Mizan Press, 1980, pp. 32–40, 91–6.

THE MODERN CALAMITIES THAT ARE LEADING TO THE deformation and decline of humanity may be placed under two main headings: (1) Social systems and (2) Intellectual systems. Within the two outwardly opposed social systems that have embraced the new man, or that invite him into their embrace, what is plainly felt is the tragic way that man, a primary and supra-material essence, has been forgotten. Both these social systems, capitalism and communism, though they differ in outward configuration, regard man as an economic animal; their differing contours reflect the issue of which of the two will provide more successfully for the needs of this animal.

Economism is the fundamental principle of the philosophy of life in Western industrial capitalist society, where, as Francis Bacon put it, "Science abandons its search for truth and turns to the search for power." The material "needs" that are generated every day and progressively increase (so that the scope of consumption may be enlarged in quantity, quality, and variety alike, to feed the vast engines of production as they race on in delirium), transform people into worshippers of consumption. Day by day, heavier burdens are imposed on a frenetic populace, so that modern technological prodigies, who ought to have freed mankind from servitude to manual labor and increased people's leisure time, cannot do even that much, so rapidly have artificial material needs outpaced the tremendous speed of production technology. Humanity is every day more condemned to alienation, more drowned in this mad maelstrom of compulsive speed. Not only is there no longer leisure for growth in human values, moral greatness, and spiritual aptitudes, but this being plunged headlong in working to consume, consuming to work, this diving into lunatic competition for luxuries and diversions, has caused traditional moral values to decline and disappear as well.

In communist society, we find a similar downward curve in human moral values. Many intellectuals, contemplating the political and economic contrasts between the communist and capitalist societies, account the former different from the latter from the standpoints of anthropology, philosophy of life, and humanism. But we see clearly that communist societies, although they have attained a relatively advanced stage of economic growth, closely resemble the bourgeois West with respect to social behavior, social psychology, individual outlook, and the philosophy of life and human nature, that what is at issue in communist societies today under the name of Fourierism,[1] *embourgoisement*, and even liberalism is nothing other than an orientation to contemporary Western man; that the intense attention to fashion and luxury now prevalent in both individual lives and the system of state production arises from the fact that, practically speaking and in the final analysis, Marxist and capitalist societies present a single kind of man to the marketplace of human history.

Democracy and Western liberalism—whatever sanctity may attach to them in the abstract—are in practice nothing but the free opportunity to display all the more strongly this spirit and to create all the more speedily and roughly an arena for the profit-hungry forces that have been assigned to transform man into an economic, consuming animal.

Thus we have: state capitalism in the name of socialism; governmental dictatorship in the name of "dictatorship of the proletariat"; intellectual tyranny in the name of the one Party; fanaticism of belief in the name of "diamat";[2] and, finally, reliance on the principles of mechanism and economism in the name of quickly attaining "economic abundance in order to pass from socialism to communism!" All are burdens that have befallen humanity in the name of a sacred, free, and creative will and that cast it like a "social artifact" into a crude but all-encompassing organization—that is, into a most blatant state of the same political and intellectual alienation that Marx spoke of in relation to bourgeois man.

The second category of modern calamities is that of ideological calamities. (Here we employ the term "ideology" in its broadest possible sense. The various contemporary ideologies, claiming as they do to be based on contemporary science, all negate the concept of man as a primary being; even those that boast of their humanism do so).

Historicism presents history as a single determinative material current that in its course constructs out of the material elements, in accordance with the inexorable laws of the historical process, something called man. Thus, in the final analysis, historicism leads to a materialistic determinism in which man is a passive element.

Biologism, which assigns precedence to the laws of nature, regards man just as it regards an animal, but sees him as the latest link in the chain of evolution; otherwise, it looks upon all human spiritual manifestations and unique qualities as occasioned by man's physical constitution, like the natural instincts!

Sociologism views man as a vegetable growing in the garden of his social environment, and thus needing the proper climate and soil; it supposes that only as the garden is changed will the human harvest change, and that, as in the preceding case, this process operates according to scientific laws beyond possible human intervention, laws governing man's actions and even his personality.

If we add to these schools those of materialism and naturalism (which view man as, respectively, a material artifact and an animal), a picture of the ideological calamities in the present age emerges.

In this context, the situation of Marxism is a confused one. Marx, in one of his phases, is a materialist, and thus in no position to regard the being man as anything but an element within the confines of the material world. (We find him writing to Engels, after studying the works of Darwin, "I accept this view as the biological basis for my philosophy of history.")

In another phase, he is an extreme partisan of sociologism. Thus he grants society its independence vis-à-vis naturalistic and humanistic tendencies and then, by arbitrarily and categorically grouping its elements under the headings of either infrastructure or superstructure (the former representing the mode of material production, and the latter, culture, morals, philosophy, literature, arts, ideology, and so forth), he in effect presents man as equivalent to this superstructure, in that man is nothing more than the sum of these parts. In short, humanity turns out to be the product of the mode of material production. Since Marx also specifies the mode of production as consisting of the tools of production, in the final analysis, the primacy of man in Marxism derives from the primacy of tools; that is, instead of humanism one might speak of "utensilism," or one might say that mankind is not considered, as in Islam, the progeny of Adam, but rather that of tools! By annexing "dialectical" to "materialism," Marx not only withholds from humanity a crown of glory, but also sets up a materialistic determinism over and above the force of historical determinism in man, which, at the level of practical application, amounts to another chain. For this truly leads to the fettering of the human will, the source of man's primacy in the world, and ultimately plunges humanity into the same pit of fatalism that upholders of superstitious religious teachings (or rather, philosophers and theologians dependent upon the political establishment) dug for it.

The chain is one and the same—its far end now affixed not to the heavens but to the earth. Thus, it is more than a casual slur to refer to this materialism as "fanatical."

We see that the calamity faced by humanity today is first and foremost a human calamity. Humanity is a species in decline; it is undergoing a metamorphosis and, just like a pupating butterfly, is in danger because of the success of its own ingenuity and labors. What is more astounding, throughout history humanity has usually been sacrificed to the idea of its own deliverance. In a kind of historical reversal, it has been the longing for deliverance that has forged the chains of human captivity and, by offering hope of release, led people into the trap!

Religion, both a powerful love and an invitation to perfection and salvation, after issuing from its primal, limpid springs and coursing through history, underwent a change in its flavor and quality; its course came under the control of those very powers that held the crown of history and that had led in the "social era."

Thus, in China, the school of Lao Tzu at first constituted a summons to deliverance from captivity in an artificial life, a fragmented intellect, and a rude civilization that drew true man into bondage, distorting and tainting primordial human nature, which in reality accords with the Principal Nature, the Tao. This school of Lao Tzu became in time entangled in the worship of innumerable gods, gods who exploited mankind financially, sapped its intellectual powers, and condemned it to endless fears and obsequies.

Confucius, in order to free the people from the thralldom of those imaginary forces, fought against superstition. He guided the people out of the embrace of senseless fantasies, endless sacrifices, vows, supplications, and debilitating self-mortifications, and toward history, society, life and reason. He set forth the principle termed li [3] as the intellectual basis for a rational organization of social life. In later times, however, this same fundamental principle was to take the form of immutable customs subject to an unthinking conformity that killed any sort of social transformation. People grew like the animals frozen in the polar ice caps; they fell into quiescence and a state of fanatical conservatism. One sociologist noted, "if we see that the society and civilization of China in the course of twenty-five hundred years has neither fallen into utter decline, nor progressed or experienced upheavals, the cause is the conservative and traditionalist rule of the Confucian mind!"

Indian religion, which had within it a clear knowledge of man coupled with a deep understanding of the unity of God, nature, and man—an understanding that infused spirit into the body of the world and served as a force for sublimating the human spirit—was transformed into a horrifying mass of superstitions, in which people were set upon by swarms of untold gods. These gods stole the last crumb of their hapless worshippers and then proceeded to condemn exponents of deliverance *(moksa)* and the high Eastern mysticism *(vidya)* to deadly superstitious austerities and to abject servitude under the official religious establishment.

The Buddha came to deliver the Hindus; he summoned them to freedom from the bondage of worshipping the astral divinities. But *his* followers became Buddha-worshippers, so much so that today, in Persian, the word *bot*, derived from "Buddha," appears in the compound *botparasti* ("idol-worship"), the common expression for the most serious form of *shirk*,[4] that is, idolatry.

The Messiah—the promised Savior—came to deliver humanity from the bonds of materialism and rabbinical ritualism, to free religion from servitude to the merchants and racists of Israel, to establish peace, love, and the salvation of the spirit. Thus he wanted to liberate the peoples who were under the spell of the superstitions of the rabbis and Pharisees and condemned to slavery under the crushing imperialism of Rome. But we have seen how Christianity itself succeeded to the throne of the Roman Empire, with the Roman Church perpetuating the imperial order, how scholasticism came to provide the intellectual underpinnings of medieval feudalism, and how it came to murder free thought, free human growth, free science. We have seen how the "religion of peace" spilled blood more freely than any known to previous history, and how, whereas man should have become Godlike (that is, spiritually and morally), God became man-like.

Finally, we come to Islam, the last link in the development of the historical religions, which arrived under the standard of *tauhid*[5] and salvation, in order that, in the words of the Muslim soldier, it might summon mankind "from the lowliness of the earth to the heights of the heavens, from servitude to each other to the service of the Lord of the Universe, and from the oppression of the religions to the justice of Islam."[6] We know how it was reshaped under the Arab Caliphate, how it became a rationale for the acts of the most savage conquerors, and how in time it became a powerful cultural force, which, in the name of jurisprudence, scholastic theology, and Sufism, cast an aura of religiosity over the feudal order of the Saljuqs and Mongols and bound the Muslim people in the chains of predestination. The road to salvation was no longer mapped out through *tauhid*, pious acts, and knowledge. Instead, it lay either through an inherited tradition of blind conformity, entreaties, vows, and supplications; or else in flight from reality, society, and life into astral worlds, a way characterized by pessimism concerning human history, progress, and the salvation of man in this world, and the repression of all natural human wants and proclivities.

During an age in which religion had emerged as a regressive force in relation to scientific and social progress—inhibiting the intellectual, spiritual, and volitional flowering of humanity; giving rise to a mass of formalities, taboos, and superstitions; presiding through its official custodians, headed by the Church and the Pope, over the fate of ideas and nations—the Renaissance (which we will take to be the upsurge of society's motivating spirit, rather than the rising of the intellectuals), by contrasting the stagnation of the Middle Ages under the rule of the religious custodians to the Golden Age of Greece and Rome, issued a call to freedom to its people through nationalism, as against the Latin imperialism of the papacy, and to humanity at large through science, as against the rigid and superstitious Catholic scholasticism.

What were the watchwords of this upsurge? Human freedom from the bonds of the all-compelling will of heaven, release of the intellect from the dominance of religious belief, release of science from scholastic dogma, a turning from heaven to earth to build the paradise that religion had promised for the hereafter, right here on earth!

What exciting slogans! Freedom of the intellect; science to be our guide; paradise on the spot! But what hands were to build this paradise on earth? Those of colonized nations, exploited human beings, with the assistance of scientific technology. So we come to science and capital.

Science was freed from subservience to religion only to become subservient to power and at the disposal of the powerful. It was transformed into short-sighted, rigid scientism, which killed the Messiah and became another lackey to Caesar. The machine that was to have been humanity's tool for ruling nature and escaping enslavement to work was transformed into a mechanism that itself enslaved man.

Finally, let us look at the gatekeeper of this paradise: capitalism, but capitalism armed with science and technology—a new magician bewitching humanity into new captivity amid the massive pitiless wheels of mechanism and techno-bureaucracies. And man? He is but an economic animal whose only duty is to graze in this paradise. The philosophy of "consume, consume, consume!"

And the watchwords? Liberalism!—that is, apathy. Democracy!—that is, "Elect those who have already chosen your lot for you." Life? Material existence. Morals? Opportunism and egoism. The goal? Consumption. The philosophy of life? Satiation of the natural appetites. The ultimate aim? A life of leisure and enjoyment. Faith? Love? The meaning of existence? The meaning of man? Forget it!

But Adam rebelled, even in this paradise on earth.

Now our conclusion is coming into view. Humanism, which all post-Renaissance humanitarian intellectuals hoped would take over the task of human liberation from religion, has become a sacred article of faith for all the atheistic schools of recent centuries. However, it loses its sacrosanct aura as soon as it is subjected to logical scrutiny and in the end proves an idle speculation, which, like some literary expression, bespeaks utopian values or Platonic wisdoms that are sublime and beautiful but have no application in the real world.

True humanism is a collection of the divine values in man that constitute his morals and religious cultural heritage. Modern ideologies, in denying religion, are unable to account for these values. Consequently, although calling themselves staunchly realist, they become more idealistic than Plato even as they entangle humanity still further in their fanatical materialism.

Poor man—always searching for deliverance and finding only disaster. In his flight from the oppression of the powerful and the slave-masters, he turned to the great religions and followed the prophets, and so endured struggles and martyrdom only to be captured by the Magi, Caliphs, Brahmans, and, most terrible of all, the dark and deadly tumult of the Medieval Church, in the midst of which the Pope, as representative of the celestial God, ruled the earth like some imperious Jehovah, holding the reins of politics, property, and faith, and making servants of intellect and science. Generations struggled and sacrificed to bring about a Renaissance, to mobilize humanity to pursue science and liberation, so that it might be freed from what had been inflicted upon it in the name of religion.

Humanity arrived at liberalism, and took democracy in place of theocracy as its key to liberation. It was snared by a crude capitalism, in which democracy proved as much a delusion as theocracy. Liberalism proved an arena in which the only freedom was for horsemen, vying with one another in raids and plundering. Again humanity became the hapless victim sacrificed to the unchecked powers that brought science, technique, and everyday life into orbit around their maddening and continually growing greed and search for profits.

The desire for equality, for liberation from this dizzying whirl of personal avarice, so horrifyingly accelerated by the machine, led humanity into a revolt that resulted in communism. This communism, however, simply represents the same fanatical and frightening power as the Medieval Church, only without God. It has its popes, but they rule not in the name of the Lord but in the name of the proletariat. These absolute despots and "sole proprietors" also claim quasi-prophetic and spiritual honors and pontificate on matters of science, belief, morals, art, and literature.

As the communist system, in the name of justice, comes to dominate those peoples who have fled the oppression and exploitation of Western capitalism, the sentiment of an old, freedom-loving Muslim poet is echoed:

> *O, would that the oppression of the sons of Marwan were returned to us,*
> *And the justice of the sons of Abbas consumed in the flames!*

But the spirit never dies. I am referring to the spirit that the Quran speaks of: not the individual soul, but the divine life-giving and animating power that, like Seraphiel's trumpet, sounds over the skeletal forms of the ages, so that they rise up from those deathly silent graves dug for the human spirit, which so longs for deliverance. Then a fresh ferment, a new resurrection begins, and humanity faces life anew in a new age.

Now that this spirit has been breathed into the corpse of this century, during which mankind reached an existential dead end, this humanity which has suffered so greatly in its search for liberation, having undergone bitter experiences with Western capitalism and struck its head against the blank wall of communism, seeks a third road between this one to the tavern and that to the temple, a third road which it is the mission of the Third World to set out upon.

What makes this future stand out in greater and more promising relief is the fact that in the capitalist and Marxist worlds alike, powerful spirits have come to self-awareness and raised their heads above the tumult and din of capitalist mechanism to decry the disastrous deformation of a humanity that, trapped in an aimless liberalism with a fake veneer of democracy, is becoming one-dimensional, impoverished, and alienated from itself and is losing its human identity.

Here, in the very teeth of the forces that have all the dimensions of society in their grasp, this spirit has called out. Its call reaches the ears of the age across the high and massive walls that have been thrown up around it, reaching further and penetrating deeper day by day. It is still too soon to depict the future that is in the making, but we may foresee its general direction.

What all the new appeals have in common is a belief that both the roads onto which Western capitalism and communism have driven humanity culminate in a human disaster, that the way to human liberation therefore consists in turning away from both of them. Apart from this shared negative view, however, one may discern a positive one in all those appeals and searches: a quest for the spirit.

We might be too optimistic if we were to interpret all this as a turning to religion, but we may speak with assurance of an aspiring spiritual tendency. There is implicit and even explicit in the words of most of the intellectuals who decry the human disaster taking place in both these (outwardly) conflicting worlds a revulsion against the materialism of today's philosophy and morals, against the distortion of the true essence of man and the loss of transcendental human values. One mourns the loss of "that Ahuran sun" that shone out from the depths of human nature, clarifying man's existence, illuminating his life, infusing spirit into the natural world, and creating love and values.

Today, in philosophy, Heidegger does not speak in the terms of Hegel or Feuerbach. In science, Max Planck, the outstanding exponent of the new physics, opposes the ideas of Claude Bernard. Heidegger is searching for Christ in humanity, and Planck is searching for God in the world of physics.

Modern literature and art, expressing alarm at the futility of modern life, review the deformation of modern man and the dark and deadly loneliness that has enveloped him. Eliot, Strindberg, Guenon, Pasternak, Toynbee, Erich Fromm, Senghor, Uzghan, Omar Mawlud—all are in some way searching for light. Even a well-known contemporary physiologist, Alexis Carrel (winner of two Nobel prizes for his work in grafting blood vessels and in preserving living tissues outside the body), speaks unselfconsciously about "grace" as a powerful factor in the moral and psychological development and harmonious growth of a person.

It even appears that a sort of messianic spirit has sprung up in the closed fortress of the communist world, and a human renaissance is taking place. This is occurring despite intensified state opposition to religion, zealous efforts by the ruling party to pacify the new generation of artists and intellectuals and bring them into line with dialectical materialist dogma, and the intimidating exercises of the apparatus of thought control to suppress "reactionary" ideas, "bourgeois" tendencies, and religious activity.

Today, in contrast to Marx, who felt human liberation depended upon the denial of God, and Nietzsche, who boasted, "God is dead," even an atheistic philosopher like Sartre speaks of God's absence from the universe "with painful regret," seeing in this a source of the futility of man and existence, the loss of values.

Thirty years ago Iqbal proclaimed, "Today, more than anything else, humanity needs a spiritual interpretation of the universe." Although it is implicit in Iqbal's words, we might add, "It needs a spiritual interpretation of humanity as well."

We are clearly standing on the frontier between two eras—one where both Western civilization and communist ideology have failed to liberate humanity, drawing it instead into disaster and causing the new spirit to recoil in disillusionment; and one where humanity in search of deliverance will try a new road and take a new direction, and will liberate its essential nature. Over this dark and dispirited world, it will set a holy lamp like a new sun; by its light, the man alienated from himself will perceive anew his primordial nature, rediscover himself, and see clearly the path of salvation.

Islam will play a major role in this new life and movement. In the first place, with its pure *tauhid*, it offers a profound spiritual interpretation of the universe, one that is as noble and idealistic as it is logical and intelligible. In the second place, through the philosophy of the creation of Adam, Islam reveals in its humanism the conception of a free, independent, noble essence, but one that is as fully attuned to earthly reality as it is divine and idealistic.

This is especially true from this standpoint: Islam does not content itself with answering only one philosophical or spiritual need, or with presenting only one ethical viewpoint; it strives to realize the world-view of *tauhid* and of human primacy within real life. Unlike the subjectivist philosophies and mystical religions, it does not accept in human existence the dichotomies of sacred and profane, belief and behavior, idea and actuality. Thus Louis Gardet says, "Islam is both a religion and a nation."

This future, which begins with the discarding of capitalism and Marxism, is neither predestined nor prefabricated. Instead, it remains to be built. There is no doubt that Islam will have an appropriate role in its construction, when it has freed itself from the effects of centuries of stagnation, superstition, and contamination, and is put forth as a living ideology.

That is the task of the true intellectuals of Islam. Only in this way will Islam—after a renaissance of belief and an emergence from isolation and reaction—be able to take part in the current war of beliefs and, in particular, to command the center and serve as an example to contemporary thought, where the new human spirit is seeking the means to begin a new world and a new humanity.

This is no extravagant proposal; it is a duty. Not only does the essential summons of Islam require it, but the text of the Quran explicitly enjoins it upon the true followers of Islam: *"God's are the East and the West. And thus We have made you a middle people, that you might be witnesses to the people, and the Prophet a witness to you"* (2:143). We see that the scope of Islam's confrontation and opposition to other ideologies, especially those that are concerned with the question of man, is as far-reaching as the very range and depth of its summons.

NOTES

1. The literal transcription here is "furalism." We also surmise that the word intended might be "formalism." (Tr.).
2. Diamat: a contraction of "dialectical materialism," the materialism that is supposed to be "the principles of belief to which education of the young, scientific research, literature and the arts, philosophy, and the scientific outlook must conform." That is to say, it is a kind of religious rule without religion!
3. This may be an error for i, "mortality," as: "The superior man comprehends righteousness [i: the "oughtness" of a situation]; the small man comprehends gain [li: profit]" (Analects of Confucius, 4: 16). (Tr.).
4. Shirk: making something a "partner" with God; setting something alongside God as worthy of worship. (Tr.).
5. Tawhid: the profession of divine unity. (Tr.).
6. This celebrated statement was made by a Muslim soldier in the army that conquered Isfahan, addressing himself to the commander of the Persian garrison. (Tr.).

CHAPTER 29

SELF-DESTRUCTIVENESS OF
WESTERN CIVILIZATION

Sayyid Abul A'la Maududi

Sayyid Abul A'la Maududi. "Suicide of Western Civilization[1]" in *West versus Islam*. Translated by S. Waqar Ahmad Gardezi and Abdul Waheed Khan. New Delhi, India: International Islamic Publishers, 1992, pp. 61–73.

THE STUPENDOUS PROGRESS OF THE WEST IN THE FIELDS of politics, trade and industry, and art and science is awe-inspiring. It looks as if the progress of these nations is everlasting and their domination over the world has been destined for all times to come. They have been conferred monopoly to rule the world and their domination and suzerainty appears to be too firm to be up-rooted.

In fact the superpowers of every age have always been considered unassailable. The Pharaohs of Egypt, the A'ad and Thamud of Arabia, the Caledonions of Iraq, the Chosroes of Iran, Conquerors of Greece, rulers of Rome, undaunted Mujaahids of Islam, and the scorching Tartars appeared with pomp and show on the world stage and each of them over-awed the world with the agility of their skill and grandeur in the same fashion. Any nation that rose to power, swept the world in a similar way. It reigned supreme over the civilized world and confounded the world to make it believe that its domination had come to stay. But as soon as the term of its domination was over and the real eternal ruler, that is Allah, decided to remove them from the world stage they fell and fell in such a way that most of them vanished altogether from the world scene. The rest who survived were subjugated by those whom they once ruled and were enslaved by those who had been their slaves.

> Many systems have passed away before you, Go about the world, and see for yourselves the end of those who did deny the messengers of Allah. (3:137)

The system of this universe is not static and stationary. A constant move, change, and cycle does not allow anything to remain static. There is extinction for every existence, unmaking for every making, autumn for every spring, descent for every ascent, and vice versa. A tiny seed flying weightless today, when it gets rooted in the soil, sprouts into a big, shady tree tomorrow. Then again becomes dead and dry and is reduced to dust. The forces of nature, leaving that dead and dry seed, start nurturing some other seed. These are all the ups and downs of life. But when a certain state is prolonged, one thinks that it is eternal. If it is the state of decline he thinks it shall go on declining, and if it is a state of progress, he thinks it shall continue for ever. But in fact it is nothing but a matter of time alone. No state is permanent and lasting.

> These are (only) the vicissitudes which we cause to follow one another for mankind. (3:140)

World events are constantly moving in a sort of cycle. Birth and death, youth and senility, strength and weakness, spring and autumn, cheerfulness and gloom, all are different aspects of this very cycle. In this cycle, everything grows and proliferates, displays force and power, exhibits beauty and bloom, and attains its climax. Then begins the anti-climax and it starts declining, withering, weakening, and at the end is eliminated by the same forces that had nurtured it.

This is the Divine way in the matter of His creation and human beings are no exception to it, be it an individual or a nation. Honor and disgrace, prosperity and poverty, ascent and descent, and other such developments occur turn by turn to individuals as well as nations in the same cyclic movement. None is exempt from this cycle of change and no state of affairs is to remain permanent, be it rising or falling.

> It was the tradition of Allah for those who passed away before you, and you shall find no change in the tradition of Allah. (33:62)

The relics of the ancient nations are scattered all over the world. The traces of culture and civilization, art and craftsmanship, skill and dexterity left behind by them show that they were in no way less advanced than the most developed nations of today, rather they were comparatively much more advanced and powerful than their contemporaries.

> They were stronger than these in might, they plowed the land and cultivated it and built on it more than these people have. (30:9)

But then what happened to them? They were puffed up by their constant rise and success, and the enormity of luxuries and favors made them proud. Prosperity proved a trial. Intoxicated by power and authority, they turned into brutes and tyrants and dug their own graves by their evil deeds. The wrongdoers followed that by which they were made sapless and were guilty (11:116). Allah gave them a long respite despite their defiance and disobedience.

There has been many wicked habitations whom at first I gave respite. (22:48)

It was not a little respite. Some nations enjoyed respite for centuries.

A day with your Lord is equivalent to thousand years as You reckon. (22:47)

But every time respite proved a new ordeal to them. They took it as an outcome of their machinations against the will of Allah and thought that they rule supreme in the world. At last the Divine fury flared up. They were deprived of all the favors. Prosperity gave way to decline and destruction. It was a super stroke from Allah which these people could neither foresee nor forestall.

They plotted thus and we too devised a plot which they could not visualize. (27:50)

The Divine move comes not from outside but works inside the man by penetrating his mind and heart. It paralyzes his reason, his consciousness, his judgment, his thought, and his senses. It blinds not his eyes but his conscience.

It is not the eyes that grow blind, but it is the hearts which are within the bosoms that grow blind. (22:46)

And when one's conscience is dead every move for his betterment goes against him. Every step he takes toward success leads him to destruction. His faculties revolt against him and he slashes himself with his own hands.

Then see what was the result of their plotting; we destroyed all of these plotters and their people. (27:51)

A clear picture of this rise and fall is portrayed in the story of the Pharaohs and the Israelites. When the Egyptians reached the height of their progress and prosperity, they started oppression and tyranny. The Pharaoh proclaimed himself as their God and subjected the weak Israelites to untold torture and tyranny who had settled there during Prophet Joseph's period. At last when the Pharaoh and his people transgressed all limits in their perversity, Almighty Allah decided to humble them and raise the down-trodden Israelites to power, which had no entity before them. Divine decree was enforced. Prophet Moses was born in the weak nation, and he was destined to be brought up by Pharaoh himself in his own palace. Prophet Moses was deputed to liberate his nation from their slavery to Egyptians. Prophet Moses pleaded the case of his people with the Pharaoh very softly, but he would not listen. He and his people were admonished by God constantly in the form of famines and draught, storms and rain of blood, attack of locusts, lice, and frogs. But their haughtiness knew no abatement.

They became proud and they were really criminals. (Quran)

When they ignored all warnings and admonitions, the Divine chastisement was enforced. Moses left Egypt along with his people and the Pharaoh and his army were drowned in the sea resulting in the total destruction of Egyptians who could not rise again for centuries.

> Therefore We seized him and his hosts, and abandoned them unto the sea, behold the end of the evil-doers. (27:40)

Then came the Israelites' turn. The real Sovereign of the universe replaced the Egyptians with them who were, till then, a depressed and wretched people.

> And we caused the people who were downtrodden to inherit, from East to West, the land we had blessed, and the most fair word of Allah was fulfilled upon the people of Israel, because of their endurance. (7:137)
> And bestowed upon them superiority over all the existing nations of the world. (2:47)

But this superiority and vicegerency on earth was subject to good deeds. It had already been conveyed to them through Prophet Moses that vicegerency and authority on earth shall no doubt be bestowed upon you but it will be observed how you behave$_2$ and this condition was not laid for the Israelites only but for all the nations bestowed with authority on earth.

> Then we made you their successor on the earth after them so that We might see how you behave. (10: 14)

When the Israelites disobeyed Allah, tampered with His word, changed the right into wrong, took to unlawful earning, falsehood, dishonesty, and breach of promises, turned greedy, cowardly and easygoing, killed their prophets, opposed everybody who called them to submit to the ultimate truth, they preferred the leadership of the wicked over the pious ones. Allah Almighty also withdrew His favors and deprived them of His vicegerency on earth. They were routed and crushed by the tyrant rulers of Iraq, Greece, and Rome, and rendered homeless. They wandered from country to country in utter humiliation. They were deprived of every authority. For the last 2,000 years, they have suffered such miserableness with the Divine curse that they find no place to live in peacefully and honorably all the world over.$_3$

> And abasement and wretchedness were imposed upon them, and they were visited with wrath from Allah. (2:61)

The tradition of Allah is being repeated today before our eyes. The torture inflicted on earlier nations as a result of their misdeeds haunts Western nations today. All possible admonitions and warnings have been administered to them. The miseries of the first world war, financial breakdowns, ever increasing unemployment, a spectacular rise in sexual diseases, disintegration of the family system, all these are very clear indications for those who have insight to conclude the repercussions of tyranny, disobedience, lustfulness, and dishonesty. But they learn not any lesson from all these calamities. They remain adamant in their rebellion against Allah. They have not the eyes to penetrate into the real cause of this malady. They try their best to remove the symptoms and not the cause. Such an attitude enhances the malady instead of its remedy. This state of affairs shows that the time of admonitions and arguments is more or less over and the final verdict of the destiny is soon to come.

Allah has imposed two big evils on the Western nations, which are dragging them toward destruction and extinction. One of them is the curse of birth control and extinction of the human race, while the other one is the curse of nationalism.

The first one is imposed upon their individuals while the other one is imposed on their states. The curse of birth control has driven the men and women mad and is persuading them to destroy their generations by their own hands. It tells them the ways of blocking conception, exhorts them for abortion, and convinces them of the benefits of sterilization meant to destroy even the seed of procreation. They become so callous that they do not hesitate nipping in the bud their own infants. In short, this evil is leading them toward gradual national suicide.

The second evil has deprived their top-ranking statesmen and army generals of the instinct of sound thinking and fair judgment. This evil developed venomous feelings of selfishness, rivalry, hatred, bigotry, avarice, and greed. It is dividing them into hostile and warring factions, who have daggers drawn against each other. This too, no doubt, is a form of Divine punishment.

Or to confront you with dissension and make you taste the violence of one another. (6:65)

It is leading them toward wholesale suicide, which will not be gradual, but sudden. It has dumped its gunpowder all over the world, and has created danger spots here and there. It is just waiting for an opportune moment. As soon as the time comes, it may trigger fire in any of the gunpowder dumps, resulting in an instantaneous devastating blast and an unprecedented havoc all over the world, which will surpass all the catastrophes of the past history.

What I am saying is by no means an exaggeration. The war weaponry that is in process in America, Europe, and Japan is quite enough to send shivers down the spines of the people in knowledgeable circles. They feel terrified to visualize the consequences of such a war. Sergel Neuman, a member of American military staff, has written an article on the impending war. According to him, it will not be a fight between armies but a sort of general massacre which would not spare the innocent population, even children and women. The research in the field of science has shifted the fight from combatants to chemical compounds and senseless weapons, unable to distinguish between combatants and non-combatants.

Now the wars shall not be fought in fields and forts, but, in cities and habitations, because, according to the modern theory, an enemy's real strength lies not in armed forces but in its cities and towns, and commercial and industrial centers. Now the airplanes shall drop different types of bombs raining explosive material, poisonous gases, germs of various diseases that would destroy millions of people—men, women, and children within no time. A single Lewisite bomb may shatter the biggest building complex of London to pieces.[4]

There is a poisonous gas called "Green Cross Gas," which, if sniffed, makes a person feel as if he has been drowned in the water. "Yellow Cross Gas" is poisonous like a snake and acts exactly like snake poison. There are 12 more such poisonous gases that are almost invisible. Their effects are not at all felt in the beginning, but by the time they are felt they become incurable. One of them is a sort of gas that spreads at a very high attitude and the pilot of any airplane crossing it loses eyesight. I believed that one ton of some such gases can destroy the whole of Paris within one hour with the help only 100 airplanes.

Recently, an electric incendiary bomb has been invented. Weighing only 100 kilograms, it is so powerful that it would generate heat to the tune of 3000 degrees Fahrenheit flaring a fire that cannot be put out by any means. The water works as petrol to such a fire and science has not yet discovered any method of extinguishing it. It is meant to be sprayed on big commercial centers to set them on fire from one end to the other. Later, to make complete annihilation sure, the airplanes would drop poisonous gas bombs on the fleeing mobs.

According to armament experts, these inventions can level the world's biggest and safest capital to the ground with the help of a few airplanes within only two hours. A population of millions of people can be poisoned in such a way that they may go to sleep unawares in the night but none of them, not a single person, may get up alive in the morning. The whole water reservoir of a country, its cattle wealth, crops, and orchards can be destroyed with poisonous matter. No effective device has been invented as yet to check these devastating attacks except to use similar devices to wipe out the opponent, resulting in the destruction of both the countries.

This is but a short resume of future war preparations. Details can be had from the book titled: *What Would Be the Character of a New War*, published after regular research by Geneva's Inter-Parliamentary Union. Its study will reveal how Western civilization has piled up, with its own hands, the means and material for its destruction. Now its life span is no more than the date of declaration of a new world war.[5]

The day a war is declared between two superpowers, take it for granted, the doom of Western civilization is sealed. A war between two superpowers would, beyond any doubt, turn into a world war. And a world war would definitely result in world-wide destruction.

> Disorder doth appear on land and sea because of the evil which men's own hands have done, that He may let them taste some part or that which they have done, that haply so they may return. (33:41)

Anyhow it is not very far off that the power and authority on earth may change hands and some down-trodden nation may come up and replace the autocrats and the oppressors. It is yet to be seen who is chosen by Allah to replace the present superpowers.

We cannot anyway guess which nation is to take over next. It is but a favor from Allah. He snatches power and authority from whom He likes and bestows it on whom He chooses:

> Say: O Allah! Owner of Sovereignty Thou givest sovereignty unto whom Thou wilt and Thou withdrawest sovereignty from whom Thou wilt. (3:26)

But this too is governed by law of Nature which has been explicitly stated in His Book. It says that a nation is toppled as a result of its misdeeds. Allah replaces it with some other nation that is not corrupt and rebellious like its predecessor.

> If you disobeyed you will be replaced by some other people who will not be like you. (47:38)

Thus, apparently it looks that the next change stands no chance for the success and rise of those backward and licentious nations that are aping Western civilization, not in its virtues, whatever little it may have retained, but in its vices, which are the real cause of its decline.

NOTES

1. An article published in the monthly *Tarjuman-ul-Quran* in Oct. 1932 by Jamadi ul-Akhir, 1352 A.H.
2. The Quran, 7:129.
3. The Israeli State was formed in Palestine a few years after this article's publication That made the people doubt the authenticity of the Quranic prophecy. But it is a known fact that the state of Israel has been established not on its own strength, but with an all out assistance and support from America, England, Russia, and France. Jews are being brought into this tiny state from all over the world. The day these Western powers are involved in any world war, and rendered incapable of supporting Israel, shall be the Doomsday for Israel and the Arab countries around shall push this bundle of filth into the Mediterranean sea. Apparently the Jews seem to have won a homeland in the heart of Arab nations with all out support of Western powers, but in fact it is the beginning of a very big calamity for them.
4. The apprehension of the late 1930's came true in 1945 when the atom bomb totally liquidated Hiroshima and Nagasaki, two densely populated big cities in Japan. It was just a sample Demonstration of the devastating weaponry, which later developed a far more powerful hydrogen bomb.
5. An example of what happened during the Second World War of 1939–1945 can be seen in the Hiroshima and Nagasaki holocaust. Lord Russell's "Scourge of the Swastika" presents much more support for the fact that a Godless civilization proves itself a thousand times more beastly than a beast.

CHAPTER 30

GRANTING CAPITULATORY RIGHTS TO THE U.S.

Imam Ruhullah Khomeini

Imam Ruhullah Khomeini. *Islam and Revolution: Writings and Declarations of Imam Khomeini*, translated and annotated by Hamid Algar. Berkeley: Mizan Press, 1981, pp. 181–8.

Imam Khomeini delivered this speech in front of his residence in Qum. Together with the declaration he issued on the same subject, it was the immediate cause for his forced exile from Iran on November 4, 1964. Source: S.H.R., Barrasi va Tahlili az Nihazat-i Imam Khomeini (Najaf, n.d.) pp. 716–26.

I CANNOT EXPRESS THE SORROW I FEEL IN MY HEART. My heart is constricted. Since the day I heard of the latest developments affecting Iran, I have barely slept; I am profoundly disturbed, and my heart is constricted. With a sorrowful heart, I count the days until death shall come and deliver me.

Iran no longer has any festival to celebrate; they have turned our festival into mourning.[1] They have turned it into mourning and are dancing together with joy. They have sold us, they have sold our independence; but still they light up the city and dance.

If I were in their place, I would forbid all these lights; I would give orders that black flags be raised over the bazaars and houses, that black awnings be hung! Our dignity has been trampled underfoot; the dignity of Iran has been destroyed. The dignity of the Iranian army has been trampled underfoot!

A law has been put before the Majlis according to which we are to accede to the Vienna Convention,[2] and a provision has been added to it that all American military advisers, together with their families, technical and administrative officials, and servants—in short, anyone in any way connected to them—are to enjoy legal immunity with respect to any crime they may commit in Iran.

If some American's servant, some American's cook, assassinates your *marja³* in the middle of the bazaar, or runs over him, the Iranian police do not have the right to apprehend him! Iranian courts do not have the right to judge him! The dossier must be sent to America, so that our masters there can decide what is to be done!

First, the previous government approved this measure without telling anyone, and now the present government just recently introduced a bill in the Senate and settled the whole matter in a single session without breathing a word to anyone. A few days ago, the bill was taken to the lower house of the Majlis and there were discussions, with a few deputies voicing their opposition, but the bill passed anyhow. They passed it without shame, and the government shamelessly defended this scandalous measure. They have reduced the Iranian people to a level lower than that of an American dog. If someone runs over a dog belonging to an American, he will be prosecuted. Even if the Shah himself were to run over a dog belonging to an American, he would be prosecuted. But if an American cook runs over the Shah, the head of state, no one will have the right to interfere with him.

Why? Because they wanted a loan and America demanded this in return. A few days after this measure was approved, they requested a $200 million loan and America agreed to the request. It was stipulated that the sum of $200 million would be paid to the Iranian government over a period of five years, and that $300 million would be paid back to America over a period of ten years. So in return for this loan, America is to receive $100 million—or 800 million tumans—in interest. But in addition to this, Iran has sold itself to obtain these dollars. The government has sold our independence, reduced us to the level of a colony, and made the Muslim nation of Iran appear more backward than savages in the eyes of the world!

What are we to do in the face of this disaster? What are our religious scholars to do? To what country should they present their appeal?

Other people imagine that it is the Iranian nation that has abased itself in this way. They do not know that it is the Iranian government, the Iranian Majlis—the Majlis that has nothing to do with the people. What can a Majlis that is elected at bayonet-point have to do with the people? The Iranian nation did not elect these deputies. Many of the high-ranking *'ulama* and *maraji'* ordered a boycott of the elections, and the people obeyed them and did not vote. But then came the power of the bayonet, and these deputies were seated in the Majlis.

They have seen that the influence of the religious leaders prevents them from doing whatever they want, so now they wish to destroy that influence!

According to a history textbook printed this year and taught to our schoolchildren now, one containing all kinds of lies and inaccurate statements, "It has now become clear that it is to the benefit of the nation for the influence of the religious leaders to be rooted out."

They have come to understand well that:

If the religious leaders have influence, they will not permit this nation to be the slaves of Britain one day, and America the next.

If the religious leaders have influence, they will not permit Israel to take over the Iranian economy; they will not permit Israeli goods to be sold in Iran—in fact, to be sold duty-free!

If the religious leaders have influence, they will not permit the government to impose arbitrarily such a heavy loan on the Iranian nation.

If the religious leaders have influence, they will not permit such misuse to be made of the public treasury.

If the religious leaders have influence, they will not permit the Majlis to come to a miserable state like this; they will not permit the Majlis to be formed at bayonet-point, with the scandalous results that we see.

If the religious leaders have influence, they will not permit girls and boys to wrestle together, as recently happened in Shiraz.

If the religious leaders have influence, they will not permit people's innocent daughters to be under young men in school; they will not permit women to teach at boys' schools and men to teach at girls' schools, with all the resulting corruption.

If the religious leaders have influence, they will strike this government in the mouth, they will strike this Majlis in the mouth and chase these deputies out of both its houses!

If the religious leaders have influence, they will not permit a handful of individuals to be imposed on the nation as deputies and participate in determining the destiny of the country.

If the religious leaders have influence, they will not permit some agent of America to carry out these scandalous deeds; they will throw him out of Iran.

So the influence of the religious leaders is harmful to the nation? No, it is harmful to you, harmful to you traitors, not to the nation! You know that as long as the religious leaders have influence, you cannot do everything you want to do, commit all the crimes you want, so you wish to destroy their influence. You thought you could cause dissension among the religious leaders with your intrigues, but you will be dead before your dream can come true. You will never be able to do it. The religious leaders are united.[4]

I esteem all the religious leaders. Once again, I kiss the hand of all the religious leaders. If I kissed the hands of the *maraji'* in the past, today I kiss the hands of the *tullab*. I kiss the hands of the simple grocer.

Gentlemen, I warn you of danger!

Iranian army, I warn you of danger!

Iranian politicians, I warn you of danger!

Iranian merchants, I warn you of danger!

'ulama of Iran, *maraji'* of Islam, I warn you of danger

Scholars, students! Centers of religious learning! Najaf, Qum, Mashhad, Tehran, Shiraz! I warn you of danger!

The danger is coming to light now, but there are other things that are being kept hidden from us. In the Majlis they said, "Keep these matters secret!" Evidently they are dreaming up further plans for us. What greater evil are they about to inflict upon us? Tell me, what could be worse than slavery? What could be worse than abasement? What else do they want to do? What are they planning?

What disasters this loan has brought down upon the head of the nation already! This impoverished nation must now pay $100 million in interest to America over the next ten years. And as if that were not enough, we have been sold for the sake of this loan!

What use to you are the American soldiers and military advisers? If this country is occupied by America, then what is all this noise you make about progress? If these advisers are to be your servants, then why do you treat them like something superior to masters? If they are servants, why not treat them as such? If they are your employees, then why not treat them as any other government treats its employees? If our country is now occupied by the U. S., then tell us outright and throw us out of the country!

What do they intend to do? What does this government have to say to us? What is this Majlis doing? This illegal, illicit Majlis, this Majlis that the maraji' have had boycotted with their fatwas and decrees; this Majlis that makes empty noises about independence and revolution, that says: "We have undergone a White Revolution!"

I don't know where this White Revolution is that they are making so much fuss about. God knows that I am aware of (and my awareness causes me pain) the remote villages and provincial towns, not to mention our own backyard city of Qum. I am aware of the hunger of our people and the disordered state of our agrarian economy. Why not try to do something for this country, for this population, instead of piling up debts and enslaving yourselves? Of course, taking the dollars means that someone has to become a slave; you take the dollars and use them, and we become slaves! If an American runs over me with his car, no one will have the right to say anything to him!

Those gentlemen who say we must hold our tongues and not utter a sound—do they still say the same thing on this occasion? Are we to keep silent again and not say a word? Are we to keep silent while they are selling us? Are we to keep silent while they sell our independence?

By God, whoever does not cry out in protest is a sinner! By God, whoever does not express his outrage commits a major sin!

Leaders of Islam, come to the aid of Islam!

'Ulama of Najaf, come to the aid of Islam!

'Ulama of Qum, come to the aid of Islam! Islam is destroyed!

Muslim peoples! Leaders of the Muslim peoples! Presidents and kings of the Muslim peoples! Come to our aid! Shah of Iran save yourself!

Are we to be trampled underfoot by the boots of America simply because we are a weak nation and have no dollars? America is worse than Britain; Britain is worse than America. The Soviet Union is worse than both of them. They are all worse and more unclean than each other! But today it is America that we are concerned with.

Let the American President know that in the eyes of the Iranian people, he is the most repulsive member of the human race today because of the injustice he has imposed on our Muslim nation. Today the Quran has become his enemy, the Iranian nation has become his enemy. Let the American government know that its name has been ruined and disgraced in Iran.

Those wretched deputies in the Majlis begged the government to ask "our friends" the Americans not to make such impositions on us, not to insist that we sell ourselves, not to turn Iran into a colony. But did anyone listen?

There is one article in the Vienna Convention they did not mention at all—Article 32. I don't know what article that is; in fact, the chairman of the Majlis himself doesn't know. The deputies also don't know what that article is; nonetheless, they went ahead and approved and signed the bill. They passed it, even though some people said, "We don't know what is in Article 32." Maybe those who objected did not sign the bill. They are not quite so bad as the others, those who certainly did sign. They are a herd of illiterates.

One after another, our statesmen and leading politicians have been set aside. Our patriotic statesmen are given nothing to do. The army should know that it will also be treated the same way: its leaders will be set aside, one by one. What self-respect will remain for the army when an American errand boy or cook has priority over one of our generals? If I were in the army, I would resign. If I were a deputy in the Majlis, I would resign. I would not agree to be disgraced. American cooks, mechanics, technical and administrative officials, together with their families, are to enjoy legal immunity, but the *'ulama* of Islam, the preachers and servants of Islam, are to live banished or imprisoned. The partisans of Islam are to live in Bandar 'abbas[5] or in prison, because they are religious leaders or supporters of the religious leaders.

The government clearly documents its crimes by putting out a history textbook that says, "It is to the benefit of the nation to root out the influence of the religious leaders." This means that it is for the benefit of the nation that the Messenger of God should play no role in its affairs. For the religious leaders of themselves have nothing; whatever they have, they received from the Messenger of God. So the government wants the Messenger of God to play no role in our affairs, so that Israel can do whatever it likes, and America likewise.

All of our troubles today are caused by America and Israel. Israel itself derives from America; these deputies and ministers that have been imposed upon us derive from America—they are all agents of America, for if they were not, they would rise up in protest.

I am not thoroughly agitated, and my memory is not working so well. I cannot remember precisely when, but in one of the earlier Majlises, where Sayyid Hasan Mudarris[6] was a deputy, the government of Russia gave Iran an ultimatum—I can't remember its exact content—to the effect that "Unless you accept our demand, we will advance on Tehran by way of Qazvin and occupy it!" The government of the day put pressure on the Majlis to accept the Russian demand.

According to an American historian, a religious leader with a stick in hand (the late Mudarris) came up to the tribune and said: "Now that we are to be destroyed, why should we sign the warrant for our own destruction?" The Majlis took courage from his act of opposition, rejected the ultimatum, and Russia was unable to do anything!

That is the conduct of a true religious leader; a thin, emaciated man, a mere heap of bones, rejects the ultimatum and demand of a powerful state like Russia. If there were a single religious leader in the Majlis today, he would not permit these things to happen. It is for this reason that they wish to destroy the influence of the religious leaders, in order to attain their aims and desires!

There is so much to be said, there are so many instances of corruption in this country that I am unable in my state at the moment to present to you even what I know. It is your duty, however, to communicate these matters to your colleagues. The *'ulama* must enlighten the people, and they in turn must raise their voices in protest to the Majlis and the government and say, "Why did you do this? Why have you sold us? We did not elect you to be our representatives, and even if we had done so, you would forfeit your posts now on account of this act of treachery."

This is high treason! O God, they have committed treason against this country. O God, this government has committed treason against this country. O God, this government has committed treason against the Quran. All the members of both houses who gave their agreement to this affair are traitors. Those old men in the Senate are traitors, and all those in the lower house who voted in favor of this affair are traitors. They are not our representatives. The whole world must know that they are not the representatives of Iran. Or, suppose they are; now I dismiss them. They are dismissed from their posts and all the bills they have passed up until now are invalid.

According to the very text of the law, according to Article 2 of the Supplementary Constitutional Law, no law is valid unless the *mujtahids* exercise a supervisory role in the Majlis. From the beginning of the constitutional period down to the present, has any *mujtahid* ever exercised supervision? If there were five *mujtahids* in this Majlis, or even one single religious leader of lesser rank, they would get a punch in the mouth; he would not allow this bill to be enacted, he would make the Majlis collapse.

As for those deputies who apparently opposed this affair, I wish to ask them in protest: If you were genuinely opposed, why did you not pour soil on your heads? Why did you not rise up and seize that wretch[33] by the collar? Does "opposition" mean simply to sit there and say, "We are not in agreement," and then continue your flattery as usual? You must create an uproar, right there in the Majlis. You must not permit there to be such a Majlis. Is it enough to say simply, "I am opposed" when the bill passes nevertheless?

We do not regard as law what they claim to have passed. We do not regard this Majlis as a Majlis. We do not regard this government as a government. They are traitors, guilty of high treason.!

O God, remedy the affairs of the Muslims! O God, bestow dignity on this sacred religion of Islam! O God, destroy those individuals who are traitors to this land, who are traitors to Islam, who are traitors to the Quran.

And peace be upon you, and also God's mercy.

NOTES

1. This speech denouncing the granting of capitulatory rights to American personnel in Iran was delivered on the anniversary of the birth of the Prophet's daughter, which under normal circumstances would have been an occasion for rejoicing.

2. The Vienna Convention of 1961—amplifying and in part replacing annexes to the Treaty of Vienna of 1815—regulates the status of diplomatic personal exchange by its signatories.

3. Marja': see n. 20 above. [Note 20 reads: Maraji': plural of marja' (more fully, marja'-i taqlid), a scholar of proven learning and piety whose authoritative rulings one follows in matters of religious practice.]

4. A reference to attempts by the Shah's regime to create dissension among the religious leaders by using a small faction of Tehran 'ulama who opposed—on allegedly religious grounds—Imam Khomeini's denunciations of Israel. See S.H.R., *Barrasi va Tahlili*, pp. 686–9.

5. Bandar 'abbas: a port on the northern shore of the Persian/Arabian Gulf to which opponents of the regime were frequently banished because of its remoteness from all urban centers as well as its inhospitable climate.

6. Sayyid Hasan Mudarris: a religious leader who was active in opposing both Russian and British encroachment on Iran during and after World War I. He has been credited with formulating the theory of "negative balance" in Iranian foreign policy; i.e., the refusal of concessions and privileges to all foreign powers. He also opposed the foundation of the Pahlavi dictatorship and was ultimately assassinated on the orders of Riza Shah in 1934. For an account of his life, see Ibrahim Khwaja Nuri, *Bazigarani-i Asr-i Tala'i: Mudarris*, new edition. (Tehran: 1359/1980).

CHAPTER 31

ISLAM AND
ITS ADVERSARIES

Abd al-Latif Sultani

Abdel Latif Sultani. "Fadila Mrabet, Kateb Yassine, and the Rocket of Islam." In *Al-Mazdaqia hia asl al-ichtirakia* (Masdaqia is the Source of Socialism), Morocco, 1975, p. 33, quoted in Francois Burgat and William Dowell, *The Islamic Movement in North Africa*. Austin, Texas: Center for Middle Eastern Studies, University of Texas at Austin, 1997, pp. 252–3.

FADILA MRABET, KATEB YASSINE,
AND THE ROCKET OF ISLAM

IN THE GROUP (OF THOSE WHO ACCUSE THE ULEMAS of fanaticism), there is notably a woman and a man who both pretend to be Algerians. The woman blackened a paper a bit with some French and called that a book *(The Algerian Woman)* [*La Femme Algérienne*, Paris, Maspéro, 1964], which she filled with enormous lies and small talk empty of any sense of Islam and Islamic morality. Her intention is to call on the Algerian woman to reject an Islam that is fanatical and archaic because it allows promiscuity between sexes no more than it allows that a woman go where she wants without her tutor *(ouali)* keeping her from it, nor all sorts of other diabolical desires. But it becomes clear from the ideas that she propagates that she is a creature of Marxism, in the service of atheistic pretensions (. . .) and the name that she uses (Fadila Mrabet) is a borrowed name. As for the man, he is a writer, a novelist who has the habit of decorating his writing with his fantasies and his falsifications in order to attract more readers. But in reality, he is far from understanding Islam. He wrote in a weekly, printed and published in Algeria but French in its language and ideas. It rarely writes of religious events and then only to speak of its disdain for them. It has become insupportable to this writer to see minarets raised over mosques from which the voice of the muezzin calls those who believe in their God to prayer (. . .). The true believer, hearing the muezzin, is filled with humility, orders his thoughts which have wandered in the labyrinth of the matter of human life, remembers his Lord with deference and respect and makes himself accomplish that which has been imposed on him in his religion. This writer, expressing the hatred that the marks of Islam inspire in him, would like the minarets to be destroyed and leveled until no trace of them remains, and so that he won't have to suffer from seeing them, like the devil suffers when he hears the voice of the muezzins, and since they are the mark of Islam and there is no Islam in him. This writer calls himself Kateb Yacine and this weekly is called *Algérie Actualité*. There appeared an article in it entitled "the Dogs of Douar" (Dogs of the Camps) (. . .). Who are these dogs of Douar in his eyes? They are the muezzin who call the faithful to accomplish the duty of prayer (. . .). Added to this ironic headline are [pictures depicting] a minaret and two American rockets in the process of taking off from their launch pads. The caption says concerning the minaret: "A rocket that does not take off from its launch pad." The review that has this headline and these photos is sold in Algeria under the eyes of the authorities. It has not been banned or confiscated (. . .) the way foreign magazines containing photographs full of impudence and license have (. . .). For as such they don't touch politics and they meet no objections from the government, even if they mock religion and the beliefs of the Umma. To this atheistic writer and to the many like him, we say that the minaret is the sign of the mosque and that, in Islam, [it] is [not only] the place where God the creator is adored, but also a place of education, of culture, of teaching, but he undoubtedly ignores all that. How many great men have left the mosque, who illuminated the path of those who walked through the labyrinths of life, who guided them to the safeguard and salvation, such as Emir Abdel kader, the Sheikh Abdel Hamid ben Hadis, and others, whose equal the universities have not been able to produce.... (. . .). The rocket of Islam, this minaret which you mock, has destroyed the palaces of the unjust and overthrown the thrones of gigantic tyrants . . . if only you knew. . . . But where would you have learned, you who have been nursed on the milk of the adversaries of Islam?[1]

NOTE

1. *Al-Mazdaqia hia Asl al-Ichtirakia* (Mazdaqia is the Base of Socialism), Morocco: n.a., 1975, p. 33.

CHAPTER 32

WESTOXICATION

Jalal Al-i Ahmad

Jalal Al-i Ahmad. *Plagued by the West (Gharbzadegi)*. Translated from the Persian by Paul Sprachman Delmar. NY: Caravan Books Modern Persian Literature Series No. 4, 1982.

1. AN OUTLINE OF THE ILLNESS

I SPEAK OF BEING AFFLICTED WITH "WESTITIS" THE WAY I would speak of being afflicted with cholera. If this is not palatable let us say it is akin to being stricken by heat or by cold. But it is not that either. It is something more on the order of being attacked by tongue worm. Have you ever seen how wheat rots? From within. The husk remains whole, but it is only an empty shell like the discarded chrysalis of a butterfly hanging from a tree. In any case, we are dealing with a sickness, a disease imported from abroad, and developed in an environment receptive to it. Let us discover the characteristics of this illness and its cause or causes and, if possible, find a cure.

Being stricken by the West has two sides: one is the West and the other, we who are afflicted by West. "We" meaning a corner of the East. In place of two "sides" let us say two poles or two ends, since we are dealing in fact with two ends of a graduated scale or rather two opposite ends of the world. In place of the "West," we can say almost all of Europe and Soviet Russia and of North America. Or let us say all of the advanced or developed countries or industrialized countries or all of the countries which, with the aid of machines, are capable of converting raw materials into something more complex and marketing it in the form of manufactured goods. These raw materials are not just iron ore or oil or gut or cotton or tragacanth. They are also myths, principles of belief, music, and transcendental realities.

In place of "we" who are a part of the other pole, let us say Asia and Africa or the backward or developing or the nonindustrialized countries or all of the countries that are the users of Western manufactured products. The raw materials for these products—those which I enumerated—have been taken from this side of the world, i.e., from the developing countries! Oil from the shores of the Persian Gulf; jute and spices from India; jazz from Africa; silk and opium from China; anthropology from the islands of Oceania; sociology from Africa. The last two from South America as well—from the Aztecs and Incas who were the victims of the advent of Christianity. In any case, something from somewhere. We are caught in the middle of all this; however, we share more points of comparison with this last group than degrees of distinction and difference.

It is not in the scope of this essay to define these two poles, these two extremes, from the point of view of economics or politics or sociology or psychology or civilization. That is an exacting task, a task for the experts. But you will notice that occasionally, out of necessity, we will call upon a general knowledge of these different areas for help. The only thing that can be said here along these lines is that, in my view, "East" and "West" are not two geographical concepts. For an American or a European, "West" means Europe and America and "East" means Soviet Russia, China, and the eastern European countries. But for me, "West" and "East" have neither political nor geographical meaning. Instead they are two economic concepts. "West" means the well-fed countries and "East" means the hungry countries. For me the state of South Africa is a piece of the "West," even though it forms the southern tip of Africa. Most of the countries of Latin America are part of the "East," even though they are on the other side of the globe. In any event, although it is correct that the exact nature of an earthquake must be learned from a seismographer in a university, before anything can be recorded, a farmer's horse (even if he is not a thoroughbred) will have escaped the area and fled to the safety of the fields. With more awareness than a sheep dog, and with vision more farsighted than a crow's, I would like to see something that others, because their eyes are closed or because they see no advantage or profit for themselves in presenting it, have overlooked and decided not to see.

Let us define, therefore, the countries of the first group with the following general characteristics (arranged in no particular order): high wages, low mortality rate, low birth rates, well organized social services, sufficient food (at least 3000 calories per day), an average annual income of more than 3000 *tomans*,[1] all the trappings of democracy, and a liberal inheritance from the French revolution.

The countries of the second group have the following characteristics (presented in neat little rhetorical bundles): low wages, high mortality rates, an even higher birth rate, no social services or the pretense of social services, malnutrition (at most 1000 calories per day), an annual per capita income of less than 500 tomans, no inkling of democracy, and an inheritance going back to the very beginnings of colonialism.

It is obvious that we belong to this second group, to the group of hungry nations. The first group, to use the phrase of Josue de Castro in his book *The Geography of Hunger*,[2] comprises all the well-fed nations. You see that between these two extremes not only is there a huge gap, but also, in the words of Tibor Mende,[3] an unfillable chasm which grows deeper and wider day-by-day in such a way that wealth and poverty, power and impotence, knowledge and ignorance, prosperity and desolation, civilization and savagery have become global extremes. One pole belongs to the well-fed, the rich, the powerful, the producers and exporters of manufactured products; whereas the other pole is that of the hungry, the poor, the weak, and the consumers and importers. The pulse of progress beats on that side of the world of ascendance and the throb of decline on this side of a world petering out. The difference does not merely arise out of temporal or spatial dimensions, nor is it measurable in terms of quantity—it is a qualitative difference. The two poles are estranged from one another. They are inclined toward mutual remoteness. On that side is a world that is frightened of its own dynamism and on this side is our world, which has not yet been able to find a way to channel its undirected and therefore wasted energies. Both of these worlds are in motion, each in a different direction.

Now, with this way of looking at things, the time when we could divide the world into two "blocks" has passed—into the two blocks "East" and "West," either communist or noncommunist. Although the first article of the constitution of most of the world's countries is still the same old dodge of the twentieth century, the way in which America and Russia (the two supposedly unchallenged head croupiers of the two blocks) gambled with each other over the Suez canal issue and Cuba shows that the headmen of two neighboring villages can still easily manage to come to terms. And of course in the wake of that, consider the nuclear test ban treaty and the other cases of cooperation. Our age, therefore, in addition to not being one of confrontation between the rich and poor classes within national boundaries, nor one of national revolutions, is also not an age of confrontations between "isms" and ideologies. Behind every disturbance or every coup d'état or revolution in Zanzibar or Syria or Uruguay one must find the colonial company or state, secretly backing the conspiracy. The local wars of our age can no longer be defined as wars of differing ideologies, not even on the surface. These days every schoolchild knows that the Second World War was just a pretext for the spread and expansion of the mechanized industries of both sides; but also, even in the Cuban crisis, the Congo, the Suez Canal, or Algeria he sees the struggle for sugar, diamonds, and oil respectively. One can see in the bloodshed in Cyprus, Zanzibar, Aden, and Vietnam the struggle to gain a bridgehead to defend the avenues of trade, which are the primary factors in determining a state's policy.

Our age is no longer one in which people in the "West" can be made to fear "Communism" and people in the "East" made to fear the bourgeoisie and liberalism. Nowadays even kings can appear revolutionary on the surface and use suspicious, i.e., "leftist" [?] language, and Khrushchev can buy wheat from America. Today all of the "isms" and ideologies have become paths leading to the exalted throne of "mechanism" and mechanization. In this respect, the most interesting development is the deviation to the far east of the political compasses of leftists and quasi-leftists all over the world; i.e., the ninety degree turn away from Moscow toward Peking. Soviet Russia is no longer "the leader of world revolution," instead it is one of the leading competitors in the nuclear arms race. Direct telegraph communications have been set up between the Kremlin and the White House, a sign that even British mediation between the two powers is no longer necessary. Even the leaders of our country are aware that the danger of Soviet Russia has decreased. At one time, the Soviet Union was grazing on the meager pastures of desolation left in the wake of World War I. Now it is the era of de-Stalinization, and Radio Moscow has actually come out in support of the Referendum of the Sixth of Bahman![4] In any case, Communist China has taken the place of the Soviet Union, because like Russia in 1930 it calls upon all the world's hungry peoples to unite in the hope of reaching the heaven of tomorrow. The Soviet Union in those years had a population of a little over 100 million; whereas China now has 750 million people. Just as Marx pointed out about his age, we today have two worlds in a state of conflict. But these two worlds have attained dimensions much wider than those of his time, and the conflict has taken on more complexity than the conflict between worker and boss. Ours is a world of confrontation between rich and poor, extending over the entire globe. Our age is one of two worlds: one engaged in making, operating, and exporting machines; the other involved in consuming, wearing down, and importing them. The arena of that conflict is the world marketplace. Its weapons are in addition to tanks, artillery, bombers, and missile launchers, which themselves are the products of the Western world, UNESCO, FAO, the United Nations, ECAFE, and other so-called international agencies, all appearing to be communal and global. But, as a matter of fact, they are the same little Western dodges that, dressed in new clothes, are used in the colonization of South America, Asia, Africa. The basis of the "Westitis" of all these non-Western countries lies here. We are not talking about the abolition of machines or their rejection, i.e., what supporters of utopian societies in the beginning of the nineteenth century fancied. Never! The world is caught up in the machine of historical determinism. Our discussion, rather, is on the way we deal with machines and technology.

The point is that we of the developing nations—the people of the second group of countries I defined—are not makers of machines. But, forced by economics, politics, and that global confrontation between poverty and wealth, we must be polite and servile consumers of the products of Western industry, or at best we must be satisfied, subservient, and low-paid repairmen for whatever comes from the West. It is this last that necessitates that we reshape ourselves, our government, our culture, and our everyday lives into some semblance of a machine. Everything of ours must meet machine specifications. And if the makers of machines, after a gradual process of change of some 200 years, have slowly become used to this new god, its heaven and its hell, what about the Kuwaitis who only yesterday found access to machines, or the Congolese or we Iranians? In what manner can we bridge this 300-year historical gap? Let us forget about the others and concentrate on ourselves. The basic point of this book is that we have not been able to preserve our "cultural-historical" personality in the face of the machine and its unavoidable onslaught. Rather we have been crushed by events.[5] The point is that we have not been able to maintain a well-thought-out and considered position vis-à-vis this monster of the modern age. The fact is that until we have actually grasped the essence, basis, and philosophy of Western civilization and no longer superficially mimic the West in our consumption of Western products, we shall be just like the ass who wore a lion skin. And we know what happened to him. While the machine-makers of today are themselves complaining and suffering, we do not complain, not even now that we are dressed up like the machine's servants—we even try to look good in our new uniforms! In any case, it is now some 200 years that we are crows acting like partridges.[6] From all that we have outlined so far, one obvious fact emerges. As long as we are solely consumers, as long as we do not manufacture machines, we shall be afflicted with the West. And the ironic part is that as soon as we are able to make machines, we shall become machine-stricken! We will be like people of the West whose cries about self-willed technology and machines are heard everywhere.[7]

Let us admit that we did not even have the will to be like Japan, which came to grips with the machine some 100 years ago. From that time, it began to rival the West in its machine-mania. It defeated the Czar in 1905 and America in 1941,[8] and, even before that, was able to take away Western markets. In the end it was destroyed with the atomic bomb as an object lesson. Now, if the "free countries" of the West have opened up a corner of the world's marketplace to Japanese goods, it is because they have invested in every Japanese industry, and also because they intend to cover all of the military expenses of defending those islands whose leaders have, since World War II, come to their senses, i.e., in matters of weaponry, troops, and military alliances, they have become total know-nothings. Or perhaps the average American wants to ease his conscience about what caused the pilot of that hellish plane to go mad.[9] The story of 'Ad and Thamud[10] was repeated in Hiroshima and Nagasaki.

There is another obvious point here. The "West" began to call us (everyone from the eastern shores of the Mediterranean to India) "The East," as soon as it awoke from its medieval hibernation, and came in search of sun, spices, silk, and other goods. At first Westerners came in the guise of pilgrims, visiting the Christian holy places (Bethlehem, Nazareth, etc.), then as warriors in the Crusades, later as merchants sheltered by the guns of ships loaded with goods, then as Christian missionaries, and finally as missionaries of urbanization and civilization. This last mission seems to have been almost preordained; after all, the word este'mar ("colonization") is from the same root as the word 'omran ("building up, settling"), and if one wants to "settle" one has to be involved with "cities."

The interesting thing is that of all the places that were settled under the boots of colonial masters, Africa was the most receptive and most promising. Do you know why? Because in addition to the natural resources, which it had in abundance—gold, diamonds, copper, ivory, and many other natural resources—its natives never had a tradition of urban settlement, nor did they have a widespread unifying faith. Each tribe had its own god, chief, customs, and language. And how diffuse! And, as a result, how receptive to domination! More important than all of this, however, was that all the natives of Africa went around naked. Wearing clothes is impossible in that heat. When Stanley, the comparatively humane English traveler, returned with this last piece of good news from the Congo, there was jubilation and thanksgiving in Manchester. After all, each year three meters of cloth for every person (just one shirt which the women and men of the Congo would wear to become civilized, and participate in Church ceremonies) translated into about 320 million yards of cloth yearly from the mills of Manchester.[11] We know that the advance scouts of colonialism were Christian missionaries, and that beside every trading post all over the world a church was constructed. The natives would be lured into them with various ploys. Now, with the withdrawal of colonialism from these areas, for each colonial agency boarded up, a church also closed.

For the colonists, Africa was also more receptive and more promising because the natives themselves represented raw materials for every kind of Western laboratory. The principles of anthropology, sociology, ethnography, dialectology, and a thousand other "ologies" could be recorded based on fieldwork carried out in Africa and Australia. The professors at Cambridge, the Sorbonne, and Leiden, by using these same "ologies," could become established in their university chairs, and see the other side of the coin of their own urbanization in the primitive areas of Africa.

But as for us easterners of the Middle East, we were neither as receptive nor as promising as the Africans. Why? If we want to be more intimate, i.e., "keep the discussion between ourselves," I must ask, rather: why were we Muslim easterners not as receptive? You see that the answer is contained in the question. Apparently within the Islamic totality itself we were not considered a subject suitable for investigation. For the same reason, the West, in its dealing with us, not only struggled against this Islamic totality (in the case of the bloody instigation of Shi'ism of Safavid times, in the creation of friction between us and the Ottomans, in the promoting of Baha'i activities in the middle of the Qajar period, in the crushing of the Ottomans after World War I, and finally in the opposition to the Shi'ite clergy during the Constitutional Revolution and afterwards . . .), but it also tried, as quickly as possible, to tear apart that unity which was fragmented from within and which only appeared whole on the surface. They tried first to turn us into raw material, as they did the natives in Africa, and afterwards bring us to their laboratories. It was because of this that among the many encyclopedias produced in the West, the *Encyclopedia of Islam* is the most important. We are still asleep but the Westerner in this encyclopedia has brought us to his laboratory. India was almost the same as Africa, with its "confusion of tongues," and the diversity of its races and religions. Then again, South America was completely converted to Christianity under the swords of the Spanish, and Oceania was a collection of islands, i.e., the best geography for sowing division. It was our lot then to be the only ones, both in the guise and the reality of an Islamic totality, to stand in the way of the advance of European civilization (read: colonialism; Christianity), i.e., in the way of the drive to the market of Western industry. The stopping of Ottoman artilleries outside of the gates of Vienna in the nineteenth century was the end of a prolonged event that had begun in 732 in Spain (Andalus).[12] How can we view these 12 centuries of struggle and competition between East and West as anything but a struggle between Islam and Christianity? In any event—in the age we live in—I, the Asian remnant of that Islamic totality, shall be accepted by the civilized (!) nations of the West and the makers of machines just as much (to the same extent) as the African and Australian survivor of primitive culture or savagery, if I, like them, agree to be satisfied with life as a museum exhibit, satisfied with being only a thing, an object suitable for investigation in a museum or a laboratory. And nothing more. God help you if you tamper with this raw material! Today the issue is not whether they want the oil of Khuzestan or that of Qatar, or whether the diamonds of Katanga are cut or the chromite ore of Kerman is processed. It is, rather, that I, the Asian and African, must even preserve my literature, my culture, my music, my religion, and everything else I possess exactly as if they were freshly unearthed antiques, so that these civilized gentlemen can come, dig, take them away, and place them in museums and say, "Yes, here we have another primitive culture!"[13]

After these introductory remarks, allow me as an Easterner with one foot in tradition and eager to jump some 200 or 300 years into the future, forced to make up for all the backwardness and stagnation and anchored in that fragmented Islamic whole, allow me to define "Westitis" this way: a complex of circumstances that come about in the life, culture, civilization, and way of thinking of a people in one spot on the globe without any kind of supporting cultural context or historical continuity, or any evolving method of integration, coming about only as a result of the charity of machines. Having defined Westitis this way, it is clear that we are among those afflicted with the disease. Since the subject of this book relates in the first place to the geographical, linguistic, traditional, and religious environment of its author, it is even clearer that if we say that once we have machines, i.e., once we make our own machines, then there will be no need for their presents or their charity, nor, as a result, will there be a need for all those things that come before and along with them.

Westitis, therefore, is a characteristic of the age in our history in which we still have not mastered machines, and in which we do not know the secret of their organization and structure; in which we still have not become familiar with the basics of machines and with the new sciences and technology; though we, forced by the market place, economics, and the flow of oil, find ourselves buying and using machines.

How did this age come about? How is it that, while we were totally isolated from the development of the machine, others made and operated them and developed, and we, when we finally woke up, saw that every oil rig was a nail driven into our coffin? How did we become West-stricken?

IV. THE FIRST SIGNS OF DECAY

It was thus, that at the same time the Renaissance dawned in the West, the mania of a medieval inquisition reared its head and the cauldron of religious disputes and wars was stirred in the Middle East. We have seen how this part of the world was emptied of rich caravans, and for this reason was forced to crawl into impoverished isolation and pseudo-mysticism. Thus, in the words of Dr. Fardid, we began right where the West left off. As the West rose we fell; the West woke up during its industrial renascence, while we fell into a prolonged hibernation. Let us admit that we play the same kinds of ideological games in our present period of "enlightenment" that the West began in the eighteenth century. While we had our constitutional movement in the beginning of this century, Europe was gravitating toward socialism and the leading ideological currents in economics, politics, and culture.

Pick up and leaf through the travelers' accounts of all of those people who, throughout the Safavid period, came here as tourists, merchants, ambassadors, or military advisers (mostly Jesuit)[14] and see what encouraging and patient witnesses they were to the settlement of the tribes! How they welcomed the great slaughter carried out by Shah 'abbas or how they reveled in Sultan Hosayn's lack of spunk! It is exactly from that time onwards that we began to crave the praise of foreign spectators who were in fact the primary instructors of our military and our men of state, during these last 300 years. And all of their praises and bravos are like the fairy tales told to tired old night watchmen so that they will sleep while thieves are busy robbing their caravans.

These are the basic sources of the flood of Westitis. Unfortunately our ears are still tuned to the conniving cries and praise of the agents of foreign governments who, once every several years, come here in the guise of orientalists, ambassadors, or advisers, and turn out debilitating decrees confirming our courage and resolution. And we are the same people who, from the time of Anushirvan, had had delusions of grandeur and had become infatuated with polite formalities. It was as a result of this new type of tourism that foreigners became acquainted with our nature and habits and learned just how to keep us impoverished and how to make loans to us and, later, to take control of our customs houses. Or how to break the Safavid monopoly on silk with the competition of their own markets and later, after they had gotten a foothold here, how, by means of the Afghan tribes, to relieve themselves of the aged Safavid warrior who was beginning to frighten people as much as a scarecrow. Next it was Nader [Shah]'s turn. He blindly attacked India just at the time when the East India Company (that is, Western imperialism) was about to set up shop in the southern part of the continent and it became necessary for the court of Muhammad Shah in northern India to be kept busy. The affair of Turkomanchay[15] (1243 A.H./1828 C.E.) which was the last roar of this ambushed paper tiger followed Nader's destruction. Then came the saga of Herat Wars (1273 A.H./1857 C.E.), the coup de grace of which was the siege of Bushire. This is how they finally threw the corpse of this warrior to the ground. In the last 50 or 60 years oil showed up on our horizon and we again found something to justify our existence. As a direct result of our recent quiescent history, the fate of our politics, economy, and culture went directly into the hands of the companies and Western nations that backed them. From the time of the Constitutional Revolution our clergy, who were the last line of defense against the foreign onslaught, had retreated so deeply into their shells in the face of the preliminary wave of mechanization and had shut out the outside world to such an extent and had woven cocoons around themselves so well, that only the Day of Judgment could rouse them. They kept on retreating, step by step.

The hanging of the spiritual leader who favored "the rule of the *Shari'at*" in the Constitutional movement was in itself an indication of this retreat.[16] I agree with Dr. Tondar Kiya who wrote that Shaikh Nuri was not hanged as an opponent of the Constitutional movement (for in the beginning he was in fact a defender of it), but as a proponent of "the rule of the *Shariat*"[17] and, I will add, as a defender of the integrity of Shi'ism. It was for this reason that in the wake of his death everyone was waiting for a writ to be issued from Najaf. And this was going on at a time when the leader of our West-stricken intelligentsia, Malkom Khan,[18] was a Christian and Talebof[19] was a social democrat from the Caucasus. In any case, from that day on we were marked with the brand of Westitis. I consider the corpse of that great man [Nuri], hanging from the gallows, to be a banner bearing the emblem of the final victory of Westitis over this country after 200 years of struggle.

Today we stand under that banner, a people alienated from themselves; in our clothing, shelter, food, literature, and press. And more dangerous than all, in our culture. We educate pseudo-Westerners and we try to find solutions to every problem like pseudo-Westerners.[20]

If, at the onset of the Constitutional Period, the danger was imminent, it has now become part of our very beings. From the villager who escaped to the city and would not return to his village because his local, itinerant barber does not have the right kind of shampoo or the village is without a cinema or he cannot buy a sandwich there—to the cabinet minister who is sensitive to dirt and grime and therefore travels 12 months out of the year to every corner of the world. And why have things reached such a state? Because the two or three generations of Iranians who came after the events of the Constitutional Period have now entered the limelight and have become teachers, cabinet ministers, lawyers, director generals, and, except for the doctors, not one of them is skilled in any trade at all. All of them, even if they were not completely relying on the foppish antics of their youth, which they spent in Paris and London and Berlin, were, at least, only harkening to the three epistles of Agha Khan Kermani[21] addressed to Jalal al-Dawla and to the other types of Westitis at the beginning of the Constitutional Period by Malkom Khan, Talebof, and others.[22] As far as I call tell these Iranian "Montesquicus" had their own solutions to the problem. Although they all probably agreed on this one point, and willy-nilly realized that the basic structure of our society and traditions would not be able to withstand the unavoidable onslaught of the machine and technology, they all accepted the wrong notion of "adopting Western civilization without Iranian modification."[23] Yet beyond this general, unsubstantiated formula, each one, in order to find a cure for the disease, followed a different path. One group offered his services to foreign embassies as sources of cultural nourishment. Another, trying to imitate the West, felt that a new Lutheranism was in order and that the old faith could gain new life through religious reform. The third called for Islamic unity at a time when the Ottomans were disgracing themselves before the world with their massacres of Armenians and Kurds. (You will pardon my discretion here; this is not the place for complete candor.)

At the outset of the Constitutional Period, the basic defect in the actions of our leaders (both those for and against the movement) was the fact that Islam, i.e., the rule of the *Shari'at*, still provided the comprehensive totality that could act as a protector or a dam against the influence of machines and the West. It was for this reason that some rose up to defend religion and others attacked it. For the same reason "Constitutional Law" and "the rule of the *Shari'at*" came to represent the two contrary notions of "religion" and "irreligion." I feel therefore that these men all approached the problem from the wrong end. Although, had we been living in those times, we would probably have repeated the idiocies of the two factions and would not be around today to judge them so harshly. Those men, after all, lived closer to the time when Mirza Bozorg Shirazi could, with a simple writ, seal the fate of the British tobacco concession and demonstrate how much of a power base and a threat the clergy was. At the beginning of the Constitutional Movement, in any case, all of those fine men were unaware that years before in Europe the god Knowhow had taken its lofty seat above the stock exchanges and banks. It had proclaimed its sovereignty and would never tolerate another God. It merely laughed at all the world's customs and ideologies. This then was the way that the Constitutional Movement, as the advance guard of mechanization, destroyed the clergy. Thereafter theological schools were (in the 20-year period) banished to one or two cities in the country. The clergy's influence on the workings of the judicial system and in parish record-keeping, was diminished, and wearing ecclesiastic robes was forbidden. The clergy, on the other hand, in the face of all this pressure not only remained silent, but continued to be wrapped up in the petty details of prayer, or the problems of ritual purity or continued to be paralyzed by nagging doubts: Did they perform the right number of prostrations or not? The only thing they accomplished was to proscribe radio and television, which had found such a wide audience that nothing could stand in their way. In fact they could have and should have been trying to arm themselves with their enemies' weapons and from their own transmitters in Qom and Mashhad (Vatican-style) challenge the Westitis of the official and semi-official media. Confidentially, if the clergy had known what a gold mine of revolutionary opposition to the rule of the "tyrannous and unrighteous" they kept alive in people with the principle "no constraint to obey those in authority"; if they were able to show the true nature of "those in authority" to the people with the media (newspapers, radio, television, film, etc.) and specifically document their general charges; and if they were able, through contact with international councils of clergy, to give their cause a certain amount of dynamism, then they would never have been so preoccupied with petty details. This only resulted in their being totally uninformed and their remaining on the sidelines of political life.[24] Let me go on. Allow me to mention, for example, the role that just one oil company has played in our politics and society during the last 60 years and then abandon these historical discussions.

The oil concession was given in the first year of the twentieth century by the Qajar king to William Knox D'Arcy, who later sold his rights to the famous company. We were embroiled in the Constitutional Revolution from 1906 on! And where was the territory covered by the contract? The southwestern foothills of the Baklitiyari mountains. The remains of the first oil well can still be found in Masjed-e Solayman. It was necessary to keep the southwestern edge of the Bakhtiyari Mountains clear of the winter migrations of the Bakhtiyari tribe, so that they could drill the first oil well easily and dig into the mountains and plains of Masjed-e Solayman. This caused the Bakhtiyari tribe[25] to move so that they, with the help of freedom fighters from Tabriz and Rasht, could march on Tehran. And if our Constitutional Revolution is half-baked, it is because the "khans" rose up in support of a revolutionary movement which in essence undermines the rule of khans. We were thus embroiled in the issues of the constitution and tyranny until World War I broke out. But meanwhile, the company had reached its oil, and the British Admiralty, which became the official concessionaire, was now assured of an oil supply. You see that I am not writing history, I am extrapolating from it; and very hastily too. You will have to look up the actual events in the history books yourself.

Later, around the year 1300 (1920 C.E.), the war had ended and the owners of the company were now the victors and the engines of war had run out of steam. Consequently, the international consumption of oil was down, and the company was forced to find customers locally. It became necessary for a strong central government to be in power to make the roads safe and clear of impediments so that the oil trucks could travel easily to Quchan, Khoy, and Makran. In every little hamlet, a gas station had to be built. And more important than these developments was the fact that, since the concessionaire was now the British Admiralty, there was no tolerance for internal disputes and for bargaining with the khans, the parliament, and the press; it only wanted to deal with one man. Hence we had the coup d'état of 1299 [1920 C.E.], military government followed by dictatorship, the forced settlement of the Kurds, the suppression of "Semitqu"[26] and the elimination of Shaikh Khaz'al who, had he behaved a bit more intelligently, could have become like one of the Shaikhs of the Persian Gulf Emirates.

In 1311 (1932 C.E.), the D'Arcy concession was more than half over and was slowly starting to run out. The principal concessionaire, the British Admiralty (i.e., the British government) had to use the existing centralized power, where one man spoke for everything from the parliament and the cabinet to the army and the gendarmerie, in order to renew the concession while the iron was hot. Taqizada[27] once again assumed his role as a "puppet" and the parliament went through the charade of first voting to cancel the D'Arcy concession and them moving to reinstate it. They did this with such fanfare that even the elders of the nation did not suspect that there was something going on. Or if they did suspect, they did not say anything about it. For we did not see any of them even lamenting what was happening and thereby removing the stain of history's condemnation from their records. Except afterwards, after matters settled down and in the years following the Shahrivar of 1941 when every ass of a person was called to account. Of course such an ugly truth had to be decorated with camouflage in style with the times. That means the reality had to be covered up. How? By threatening people with beatings, they forced them to dress the same, removing the pressed felt hats from the men and the veils from the women. This was done in the name of the latest development in civilization! They constructed a nationwide rail network, not with oil revenues but with revenues from the tax on sugar! What is more, the biggest reason for his railway was to get help behind the Stalingrad front during World War II.

Then came the year 1320 (1941 C.E.) and Europe was again at war. There was the danger of Rashid 'Ali Gilani[28] and the government's flirtation with the Axis powers as it tried to demonstrate maturity, but actually succeeded in betraying its senility. After all, even if they cannot stand each other, cows kept in the same barn eventually begin to smell alike. Of course this is no longer a laughing matter. We have all seen what kind of situation came next. All of the authority, majesty, military power, the security forces, and gendarmerie [of Reza Shah] fell apart one day. Of course, if Napoleon was satisfied with being exiled on Sainte-Helene, it is obvious that an Iranian emperor could put up with the Mauritius. After the Allies, it was America's turn; America, which long before World War I had sprung to life and was "compelled" to have its gunboats refuel in the Persian Gulf. If you were in their place would you pay for fueling ships involved in the victory over Fascism (i.e., the salvation of Russia and England) with dollars out of your own pockets? Paid to British Petroleum at that! The context for American intervention in the matter of the southern oil fields comes into being right here; especially in the Azerbaijan affair. It was American political clout that eventually prodded the United Nations into action and forced the Soviet Russians to evacuate. Inevitably there was unrest again, cries for liberty, and talk of a northern oil concession as well. In a way, these were scarecrows, guarding fiefs that the British did not want to hand over to America. And this brief liberty lasted until 1329 (1954 C.E.).

This is what is called cooperation in politics and economics, i.e., following the directives of the oil companies and the Western countries. This is the ultimate symptom of Westitis in our time. In this way Western industry plunders us, rules us, and determines our fate. It is obvious that when national economic and political autonomy is given to foreign companies they determine what to sell and what not to sell. Of course the best thing for these companies, which want to be permanent sellers of their goods, is to make sure that consumers are never able to do without them. God keep the oil flowing! They get the oil and, in return, they give you whatever you desire, from pigeon's milk to human souls—even wheat. This mandatory exchange of goods occurs also on a cultural level in language and literature. Pick up and thumb through any of our so-called serious literary journals. Where is there anything about this part of the world? Or about the East as a whole? About India or Japan or China? They are all filled with reports about the Nobel prizes, about the Papal elections, about Françoise Sagan, the Cannes film prizes, the latest Broadway play, and the newest film from Hollywood. As for the illustrated weeklies, what can I say? And if this is not Westitis, what is it?

NOTES

1.   In the mid-1950s, worth about $370.00.
2.   Boston: Little, Brown and Company, 1952.
3.   Tibor Mende, *Reflexions sur l'histoire d'aujourd'hui: Entre le peur et l'espoir.* Paris: Editions du Seuil, 1958. The author is paraphrasing material from this book.
4.   January 27, 1964, known as the "Day of the Revolution of the Shah and the People," when, according to government figures, 5,598,711 people voted for the six principles of the White Revolution.
5.   I have illustrated this very issue in *Jazira-ye kharg* (Tehran: Danesh, 1960).
6.   If we take for granted the identity of crows and partridges.
7.   For example see *La France contre les robots* by George Bernanos (Paris: Plon, 1970).
8.   This is not exactly accurate, even though Japan initially caused great damage to the American navy.
9.   The name of the pilot was Claude R. Eatherly. See the book *Avoir detruit Hiroshima,* ed. Robert Laffort (Paris). Claude R. Eatherly was not the pilot of the Enola Gay, he was the pilot of the advance plane, the Straight Flush.
10. The pre-Islamic Arabian tribes all traces of which were wiped out.
11. *Du Zambeze au Tanganika, 1858–1872: par Livingstone et Stanley*, Paris, 1958.
12. I am referring to the defeat of 'abd al-Rahman Omavi (the head of the Caliphate of Andalus) at the hands of Charles Martel, the French commander, at Poitiers and to

the halt of the expansion of the Western Islamic caliphate. Note that "Martel" is today the name of a well-known cognac.

13. My respected friend Thaminra Baghchaban, the music scholar, writes the following in unpublished notes on the Tehran Congress of Music in January 1961: For D. L. (the French delegate) there would be nothing more fascinating than if we Iranians were living in the age of the Sassanian kings and were the proper subjects of study for him. He would then come from the heart of the twentieth century with sensitive instruments and latest in tape recordings to the Sassanian court to record the performances of minstrels like Barbad and Nakisa and would return directly to Paris on an Air France jet from the airport near the Sassanian capital constructed especially for orientalists and authorities on poetry and music.

14. Their names are listed in a tumar (document), and the best source for information on all of them is *Zendagi-e Shah 'abbas* [The Life of Shah 'abbas] by Nasrallah Falsafi which was published in three volumes. The interesting thing is that the primary and biggest sources of Orientalist knowledge are these same travelers accounts and most orientalists were themselves the disciples of the narrators of these accounts! Read Falsafi's book and you will know what I am talking about.

15. This treaty ended a war with Russia which started when Iran attacked Russian possessions in Transcaucasia. As part of the Treaty of Turkomanchay, Russia secured part of Armenia and Iran recognized Russia's exclusive right to have a navy on the Caspian Sea and granted Russia commercial concessions.

16. Al-e Ahmad is referring to Shaikh Fazlallah Nuri (hanged July 31, 1909). According to E. G. Browne (*Persian Revolution*, Cambridge, 1966, p. 148), Shaikh Nuri denounced the constitutionalists as "atheists, free thinkers, Babis, etc." His opposition was responsible for stirring up reactionary mobs against attempts at constitutional reform.

17. I am quoting freely from the *Biography of Shaikh Nuri* by Tondar Kiya. See the introduction to the latest issue of *Shahin* (Tehran, 1335), pp. 319–21.

18. Mirza Malkom Khan was an opponent of the Qajar king Naser al-Din Shah and oversaw the publication of an anti-Qajar newspaper *Qanun* (Law) while in exile in London. Some writers contend that Malkom Khan's close ties with the British and his religion (Armenian Christian) make his calls for local reform seem suspect.

19. Mirza 'abd al-Rahim Talebof Tabrizi was educated in Tiflis and was one of the first Iranian writers to use a simplified literary Persian in translations and original works. He was a prolific antimonarchist who called for constitutional government in Iran in many of his writings.

20. See the article "Taskhir-e tamaddon-e Farhangi" [The Domination of Foreign Civilization] by Sayyed Fakhr al-Din Shadman (Tehran, 1326). The author is a far better writer than I and, years before the writing of these pages, tried to find a cure for "Westernization" [fokoli-mabi, lit., "being like the faux col wearers"]. He suggested a serious education in our mother tongue and the translation of philosophical, scientific, and literary works of the West. Even though he was well-acquainted with the disease, his prescription proved ineffective, because thousands of foreign books have been translated from that time until now, and we have read each one of these as a mine of Western information, but [the fact that] we still grow more like "faux col wearing" [people] or as I call [them, "prisses"], is itself a clear symptom of a larger ailment, which is West-strickenness. Perhaps the person who, before all others, pointed the way to the basic cause of the problem was Dr. Muhammad Baqer Hushyar who, although known as a Baha'i, in 1327 [1948] wrote the following: Through a crack in the door, you have seen how all Europeans are literate, but you do not see

how well-entrenched their traditional culture is, and you do not know that their entire educational establishment from the primary grades to the university is based on the Church. You have by means of the Western intelligentsia and in your overzealousness destroyed this foundation in your own country. From the article "Amuzesh-e hamagani va rayegan" [Free Public Education] in *Amuzesh va Parvaresh* (Tehran, 1327).

21.   Mirza Aqa Khan Kerman is known as a liberal reformer who was active in the last part of the reign of Naser al-Din Shah (ruled 1848—96). It is also known that he openly doubted the usefulness of the clergy in a constitutional revolution. The text reads "seh maktub," "three letters of Kermani" instead of "epistles."

22.   Read the treatises *Eslam, Akhond va Hatef al-Gheyb, Haftad o do Mellat, Resaleye yak kalma, Siyasat Talebi,* and *Siyahatnama-ye Ebrahim Baeg,* as well as most of the [works of] missionaries of Westernism and destroyers of superstition in the name of religion. In my opinion, they were the ones who smoothed the way for Westitis. [Jalal al-Dawla was a Qajar prince who opposed the monarchy during the first part of this century.]

23.   These are the very words of Malkom Khan from his collected works edited by Molut Tabataba'i (Tehran, 1327). See also *Fikr-e Azadi* [The Idea of Freedom] by Feridun Adanuvat (Tehran, 1340) in which he, with that special skill of his, condemns one group of Freemasons and exonerates another. In my opinion, the Freemasons are all cut from the same cloth.

24.   In the interval between the first and second printing of this volume, a book was published with the title, *Marja'iyat va rawhaniyyat* [Religious Authority and the Clergy] (Tehran, 1341). It contains all the accustomed verbosity of the clergy, but it also reveals a relatively good appreciation of these problems and responsibilities and of possible solutions. See especially the articles of M. Bazargan, professor at the University, and Sayyed Mahmud Talaqani, the Imam of the Hedayat Mosque, both of whom proposed, in place of one source of religious authority, a kind of holy writ-issuing council. And if we accept that his volume with all of its faults was a kind of presager of the events of the 15th of Khordad 1342 [the bloody Moharram riots of the summer of 1963], I can now, one year later, find the boldness to inform the leaders of the religious establishment that:

A.   If the clergy continued to ignore their own principles (one of which I mentioned);
B.   If they remain satisfied with the minutiae of religious life, proscribing this or that tiling or person; and
C.   If they continue to forget that Shi'ism with its principles of ijtehad [application of judgment in religious matters] and issuing writs is much better able to deal with new developments than Sunnism (in spite of the fact that the writ concerning women's freedom was issued by Shaikh Muhammad Shaltut, the head of al-Azhar, not Shi'ite divines)—in any case if the clergy, taking into account the conditions of the time, cannot break out of those early Constitutional Period cocoons, we have no choice but to accept the fact that this last barricade against West-strickenness has lost its vitality and turned into some fossilized remain which belongs in a museum, or, at best, has become the last refuge of the country's reactionary forces.

25.   Remember that among the stockholders in the British Petroleum Company were the chief, Asa'd Bakhtiyari, as well as Moshir al-Dawla (Nasrallah Khan). And if they rubbed out this Sardar Asa'd in the time of Reza Shah, do you not think that he, like

Shaikh Khaz'al who had territorial claims in Khuzestan, had claims in the oil-rich winter grounds of the Bakhtiyaris and was causing problems for the government? Again it is just like the case of the Hayat Davudis [a people living on the Persian Gulf] who had claims on Kharg Island and were executed because of this. To find out more about these matters see *Talaye Siah ya bala-ye Iran* [Black Gold or the Bane of Iran] by Abu al-Fazl Lesani.

26. Esma'il Semitqu was the leader of a group of Kurds who rebelled in western Azerbaijan, and was killed by government forces in 1929.

27. Sayyed Hasan Taqizada, a noted scholar, was the first member of the constitutional assembly from Tabirz. After Reza Shah's abdication, he became Iran's ambassador to England.

28. In 1941 Rashid 'Ali (Gilani) was the pro-German leader of an independent government in Kordestan. He was later exiled.

CHAPTER 33

A MORALIZING
FUNDAMENTALISM

Abd al-Latif Sultani

Abdel Latif Sultani. "A Moralizing Fundamentalism, Women." *Al-Mazdaqia hia asl al-ichtirakia* (Masdaqia is the Source of Socialism), Morocco, 1975, quoted in Francois Burgat and William Dowell, *The Islamic Movement in North Africa.* Austin, Texas: Center for Middle Eastern Studies, University of Texas at Austin, 1997, pp. 251–2.

WOMEN

THE SAME HARMFUL EFFECTS THAT WERE PRODUCED BY the Mazdak sect in Persian society (licentiousness, usurpation, injustice, etc. . . .) are reproduced [in the modern age] by socialism and Communism in the countries that are afflicted by them. Injustice and debauchery in all forms are common there. Liberties that call on the good and fight against evil are smothered there, while those who want to do evil or aid it are given complete freedom. Abandoned children are legion, the result of this promiscuity between the sexes instituted under the cover of progressivism, of liberation and emancipation, etc. . . . King Choroes I the Great (Sassanid Emperor of the fourteenth century before Jesus Christ) summed up the results: "The most vile species mixed with the most honorable elements. The low people, who did not have the audacity to reveal themselves before, had access to the most precious women. . . ."

[The same today], women go out in the streets with the finery that has been given them, to meet whoever seems good to them, to speak with whom they want, to work in offices or elsewhere. But it is there that the evil and corruption of society hides. It is not just the wives and daughters of rich people and the ulema and men of religion who have begun working in business and offices, who thanks to that which God has given to their fathers and husbands have no reason to work, if it is not for love of gain, financial or other; and the woman or the young girl who does not work in an office has become like death. Honor, spirit of chivalry, chastity, modesty, all that has vanished, and the commandments belong to God in the first and last resort.

Several newspapers have given to those who defend Islam and its morality a qualification—Tartuffe, in reference to a play by Moliére—which does not correspond to reality. The reason for it is that in my Friday sermon on November 5, 1965, I evoked the military parade organized in Algiers on November 1 in commemoration of the revolution of 1954. In this parade, which we saw on television, we had not rejected the force of our army. What we denounced, in contrast, and what we insist not be produced again, is that young women dressed in a scandalous fashion were inserted into the middle of the parade. Only a small part of their bodies was covered. In effect, the young woman who represented each of these countries and appeared in front of the troops wore a miniskirt! That cannot be accepted or allowed to pass in silence. Who should be blamed for it? The one who denounces the inadmissible? No, all the blame should go before any other consideration to the one who brought that young woman here to throw her into this enormous army of young men and in front of the spectators. Her father, who accepted the showing of the body of his daughter and letting her march nearly nude in front of the spectators and cameramen working for foreign television, is just as much to blame. The truth is that certain Muslim governments, because of the lack of a sufficient Islamic religious education, are not up to the level of their Umma.

CHAPTER 34

ON THE ISLAMIC HIJAB

Murtaza Mutahhari

Murtaza Mutahhari. *On the Islamic Hijab*, translated by Laleh Bakhtiar. Tehran: Islamic Propagation Organization, 1987, pp. 47–64.

THE ISLAMIC HIJAB—PART I
THE HIJAB BRINGS DIGNITY TO A WOMAN

THERE IS ONE ISSUE THAT REMAINS TO BE DISCUSSED. It is one of the criticisms they have made against the *hijab*, which says that the *hijab* deprives the honor and respect of a woman. You know that human dignity has become one of the important goals of humanity since the words about human rights have developed. Human dignity is respected and it must be followed; all human beings share in this whether man or woman, black or white, or whatever nation or creed. Every individual has this right of human dignity.

They say that the Islamic *hijab* opposes a woman's dignity. We accept the right of human dignity. The discussion is whether or not the *hijab*, i.e., the *hijab* that Islamic precepts mention, is disrespectful to women, an insult to her dignity. This idea came into being from the idea that the *hijab* imprisons a woman, making her a slave. Enslavement opposes human dignity. They say because the *hijab* was introduced by men to enable them to exploit women, men wanted to captivate woman and imprison her in a corner of her home, thus, it is to have overlooked or insulted her human dignity. The respect, honor, and nobility of a woman call for not having a *hijab*.

As we have said and we will further describe later, that is, we will deduce from the verses of the Holy Quran that we have nothing that would serve to imprison a woman and the necessities of the Islamic *hijab* are not to imprison a woman. If a man has duties in his relation to a woman or a woman has duties in relation to a man, the duty is in order to strengthen and solidify the family unit. That is, it has a clear purpose. In addition, from the social point of view, it has necessities. That is, the well-being of society demands that a man and a woman commit themselves to a special kind of association with each other or the ethical sanctities and ethical balance and the tranquillity of the spirit of society, demand that a man and a woman choose a special way of relating to each other. This is called neither imprisonment nor enslavement nor does it oppose human dignity.

As we observe if a man leaves his house naked, he is blamed and reproached and perhaps the police will arrest him. That is, even if a man leaves his house with *pajamas* on, or with just underpants, everyone will stop him because it opposes social dignity. Law or custom rules that when a man leaves his house, he should be covered and fully dressed. Does this oppose human dignity to tell him to cover himself when he leaves the house?

On the other hand, if a woman leaves her house covered within the limits that we will later mention, it causes greater respect for her. That is, it prevents the interference of men who lack morality and ethics. If a woman leaves her house covered, not only does it not detract from her human dignity, but it adds to it. Take a woman who leaves her home with only her face and two hands showing and from her behavior and the clothes she wears there is nothing which would cause others to be stimulated or attracted toward her. That is, she does not invite men to herself. She does not wear clothes that speak out or walk in a way to draw attention to herself or does not speak in such a way as to attract attention.

Sometimes the clothes of an individual speak. His or her shoes speak. The way she or he talks says something else. Take a man, for instance, who speaks in such a way so as to say, "Fear me," or dresses in such a way opposite to that which is customary. That is to say a traditional cloak, a beard and a turban, etc., communicates to the people, "Respect me."

It is possible that a woman may wear clothes in such a manner that a human being, a respected human being, could freely associate with other people. It is also possible that she may wear certain clothes and walk in a way that stimulates, that says, "Come and follow me." Does the dignity of a woman, the dignity of a man, or the dignity of society not cause a woman to leave her home serious, diligent, and simply dressed in the manner that does not draw the attention of everyone she passes by?

She should be such that she does not distract a man and turn his attention from what he is doing. Does this oppose a woman's dignity? Or does it oppose the dignity of society? If a person says something, which existed in non-Islamic societies, that the *hijab* was to imprison women, that a woman must be placed in a locked house and she should have no right of association outside the home, this does not relate to Islam. If Islamic precepts were to say that a woman is not permitted to leave her house; if we were to ask whether it is possible for a woman to buy something from a store where the seller is a man and they said no, it was forbidden; if a person asked, "Is a woman permitted to participate in meetings, religious gatherings?" and we were to say no, it is not permitted; is it possible for women to meet each other?; if someone were to say all of these were forbidden, that a woman must sit in a corner of the house and never leave her home, this would be something, but Islam does not state this.

Our beliefs are based on two things. One is based upon that which is good for the family. That is, a woman must not do anything that would disturb her family situation. For a woman to leave her house to go to her sister's house if her sister is a corrupt and licentious person or even to visit her mother wherein the effects of the visit bring chaos to the house for a week, they say no to such circumstances. The family must not be disturbed.

The second basis is that leaving the house, according to the Holy Quran, must not be in order to flaunt oneself, to disturb peace and tranquillity of others, or to prevent the work of others. If it is not with the intent to do these things, there is no problem.

THE COMMAND TO ANNOUNCE YOUR ENTRANCE TO SOMEONE'S HOUSE

Now we will discuss the relevant Quranic verses and after we clarify what traditional commentators have explained about the verses, things will be made clearer with the help of traditions that have been narrated on this topic and the edicts of the religious jurisprudents made on this issue. The verses relating to the *hijab* are found in *Surah Nur* and *Surah Ahzab*. We will mention all of them.

We will begin our discussion with the verses from *Surah Nur*. Of course the verses that relate directly to the *hijab* are verses 30 and 31 of *Surah Nur* but there are three verses before this which are more or less introductory to the *hijab* and relate to this issue.

"*O believers, do not enter houses other than your houses until you first ask leave and salute the people thereof; that is better for you; haply you will remember*" (24:26).[1] This verse describes the duty of a man who is not *mahram*, to the house of another person, that is, the house of a person whose wife is not *mahram* to him. Of course, there are rules regarding those who are *mahram* and we will mention them later. Also there are some places where it is not particular to those who are *mahram*. It relates to how a person who wants to enter the house of another should do so.

To begin with, let me say that during the Age of Ignorance before the Holy Quran was revealed, the present situation of houses did not exist with locks, etc. Doors are closed basically because of the fear of thieves. If someone wants to enter, he rings the doorbell or uses the knocker. In the Age of Ignorance this situation did not exist. It was more like the situation in villages. People like myself who lived in the village know that there were basically no doors shut. The doors to the courtyard are always open. In many places it is not even the practice to lock the doors at night. In Fariman, a village near Tehran where I lived, I do not remember the door to the yard being closed even once and there was very little theft.

History shows that, particularly in Makkah, they often did not even put doors on a house. In Islam a law was passed that a person may never own the houses of Makkah. Of course, there is a difference of opinion among the religious jurisprudents. The Imams and the Shafe'ites agree that in Makkah, the land cannot belong to any one person. That is, it belongs to all Muslims and the land of Makkah cannot be bought and sold. The houses belong to all the people. It has the ruling of a mosque. In *Surah Hajj* it says that the people who live there and the people who come from outside that area are all the same.

The rents that people collect today in Makkah are in accordance with neither the Shi'ite jurisprudence nor with much of the jurisprudence of Sunnis. It must have an international ruling. They have no right to establish limits there and not allow a person to enter. It is like the room in a mosque, someone may have a room there. It belongs to him, but he has no right to prevent others from entering. The person has no right to close off an empty room. Of course, if a person is using it, he has priority. The first person who gave the order for doors to be placed on the houses was *Muawiyah*. This had previously been forbidden to be done to the houses of Makkah. This was the general situation.

It was not the custom among Arabs in the Age of Ignorance to announce that they wanted permission to enter. They felt it was an insult to seek permission to enter. The Holy Quran says in another verse, if you go and seek permission and it is not granted, return. This may be considered to be an insult by some but this emphasis in the Holy Quran is one of the introductory aspects of the *hijab* because every woman in her own home is in a situation that she does not want to be seen or she does not want to see a person. A verse was revealed. *"And when you ask his wives for something, ask them from behind a curtain (hijab)"* (33:54).[2]

Thus, a person must first seek permission to enter and then in agreement with the owner, the person enters—even if the other party knows that he wants to enter. The Holy Prophet said: "In order to announce your entrance, recall God's name in a loud voice. I later realized the words *'ya Allah'* that Muslims say, for instance, to enter, is the implementation of this command.

Thus, announce and how much better it is when this announcement is made by the recitation of God's name. The Holy Prophet continuously did this and he was asked, "Is this a general ruling that we should use when we enter our sister's house, our daughter's house, our mother's house?" He said, "If your mother is getting undressed, would she want you to see her then?" They said, "No." He said, "Then this same ruling holds for one's mother's house. Do not enter without announcing your entrance."

When the Holy Prophet would enter, he would stand behind the door of the room in a place where they could hear his voice and would call out, *"Assalamo alaikum ya ahlal bait."* He said, "If you hear no answer, perhaps the person did not hear you. Repeat it again in a loud voice. Repeat for a third time if you receive no response. If, after the third time that you announce yourself, you hear no response, either that person is not home or the person does not want you to enter; Return." The Holy Prophet did this and many stories have been narrated about this, such as when he wanted to enter his daughter's house, he would call out salutations in a loud voice. If she responded, he would enter. If he called out three times and received no response, he would return.

There is something here to note which is the difference between *dar* and *bait* in Arabic. *Dar* is that which we call the courtyard, and they call a room *bait*. The Holy Quran refers to *bait*, that is, when you want to enter the room of a person. Since the doors to the courtyards were open, the courtyard clearly did not assume an area of privacy. That is, if a woman was dressed in such a way that she did not want anyone to see her, she would not be so dressed in the courtyard. She would go into a room. The courtyard has the ruling of a room. The door is closed and it normally has high walls. Women still consider the courtyard to be, to a certain extent, a place of privacy. Now *dar* has the ruling of *bait* because *bait* basically means the place of privacy where a woman does not want a strange person to see her.

"This is purer for you." That is, the commands We give are better for you, contain goodness, are not illogical. "Know that this is good."

"And if you do not find anyone therein, enter it not until leave is given to you and if you are told "return." That is purer for you; and God knows the things you do" (24:27). *"There is no fault in you that you enter uninhabited houses wherein enjoyment is for you. God knows what you reveal and what you hide "* (24:28).[3] This was very difficult for the Arabs to understand. To seek permission when they wanted to enter a house was itself difficult and then to be told to return and to return was next to impossible. It was an insult.

In the verse, *"there is no fault in you . . ."* an exception arises. Does this ruling apply whenever one wants to enter any or only a person's residence. The Holy Quran says this is not a general ruling and only applies to someone's home.

A home is a place of privacy, the place of one's private life but if it was not, there would be need to seek permission. If there is, for instance, a *caravanserai* and you have business, do you have to seek permission, etc. No. Here it is not necessary to enter by seeking permission. What about a public bath. There is no need here. "There is no fault in you . . ." if it is not a place of residence in which you have business. "God knows what you reveal and what you hide."

From the word "uninhabited" one can understand that the philosophy of why a person cannot enter the home of another without announcing it first is because of the wife as well as the fact that the home is the place of one's privacy. Perhaps there are things that one does not want someone else to see.

Thus, when a person enters the privacy of another's home, the entrance must be announced. A person must, in some way, announce that he wants to enter even if the person knows that the other has allowed him to enter. He is your friend. He knows that you are going to enter. You know that he is totally in agreement with your entering. Still, you should realize that you are entering upon his privacy.

THE COMMAND TO "CAST DOWN THEIR LOOK"

Say to the believing men that they cast down their look and guard their private parts; that is purer for them. God is aware of the things they do. (24:30) [4]

Say to the believing women that they cast down their look and guard their private parts and reveal not their adornment except such as is outward and let them cast their veils (khumar) over their bosoms and reveal not their adornment except to their husbands, their fathers, or their husband's fathers or their sons or their husband's sons, or their brothers or their brothers' sons, or their sisters' sons or their women or what their right hands own, or such men as attend to them, not having sexual desire, or children who have not yet attained knowledge of women's private parts; nor let them stamp their feet, so that their hidden ornaments may be known. And turn all together to God, 0 you believers, so you will prosper. 5 (24:31)

In the phrase, "tell the believing men to cast down their look," there are two words that we have to define. One is *ghadh* and the other is *absar*. A person who might say *absar*, the plural of *basar*, needs no explanation because it means eyes, but *absar* essentially means "sight." If it had said *'ain* as in *ghamdh'ain* it would have meant "close their eyes." It would have had a particular meaning in this case. What does *ghadh basar* mean? *Ghadh* means "lower," "cast down," not "cover" or "close." We see this in another verse, *"Be modest in thy walk and lower (yaghaddwu) thy voice; the most hideous of voices is the ass's"* (31:19). [6] This does not mean to be silent. A person's voice should be moderate. In the same way, "to cast down one's look" means not to look in a fixed way, not to stare.

In a famous tradition of Hind ibn Abi Halah, which describes the Holy Prophet, it is recorded, "When he was happy, he would cast down his glance."[7] It is clear it does not mean he closed his eyes.

Majlisi in *Bihar* interprets the sentence about the Holy Prophet thus: "He would cover his gaze and put down his head. He did this so that his happiness would not show."

Hazrat 'Ali in the *Nahj-ul-Balaghah* says to his son Imam Hasan, when he gave a banner to him in the battle of Jamal, "Even if the mountains are uprooted, do not leave your place. Clench your teeth (so that your anger increases), bare your head to God and nail your feet to the ground. Survey the enemy's forces and cast down your look,"[8] That is, "do not fix your gaze on the enemy."

There are essentially two ways of looking. One is to look at another with care as if you were evaluating the person by the way he looked or dressed. But another kind of looking is in order to speak to that person and you look since looking is necessary for conversation. This is a looking that is introductory and a means for speaking. This is an organic looking while the former is an autonomous kind. Thus the sentence means: "Tell the believers not to stare at or flirt with women."

ON THE COMMAND TO GUARD
THEIR PRIVATE PARTS

In the next sentence it says: *"Tell the believing men . . . to guard their private parts"* (24:30). To guard from what? From everything that is not correct, guard against both corruption and the glance of others. As you know, it was not the custom among Arabs in the Age of Ignorance to hide their private parts. Islam came and made it obligatory to cover this area.

It should be noted that the present Western civilization is moving directly toward the habits of the pre-Islamic Arabs in the Age of Ignorance and they are continuously weaving philosophies justifying nakedness as a good thing. Russell in "On Discipline," says that another illogical ethic or taboo is that a mother and father tell their children to cover themselves, which only creates a greater curiosity in children, and parents should show their sexual organs to children so that they become aware of whatever there is from the beginning. Now, they do this.

But the Holy Quran says, "And guard your private parts," both from corruption and from the view of others. Covering one's private parts is obligatory in

Islam except, of course, between a husband and wife and it is among the most disapproved acts for a mother to be naked before her son or a father before his daughter.

"That is purer for them. God is aware of the things they do"[9] (24:30). The Holy Prophet said that from childhood a certain event occurred several times. He sensed that there was another kind of power within him and it would not allow him to do things that were being done during the Age of Ignorance. He said once when he was a child he was playing with the children. Masons were building a house for one of the Quraish nearby. The children enjoyed helping the builders by bringing them stones, bricks, etc. The children would carry them in their long white skirts (underneath which they wore nothing) and then place them before the builders. In doing so, their private parts would be revealed. The Holy Prophet related that he went and put a stone in the skirt of his long chemise and when he wanted to rise, something stopped him and hit against the skirt of his dress. He repeated it and he had the same feeling. He then realized that he should not do this and he did not try again.[10]

"Say to the believing women that they cast down their look . . ."(24:31). You see that in these two verses, the ruling for a man and woman is the same. This is not something particular to men. For instance, if women were forbidden from looking and not men, there would have been a distinction that such and such was all right for men but not for women. It is clear, then, that when there is no distinction made between men and women, it has another purpose which we shall discuss in the next lesson.

LESSON FOUR: THE ISLAMIC HIJAB—PART II
THE COMMAND NOT TO REVEAL
THEIR ADORNMENT "AND TO GUARD
THEIR PRIVATE PARTS"

The word *farj* is used in Arabic to refer to both a man and a woman's private parts. The fact that men and women have both been commanded to guard their modesty, to guard their private parts is in relation to two things: the view of others and this includes everybody except a husband and wife, and the other is that one should guard one's modesty from corruption, from adultery. If we look at the external form of the verse, perhaps we would conclude that it only refers to corruption but because, from the time of the Prophet's companions and the very first commentaries of the Holy Quran, it has been clearly recorded that wherever the Holy Quran says, "guard their private parts,"[11] it means from adultery except in those verses where it is to guard the private parts from the view of others. Thus, this verse either refers to the collective view or it refers to the view of others if we take the traditions into account. There is no difference of opinion here.

The third duty is not to reveal "their adornment . . ." which refers to that which is separate from the body like jewels and gold as well as things that are attached to the body like *hena* and collyrium.

THE EXCEPTIONS

As to the fact that they should "reveal not their adornment," there are two exceptions in the Holy Quran. The first is "except such as is outward" and the second is "except to their husbands . . . etc." Both of these have discussed further, in particular, the first exception.

Women should "not reveal their adornment . . . except such as is outward." What does this refer to? Is it beauty that is most often hidden under clothes that must not be revealed? Then what is that which "is outward"? From the beginning of Islam, many questions arose in relation to "except such as is outward" which were asked from the companions of the Holy Prophet and the helpers and many Shi'ites asked the infallible Imams. There is almost total agreement regarding this point. That is, whether one is a Sunni who refers to the companions and helpers of the Holy Prophet or one be a Shi'ite who refers to the recorders of those traditions, there is more or less agreement that which "is outward" is collyrium, a ring and, in some cases an anklet—that is, adornments that are used on the two hands and the face. This then shows that it is not obligatory for women to cover their face or their hands. Things that adorn them may appear as long as they are part of common usage. The adornments that are applied to the hands and face are not obligatory to be covered.

There are a great many traditions in relation to this. It was asked from Imam Sadiq what may be displayed of adornments. That is, those things that are not obligatory to cover. He said, "It refers to collyrium and a ring and they are on the face and hands."[12] Abi Basir said he asked Imam Sadiq about the exception and he said a ring and bracelet.[13]

There is a tradition recorded by a person who was not a Shi'ite but because of his reliability, he is referred to and quoted by the "ulama." He says that he heard from Ja'far ibn Muhammad (A.S.) that the exception is the face and the hands. These are all similar in what they say. When the face and hands do not need to be covered, then their adornment, even less so.

There is another tradition narrated by 'Ali ibn Ibrahim from Imam Baqir, peace be upon him. He was asked about this exception and he said it includes the woman's clothes, collyrium, ring, and coloring of the palms of the hands and a bracelet.[14] Then the Imam said that we have three levels of adornment, the adornment all people may see, the adornment that *mahram* may see, and the adornment for one's spouse. That which may be displayed for the people is the face and hands and their adornment such as collyrium, a ring, a bracelet but the adornment that may be displayed before someone who is *mahram* is the neck and above including a necklace, an armlet, hands, plus an anklet and anything below the ankles. There is, of course, a difference of opinion as to what can be revealed before someone who is *mahram*. That which can be concluded from the totality of the traditions and according to the edicts of the religious jurisprudents is that no one is *mahram* other than one's husband from the navel to the knees. That is, a woman must cover herself from the navel to the knee, from even her father or brother and from the navel above, it must be covered from everyone except one's father. But for the husband, a woman may display her whole body.

We have other traditions in this area as well such as the fact that women must "veil their bosoms." Before the revelation of this verse, women would wear a scarf but they would place the ends behind their head so that their earrings, neck, and chest would show since their dresses were most often v-necked. With the revelation of this verse, it became clear that they had to cover their ears, neck, and chest with their head covering. There is a tradition recorded by Ibn 'abbas, the well-known transmitter of traditions, that it is obligatory for women to cover their chests and neck.[15]

The first exception we have referred to relates to what is not obligatory to be covered. The second exception refers to those before whom it is not obligatory to cover, such as fathers, husbands, children, etc.

IS "LOOKING" PERMISSIBLE FOR MEN?

In this area there are two points to be recognized and separated, at least mentally. One is what is obligatory for women to cover and what is not. If we say that it is not obligatory for women to cover their face and hand, does this agree with the saying that it is advisable for men to lower their gaze? Or is that something separate? Is it something that needs to be discussed separately? Is it possible that it is not obligatory for women to cover, even though this is definite in jurisprudence, but that it be advisable for men to lower their gaze?

We know from the lifestyle of the Holy Prophet that it is not obligatory for men to cover their head, hands, face, or neck. Does this mean that it is also not advisable that men lower their gaze if they are walking down the street and women are passing? These are two different issues and must be discussed separately.

Another issue is that in areas other than the ones we mentioned as exceptions, which the traditions have commented upon and in which the verse itself states what the limitations are, the face and the hands are among the absolute necessities of Islam whereby covering everything but them is obligatory for women. Of course, this itself has an exception, which we will discuss in the next verse, which is that if women reach beyond a certain age, it is no longer obligatory for them. But, in general, covering the hair of a woman is among the compulsory precepts of Islam. It is clear that much of the hair that shows, by which one would conclude that a woman's head is "uncovered," is clearly not permissible to show in Islam. Covering the neck, the chest, the arms above the wrists, the feet (which is debated) from the ankles above are all among the obligatory aspects of Islam. There is no controversy here.

But there is another point. We said that we have to discuss separately whether or not lowering the gaze is advisable. If the look is of a flirting nature, looking with the anticipation of pleasure, this is another clear issue, which is among those which are forbidden. Not only is it forbidden to look at strangers or persons to whom one is not *mahram*, but even those who are *mahram* as well. If a father was to flirt with his daughter, it is forbidden and perhaps an even greater sin. It is forbidden for a father-in-law to look at his son's wife with lust. It is forbidden for a man to look at another man with lust. That is, in Islam, lust is exclusively allowed between marital partners. It is not permissible in any form anywhere else between anyone else.

But this should be distinguished from *riba'*, which means to look but not with the intention of lust nor to really see or view the other person. It is a special state that could be dangerous. That is, the fear exists that the look will cause a person to deviate to a forbidden state. This, then, is also forbidden and there is no difference of opinion on this.

Thus, if a person says it is advisable to look, a lustful look is not meant or a look that holds the fear that it may lead to something forbidden.

Now we will discuss "looking." We have a tradition recorded by 'Ali ibn Ja'far, the brother of Imam Riza. He asks to what point a man can look at a woman who is not permissible to him? He said, "Her face and her hands and her feet."[16] Of course, face and hands are clearly so, but the jurisprudents have not issued edicts about the feet.

There is another tradition about a man who is on a trip and dies. There is no man present to give him the obligatory bath for the dead nor are any *mahram* women present. What should be done for the obligatory bath? The opposite has also been questioned, a woman on a trip who dies and there are no *mahram* men present to give her the bath. When in both cases they asked the Imam, Imam Sadiq said about the first case, "Those women may touch and wash that part of the man's body which was permissible for them to see when he was alive." The same thing is said about a woman who has died. The men who were not *mahram* can only wash that part of her body which they could look at when she was alive. The Imam said that if they touch the face and wash her face and her hands, this is sufficient. It is not necessary to wash her whole body. Thus, a man may look at a woman's face and hands when she is alive.[17]

We also find this in the tradition in *Mustamsak*, which Ayatullah Hakim relates about Hazrat Fatimah, peace be upon her. One is the tradition regarding the companion Salman who once entered her house and saw that she was grinding barley and her hands were bleeding. This tradition makes it clear that the hands were not covered and that it was not forbidden to look at her hands because if it had been, neither would Salman have looked at them nor would Hazrat Fatimah, peace be upon her, have left them uncovered.

More authentic than this is a tradition of Jabir that appears in *Kafi*, in *Wasa'il* and all of the reliable books on traditions that the *ulama* narrate. Jabir narrated that he went with the Prophet of Allah to enter Hazrat Fatimah's house. The Holy Prophet had said that a person should seek permission to enter another's house, even if it belonged to one's mother, and that the only exception is that one need not seek permission to enter one's wife's room. "When he arrived at her house, he did not enter but called out, '*Assalamo alaikum ya Ahl-al-Bait.* Hazrat Fatimah answered from inside the house. The Holy Prophet asked, 'Do you allow us to enter?' She said, 'Yes enter.' He asked, 'Should the person with me enter?' She said, 'No. Then wait until I cover my head.' Then she said, 'Enter.' Again the Holy Prophet asked 'Should the person with me enter?' And she said, 'Yes.'" Jabir says that when he entered he saw that Hazrat Fatimah's face was sallow colored. "I became very sad when I realized it was because of lack of food. I said to myself,

"Look at how the caliph and a king's daughter is brought up and the daughter of the Prophet of God!"[18]

This shows that Hazrat Fatimah neither covered her face nor her hands. Otherwise, Jabir's look would have been forbidden.

Among the traditions, we have a great many which, when they ask of the Imam, he says that one cannot look at the forearm of a woman or at a woman's hair. All of these are mentioned but nowhere does it say about the face and hands.

Another issue is *ihram* (Hajj pilgrim's garb), where it is forbidden for women to cover their face and therefore we realize that it is not obligatory. It could not be that there is something that is obligatory but not so in the *ihram* and forbidden here.

"Let them cast their veils over their bosoms," the verse itself expresses the limits and does not include the face and hands. On the other hand, those who say "looking" is absolutely forbidden have given as a reason the very thing that has been given for it not being forbidden. They refer to the verse, "say to the believing men to cast down their look." He answers that in the first place the verse does not say what not to look at. Secondly, it says *min* which means "from something," and, thirdly, *ghadd* means "cast down" or "lower."

There is another tradition that is referred to and those who say that it is forbidden to look should note it. A man wrote a letter to Imam 'Askari, peace be upon him, where he said that there is a woman who wants to confess something and others want to listen to her confession to bear witness to it. Must she confess behind a curtain and the others listen from behind a curtain to then justly say that it was her voice. The Imam said, "No. She should come forward to bear witness but she should cover herself so that only the roundness of her face shows."

Another tradition that they present is an often quoted tradition. It is called *Sa'd Iskaf* in reference to a man who went to the Prophet with his face bleeding and said that he had a complaint to make. The Holy Prophet told him to speak. He said he was walking down the street of Madinah and saw a woman coming toward him who was very beautiful and who had tied her scarf behind her head, and her chest was visible. As she passed, he turned his head to look at her and did not see what was in front of him. Something was sticking out of the wall and it struck his face and injured him. The verse was then revealed, *"Say to the believing men to cast down their look."* But this means women like this and not all women. The verse tells what must be covered and it is not more or less than this.

Another reason they give is that it says in the traditions, "Is there anything which has not committed an illicit act for the illicit act of the eyes is to look?" The answer is that this is referring to looking with lust, not just looking; like the tradition that says "looking is like an arrow of satan," and, of course, they refer to looking with lust.

There is another tradition, which I have read in the books on traditions of the Sunnis. It says the Holy Prophet was on a journey, probably the Farewell Pilgrimage, and he placed ibn 'abbas behind himself. Ibn 'abbas was a young boy. He continued to look at the women who passed back and forth in the *ihram*. The Holy Prophet realized that he was doing this and he turned the boy's face away. Ibn 'abbas then began to look from that direction. The Holy Prophet again turned the boy's face away.

According to the Shi'ite sources, the tradition differs. It says that he was a very handsome young boy and the Holy Prophet was riding, probably on a camel. A woman from the Khasamiyyah tribe came to ask the Holy Prophet a question. She asked and the Holy Prophet answered. Then the Holy Prophet realized that her eyes were fixed upon Fazl ibn 'abbas and Fazl ibn 'abbas was staring at her. The tradition states that the Holy Prophet turned Fazl's face away saying, "A young woman and a young man, I am afraid satan will enter."[19]

They say that because of this, it is clear that it is forbidden to look like this. There is no doubt about it. This is love making and it is forbidden. Shaikh Ansari says that from this tradition it is clear that it was not obligatory for women to cover themselves and it was not forbidden in general for men to look. Otherwise the Holy Prophet would not have looked but he was looking at her as he was answering her questions and saw that her eyes were fixed on Fazl ibn 'abbas and his on hers.

Ayatullah Hakim narrates another tradition. A man by the name of 'Ali ibn Salah said to Imam Riza, peace be upon him, "I have a problem. I look at beautiful women and it makes me happy to do so but I have no bad intentions." The Imam said, "There is no problem as God is aware of your intentions and you have no ill intentions but fear an illicit act."

NOTES

1. The Quran, 24:26.
2. Ibid., 33:53.
3. Ibid. 24:27–28
4. Ibid., 24:30.
5. Ibid., 24:31
6. Ibid., 31:19.
7. *Tafsir ul-Quran, Safi,* 24:31, narrated from a tradition of 'Ali ibn Ibrahim Qummi.
8. *Nahj al-Balaghah,* Sermon 110.
9. Ibid., Sermon 227.
10. Ibn Abil Hadid, *Sharhe al-Nahj al-Balaghah,* Sermon 190.
11. The Quran, 24:30 and 24:31.
12. *Kafi,* vol. 5, p. 521 and *Wasail,* vol. 3, p. 25.
13. Ibid.
14. *Tafsir ul-Quran, Safi,* 24:31.
15. "Majma 'al-Bayan," The Quran 24:31.
16. "Qurb al-Asnad," p. 102.
17. *Wasail,* vol. 17, p. 135.
18. *Kafi,* vol. 5, p. 528 and *Wasail* 71, vol. 3, p. 28.
19. *Sahih Bukhari,* vol. 8, p. 63.

BIBLIOGRAPHICAL SOURCES

Abd al-Raziq, Ali. "The Unity of Religion and Arabs." *al-Islam wa-Usul al-Hukm* (Islam and the Principle of Government). Cairo: Matba'at Misr, 1925. Translations in text by Kamran Talattof.

Abduh, Muhammad "Quranic Exegesis" (Tafsir al-Quran al-Hakim). *al-Manar,* vol. 8, no. 24, pp. 921–30, February 10, 1906. Translations in text by Kamran Talattof.

———. "The True Reform and its Necessity for Al-Azhar" (al-Islah al- Hakiqiqi wa al-Wajib lil al-Azhar). *al-Manar,* vol. 10, no. 28, pp. 758–65. Translations in text by Kamran Talattof.

Abrahamian, Ervand. 1993. *Khomeinism: Essays on the Islamic Republic.* Berkeley: University of California.

Adamiyat, Fereydoun. 1976. *Idi'olozhi-ye Nahzat-i Mashrutiyat-i Iran* (The Ideology of the Constitutional Movement in Iran). Tehran, Iran: Payam Publications.

Adams, Charles C. 1933. *Islam and Modernism In Egypt: A Study of the Modern Reform Movement Inaugurated by Muhammad 'abduh.* New York: Russell and Russell.

———. 1966. "The Ideology of Mawlana Maududi." In *South Asian Politics and Religion.* Donald Eugene Smith, ed. Princeton, NJ: Princeton University Press.

Afghani, Sayyid Jamal al-Din. Excerpt from Nikki R. Keddie, ed. 1968. *An Islamic Response to Imperialism: Political and Religious Writings of Sayyid Jamal al-Din al-Afghani.* Berkeley and Los Angeles: University of California Press, pp. 181–87.

Ahmad, Aziz and G. Grunebaum. 1970. *Muslim Self-statement in India and Pakistan 1857–1968.* Wiesbaden: O. Harrassowitz.

Ahmad, Aziz. 1967. *Islamic Modernism in India and Pakistan: 1857–1964.* London: Oxford University Press.

Aligarh Institute Gazette. "The Present Economical Condition of the Musalmans of Bengal." In *Aligarh Institute Gazette,* vol. 12, nos. 73, 74, 75, 77, and 79.

Al-i Ahmad, Jalal. 1966. *Mudir-i Madrisih.* Tehran: Amir Kabir.

———. 1978. *Khasi dar Miqat.* Tehran: Intisharat-i Ravaq.

———. 1979. *Karnamah-i Sih Salih.* Tehran: Intisharat-i Ravaq.

———. 1982. *Plagued by the West,* translated by Paul Sprachman. New York: Center for Iranian Studies, Columbia University.

———. 1982. *Plagued by the West (Gharbzadegi).* Modern Persian Literature Series No. 4. Translated from the Persian by Paul Sprachman. Delmar, NY: Caravan Books.

Ali, Moulavi Sayyid Amir [Maulavi Sayed Ameer Ali]. 1922. "The Apostolical Succession." In *The Spirit of Islam: A History of the Evolution and Ideals of Islam with a Life of the Prophet.* London: Christophers.

———. 1922. "The Rationalistic and Philosophical Spirit of Islam." In *The Spirit of Islam: A History of the Evolution and Ideals of Islam with a Life of the Prophet.* London: Christophers.

al-Manar. Various issues.

al-Urwa al-Wuthqa. Various Issues.

Amin, Qasim. 1992 [1899]. Introduction: "The Status of Women in Society: A Reflection of the Nation's Moral Standards." In *The Liberation of Women,* translated by Samiha Sidhom Peterson. Cairo, Egypt: The American University in Cairo Press.

Baljon, J. M. S., Jr. D. D. 1970. *The Reforms and Religious Ideas of Sir Sayyid Ahmad Khan.* Lahore, Pakistan: Sh. Muhammad Ashraf.

Baron, Beth. 1994. *The Women's Awakening in Egypt.* New Haven: Yale University Press.

Binder, Leonard. 1988. *Islamic Liberalism: A Critique of Development Ideologies.* Chicago: University of Chicago Press.

Browne, Edward G. 1910. *The Persian Revolution of 1905–1909.* New York: Barnes and Noble.

Chiragh [Cheragh] Ali, Moulavi. 1883. *The Proposed Political, Legal, and Social Reforms in the Ottoman Empire and Other Muhammadan [Mohammadan] States.* Bombay: Education Society Press.

———. "The Popular Jihad or Crusade; According to the *Muhammadan* [Mohammadan] Common Law." In *A Critical Exposition of the Popular "Jihad."* Karachi, Pakistan: Karimsons, 1977. pp. 114–61.

Cromer, Evelyn Baring. 1908. *Modern Egypt,* vol. II. New York: Macmillan.

Dabashi, Hamid. 1993. *Theology of Discontent: The Ideological Foundations of the Islamic Revolution in Iran.* New York: New York University Press.

Dar, Bashir Ahmad.1957. *Religious Thought of Sayyid Ahmad Khan.* Lahore, India: Institute of Islamic Culture.

Davari, Riza. 1988. *Difa' az Falsafah.* Tehran: Daftar-i Pizhuhish-ha va Barnamah'rizi-i Farhangi.

Enayat, Hamid. 1982. *Modern Islamic Political Thought.* London: Macmillan.

Enayat, Hamid [Inayat, Hamid]. 1979. Sayri da Andishah-'i Siyasi-i Arab Az Hamlah-'i Napuli'un bih Misr ta Jang-i Jahani-i Duvum. Tehran: Amir Kabir.

Esposito, John. 1983. *Voices of Resurgent Islam.* New York : Oxford University Press.

———. 1995. *The Islamic Threat: Myth or Reality?* New York: Oxford University Press.

Farhan, Ishaq A. 1997. "Interview with Ishaq A. Farhan, the Leader of Islamic Action Front Party." (Hizb Jibhih al-Amal al-Islami). By Mansoor Moaddel in Amman, Jordan, spring.

FIS. 1989. "Encart Central: Front Islamic du Salut: Le Programme." *La Tribune,* no. 11, July 25. Translated by Nicky Peters.

Hairi, Hadi. 1977. *Shi'ism and Constitutionalism in Iran.* Leiden, Netherlands: E. J. Brill.

Hali, Altaf Husain. 1979 [1901]. *Hayat-i-Javed.* Delhi, India: Idarah-i Adabiyat-i Delli. Translated by K. H. Qadiri and David J. Matthews.

Harrison, Christina. 1964. *Nationalism and Revolution in Egypt: The Role of the Muslim Brotherhood.* Hague: Mouton.

Hourani, Albert. 1983. *Arabic Thought in the Liberal Age (1798–1939).* Cambridge: Cambridge University Press.

Hussain, Muhammad Hadi. 1970. *Syed Ahmed Khan: Pioneer of Muslim Resurgence.* Lahore: Institute of Islamic Culture.

Keddie, Nikki R. 1972. "The Roots of Ulama Power in Modern Iran." In *Scholars, Saints and Sufis.* Nikki R. Keddie, ed. Los Angeles: University of California Press, 211–229.

Kepel, Gilles. 1985. *Muslim Extremism in Egypt: The Prophet and Pharaoh.* Berkeley: University of California Press.

Kirmani, Nazim ul-Islam. 1945/1324. *Tarikhi Bidari-ye Iranian* (The History of the Awakening of Iranian). Tehran, Iran: Ibn Sina Publications.

Khan, Sayyid Ahmad. 1972. Selected essays by Sir Sayyid Ahmad Khan from the journal *Tahzib al-Akhlaq*. Translation in this text by Kamran Talattof, et al.

Khomeini, Ruhullah [Khumeini, Imam Ruhullah]. 1981. "The Nature of the Islamic State and the Qualifications of the Head of State." In *Khumeini[Khomeini] Speaks Revolution*. Compiled by Mohiuddin Ayyubi. Translated by N. M. Shaikh. Karachi, Pakistan: International Islamic Publishers.

———. 1981. "The Necessity for Islamic Government." In *Islam and Revolution: Writings and Declarations of Imam Khomeini*, translated and annotated by Hamid Algar. Berkeley: Mizan Press.

———. 1981. *Islam and Revolution: Writings and Declarations of Imam Khomeini*, translated and annotated by Hamid Algar. Berkeley: Mizan Press.

Khuri, Raif. 1983. ed. "Selection III: Rifa'a Rafi' al-Tahtawi, 1216–1290 (1801–1873)." In *Modern Arab Thought: Channels from the French Revolution to the Arab East*. Princeton: Kingston Press.

Malik, Hafeez. 1980. *Sir Sayyid Ahmad Khan and Muslim Modernization in India and Pakistan*. New York: Columbia University Press.

Maududi, Sayyed Abul Ala [Maudoodi, Syed Abul Ala], 1992. "Fallacy of Rationalism I and II." In *West Versus Islam*. Translated by S. Waqar Ahmad Gardezi and Abdul Waheed Khan. New Delhi, India: International Islamic Publishers.

———. 1986. *A Short History of the Revivalist Movement in Islam*. Lahore, Pakistan: Islamic Publications.

———. 1992. "Suicide of Western Civilization." In *West versus Islam*. Waqar Ahmad Gardezi and Abdul Waheed Khan. New Delhi, India: International Islamic Publishers.

Mitchell, Timothy. 1988. *Colonising Egypt*. Cambridge: Cambridge University Press.

Moaddel, Mansoor. 1992. *Class, Politics, and Ideology in the Iranian Revolution*. New York: Columbia University Press.

———. 1998. "Religion and Women: Islamic Modernism versus Fundamentalism." In *Journal of the Scientific Study of Religion*, vol. 37, no. 1, 108–1030.

Moin, Baqer. 1991. *Khomeini: Sign of God*. London: Tauris.

Muslim Brotherhood. 1997. "Why does the Muslim Brotherhood Boycott the 1997 Parliamentary Elections?: A Statement to the People" (pamphlet). Muslim Brotherhood Headquarters, Amman, Jordan. 13 July.

Mutahhari, Murtaza. 1985. *Fundamentals of Islamic Thought: God, Man, and the Universe*. Berkeley: Mizan Press.

———. 1987. *On the Islamic Hijab*. Translated by Laleh Bakhtiar. Tehran: Islamic Propagation Organization.

Nu'mani, Allama Shibli. *Sirat un-Nabi*. vol. I. Translated by M. Tayyib Bakhsh Budayuni. Delhi: Idarah-i Adabiyat-i Delli, reprint 1983 [orig. 1979], pp. 36–63.

Na'ini, Mirza Muhammad Hussein. 1909. *Tanbih al-Umma wa Tanzih al-Millah* (The Admonition of the Umma and the Enlightenment of the Nation). Baghdad.

Qutb, Sayyid Shaheed [Sayyid Qutb Shaheed]. 1988. "Islam and Culture." In *Milestones*, 2nd ed. Translated by S. Badrul Hasan, M.A. Karachi, Pakistan: International Islamic Publishers Ltd.

———. 1988. "Jihad in the Cause of Allah." In *Milestones*, 2nd ed. Translated by S. Badrul Hasan, M.A. Karachi, Pakistan: International Islamic Publishers Ltd.

———. 1964. *Ma'alim fi al-Tariq*. Cairo: Maktabat Wahbah.

Ruedy, John. ed. 1994. *Islam and Secularism in North Africa*. New York: St. Martin's Press.

Ruhani, Hamid. 1982. *Bar'rasi va Tahlili az Nahzat-i Imam Khumayni*. Tehran: Rah-i Imam.

Shariati, Ali. 1980. "Modern Calamities." In *Marxism and Other Western Fallacies: An Islamic Critique*. Translated by R. Campbell. Berkeley: Mizan Press.

Shibli Numani. 1970 [1330HQ]. *Sirat al-Nabi*. Translated by Fazulur Rahman. Karachi: Pakistan Historical Society.

Sivan, Emmanuel. 1990. *Radical Islam: Medieval Theology and Modern Politics*. New Haven: Yale University Press.

Smith, Charles. *Islam and the Search for Social Order in Modern Egypt: A Biography of Muhammad Husayn Haykal*. Albany: State University of New York Press, 1983.

Sultani, 'abd al-Latif [Abdel Latif]. "Fadila Mrabet, Kateb Yassine, and the Rocket of Islam." In *Al-Mazdaqia hia asl al-ichtirakia* (Masdaqia is the Source of Socialism). Morocco, p. 33. Quoted in Francois Burgat and William Dowell. 1997. *The Islamic Movement in North Africa*. Austin, Texas: Center for Middle Eastern Studies, University of Texas at Austin, pp. 252–3.

———. 1975. "A Moralizing Fundamentalism, Women." In *Al-Mazdaqia hia asl al-ichtirakia* (Masdaqia is the Source of Socialism). Morocco. Quoted in Francois Burgat and William Dowell. 1997 *The Islamic Movement in North Africa*. Austin, Texas: Center for Middle Eastern Studies, University of Texas at Austin.

———. 1982. *Fi sabil al-'aqidah al-Islamiyah*. Qusantinah: Dar al-Ba'th.

Talattof, Kamran. 1997. "Iranian Women's Literature: From Pre-revolutionary Social Discourse to Postrevolutionary Feminism." *International Journal of Middle East Studies*, vol. 29, no. 4, November.

———. 1999. *The Politics of Writing in Iran: A History of Modern Persian Literature*. Syracuse: Syracuse University Press.

Turner, Bryan S. 1974. *Weber and Islam*. Boston: Routledge & Kegan Paul.

Wajdi, Farid. 1901. *Al-Madaniyah wa al-Islam*. Egypt: Matba'at Hindiyah, pp. 23–47. Translations in text by Christine Dykgraaf and Kamran Talattof.

INDEX

CPSIA information can be obtained at www.ICGtesting.com
Printed in the USA
LVOW11s0913040214

372251LV00005B/550/A